Tirailleurs

Tirailleurs

A History of The 4th Louisiana and The Acadians of Company H

THOMAS H. RICHEY

Writers Advantage
New York Lincoln Shanghai

Tirailleurs
A History of The 4th Louisiana and The Acadians of Company H

All Rights Reserved © 2003 by Thomas H. Richey

No part of this book may be reproduced or transmitted in any form or by any means, graphic, electronic, or mechanical, including photocopying, recording, taping, or by any information storage retrieval system, without the written permission of the publisher.

Writers Advantage
an imprint of iUniverse, Inc.

For information address:
iUniverse
2021 Pine Lake Road, Suite 100
Lincoln, NE 68512
www.iuniverse.com

ISBN: 0-595-27258-4

Printed in the United States of America

This book is dedicated to Agnes Hilda Blanchard, who loved to tell stories to her grandson about the old folks.

SECOND SERGEANT TRASIMOND LANDRY
Photo taken in the spring of 1861 by Andrew David Lytle.
This copy was furnished by Mr. Lew Cazes.

Contents

Introduction 1
1. Preparing for War 3
2. Guarding the Coast 13
3. Shiloh Church 33
4. First Siege of Vicksburg 59
5. Battle of Baton Rouge 65
6. Port Hudson 88
7. Siege of Jackson 113
8. Battles for Atlanta 139
9. Jonesboro 165
10. Nashville 180
11. Prison Camps 191
Epilogue 197
Appendices 199
Roster for The West Baton Rouge Tirailleurs 213
Physicians Associated with The 4th La Volunteers 295
Notes 297

Maps

Shiloh Battlefield First Day 57
Shiloh Battlefield Second Day 58
Battle of Baton Rouge August 5, 1862 78
The Port Hudson Area 112
Mobile Bay 138
Kennesaw Mountain Area 164
Atlanta and Jonesboro 178
The Long March 179

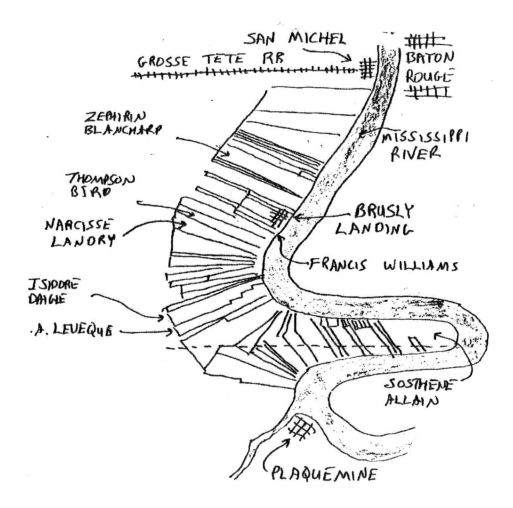

Introduction

This is a tale of a company of soldiers called the West Baton Rouge Parish Tirailleurs. "Tirailleur" (TEE-ray-your) is a French word meaning "rifleman." A "company" is a unit, usually of about one hundred men, making up part of a "regiment," which has about a thousand men. (See Appendix D) Their ranks were made up primarily from the southern half of West Baton Rouge Parish. This unique group of men fought gallantly in the War Between the States. Their uniqueness stems from their origins as French-speaking Acadians. More than three fourths of the company had Acadian surnames. There were some Anglo-American (*les Américains*) names in the company, but most of these men were married to Acadian or French-Creole women.

There were four distinct social classes in antebellum West Baton Rouge Parish: French Creoles, Acadians, Anglo-Americans, and slaves. All had well-defined cultural differences. The French Creoles were descendents of Frenchmen who had migrated to Louisiana from France. The Acadians were descendents of Frenchmen who had migrated from Nova Scotia. The French Creoles and Acadians shared the French language and Catholic religion, but that was about all. The rich lands along the west bank of the Mississippi River created a group of Acadians that had adopted many of the materialistic ways of the French Creole. Rather than pursue the traditional Acadian (*les petits habitants*) lifestyle of subsistence farming they became large landowners, slave holders, and planters. They have been called "Genteel Acadians."

The history of the Acadians began in seventeenth century France. They left France for an area of Canada known as Acadia (Nova Scotia). Existing peacefully with the local Indians, the group was physically and culturally isolated from their French homeland for 150 years. This long interval was punctuated by turmoil created by the English and New Englanders. This eventually led to the expulsion of ten thousand Acadian farmers. In the great Acadian dispersion of 1755, approximately one third died, one third went to France and Canada, and one third ended up in Spanish-held Louisiana. The largest single group of Acadians arrived by ship from exile in France in 1785. Years of isolation and persecution by the English had created a close-knit group of people with their own distinct culture.

After President Thomas Jefferson purchased Louisiana from Napoleon, English-speaking farmers began to acquire lands all along the Mississippi and, in particular, West Baton Rouge Parish. They mostly lived in the northern half of the parish.

This is also the story of the 4th LA Infantry Regiment. This regiment fought gallantly at Shiloh, the First Siege of Vicksburg, the Battle of Baton Rouge, the Siege of Jackson, Pickett's Mill, New Hope Church, Lost Mountain, Kinnesaw Mountain, Ezra Church, Atlanta, Utoy Creek, Jonesboro, Calhoun, Florence, Nashville, and Mobile. The primary sources for this story are diaries, letters, and recollections of members in various companies of the regiment.

Sources include the diaries of Robert Patrick, Wyllie Micajah Barrow, Edmond Enoul Livaudais, John Jackman, Dr. J. M. Craig, Sarah Morgan, William Young Dixon, Isaac Erwin, James Marston, and D. C. Jenkins, and also the letters of Alexis Hebert, Theodore Lejeune, John A. Morgan, J. G. Kilbourne, C. J. Loe, John Doyle, Silas T. White, James B.Corkern, Samuel Hunter, Francis Palms, and Jimmy Knighton. Other sources are the recollections of H. W. Allen, John I. Kendall, A. P. Richards, Samuel Lambert, Frank L. Richardson, Samuel G. French, Lionel C. Levy, Douglas John Cater, Ambrose Bierce, William Watson, and Phillip Dangerfield Stephenson.

Prior to the war, the Acadians of Brusly Landing were prosperous, well-educated gentlemen. They were Southern patriots who had lost everything in postbellum Louisiana reconstruction. They entered the fire and fury of the War Between the States with all its suffering, wounding, disease, and death. They fought gallantly and without complaint. However, their bravery and steadfastness have been mostly forgotten. The writer's hope is that the Tirailleurs might earn a place in the memory of the South.

The man who led the Tirailleurs through most of the war was Trasimond Landry. This book will follow him, his family, and the Tirailleurs (Company H, 4th LA), through the War Between the States.

I would like to thank the following for their invaluable help in researching this book: Lew Cazes; Tommy Landry; Jane Landry Comeaux; LSU Press; librarians at Hill Memorial Library (LSU); Louisiana State Archives and the Louisiana State Library; Ms. Nancy Mertz (Midwest Jesuit Archives); Dr. Charles Boyle (Springhill College); Tom Clancy, S. J. (Loyola University); Yvonne Arnold (University of Southern Mississippi); Melinda McMartin (American Jewish Archives); Patrick Ailliot; Rebecca Wickliffe; Michael Cherry; Drew Burk; Albert Arnold Gore, Jr.; Johnnie Ruth Richey; Michael Hopwood, Jr.; West Baton Rouge Parish Museum; West Baton Rouge Genealogical Society; Glenda Norwood; park rangers at Shilo Battlefield Park and Kennesaw Mountain Park; James A. Wooten, interpretive ranger at Picken's Mill State Park, Georgia; and especially to Mrs. Iris Lejeune of Brusly Landing.

1.

Preparing for War

April 8th, 1865, was a day of terror. Isidore Daigle clawed at the ground trying to dig his way to safety. He had to get away from the screaming, searching shells that were pounding his rifle pit. His trench-mates, Jean Baptiste, Emile, and Amedee, joined in throwing up dirt, digging deeper and deeper towards safety. The Tirailleurs burrowed into the Earth's marsupium like hairless opossum grubs. Ten yards away a fifteen-inch, two-hundred pound mortar ball crashed into the fort, plowed six feet into the ground, and exploded.

The earth trembled. The concussion caved in the walls of their rifle pit. The four Acadians coughed and gasped for air as they struggled to free themselves from the sandy soil. Blood trickled from their noses. The terrible roar of Yankee artillery was dulled, now filtered through ruptured ear drums. The four Rebel soldiers were all alone, or might as well have been. The powder smoke limited their vision to less than a dozen yards.

Through the soot-filled atmosphere, Isidore could see Father Turgis. The priest dragged a wounded artilleryman into their pit and ordered them to care for him. Isidore pleaded with the little priest to stay with them. Artillery shells burned holes in the surrounding air as the priest moved off, looking for more wounded. The fort in the center was being mercilessly pounded. More huge mortar rounds whistled in, along with Parrott shells, minnie balls, and rounds from Farragut's gunboats offshore. The 2,300 Rebels at Spanish Fort were in a trap that would soon spring 30,000 Yankee infantrymen at them.

They all knew the Cause was lost, but fought on anyway. In the midst of his terror these thoughts held in Isidore's mind. How could his young life have come to this? How could he have been led to this hell? Water! If he only had a small drink of water things would be better. Somewhere in the back of his neck his throat demanded water. He could drink a river.

+   +   +

Late January, 1861.

The river stretched out in front. It was full from bank to bank. The high water would make for a swift run to Baton Rouge. When the Mississippi River was at flood stage a steamboat could run through cutoffs and shave days off the trip. The *SS Eclipse* was a fast steamer, but not fast enough for four of its passengers.

The times were electric in 1861, especially for these college students on their way home. The term at St. Joseph's College in Bardstown, Kentucky, had ended in January. Trasimond Landry, Alex Allain, Isidore Daigle, and his brother Prudent were headed home. They had traveled from Bardstown to Louisville by train. By steamer, they traveled the Ohio River and then the familiar Mississippi River.

These young men were all of French descent. Trasimond Landry was born on his father's plantation, August 7, 1839. He was the third son of Narcisse Landry, a direct descendent of Rene Landry and Marie Bernard of Port Royal, Acadia. Being the oldest of the group, he was their tacit leader and would be the only one to become an officer. Alexander Pierre Allain was the son of a wealthy sugar planter, Theophile Allain. Alex excelled at mathematics and planned to offer his services to his new country as an artillerist. He was Colonial French (Creole).

Sixteen-year-old Isidore and twenty-one-year-old Prudent Daigle were also the sons of a sugar planter. Their father had died six years earlier and "Stonewall" plantation had been sold to settle his estate. They were descended from an original Acadian settler, Olivier Daigle. The Daigle brothers would do nothing without the blessing of their older brother, Louis. These young men were headed home to Brusly Landing, Louisiana.

All four were broke and traveling deck class. They spent most of the trip on the boiler deck smoking their pipes, telling tales, and discussing their future military careers. They had no understanding of the still forces that lead men to war. There was even less understanding of the terrors they would face in their pursuit of glory.

The *Eclipse* was a first-class steamer. Huge clouds of black smoke billowed from her twin stacks. Giant paddle wheels pushed her swiftly southward. On the eighth day, the boat stopped briefly at Natchez. Nearing Baton Rouge, the dense gray forests bordering the river gave way to endless fields of sugar cane on both sides. The grinding season was ending, and the river was covered with a smoky haze. For the next hundred miles the river banks were clouded by huge burning piles of bagasse. It was from these fires that Brusly Landing derived its name. *Bruler* is a French verb meaning, "to burn." In 1861, it was spelled "Brusly."

The Bardstown students debarked at Baton Rouge and took the ferry to San Michel. San Michel was on the right bank of the river opposite Baton Rouge and was the political center of West Baton Rouge Parish. (1) They were met by their families and were soon at Brusly Landing in the independent country of Louisiana.

Narcisse Landry's sugar plantation was south of Brusly Landing. Narcisse was getting old, and since 1856 the duties of running the plantation had passed to his eldest son, Belisaire. On their plantation, the twelve whitewashed slave cabins were neat and comfortable. Each cabin was twenty-one feet squared. To the rear of the sugar house was a large vegetable garden and hot house. Belisaire provided the forty-two slaves with weekly rations of pork, flour, coffee, and tobacco. (2) He made certain they received regular medical care. Dr. Thomas Vaughn was kept on a retainer for $125 per year. He examined the slaves every six weeks.

The plantation was very diversified. Sugar was the cash crop, but the Landrys also raised most of their own food for themselves and their field hands. There were beef cattle as well as sheep, hogs, chickens, turkeys, and geese. Fish and turtles were netted in the river and crawfish in the swamp. The rich, black-gumbo clay on the Mississippi's west bank would grow almost anything. To feed the mules, oxen, and horses, two crops of corn were planted. Oats, rice, and tobacco were also important. Great care was placed in the cultivation of sweet potatoes and peas. In a large vegetable garden were pumpkins, squash, melons, snap beans, butter beans, peppers, and okra. There were traditional Acadian orchards with pears, peaches, figs, apples, and citrus. Each year fifty hogs were slaughtered and smoked (requiring five hundred pounds of salt to cure). Several female hands spent most of their time weaving. Beef hides were tanned to make harnesses. In an average year, the Landrys produced sixty-five hogsheads of sugar. Narcisse owned a one-third interest in a stone mill and bartered for his wheat flour.

In September and October the cane was planted. Hands used knives to cut off leaves from the planting cane, plows opened furrows, cane stalks were placed lengthwise in these windrows, and another plow covered them up. New cane sprouted from the buried seed cane. Every two weeks each part of the cane field was weeded until it possessed a garden-neat appearance. This weeding and cultivating went on for six months. By July, the cane was tall enough to shade out weeds.

All during the year the hands were kept busy cleaning ditches, improving drainage, reconditioning roads, and repairing levees. In September, they attacked the swamp in the rear of the plantation for firewood. Huge loads of wood were necessary for fuel in the sugar-making process. Usually one third of the fields were planted each year. This newly-planted cane could be cut and re-cut for several years. From October through December, and often into January, everyone was consumed by the sugar-making process. The work went on eighteen hours a day. This was the "grinding season."

In the fields, the strongest hands used hooked machetes (*couteau de cane*) to cut and strip the ten-foot cane stalks. Other men and women loaded the cane onto carts. These carts were pulled to the sugar house by teams of mules. The sugar-making process was quite complicated. The stalks were fed into steam-powered presses which ground the cane and squeezed out the sweet juice. The juice then went to the evaporating pan, then through filters and clarifying tanks, then on to the granulating pipe, and finally to the vacuum pan. It took three cords of wood to produce one hogshead of sugar. A hogshead was a large wooden barrel which held one half-ton of sugar or seventy gallons of molasses. Tariffs protected the sugar planter from competition from the Caribbean sugar producers. Sugar planters got rich, but of course the rest of the country paid higher than necessary prices for their sweetener. Cotton planters, with no federal tariff protection, were more likely to whine about the high prices of protected goods from New England than the sugar planters. Both groups equally resented strident Yankee Abolitionism.

Yearly state tax revenues from the parish amounted to about $10,000. Of this money, $5,000 was devoted to public schools. The parish was divided into five school districts. These schools were well managed and efficient and had a much better reputation than public schools in the interior parishes. (3)

In the antebellum period, private college preparatory schools appeared in the area. As early as 1846, the West Baton Rouge English and French Academy was operating at Brusly Landing. "All the necessary branches (either English or French), will be sufficiently taught to give to the pupils all the necessary qualifications to enter any university. For one language only, $7.50 per month; for English and French, $10 per month; and Latin language, $8 per month." (4) The Baton Rouge Classical and Commercial Boarding and Day School began operating on January 1, 1846. In the list of references was The Right Reverend Leonidus Polk, D. D., Bishop of the Diocese of Louisiana. (5) A Methodist college and a Jesuit college were also established in the mid-1840s in Baton Rouge.

Narcisse Landry's children were home schooled. When they were older, they were sent to boarding schools. Narcisse knew that the secret to maintaining wealth and power was through education. Bilingualism was another key to economic security, and all of his children were fluent in English.

Trasimond Landry studied at the Jesuit College of St. Peter and Paul of Baton Rouge. When the college closed in 1855, he transferred to Jefferson College. He again transferred on September 30, 1859, to St. Joseph's College in Bardstown, Kentucky. (6) Bardstown was thirty miles below Louisville, Kentucky, and was the location of St. Joseph's Cathedral, constructed between 1816 and 1819. St. Joseph's College was established there in 1823. Spaulding Hall and Flaget Hall still stand on the old campus. Nazareth College for Women was a short, thirty-minute buggy ride south of St. Joseph's. (See Appendix F)

It was at Bardstown that Trasimond learned to play baseball (*jeu de plotte*). Football was also popular at St. Joseph's, and in the winter Trasimond took up ice-skating. He was an inch short of six feet tall, with an athletic build. He weighed 150 pounds and was fast and strong. He had a straight nose, high cheekbones, a sparse brown mustache and a goatee the same color as his straight hair. His gray eyes advanced intelligence and a will not easily turned from its purpose. In the South, the average height of *les Américains* was five feet, eight inches, and the average weight was 146 pounds. The average height of a male Louisiana Acadian was five feet six inches and the average weight was 136 pounds.

Trasimond Landry's future was to change from study and sports to soldiering. The same would be true for his fellow Acadians from Brusly Landing. Trasimond Landry and Prudent Daigle would become members of a local militia company, the Tirailleurs.

In the antebellum era, most communities organized militia companies. This tradition began under the French government and continued under Spanish and American rule. These units were more like social clubs than military formations. They all had colorful uniforms and on special occasions they formed up and paraded for community gatherings. Memberships in some formations were highly sought after and carried an amount of prestige. In these units the members had meetings, paid dues, elected officers, built meeting houses, and even voted to approve new members. (7) In the slave-holding South they were always ready to support the local law-enforcement agencies in cases of slave uprisings.

The Tirailleurs was established in 1841 and led by West Point trained Captain Gustave Rousseau. It was originally raised in Iberville and attracted members from Brusly Landing. In the Mexican War (1846–1848) they were part of the 2nd Regiment, Colonel Persifor Frazer Smith's Brigade, Louisiana Volunteers. The West Baton Rouge Guards (Captain William Blount Robertson) was organized in 1846. (8) (9) (See Appendix C)

The Tirailleurs were serious about their military preparation. The officers recruited Lewis Woods of Plaquemine to drill them. Private Woods was almost six feet tall and ramrod straight. He was eighteen years old and weighed 119 pounds. Private Woods had spent six months in a military academy before enrolling in the Class of 1859 at the United States Military Academy at West Point. He was fifth in his class of seventy five. (10) Woods was bilingual and drilled the Acadians in French and English.

In early January 1861, Colonel Braxton Bragg, of Governor Thomas O. Moore's staff, assembled four militia companies from Baton Rouge: the Pelican Rifles, National Guards, Creole Guards, and the Baton Rouge Fencibles. The Ed Moore Rangers, a company from Grosse Tete, came over on the ferry. That same day, the Delta Rifles and fifteen Tirailleurs arrived. These companies bivouacked on the neutral ground of North Boulevard near the Capitol, five blocks south of the Federal arsenal. Their mission was to seize the arsenal and capture its fifty thousand small arms, four howitzers, twenty pieces of heavy artillery, a battery of six-pounder guns, a battery of Napoleons, immense piles of shot and shell, and enough gun powder to start a war. (11)

Unknown to them, Governor Moore had also sent for militia from New Orleans. When the Creole Guards, Pelican Rifles, and other companies heard of the arrival of the New Orleans troops, their pride was wounded and they left for home. The Delta Rifles remained with the Tirailleurs and the Baton Rouge Fencibles. Six hundred men of the Washington Artillery, acting as infantry, took possession of the Federal arsenal. The one-armed U. S. Major Joseph A. Haskins and his sixty artillerymen and twenty ordinance men surrendered without firing a shot. (12)

In March 1861, there was a popular vote on the issue of secession. This vote was to decide whether the state should remain in the Union and act as a solid body in Congress, or to separate entirely from the Union. West Baton Rouge Parish citizens voted 227 for secession and 550 for cooperation. (13) Like the Second Law of Thermodynamics, heat always tends to transfer from a hot object to a cooler one. So the heated rhetoric of the Southern "fire eaters" swept cooler heads into the path to war. Statewide, the secession forces prevailed. There were some who suspected that the secessionist forces stole the election. (14) By now everyone knew that war was inevitable.

In his inaugural address, Lincoln vowed not to fire the first shot. By reinforcing Fort Sumpter by sea, he skillfully maneuvered Southerners at Charleston, South Carolina, to fire first: 4:30 P.M., April 12, 1861. His call for 75,000 volunteers drove the upper tier of Southern states into the Confederacy. Lincoln acted quickly to suspend the writ of habeas corpus and closed many newspapers in the North, especially in Maryland. He then sent his navy to blockade Southern ports.

Sending the men to war begged the question of who would manage the slaves. The fear of slave uprisings and another Santo Domingo was always in the back of the mind of any Southerner in 1861. Narcisse Landry was fifteen years old when a slave uprising near New Orleans was put down. The leaders were decapitated and their heads were put on the ends of long poles along the river road. One of these poles was placed at Plaquemine as a warning to the local slave population. The would-be Spartacus, Nat Turner, and his rebellion in 1831 Virginia, as well as the more recent exploits of John Brown, added to this long-held paranoia.

Men who for reasons of age or health that were unable to go to war organized themselves into a "corps of police" to watch the slaves. Patrols had been a common practice in slave states. With the advent of war, they were beefed up and taken more seriously. Every white male between the ages of sixteen and sixty was compelled to do patrol duty. This was one of the many hidden costs of maintaining the slave economy.

Clerk of Court W. B. Chamberlin was appointed "Chief of Police." The chief was to appoint ward captains (*chefs de patrole*), lieutenants, and deputies. The patrols were to make rounds at night from one end of the ward to the other. They were to arrest any Negroes without a pass and it was their duty to search slave quarters. Slaves with any weapons had them confiscated. Any slave owning a dog was ordered to part with it. (15)

The Sunday, April 21st edition of the Baton Rouge *Daily Advocate* ran this article: "It is with pleasure, we note an instance of patriotic liberality in our parish, worthy of the highest praise. In order that the fine company of Tirailleurs, recently formed under command of Captain F. A. Williams, at Brusly Landing, should be properly and effectively armed, Mr. Thompson W. Bird, one of our most spirited and patriotic citizens, has generously presented each member of the company with a fine Enfield rifle. Armed with this terrible weapon, the Tirailleurs will do good service in the cause of Southern rights and institutions." T. W. Bird was the father of Second Lieutenant A. J. Bird of the Tirailleurs. (16)

The Tirailleurs dressed in gray wool with long trousers and brogans. Their belt, with the brass Pelican buckle, held a standard bayonet scabbard, cartridge pouch, and cap pouch. They wore kepis with short bills in keeping with the then-current European tradition. They carried knapsacks and haversacks. The knapsack was stuffed with all things thought to be necessary in the field: extra clothes (*ligne*), comb (*peigne*), stationary (*papier a écrire*), tobacco (*tobac*), toothbrush (*brosse à dents*), tourniquet, and bandages. On top of this was folded two blankets (*courveture*) and a rubber cloth (*courverture de gumelastic*). All this weighed between fifteen and twenty-five pounds. The Tirailleurs also carried a canteen (*flacon*). Some carried revolvers and Bowie knives as well.

Each mess consisted of four to eight men or more and carried a camp chest (*coffre de camp*) containing a skillet (*poelön*), coffee boiler (*grègue a café*), lard bucket (*baquet de graisse*), coffee box (*bôite de café*), salt box (*bôite de sale*), sugar box (*bôite de sucre*), meal box (*bôite de farine*), knives (*couteau*), forks (*fourchette*), spoons (*cuillere*), and cups (*pinte*). Each mess carried an axe (*hache*), and a water bucket (*baquet de l'eau*). The men chipped in money and formed a mess fund for purchasing food not supplied by the army. More than one man brought along a slave (*esclave*) to do the cooking. Most of this paraphernalia would be discarded when real campaigning started. (17)

On April 26, 1861, there was a big celebration at Brusly Landing with a huge crowd of citizens. The full strength of the company was out. Bands were playing and flags were flying for the celebration. Captain Rauhman's company of National Guards of East Baton Rouge arrived by ferry for the celebration. The National Guards were made up primarily of German immigrants from East Baton Rouge Parish. The Delta Rifles arrived in their "distinctive" green uniforms, their sleeves trimmed with long fringe. The tunic was also trimmed with fringe that reached below the knees. The companies were put through the battalion drill by Captain Favrot, much to the delight of the crowd. There were many in attendance from Iberville and East Baton Rouge parishes.

A new company flag was sewn by the beautiful daughters of the Widow (*Veuve*) Bujol. The presentation of the flag was made, followed by speeches and celebration. Then the band played the *Marseillaise*. Following the presentation the crowd retired to a sumptuous repast. There was a blessing by Father Victor Clerouin. Thirteen pigs hung in front of huge fires, and speeches and toasts continued. A feast of *vin, sauce pecante, viande de chevreuil, couchon farci*, and hot coffee was consumed. Following dinner, the Tirailleurs accompanied the other companies to the landing, where they boarded a steamer for home.

On May 6th, a meeting was held at the Harney House Hotel in Baton Rouge. All the officers of the prospective 4th LA were in attendance. Informal elections were held. Forty-two-year-old Robert J. Barrow was selected as colonel, H. W. Allen was selected lieutenant colonel, and twenty-eight-year-old Samuel Eugene Hunter was selected major. All three wore the patriotic symbol of tricolor rosettes in their hats.

Colonel Barrow insisted on a dark blue flag with a white star in the center for the regimental ensign. Barrow was a descendant of William Barrow, a cofounder of the West Florida Republic. September 11, 1810, citizens of East and West Feliciana and East Baton Rouge declared their independence from the

Spanish, captured Baton Rouge, and ran up the Bonnie Blue flag over Fort San Carlos.

On Sunday, May 19, 1861, a special Mass was said for the Tirailleurs at St. John the Baptist Church by Father Clerouin. It was a solemn moment when the little French priest blessed the company's flag. The next day, the company was to travel to New Orleans as part of the 4th Regiment of Louisiana Volunteers. In the morning a crowd began to gather at Brusly Landing. Everyone who could possibly leave home was there to bid an affectionate farewell to the Tirailleurs. The men of the company were fully armed and equipped, awaiting the arrival of the steamship *J. S. Cotton*. The *Cotton* had been up river to pick up the Delta Rifles. Captain Rauhman's National Guards were to travel as well, but were delayed. (See Appendix A for roster).

The editor of the Baton Rouge *Gazette and Comet* wrote, "The citizens of this and the neighboring parish were called upon to witness another painful departing of brothers and sons for the war of conquest, subjugation and extermination now being waged against us...A herd of hirelings under the mandate of an imbecile [Lincoln] and weak despotism march against us, to force us into slavish servitude, under the pretext of preserving liberty! What madness! What folly! Our position is one in which we have all to lose by defeat, and nothing to gain by victory, except that independence which is our Divine right." (18)

The flowers of chinaberry trees filled the air with their perfume. It was now 11 A.M. and the steamboat came into view. Its arrival was greeted with cheers. In a few minutes the steamer rounded to, and families parted sadly. The women were there in their bonnets (*garde-soleil*) and the men in their Sunday best. Narcisse was there as well as Trasimond's sister Marie and her husband, Francis. Trasimond's sister Victorine had her three children and husband Gustave. Belisaire parted with his wife, Manette. Sisters Adele and Josephine were there. Second Sergeant Trasimond Landry hugged them all and said his goodbyes. Young Simon Alcide hugged his brothers and said he would join them soon. They laughed at the fifteen-year-old baby brother. The war would surely be over before he was old enough to join. The order was given to "*Alignez vous! Rassemblement!*" (Fall In!)

When the *Cotton* arrived at Brusly Landing the Tirailleurs were drawn up in a line. The command was given, "*Marchez!*" In a few moments the company was aboard. The stage plank was lifted and the steamer backed into the river and straightened herself up. She rounded to the north and then passed back in front of Brusly Landing to the cheers of onlookers and the waving of handkerchiefs. Flags were flying from the jackstaff and black smoke boiled from her stacks. The hurricane and boiler decks were full of waving and cheering gray-clad Southern patriots. Mark Twain wrote, "From this point in the river, south, begins a pilot's paradise: a wide river hence to New Orleans, abundance of water from shore to shore, and no bars, snags, sawyers, or wrecks in this road." (19)

Downriver, residents of Plaquemine were awaiting passage of the *Cotton*. As it went by, "Old Black Bess," the city's salute cannon, was fired. Passing down the river by almost every home, handkerchiefs and hats were seen waving. The inhabitants of the entire coast seemed to be on watch to cheer on these new volunteers. In 1861, the levee was not very high (fifteen feet wide at the base, five feet high, with a three-foot crown) and passing down the Acadian and the German Coasts was like touring a long, spread-out village. Most plantations fronted the river for a few arpents, then stretched back across the natural river levee to the swamps. Each plantation home would front the river and could be easily seen from the steamers. After Plaquemine was Donaldsonville, then College Point, Bonnet Carre, Red Church, Harry Hills, Carrollton, and then on to New Orleans. Captain Baranco and his crew on the *Cotton* made the six-hour trip as pleasant as possible for the Tirailleurs. (20)

Near New Orleans, three steamers were passed conveying Colonel Paul Hebert's 3rd Regiment of Louisiana Volunteers. It was dark at the time, but the men cheered each other. Company K of this regiment was the Pelican Rifles of Baton Rouge and they were on their way to Arkansas and the Battles of Oak Hill and Pea Ridge.

The companies arrived in New Orleans well after dark. They were not allowed off the steamer. The next morning at a very early hour they were ordered to the Jackson Railroad for transportation to Camp Moore. In the early morning, the companies marched through the cobblestone streets of New Orleans to the train depot. On reaching the station they found cars waiting for them and were whisked away to Camp Moore.

The Confederacy had established the "Twenty Negro Rule." Any plantation with twenty or more slaves could have their overseer exempted from military service. Sergeant Amedee Landry, Narcisse Landry's second son, was dropped from the rolls of the Tirailleurs. It was necessary for him to return home to act as overseer of the plantation.

2.

Guarding the Coast

The original training camp for Louisiana troops was Camp Walker at the old Metairie racetrack. The low, swampy ground and poor water forced Governor Moore to look elsewhere for a camp. In mid-May 1861, Camp Moore was established in the piney woods of northern St. Helena Parish. It was bordered on the south by Beaver Creek, on the east by the Tangipahoa River, and by the railroad on the west. There was good, fresh water from Beaver Creek and the Tangipahoa River. The companies cleared off underbrush for a shady campsite about one half mile from Tangipahoa Station, immediately on the railroad. At the time, the 4th LA, 5th LA, 6th LA, and 7th LA regiments occupied the camp. There was a welcomed scarcity of annoying mosquitoes (*maringouin*), but plenty of ticks (*pou de bois*) and red bugs (*des bête rouge*). (1)

Supplies began pouring in by rail from New Orleans, including barrels of vinegar, flour, mess pork, hard bread, and corn meal; sacks of coffee and salt; tierces of sugar and rice; hogsheads of molasses and bacon; boxes of soap and candles; casks of beans; and bales of hay. At the depot were bundles of canteens, knapsacks, haversacks with straps, and tin cups. There were bales of bedsocks and blankets, and boxes of mosquito bars.

Many problems faced General Elisha L. Tracy, the camp commander. Chief among them was establishing discipline in the raw volunteers. Whiskey and wine was in abundance and the Tirailleurs were not the least temperate. The camp had only been in existence for several weeks when the West Baton Rouge companies arrived. The men were called out at daylight by the drum beat. Roll was called. They were put to work constructing camp facilities and drilling. Dress parade was held every evening to the lively strains of Bernard Moses' camp band. To the men it was like a big camp out. There was plenty of spare time for poker, baseball, swimming, and letter writing. There was good clay for making pipes. Securing a pass to visit New Orleans was easy. At 9 P.M. roll was called again, and the troops were given fifteen minutes to get to bed and put out their candles.

Private John Morgan (Hunter Rifles A) wrote his sister on May 16, 1861: "There were two deaths in camp yesterday. One from sunstroke or apoplexy and the other from being run over by the cars (of a train) when drunk the night before. They were both Irishmen and were not grieved after much." (2) The two men were members of Wheat's Battalion.

On May 25, 1861, at Camp Moore, the West Baton Rouge Tirailleurs were officially mustered into service as Company D (later to be Company H) of the 4th Louisiana Infantry Regiment. These boys and young men from the tranquil sugar bowl of Louisiana were now committed to become participants in the defining event of the American nation.

The 4th LA was organized through the efforts of H. W. Allen, a colonel in the Louisiana State Militia. Allen was an experienced politician who had lobbied and jockeyed himself into the position lieutenant colonel of the newly formed 4th LA. In 1842, he had raised a company of Mississippi volunteers that traveled to Texas during a border threat from Santa Anna. (3) He was born in Virginia in 1820, and moved to Mississippi via Missouri. He was also a teacher and a self-trained lawyer. After the death of his wife, he moved to West Baton Rouge Parish and became a very prosperous sugar planter and politician.

The 4th Louisiana enrolled 862 men, organized into ten companies:

Colonel: Robert J. Barrow
Lieutenant Colonel: Henry W. Allen
Major: Samuel E. Hunter

Company A, National Guards (East Baton Rouge) Capt. Rauhman
Company B, Lake Providence Cadets (Carroll) Capt. Whicher
Company C, Delta Rifles (West Baton Rouge) Capt. Favrot
Company D, Tirailleurs (West Baton Rouge) Capt. Williams
Company E, West Feliciana Rifles Capt. Tooraen
Company F, St. Helena Rifles Capt. Taylor
Company G, Beaver Creek Rifles (St. Helena) Capt. Wingfield
Company H, Lafourche Guards (Iberville) Capt. Vick
Company I, Hunter Rifles B (East Feliciana) Capt. Hilliard
Company K, Hunter Rifles A (East Feliciana) Capt. Pullen
St. Mary Cannoneers (4)

In late May, there were rumors that the regiment would be sent to Ship Island, but the men were sure that they would be sent to Virginia. They were wrong. Some companies left Camp Moore on June 6th. On June 7th, they prepared for their departure to the Mississippi Coast with a celebration. A huge kettle of jambalaya was prepared, along with as much wine and liquor as they could supply themselves. On June 8th, tents were taken down, blankets rolled, and camp chests packed. The Tirailleurs lined up along the railroad track to await the train. Dr. Langworthy remained at Camp Moore to care for soldiers with measles (*rougeole*). Among them was J. L. Belue, St. Helena Rifles, who died of measles at Camp Moore.

The regiment went by rail in open cars to New Orleans to await a steamer. There was great enthusiasm and exhilaration. Cheering crowds lined the route in a Mardi Gras-like atmosphere. Ladies stood on balconies to bid the regiment good-bye. The regimental band struck up a lively rendition of *The Bonnie Blue Flag* as the new regiment marched through the hot New Orleans' streets. The men marched to the Carrollton Railroad and took cars to the lake end of the line. The bulk of the regiment spent two nights on the pier with very little to eat. While awaiting the steamer *Creole*, they suffered in either the rain or the hot sun, and were constantly attacked by mosquitoes. (5) The Tirailleurs arrived later with the left wing of the regiment and went straight to the steamer. Standing on the wharf was Gustave Grogne. He was an un-enrolled, unpaid member of the Tirailleurs. Gustave preferred this status to official enrollment. Captain Williams let him stay on because he was willing to work, drill, and fight.

The steamer *CSS Gray Cloud* arrived on Sunday morning, June 9th, and took off with the Tirailleurs and three other companies for the Mississippi Coast. "All Aboard!" The shrill steam whistle blew. The hawser was cast loose and the steamer pulled away from the pier. Just after the *Gray Cloud* had left her wharf, Lieutenant A. J. Bird fell overboard and drowned. Lieutenant Colonel Allen sent a resolution of condolence, to be printed in the *Sugar Planter*. All commissioned officers were to wear black crepe on their left arm for thirty days, and the regimental flag was flown at half-mast. (6)

Second Lieutenant Abraham John Bird left a widow, Marie Eliza Dupuy, and one son, Abraham John Jr. The drowned Confederate's grandmother was a sister of Jim Bowie. (7) He was wearing a heavy Bowie knife when he fell overboard. Lieutenant Bird was the first West Baton Rouge soldier to die in wartime since the death of Ulysse Landry at Matamoros, Mexico, July 16, 1846. Ulysse was a Tirailleur.

There were now sixty-nine men present for duty in the Tirailleurs. Belisaire Landry was elected second lieutenant and Sosthene Aillet moved from first sergeant to third lieutenant.

On the trip to Mississippi City, Sergeant Sosthene Aillet paced the deck. Trasimond noticed how uneasy and nervous he was and asked Belisaire about him. His brother explained that Aillet probably took Lieutenant Bird's accident as a bad omen. Bad luck meant a stormy sea voyage ahead. He then went on to recount an old story. When the Tirailleurs left for Mexico on May 15, 1846, they traveled to New Orleans. From there they struck for Port Isabel, Texas. One day out of New Orleans their ship, the *U.S.S. New York*, was lashed by a storm. Even the ship's captain thought they were lost. Ever since that terrible storm, Aillet avoided sea travel.

Around noon, the steamer reached the mouth of the Rigolets. The *Gray Cloud* passed Fort Pike's twelve-foot brick walls. Fort Pike's sixteen heavy guns were surrounded by barracks and white tents. Passing the fort, the steamer pulled into a wood yard. Crewmen loaded wood for two hours while swarms of mosquitoes feasted on the soldiers. They arrived at Mississippi City before dark.

On June 29, 1861, there was a major reshuffling of the non-commissioned officers. Trasimond Landry's rank was reduced from second sergeant to private at his own request. Several other non-commissioned officers requested relief. (8) At the beginning of July another outbreak of measles hit the regiment. The Delta Rifles and West Feliciana Rifles were particularly hard hit. (9)

John McGrath, Company C, wrote this for the *Baton Rouge Daily Advocate*, January 13, 1915:

"General Twiggs sent for Lt. Col. Allen, then in command of the 4th LA, and ordered him to construct sand fortifications on the island (Ship Island).

'Will laborers be there when we arrive?' asked Col. Allen.

'Laborers? Why your soldiers will do the work,' said Twiggs.

'Soldiers! My God, General, my men are gentlemen. Do you expect gentlemen to do the work of laborers?' said Allen.

'Gentlemen. Gentlemen be damned. They are soldiers. You take your damn gentlemen over to the island and put them to work at once. Gentlemen!'

Allen did so, and young men who had never so much as saddled their own horses or even laced their own shoes were soon filling and carrying them [sandbags] under a blistering sun." (10)

On July 7th, the Tirailleurs boarded the *CSS Oregon*. The *Oregon* sported an eight-inch Columbiad and a twelve-pounder Howitzer. They landed safely at Ship Island along with bales of sandbags, spades, pick axes, lumber, and kegs of nails. What they found there was a half-finished masonry fort and a bunch of burned-out buildings. In mid-July all companies except the Delta Rifles and the West Feliciana Rifles were on Ship Island. (11) They were stationed on this desolate spot digging fortifications—just the start of many days of back-breaking toil the Tirailleurs would see during the war. Their willingness to work was a tribute to their dedication to the Cause.

Private Silas T. White, Hunter Rifles A, wrote: "Ship Island is about twenty-five miles long and one (mile) wide. The eastern end is finely timbered and a little elevated, but the western part, for the space of five miles, is a barren tract with a few patches of saltwater grass. There in the place where the camp and fort is situated is one of the hottest places I ever saw." (12)

On July 9th, excitement spread through the camp. The light-house sentinel sounded the alarm. The *U.S.S. Massachusetts* was advancing toward the island under full sail. Cannoneers moved to their posts with Lieutenant Colonel Allen in command.

From the deck of the *Massachusetts,* Commander Melancton Smith could see thirty-nine tents, three Confederate flags, and four gun emplacements. That day the National Guards, under Captain Rauhman, stood the fire of the Yankee warship. With a single piece of artillery the company compelled the Yankees to withdraw. Shells from the Columbiads on the island were reaching the *Massachusetts,* but her shells fell short.

On July 13th, the *Massachusetts* returned, but the soldiers of the 4th LA were watching. Several Confederate gunboats stood to and tried to lure the Federal ship into the range of the fort's cannon, but were unsuccessful. To cheers from the men of the 4th LA, the *Massachusetts* broke off and sailed out of sight. (13)

Earlier that same day, a steamer arrived at the island with the Washington Light Infantry. Arriving on the same steamer was a member of Hunter Rifles A. He wrote, "My first idea of this place was that I had come to a place of punishment." (14)

"We have seven thirty-pounders, one sixty-four-pounder, and one ninety-six-pounder, besides two Howitzers in the fort," wrote Private White. "I saw four more guns taken from the boat when we came to Biloxi yesterday (July 24th). There are about 800 men on the island, a plenty to whip 10,000 Yankees." (15) Another soldier wrote, "It is my candid opinion that 100 men could hold this fort for weeks from any army of men Old Abe will ever send in these waters." (16)

The soldiers had confidence in their fort. The base was four feet wide and four feet high and topped with three feet of sandbags. Thirteen cannons had been mounted. There was ample protection for artillerists. A Hunter Rifle member wrote, "Lincoln certainly never intends an attack upon this place, for it would be reckless folly." (17)

Mail arrived, July 20th. Private Prudent Crochet read a letter from his new wife, Adolphine. She was pregnant and informed him that the Police Jury had awarded them $78 from the Poydras Fund. She promised to put the money to good use. Julien Poydras was a Frenchman who had made his fortune in Colonial Louisiana. He never married, and on his death willed $30,000 to the parish. The interest earned from the money was to be given to all the girls of the parish as dowries. Preference was to be given to the poor. (18)

Private Theodore Lejeune wrote home to his sweetheart from Ship Island, July 26, 1861. "Here they make a delicious soup. And we come to be true rascals. Almost every day on Ship Island, pigs and sheep are killed. They belong to a widow, A. Zelofie. I can say that the Tirailleurs are not going to starve as long as the widow has pigs on the island. There is not a single tree where we are, only much white sand. Consequently, almost all of us have turned into mulattos (*tournez mulâte*). My compliments to all the Damoiselles and to your family." (19)

A package arrived from Brusly for Arthur Blanchard. Arthur was of medium height, but very slender. He had blue eyes and straight blond hair. Pink blemishes of acne confirmed his youth. By 1861 standards, his inheritance had left him quite wealthy. Arthur was no fool. He took half his fortune and purchased 8% Confederate bonds. He converted the other half to gold and buried it somewhere on his brother's property. His sister-in-law, Emma, sent him a can of syrup and a box of marchpane. Arthur's widowed mother had died when he was eighteen years old and his older brother, Theodore Elie Blanchard, and his wife, Emma, acted *in loco parentis*. Emma was the sister of Corporal Paul Babin. She sent news of her new baby, little Thomas Victor Blanchard.

Trasimond's sister, Josephine, wrote him about his new niece, Marie Josephine Rivet. She was born July 27, 1861.

Around their driftwood campfires, the sea breezes kept the mosquitoes away. Forty-one-year-old Jackson Libby was a Mexican War veteran of Captain William Blount Robertson's West Baton Rouge Guards. He had a long red beard and a shiny bald head, altogether an unlikely looking prospect for a soldier. His nose was red from continuous sunburn. The campfire sizzled as he spit tobacco juice into it. A Norfolk whine made him difficult to understand at times, but he was a great storyteller. Ship Island reminded him of Brazos de Jayo, an island off the Texas coast, from which island the volunteers joined the army of General Zachary Taylor.

A fresh copy of the *Sugar Planter* was passed around the camp. A group with the curiously redundant name of "The Confederate League" had been formed. The paper reported that their agents were making their rounds about Brusly Landing, stopping by each plantation home and soliciting subscriptions for the war effort. The editor of this local paper wrote, "Remember that you but *lend* so much money to the government for which you receive eight percent interest. If successful in our war of independence, your money will be faithfully returned; if not successful, of what value will be your lands and negroes (sic)." (20) While on the Mississippi Coast the West Baton Rouge Police Jury met and offered a resolution of monthly assistance to volunteers of the Tirailleurs "requiring pecuniary assistance." (21) (See Appendix H)

The paper also noted that the parish women of West Baton Rouge were organizing a sewing society to make clothing for new volunteers. The looms in the state prison at Baton Rouge supplied the cloth. Celine Fremaux wrote, "When ladies met it was to sew for the soldiers or to make lint and bandages. Rolled bandages were made five yards long and of three widths...the lint was put in one-pound packages. Every soldier's knapsack contained a set of bands and a package of lint." (22)

Wednesday, August 7th, was Private Trasimond Landry's twenty-first birthday. It had rained hard for the previous two days. The wind whipped across Ship Island, collapsing many of the tents. That morning the sun rose, lighting up the whole expanse of the white beach. Sea birds hung over the camp garbage dump. The fortifications at Ship Island were not yet completed and work continued daily. Filling sand bags all day in the subtropical sun had bronzed Trasimond's skin. In the afternoon, he and his mess mates went crabbing. Two island pigs had been killed that week and the pork made good crab bait. In late July, news reached the regiment describing a great victory at Manassas, Virginia. A few weeks later came news of General Benjamin McCullock's defeat of the Union General Lyons at the Battle of Oak Hill. The men knew that the Pelican Rifles of Baton Rouge had been in this battle.

On August 8th, General Twiggs sent West Point-trained Colonel Johnson Duncan to Ship Island. Twiggs expected a Yankee attack. At the time, the disposition of the 4th LA was: Pascagoula, two companies (200 troops), Ocean Springs, two companies (100 troops), Biloxi, two companies (180 troops), and Ship Island, four companies (360 troops). (23) By August 10th, the Hunter Rifles were at Biloxi. At dress parade, Ira Bowman accidentally shot Tom Moore. Moore lost his arm.

On August 17th, there was a hard rain and a hard wind. That same day, the *Sugar Planter* wrote a long editorial bemoaning the fate of the 4th LA. Calling the regiment one of the finest regiments ever formed, it should have been "rapidly hurried off to the scene of action rather than doing guard duty on the Mississippi coast." (24)

The editor lamented the fact that "in many instances, the scum of towns and cities, the outpouring of work houses and shops have been sent off to fight for that which they have no interest." Here the editor was referring to regiments from New Orleans made up of lower classes, who had made a good account of themselves in Virginia. They were unruly, but were affectionately referred to as "Lee's Tigers." (25) It is from this group of soldiers that Louisiana State University takes its mascot, the Bengal Tiger. The paper contended that the South would best be served by letting the sons of gentlemen and planters do the fighting. Major Roberdeau Wheat's Battalion of Tigers were at Camp Moore with the 4th LA, but were kept out of the main camp. They were too rough a set of neighbors, and on one occasion at camp the 4th LA was called out to put down a near mutiny among the Tigers.

Most volunteers expected to be sent off to Missouri or Virginia for immediate action. They were all sure that the war would be over in three to six months and were eager to fight. They had not bargained for belonging to a coast guard, and many asked for transfer. Many just walked away, joining regiments with better prospects for action. They had begun referring to themselves as the "Crab Catching" Regiment. Colonel Barrow had repeatedly made requests to Secretary of War William Seddon to assign the 4th LA to a brigade more likely to see combat. He received no help from Governor Moore, who liked the idea of Louisiana troops being close to home. (26) Four new recruits arrived in early July. There were now seventy-three Tirailleurs.

August 27th, J. B. Corkern wrote, "There will soon be 3,300 Mississippi State troops here. We have little prospect of an engagement with the enemy. General Twiggs wants us to remain in his division of the army and will do everything in his power to retain us." (27)

By mid-September, Ship Island was occupied by four companies of the 4th LA, two companies from Baton Rouge commanded by Lieutenant Oliver Semmes, and the Washington Light Infantry. The Tirailleurs had been sent to East Pascagoula in late August. Without the support of shallow draft gunboats, Colonel Duncan recommended abandonment of Ship Island. This was done between September 13th and the 17th. (28) Francis Palms, Delta Rifles wrote, "Before our troops were one mile from the burning fort, the enemy's ships were seen nearing the island." (29) The loss of Ship Island effectively cut off communications between Mobile and New Orleans. (30)

After leaving the island, the regiment was split up. The West Feliciana Rifles were sent to Pass Christian (Camp Barrow). The Hunter Rifles went to Biloxi (Camp Neafus). The Delta Rifles were sent to Ocean Springs (Camp Beauregard). The Lafourche Guards, Beaver Creek Rifles, St. Helena Rifles, and Lake Providence Cadets were sent to Mississippi City (Camp Davis). The Tirailleurs and National Guards went to East Pascagoula. Military camps had not been seen in East Pascagoula since 1848. That year the army from Mexico had returned and encamped there.

Hunter Rifles B left Ship Island early for Biloxi. Jimmy Knighton wrote home describing the huge grapes and muscadines grown by the locals. He had gained seven pounds while at Biloxi. Rumors were circulating in camp that the 4th LA would soon be sent to New Orleans to construct fortifications. (31) The Hunter Rifles were camped on the property of Byrn Vance. In bad weather, they were allowed to stay in the vacation cottages on the property. (32)

At East Pascagoula there was plenty of guard duty and drill for the Tirailleurs. Dress parade was at 5 P.M. and was usually attended by many of the local belles. The local Mississippi rednecks (*chou rouge*) were fascinated by the Tirailleurs. One local was remembered as saying, "Why, them officers spout out some gibberish, and them Frenchies just march around smartly like they know what he's a sayin."

September 24th, Rosemond Hebert and his cousins, Alexis and Raphael Hebert, had permission to visit Mobile. Mess mate Gustave Grogne came along as well. They took the stagecoach and made the thirty-mile journey in less than one day. They entered Mobile down a white oyster-shell road which passed Springhill College. Alexis remembered that Lieutenant Bird had attended college there. They passed Camp Moore, about a mile from the city. There were many companies of new Alabama recruits out drilling.

Their first stop was at the home of a LaGrange College classmate of Raphael. They were invited to stay and eagerly accepted. Mobile hospitality impressed the Acadians. The Mobilians always did what they could to brighten the lives of their soldiers and sailors visiting there on leave. The Acadians took to the city immediately. While the three Heberts explored the city, Gustave spent his time at the Battle House Hotel exploring the Mobile prostitutes. He had a taste for officer's brothels. After three days of oysters and admiring the pretty Mobile girls, they heard the stage horn blow. The troupe left for East Pascagoula.

Discipline was relaxed at East Pascagoula. The men did guard duty and company drill, but spent the majority of their time amusing themselves. Trasimond organized a baseball team and played many games, sometimes with four bases, sometimes with only two. The Tirailleurs did a great deal of fishing. They caught crabs, fished, and speared flounder at night. They preferred fish when wine was available. Belisaire was fond of saying, "*Le poisson sans boissan est poison.*" (Fish without a drink is poisonous). Great card games flourished. Fiddle music was supplied by Private Sam Leveque, and musicians from both companies organized an *ad hoc* battalion band. Reading and letter writing went on daily. All but one of the Tirailleurs were literate, though many spoke only French. The troops relished receiving mail and the best way to get a letter was to send a letter. Stationary had not yet become scarce.

Since the war started, most of the summer homes at East Pascagoula had become deserted. The company camped on the grounds of the only hotel, which had closed due to lack of business. There was milk, oysters, and chicken daily, and the company attended Mass each Sunday. Myrtis Naquin died of illness at Mississippi City. His body was shipped to Thibodeaux, and his funeral was attended by 2,000 people as well as several military companies. (33)

On October 9th, the company was ordered to Ocean Springs, where they arrived on the 10th. (34) Alexis Hebert was a twenty-one-year-old big-eyed Acadian with impeccable manners and sensitivity. He was a dutiful spirit with an earnest regard for God and family. He wrote his father, "We have left Pascagoula. The fellows have been very much missed by some of the ladies in particular there are several of the company who courted well, and also who made some of these girls weep." (35) J. B. Corkern wrote, "This is a very desolate place (Ocean Springs) presenting no inducements to our enemy to land and what the object of sending us here I cannot surmise." (36)

The weather was turning cold and the days were getting shorter. An early morning duck (*canard*) hunt on Bayou Bonheur was a common diversion. Francis Palms wrote, "The camp is beautiful, being located in the shade of wide spreading oaks facing a beautiful bay of clear limpid water, but the place is deserted of its inhabitants." (37) Tents were leaky and there was no wood available to floor them. The companies were next ordered to Mississippi City.

The Ocean Springs companies waited as the *Oregon* hove into view at 10 A.M., October 14th. The troops broke camp and boarded at sundown. The steamer did not leave until the next day as she waited for a high tide.

October 22, 1861, Alexis Hebert wrote dutifully to his father. He thanked him for the underwear (*leinge*) that he had sent by way of Captain Williams. There was a gentle hint that he and his older brother, Raphael, Jr., would like a rubber (*gumelastic*) overcoat. He mentioned an episode in which a member of the Hunter Rifles was accidentally shot. William Stone was cleaning his pistol when it fired, striking Sergeant Charles Ratcliff in the head. Ratcliff died the next day. The regiment formed up for a military funeral procession. Bernard Moses' brass band played funeral music as the regiment accompanied the dead sergeant to the wharf. His body was taken aboard the *CSS Creole* and sent for burial at Pass Christian.

Alexis also wrote describing the local cafe, "There are three billiard tables and we play all the day, but there is only lemonade to drink." Colonel Barrow had closed all the bars. There was also mention of a sea battle between the *CSS Florida* and ships of the Union navy off the coast at Mississippi City. (38)

The regiment was ordered to Berwick City, Louisiana, October 9, 1861. By October 29th, the entire regiment was assembled at Mississippi City. They camped in a thick grove of pines near the beach on the grounds of the Barnes Hotel. The 4th LA was being sent to guard the mouth of the Atchafalaya River against Union attack. The port was important for the cattle trade with Texas and for the salt trade. If lost, the Union navy could travel up the Atchafalaya in shallow draft boats and get into the Red River system and the Mississippi, thus bypassing New Orleans. General Mansfield Lovell took over command of Southern Department No. 1 after seventy-four-year-old Major General Twiggs resigned. (39)

The right wing of the regiment left the Mississippi coast for New Orleans on the steamer *Creole* in mid-October. The left wing, with the Tirailleurs, left on the *CSS Oregon*, October 31st. After arriving in New Orleans, the troops were marched off to Washington Square and from there to the Opelousas and Great Western Railroad. (40) The train passed out of New Orleans, through Boutte, Allemands, Lafourche, Thibodeaux Junction, Chacahoula, Donner, Tigerville (Gibson), across Bayou Boeuf, and on into Brashear City (Morgan City). They arrived in Brashear City in the early morning of November 1st. From there they crossed the bay by steamer to Berwick City. As usual, their baggage followed later.

The weather had become cold, but was milder than West Baton Rouge weather. Practically all the plantations from Berwick City to Franklin were well into their grinding season. The odor of woodsmoke was everywhere. Aside from citrus orchards, the local plantations grew cane almost exclusively. The profits were substantial enough to buy their corn from northern parishes by the barge loads.

The quiet little town of Berwick City had three bar rooms, a bakery, two stores, and an oyster house. There was an old hotel overlooking the bay. Tall, moss-draped cypress, all green, but with a faint redness, could be seen everywhere. Dotted here and there were box elders. The water's edge was choked with thick growths of willows. There was a frost November 2nd, All Souls Day (*le Jour des Morts*).

The regiment was again split up: five companies at Camp Lovell (Berwick City), two companies at Fort Chène, one at Fort Berwick, and two at Fort Hunter (Franklin). (41) Fort Berwick was four miles below Berwick City at the junction of Wax Bayou and the Atchafalaya River. Work consisted mostly of mounting heavy cannon around the bay. There were always at least four companies in camp at Berwick City. Regular drills and dress parades continued. Tobacco was plentiful. Bar rooms were placed off-limits and guards stationed to prevent temptation. Bernard Moses' regimental band was always in attendance at parade. (42)

Lieutenant Belisaire Landry had a fifteen-day furlough, October 17, 1861. (43) At home in Brusly Landing, the frost had killed potato vines and pumpkins stood out starkly in the garden. Hands were windrowing seed cane behind double plows. Other hands were picking peas. All the white corn had been shelled, ground, sifted, and put into barrels. The rice had been cut and was soon to be threshed. Sweet potatoes needed digging. The second week in November the Landrys started bringing in their cane. Friends in New Orleans were complaining of food becoming scarce. Flour prices in New Orleans were high. Fats, soap, starch, and candles were now very expensive. Many whites were suffering from the economic upheavals and dislocations that accompany war. Manette informed Belisaire that the townsfolk were sending coats and winter clothing to the Tirailleurs by way of Mr. W. B. Chamberlin. She also sent blankets for them and some extras for men with no families. Sixteen-year-old Simon Alcide Landry spent his time gathering up scrap iron and brass to be sent to the army.

On November 12th, J. B. Corkern wrote, "We get an abundance of sugar cane and oranges for the gathering and can catch very good freshwater fish. The mosquitoes are very bad." (44) Thanksgiving Day, November 13th, the weather was warm with a breeze from the south. The *CSS Mobile*, a gunboat on patrol on Berwick Bay, took on twenty or so privates from the 4th LA. They were to be used as marines aboard the gunboat. (45)

On December 1st, six men from each company were detached to blockade the channel leading from the Gulf of Mexico into Berwick Bay. The work detail cut live oak trees to be sunk in the channel, forming an obstruction forty feet wide at the base and eight feet wide at the top. (46) They camped aboard the *CSS General Rusk*. The work went on until early January, 1862. The local police jury grudgingly paid these soldiers $1.50 per day for their labor. (47) Also at this time, three Tirailleurs, August Buquoi, Hubert Hebert, and William Gassie, were discharged on account of physical disability.

On December 8th, Marie Therese Kirkland was in camp visiting her fiancé, Lieutenant J. A. Leveque. On December 10th, he accompanied her to New Orleans. They would be married the next December. The regiment at this time was still looking fresh and new. All had their distinctive uniforms, equipment, and shoes. There was still much concern among the troops that they would miss out on the war entirely.

In early December, rumors floated around camp that Berwick City would be their winter quarters. Corporal Paul Babin, a carpenter, had spent December working on a barrack for the company. The regiment had completed six large structures before Christmas. These huts became the men's homes. They were warm and had the smell of smoke and sleep.

On Christmas Eve, the sun went down in a glorious red sky. In December, the surrounding army of cypress had gone from green to red. The evening was spent with mess mates around a warm fire telling stories. Private Jackson Libby joined the Acadians' campfire. He enjoyed entertaining the young volunteers with tales of Mexico. Except for Ursin Leblanc, no one knew if his stories were truthful or not. He was a Yankee by birth, born in Limington, Maine. He had the revolting habit of occluding one nostril with his finger and blowing snot out of the other. The process was then reversed and repeated on the other side.

Trasimond sat back quietly and puffed on his pipe, thinking of all the amazing changes that had taken place in his life over the last year. The memories and sounds of home echoed softly through his mind. Samuel Leveque was nearby, tuning his fiddle. Whenever he took it from the warm huts into the cold night air, the strings contracted, putting it out of tune.

Gustave Grogne was in camp. Gustave pulled out a letter and with a wide grin that reached his eyes, made a production of sniffing the perfumed envelope. He often read the letters from the damoiselles aloud in a dramatic style. This elicited cat calls from the other soldiers. Some were impressed with Grogne's sexual exploits; others simply dismissed him as an accomplished liar.

Looking up into the black sky, Arthur Blanchard could see the big "W." Paul Babin claimed it looked more like a big "M." Trasimond explained that it was the constellation of Cassiopeia, Queen of Ethiopia. He showed them Cepheus, the king, and to the eastward night sky, their daughter, Andromeda. Trasimond told of how Perseus saved the beautiful Andromeda from the sea dragon. Paul Babin thought this was much like the gallant Southern soldiers saving Southern womanhood from the invading Yankee dragons. Trasimond agreed that this may be so, but pointing in the air with his pipe, he cautioned Paul Babin that Andromeda's mother was black. They all laughed. The men stayed up late that night listening to Sam Leveque's fiddle, singing and drinking wine. Late that night, the ash glowed red as Trasimond tapped out his pipe.

Food was plentiful in their winter camp, and most meals were taken alfresco. Micajah Barrow of Company D described his Christmas dinner as "Turkey, chicken, claret, rice, gumbo, and custard—quite a Christmas dinner for camp." (48) One Delta Rifles private described a Christmas meal of roast chicken, ham, milk, eggs, lobsters, cabbage, preserved pears, pumpkin and apple pie, "and plenty of wine and strong coffee." (49) Another private wrote home, "The people are generally very hospitable to us. They have sent us at different times all kinds of vegetables, potatoes, and one or two bbls. of molasses since we have been here." (50)

Christmas night, Private Henry Walsh of the Deltas was shot while visiting Brashear City. Mistaken for an intruder, an Irishman unloaded a double barrel shotgun at him. Dr. Pope had to amputate his arm. (51)

After spending Christmas at Berwick City, Trasimond Landry, Adelard Courtade, and Arthur Blanchard went on a pass to New Orleans. It was Friday, December 27th. They arrived that afternoon and took a room at the St. James Hotel. They then went down to the market for coffee. Their next stop was to purchase a set of violin strings for Private Leveque. The rest of the day was spent in and out of taverns and frolicking around New Orleans. Saturday, they spent the day exploring the city. They visited the shipyards and got a look at the ironclad *CSS Louisiana*. That night there was a thunderous explosion that shook the city, rattling windows and jarring the citizens. The powder mill located in the Marine Hospital had exploded. Eight thousand pounds of gunpowder had accidentally ignited and destroyed the works. Prices were high in New Orleans and they were running low on money. After attending Mass they returned to Berwick City.

Private Joachim Daigle became ill at Berwick City and was sent to New Orleans. He would die from pneumonia. Private Rosemond Hebert received a one-week furlough, December 29th. He was homesick and anxious to visit his widowed mother. (52) His two cousins, Alexis and Raphael Hebert, also had passes, as well as mess mates Prudent Daigle and Theodore Lejeune.

On the 29th, the five Tirailleurs crossed the bay to Brashear City. They paid the $2.00 for a round trip ticket and caught the train to New Orleans at 1 P.M. They arrived at dark in New Orleans and took a room at the St. James Hotel. After breakfast the next morning they boarded the *Cotton*. The fare was $3.00. The whistles blew and she sailed at 9 A.M. They arrived at Brusly Landing late that evening. These five *soldats Acadien* spent one week eating, sleeping, and partying, but mostly partying. Too soon it was time to return to Camp Lovell. At the pier at Brusly Landing, Odile Landry Hebert kissed her sons goodbye. She was a plump Acadian matron who wept continuously as she said her goodbyes. Raphael, being the oldest, embarrassingly took instructions from her to take care of Alexis.

Prudent, Alexis, Raphael, Theodore, and Rosemond boarded the *Cotton* at noon, January 5th. Three of these young men would be dead in a few months. Also returning from leave was Louis Dupuy and Charles Hebert. They arrived back in Brashear City the next day.

On January 31st, Private Palms wrote, "It has rained constantly for the last four days, and during this time we have almost starved. We have not drawn any meat until today. The boys became very indignant. Our captain has gone to New Orleans—probably home." (53)

On February 1st, a member of Hunter Rifles B got his foot caught as he jumped from a train car. His leg was crushed. It was amputated by Dr. Langworthy. A week later he died. (54)

On February 2nd, Private White wrote, "The weather has been very bad for several days, which makes it very muddy in this part of the state, which is nothing more than a frog pond." (55)

By February, the company was tiring of Berwick City. The camp was muddy and not as pleasant as the Mississippi coast. February 10th brought a strong frost. It had rained for two weeks. Private Raphael Hebert kept busy trying to make caramel (*bouillir du sirop*). Gustave Grogne had gone off to New Orleans with the daughter of a local farmer. No one expected him to return.

Private Palms wrote, "Camp life is truly becoming tiresome every day. When I am not on duty I don't know what to do to kill the time. The days seem to grow longer and longer as the day for our discharge approaches." (56)

Colds and fevers began taking a toll on the troops. Colonel Allen was drilling the men in "double quick" time. On February 13th, the regiment received orders from General Ruggles. The men were ordered to hold themselves ready to move on one hour's notice.

Fort Donelson fell, February 16, 1862. This was the site of the first major Confederate defeat in the War Between the States, a most disgraceful event.

Fort Donelson, on the Cumberland River, protected Nashville from Yankee gunboats. The fall of this strategic fort opened the Cumberland and Tennessee Rivers to the Union army and navy. This was a great victory for Grant.

Ulysses Grant was a Mexican War hero, but was a loser in civilian life. When the war began, he rented his house, leased out his Negro slaves, and took a general's commission in the Yankee army. Overnight he had become Lincoln's first winning general.

Flushed with their recent victories, Grant's army then metastasized toward Pittsburg Landing on the Tennessee River. Pittsburg Landing was the closest all-weather landing to the vital railroad junction of Corinth, Mississippi. Confederate General Albert Sidney Johnston was determined to protect it and to push Grant back. In February, second-in-command General P. G. T. Beauregard wired Governor Moore in Louisiana and asked for all the equipped troops he could send for ninety days.

A. S. Johnston was a fifty-nine-year-old Kentuckian and West Point graduate who had fought in the Black Hawk War, the War for Texas Independence, and the Mexican War. After secession he became a full general in the regular army of the Confederacy. He was placed in command of all Confederate forces west of the Alleghenies. (57)

To add to General Johnston's forces, the 4th LA was ordered in mid-February 1862 to Jackson, Tennessee. They were to become part of General Braxton Bragg's Second Corps. On February 20th, the St. Helena Rifles, Hunter Rifles A and B, and the Lake Providence Cadets marched to the railroad to entrain for New Orleans. (58)

The camp was quiet now. The regimental band went off with the first four companies. On February 22nd the weather was very warm and cloudy. A warm wind blew up the bay from the Gulf. That day the Tirailleurs and the remainder of the 4th LA entrained at 9 A.M. Twenty members of the 4th LA were left behind in the hospital. The train jostled and creaked through the now-desolate cypress forests. The leafless, moss-covered branches looked down on a red forest floor. The train arrived in New Orleans at 4 P.M. The next three nights were spent at the old, musty Orleans Cotton Press warehouse. Rumors in camp were that the 4th LA was to be sent to Columbus, Kentucky, or Nashville, Tennessee.

Lieutenant Joseph Augustus Leveque was an 1855 graduate of Pennsylvania Medical College. He was a refined French Creole gentleman whose family had married into and adopted the culture of the West Baton Rouge "Genteel Acadians." While in New Orleans, he stayed with relatives and visited ailing Captain F. A. Williams. Dr. Leveque had many friends in New Orleans and was an acquaintance of General Beauregard. He visited Archbishop John Odin, a friend of his aunt. His aunt was Madame Evelina Leveque, Mother General of the Religious of the Sacred Heart. Leveque was there to ask for a Catholic chaplain for his men.

The war had not stopped the citizens of New Orleans from their festivities, which the Tirailleurs joined in. There were balls, parties, theater, and operas. Carnival season was not ignored. There was a huge Mardi Gras ball February 22nd and the Tirailleurs enjoyed the Carnival parade held that night. Governor Moore, however, prohibited all forms of street masking due to a spy scare. (58) The next day, Private Landry felt as if someone had driven a spike through his head. The Tirailleurs were suffering from hangovers. On February 24th, the regiment was assembled in Annunciation Square for dress parade. Speeches were made to the regiment and the crowd, and orders were read to be ready to travel to Tennessee in the morning. With Lent starting, Private Leveque sent his fiddle home. Acadians didn't make music during Lent.

On Tuesday, February 25th, the 4th LA entrained for Jackson, Tennessee. A bugle sounded assembly. "Fall in! Fall in!" A cheer arose from the men as they scrambled into formation. "Attention!" "Take Arms!" "Carry arms!" "Right Face!" "Forward! March!" With a flourish of patriotic zeal, the band struck up *Dixie*. The last man on the train was Gustave Grogne. He left the poor farmer's daughter sobbing at the depot.

Prior to the war, Gustave was a hotel and restaurant supplies salesman. He sold dinnerware and kitchen supplies for wholesale merchants from New Orleans. He traveled the river as far north as Memphis and frequently traveled the New Orleans to Jackson railroad, selling his wares. Part of his circuit included hotels along the Mississippi Sound and as far east as Mobile. His commissions were substantial and he supplemented his income handsomely by gambling. As a consequence of his travels he had many romantic contacts throughout the Deep South. He had also been in two duels.

They left New Orleans at 3 P.M., their canteens filled with brandy. The first leg of the trip to Tennessee saw a loud, raucous bunch of Acadians singing, laughing, and partying. At each stop they hung out of the car windows waving their caps and looking at the puzzled faces of the ladies as they introduced themselves in Acadian French. Many threw notes to the girls with their names and addresses. The whole rail line through the parish of St. Helena was lit up with bonfires and the citizens were out cheering on their Rebel heroes. It was dark before they arrived at Camp Moore.

The troops left with two days cooked rations, but the food was put into the baggage train, which left several hours after the passenger train. The men were without anything to eat of any consequence for two days. At every stop troops would detrain to buy food. The Tirailleurs arrived in Canton, Mississippi, at 8 A.M. on the 26th. The troop train was welcomed by young ladies waving little Confederate flags. The Tirailleurs detrained and explored the little village. Many of the townsfolk fed the hungry soldiers. They changed cars and left Canton at 8 P.M. All through Mississippi the 4th LA was warmly welcomed.

There was food at a stop in Grand Junction, Tennessee. Most of the Tirailleurs made for the Percy Hotel and dined. It was obvious to the soldiers that the folk in this part of Tennessee were not as friendly as the Mississippians. This town was about fifty miles south of Jackson, Tennessee. The cars left Grand Junction at 2 P.M. on the 27th. Due to curves in the tracks five miles out, the men had to get out and push the train. They arrived in Jackson, Tennessee, at 5 P.M. (60)

The 4th LA camped in an oak grove on the Jackson fairgrounds and stayed there for two weeks. They camped in the open that first night. While at Jackson, Colonel Barrow resigned for health reasons. Elections were held and H. W. Allen was elected colonel. The Clinton lawyer, S. E. Hunter, became the lieutenant colonel and Thomas Vick became major. (61) Colonel Allen was also appointed military governor of Jackson by Major General Beauregard. Braxton Bragg had his Second Corps headquarters in Jackson. Martial law was declared. In their role as "town police," a "great deal of liquor was confiscated by our boys." (62)

The local townsfolk sent up hams, crackers, butter, and bread. The company baggage arrived with their tents the next day. New tents and new blankets were supplied in Jackson. Trasimond, Arthur Blanchard, and Prudent Daigle set up their tent and put in a board floor to keep off the damp ground. The weather was mild but soon turned cold. They drilled to the sound of the bugle and dress parade was held as usual. The Tirailleurs had lost their West Point private, L. E. Woods. He transferred to Miles' Legion and was elected first lieutenant of Company A. (63) Captain F. A. Williams of the Tirailleurs was not well, and remained in New Orleans. He had been nagged by illness off and on since July 1861. General Beauregard was in camp, and there were rumors that the 4th LA was to become Beauregard's bodyguard. (64)

After breakfast, March 1st, there was regimental drill. The men of the Tirailleurs had plenty of spare time and explored Jackson, which was about the size of Baton Rouge. Local farmers were busy planting corn. Many of the Tirailleurs had never seen such wheat fields as those that surrounded the city. Private Palms wrote, "The country is hilly and very picturesque, and this section is also noted for its beautiful women." (65) The next day it rained, and the next it froze.

On March 11th, orders came to send all excess baggage to warehouses at Grand Junction. While awaiting the arrival of A. S. Johnston's army, Beauregard worked to concentrate his forces at Corinth, Mississippi. The 4th LA was ordered south to Bethel, Tennessee. Mardi Gras day was spent packing up.

The Tirailleurs took cars from Jackson by moonlight at 10 P.M., March 14th. Three miles from Henderson Station, the Yankees had burned a rail culvert, which caused a cold delay. It began to rain, soaking the men who were cramped onto the open flat cars. They arrived at Bethel, Tennessee, at dusk, wet through and through. Bethel was midway between Jackson, Tennessee, and Corinth, Mississippi. The regiment occupied this town for a few days, then moved to Corinth. The stop at Bethel was a move by General Beauregard to counter a feint by the Yankees. Private White wrote, "I have had to sleep out two nights lately without tents in the rain and cold too, but I am willing to sleep in the rain and even do more so it is to the advancement of our cause of Liberty." (66)

At Bethel they received provisions which would last four days. The Acadians were loaded into cars at 11 P.M., March 17th, and headed for Corinth. The cars were packed and Private Landry was required to ride on the top of the car. On the trip it began to rain. The men wrapped themselves in blankets and traveled all night. For those riding on the tops of cars, the smoke and cinders from the locomotive were suffocating. Six miles from Corinth a collision occurred between two trains ahead of theirs, creating three-hour stop. The train then passed the bodies of soldiers killed in the wreck. They arrived in Corinth at 4 P.M., after the most miserable train ride of the war. Corinth was a small village located at the junction of the Mobile and Ohio, and the Memphis and Charleston railroads.

The Tirailleurs of the 4th LA were now in a brigade commanded by Colonel Randall L. Gibson. This brigade was part of Daniel Ruggle's Division of Braxton Bragg's Second Corps. On the eve of the Battle of Shiloh, men in the ranks had no idea of where they were or who was commanding their division or corps. Soldiers in the ranks knew very little of what was going on outside of their regiment. (67)

Randall Lee Gibson was colonel of the 13th LA Infantry Regiment. He was the son of a wealthy Terrebonne Parish planter, and graduated from Yale University in 1853. After studying law, he returned to Louisiana to run his father's plantation. Completing a stint as a military aid to Governor Thomas O. Moore, he was named captain of the 1st LA Artillery. He resigned this post to become colonel in the 13th LA. (68) He was very striking and presented a fine and admirable appearance.

General Daniel Ruggles was a fifty-two-year-old native of Massachusetts and a West Point graduate. He was a veteran of the Seminole War and the Mexican War and married into a Virginia family. He resigned from the Union army and was commissioned a brigadier general in the Confederate army. (69) Robert Patrick of the Hunter Rifles was a clerk for Ruggles, and wrote, "He is an old brute. Being an old army officer and a New Englander, he had no conscience nor mercy on anyone." (70)

Braxton Bragg was born in North Carolina in 1817. He was a West Point graduate and fought in the Seminole and Mexican Wars. In 1856, he became a Louisiana planter. Appointed a brigadier general with the onset of the war, he was sent to Pensacola. The politically well-connected Bragg was promoted to major general in September 1861, and was appointed to head A. S. Johnston's Second Corps, Army of Mississippi. (71)

Robert Patrick of the Hunter Rifles also clerked for Bragg. He wrote in his diary, "Bragg is not fit for a general....he is fit only for command of a brigade. If Jeff Davis will just let Bragg alone, I think he will do us more damage than the enemy, and I believe that he is cowardly too. I know one thing, that he is a perfect tyrant, and I never saw a tyrant yet but what was a coward." (72) If Jeff Davis had had the same insight demonstrated by Private Patrick, the war in the West may have come to a different conclusion.

Colonel Allen was very well liked by the soldiers. He was accessible to the men in the ranks and was approachable at any time. He joked with the soldiers and even participated in their practical jokes, all the while drilling them harder and harder. He was also mindful that he was the leader of well-educated sons of wealthy planters. Many of the lowliest of privates in the 4th LA were heirs to more wealth and status than their commanding captains, colonels, or generals.

After a prolonged gestational period of ten months, Colonel Allen's 4th LA was to be born on the battlefield at Shiloh.

3.

Shiloh Church

Order of Battle, Shiloh Church
Army of the Mississippi, Lieutenant General A. S. Johnston
    Second Corps, Major General Braxton Bragg
        First Division, Brigadier General Daniel Ruggles
            First Brigade, Colonel Randall L. Gibson
                1st Arkansas, Colonel James F. Fagan
                4th Louisiana, Colonel H. W. Allen
                13th Louisiana, Major A. P. Avegno
                19th Louisiana, Colonel B. L. Hodge
                Bains Battery, Captain M. Bain

At Corinth there were troops everywhere. Private Landry had never seen so many men in one place at one time. Open fields and woods were filled with white tents. The 4th LA camped north of town on March 22nd. A slow rain, mingled with sleet, fell all day long. (1) The next day the 4th LA was ordered one mile south of town beside the Memphis and Charleston Railroad. Camps stretched out along the railroad for seven miles. A campground was cleared out and the men remained there for nine days. The campsite was on an oak ridge about 250 yards from a good creek. Trains passed day and night loaded with troops, supplies, cannon, and mules. Corinth was well-fortified by General Beauregard. It was to become the base of operations against Grant.

    Silas T. White wrote, "It is said that the Yankees have their baggage marked 'Corinth or Hell,' and according to my opinion, they will see the latter place long before they see Corinth." (2)

    On March 23rd it snowed. That day, Alexis Hebert paid a sutler thirty cents for two sheets of writing paper. He sat down on a tree stump and wrote his father. "It is reported that (Albert Sydney) Johnston is coming with his troops. I tell you that there are cannons here in quantity, and nice ones....In all directions, there are coming every day infantry and cavalry. The rail cars are always full. A battle is expected here in a few days." He added, "We have forgotten Lent these days. We read in the newspapers that they talk of Mardi Gras and we have gone until today without having made vigil a single time, although we always do enough penance as there is nothing to eat here other than some biscuits." (3)

John Morgan wrote on March 26th, "There are over 100 regiments here now and they keep coming every day. They are putting all the Louisiana troops together here. Our men do not like to be put with the Tennessee troops." (4)

On March 27th, the 13th LA arrived and camped nearby. At Corinth the men were again put to work on fortifications: trenching, felling trees, and constructing abatis. All the regiments of Bragg's Corp were issued new battle flags. The flag was a blue St. Andrew's Cross with twelve six-pointed stars on a red field with a wide yellow border on three sides.

On March 29th, the *Bataillion des Gardes d'Orleans* (Orleans Guards) arrived from Grand Junction and camped near the 4th LA. The Orleans Guards had enlisted for ninety days and were dressed in blue uniforms. This unit of elite Creole gentlemen claimed P. G. T. Beauregard as a former member. They were assigned to Colonel Preston Pond's Brigade of Ruggle's Division. A member of the Guards was Daniel Leveque, brother of Lieutenant J. A. Leveque.

Even before the battle, casualties from illness mounted. At Corinth, the limestone water was plentiful but unhealthy. Sergeant Silas Grisamore of the 18th LA did not hold back when he wrote, "The water we had to drink was the most abominable stuff that was ever forced down men's throats. It was obtained from wells and holes about the camps and was of a bluish color and greasy taste....It was a kind of liquid resembling coal tar, dish water, and soap suds mixed." (5)

On his twenty-first birthday, Lieutenant Donelson Caffrey Jenkins, of the Lake Providence Cadets wrote in his journal: "March 30th, 1862, Sunday. Our regiment received a visit today from General Beauregard, enthusiastically received. I was very much pleased with him. A tall man, rather striking physiognomy, keen black eye, black mustache, and white hand, sits a horse splendidly, plainly dressed. Gave a short speech as follows: 'Gentlemen of the Fourth Regiment. Never before did I feel better than I do now. Never did I feel so confident of victory as I do now. All that I regret is that the enemy is so far from us and the roads are so bad we cannot get at them, but have patience and we'll get at them. And when we do, the injury will be satisfied in the result.' He has a way with company." (5)

General Beauregard visited for a short while with the companies of the 4th LA. One face familiar to him was First Lieutenant J. A. Leveque. Beauregard was quite pleased to speak to soldiers in his native tongue and was introduced to the Mexican War veterans Lieutenants Sosthene Aillet and Belisaire Landry. It was rumored that Beauregard had been ill. To Lieutenant Leveque, he looked as he always had, with maybe a little more gray in his hair. That day, the Tirailleurs were ordered to take from their knapsacks anything that was not absolutely necessary.

Pierre Gustave Toutant Beauregard was born in St. Bernard Parish, Louisiana, in 1818. He was a West Point graduate and served in the Mexican War. After secession, the Confederate army put him in charge of fortifications at Charleston, South Carolina. He was in command of the Rebel attack on Fort Sumter and was second in command at the great victory of First Manassas. He was then sent west and became busy fortifying Corinth and making preparations to attack General Grant. (7) Finally, A. S. Johnston joined his forces with Beauregard; the army began to move.

On March 31st, the men heard the long roll of the drum. "Fall in! FALL IN!" The 4th LA, 13th LA, and 19th LA marched out of Corinth ahead of the other Louisiana regiments to do picket duty around Monterey, Tennessee. On April 2nd, the 4th LA was on picket and later relieved by the 2nd ARK. Short on rations, Gustave Grogne was a welcomed sight. He showed up before supper time with a pig. Gustave always wore a top hat and coat with tails. He kept a deck of playing cards in a pocket of his silk vest. His coat sleeves and pants were muddy, indicating that the pig had put up some resistance.

There were reports of Yankees being seen, and some minor skirmishes were occurring around the area. Three Zoauves from the 13th LA deserted at Monterey. They were Frenchmen and were brought in by Dreux's Cavalry. A court martial was quickly convened and the three were sentenced to be shot. (8)

The night of the 3rd was spent in a wet, swampy area. On April 4th, the march to Pittsburg Landing began. The men left Monterey that evening and marched three miles. D. C. Jenkins wrote in his diary, April 4th: "Roads very bad. Met the 5th Company Washington Artillery. Roads blocked with trains stopped. Continued our march until 12 P.M. Camped in an old field. Raining hard, no tents or protection of any kind." (9)

Thomas Chinn Robertson wrote his mother, "We were obliged to sit for two reasons: first, we were momentarily expecting to receive orders to march forward, and second, the rain which poured down in torrents would have prevented us from sleeping...." (10)

On Friday, the 4th LA's march was held up at Michie's Farm. The men waited off the road while Polk's Corps passed. The yellow flag flew over Michie's house, which was being converted into a hospital. That night, the brigade marched out toward Pittsburg Landing on the Corinth Road. From Michie's, the march down the ridge road seemed to be heading distinctly downhill.

The backs of the Tirailleurs chaffed from their knapsacks. Rain delayed the advance and the creeks were swollen. The attack on the Union force was planned for Saturday, but the delay dragged on. The Rebels were in a race to engage Grant's army before he could combine forces with Union General Don Carlos Buell.

Finally, by Saturday night, the brigade was encamped a mile from the Union lines. They broke ranks and stacked arms. No fires were allowed and silence was enforced under penalty of death. The 4th LA camped in woods a little to the left of the Corinth Road. That night, the sky had cleared and a cold front was passing through. The men huddled up next to each other to keep warm.

Captain Williams was on sick furlough and First Lieutenant Leveque was in charge. The soldiers looked forward to a victory that would put an end to the war, but not before they captured their share of glory. The war had to end soon. After all, their enlistments would be up in fifty days.

Trasimond could see the lights of the warm Yankee fires and hear singing in their camp. There were sounds of Union axes cutting firewood and dogs barking. He could hear the loud beating of drums near the hour of tatoo. Wrapped in his blanket, he sat on his knapsack to keep off the wet ground. His left hand fumbled with a Sacred Heart medal as he said an "Act of Contrition" to himself. Trasimond knew that he would very soon face his destiny in a great battle.

The letters of Jimmy Knighton illustrate how little the foot soldier knows. On April 1st, he wrote, "We have between 80 and 100,000 men here at Corinth." On April 5th, he wrote, "The Federals are reported to be 120,000 strong." Actually, both sides would be fairly evenly matched on the first day at Shiloh, roughly forty-five thousand on each side. (11) The Rebel brass were not worried about Grant's numbers. They knew that Grant had his back to the Tennessee River and that he was hemmed in on both flanks (Owl Creek and Lick Creek). No matter what their number they could only send so many men to the front. They were, however, worried about Buell's numbers and knew that they had to whip Grant before Buell arrived with re-enforcements.

Junior Second Lieutenant Sosthene Aillet kicked Private Landry on his shoes and said, "*Allez vous*" (Let's go). Trasimond had slept very little, and it was still dark at 5 A.M. on this cool Sunday. Slowly the gray light trickled into the camp. The sergeants solemnly distributed sixty rounds of ammunition to each man. The air was damp and heavy. With the first scarlet rays of morning, the Tirailleurs formed up in a line of attack. For where, no one knew. There were no bugles or drum rolls. That day, there were 575 men of the 4th LA present for duty. There were fifty Tirailleurs in the ranks. While the men ate a cold breakfast from their haversacks, back at staff headquarters, General A. S. Johnston told his escort, "Tonight we will water our horses in the Tennessee River." By 2:30 P.M., Johnston would be dead.

The morning broke with a clear and cloudless sky. Hardee's Corps stepped off first and fanned out on both sides of the Corinth Road, heading toward Shiloh Church and the enemy's camps. Hardee's Corps would deliver the most devastating strategic surprise of the war. Federal soldiers were preparing breakfast when suddenly deer, rabbits, and foxes started running into their camp and through their breakfast fires. Hardee's Corps struck the Union camp in Rea's Field first and sent the 53rd OHIO reeling back. The Rebel generals were astounded to find that Sherman had not thrown up breastworks.

At 7 A.M. Bragg's Corps began to move. The 4th LA in Gibson's Brigade was grouped with Pond's Brigade and Anderson's Brigade of Ruggle's Division. In funneling into the battlefield, Gibson was ordered to the right and onto Seay's Field, forever separating from Pond and Anderson. He was ordered to find Hindman's Brigade and assist them on the right.

The Tirailleurs were in their part of the line in Seay's Field. The Washington Artillery was on the left, then the 4th LA, the 13th LA, the 1st ARK, and the 19th LA. (12) The 1st ARK were veterans of the First Battle of Manassas. Other than prisoners being taken to the rear, the Tirailleurs had yet to see a Union soldier, but from Union artillery, enemy shells began plopping and exploding all around the area. Some men in the brigade were killed by cannon fire in Seay's Field. Wounded began streaming back towards the rear.

It was a grand sight seeing long lines of troops in their various colored uniforms: some gray, some butternut, and some blue. Officers were mounted on their fine horses, battle flags were unfurled, and bugle calls directed the army forward. Ammunition wagons and artillery followed closely behind this line. The scene had the thrill of an adventure soon to unfold. Rifle shots and cannon fire could be heard to the front. The hollow boom of cannon and the popping sounds of musketry gradually increased. Private A. P. Richards of the St. Helena Rifles wrote, "The morning of the 6th opened that grand and magnificent panorama of war which only those who were participants can appreciate—a veritable onslaught of fire, shot, and fury." It was 8 A.M. (13)

The battlefield was a hardwood forest with gently rolling hills and a few ravines. Its main feature was a dozen or so cleared fields of five to ten acres. These fields had been cleared and farmed for generations by Cherokee Indians.

When the Indians were disposed of by Andrew Jackson, white subsistence farmers moved onto their plots. The woods were mostly oaks, draped with Spanish moss and a few scarce loblolly pines. There were tufts of oak flowers, but no leaves. The race to leaf-out had been won by scarce hackberries and yellow poplars. Beech trees still had hold of their yellowed leaves. On the edges of the cleared plots, cedar trees had a toe-hold and redbuds left bold shows of purple on the forest skirt. Dogwoods were plentiful and in full bloom. Scattered sparsely were flowering wild plum and the bold white flowers of the serviceberry.

The men were nervous and over-alert. Private Landry witnessed a Rebel courier shot off his horse. He was mistaken for a Yankee and fifty bullets struck him, fired from Confederate rifles. (14) At that moment you could see it in every Tirailleur's face. This was not drill. This was battle, and they were now in its embrace.

Forty-five thousand Confederate soldiers continued stalking toward the Union lines. Like a gravitational wave—unseen and unfelt yet powerful—the men were drawn into the conflict. Firing increased to the left. The combat had become general. In Seay Field, the sky was hung with white puffs of smoke. With the first screaming shells, arteries began to pound, hands became wet, shoulders curled forward, and the chin lowered to meet the chest. The senses became swollen, pounding, and razor sharp.

The 4th LA crossed Seay's Field and into the woods to the right of the Corinth Road. These Tennessee woods had a soft loamy floor with a fresh carpet of last winter's leaves. It was easy going, with little undergrowth. The local farmers loosed cattle and hogs to roam freely and forage for themselves. This left little chance for undergrowth to flourish. Only an occasional fallen cedar trunk broke their step. Gibson was trying to find Hindman's division, and at 8:30 A.M. moved into the lower end of Rea's Field.

Rea's Field was 800 yards long. At the opposite end was a well-placed six-gun Yankee battery. This was the 1st Illinois Light Artillery, commanded by Captain Allen Waterhouse. His gunners were pounding the Rebels who were advancing, in the open, up Rea's corn field.

The air was full of thunder as the 4th LA suffered its first casualties. James Dupriest and Robert McKie of Hunter Rifles A were kneeling side by side when a cannon ball struck them, killing both. A Yankee 5.4 inch solid round bolt from a twelve-pound bronze Napoleon was fired across the battlefield. The shot traveled seven hundred yards and was aimed to ricochet. The ball hit the ground once, then skipped, hitting the ground again. As the ball rose again into the air it hit Private Dupriest in the left chest, fracturing ribs in front and back and smashing his spleen. The ball then struck private McKie in the anterior chest, crushing his heart and lifting him out of his boots. He died instantly. Private Dupriest was dragged behind a tree. His flail chest sinking in with every breath, he lapsed into shock and died several hours later. (15)

As Allen led the regiment forward, a huge eight-inch shell demolished a tree in front of him. The shell landed in the ground at his horse's feet. His horse reared and struck at the air with its forefeet. As Allen spurred his mount and leaped the shell crater, he called his men forward. (16) The regiment had advanced up Rea's Field to the abandoned camp of the 53rd OHIO. The standing tents were riddled with shot holes. Confederate dead and wounded of the 6th MISS and 23 TN were scattered among the tents. Colonel Allen ordered the men to lie down in the middle of the Federal camp to allow rearward artillery to fire over their heads. The Washington Artillery opened up on Waterhouse, who had moved his battery across Shiloh Branch Creek and onto an elevation with an excellent command of the entire field. Private Landry's heart began to beat faster. Friendly artillerymen were firing from behind him and Yankees were firing at him.

Colonel Allen moved the men away from the artillery and into a ravine on their right. They watched from woods as Allen sat upon his horse in Rea's Field like a war god. Through glasses and under fire he viewed the field, sitting upon his horse like an equestrian statue. This purposeful display of fearlessness gave the men confidence in their leader.

The brigade was then ordered to charge the battery. With a yell, they advanced. Before the 4th LA reached Shiloh Branch Creek, Waterhouse was suddenly surrounded by the 13th TN and his guns captured. The men rested and filled their canteens from Rea's Spring. It was 9:30 A.M. Sherman's lines were now on the verge of collapse.

Gibson was ordered to move his regiment farther to the right and moved into a place called Lost Field. It was the abandoned camp of the 4th ILL Cavalry. At this time, Hindman was in the woods to the left of the 4th LA with Brigadier General A. P. Stewart of the 4th TN. Hindman ordered Stewart to attack a battery in the next field, Review Field. At this time, Aaron Verter, a young aid of General Hindman, had taken Waterhouse's battle flag and rode across the front of the 4th LA. Lieutenant Verter had been a member of the Lake Providence Cadets before becoming Hindman's aide, and was a nephew of General Van Dorn. It was 10 A.M. Verter was dressed in a blue Rebel uniform and was wearing a captured Yankee hat. He was mistaken by the 4th LA as a Yankee ensign. He rode toward the 4th LA on a white horse from left to right at a gallop. Someone cried out, "Yankee! Stop him!" He was shot and killed by men from the St. Helena Rifles and the Lafourche Guards. (17)

The 4th TN regiment, posted in the woods to the right of the 4th LA, knew the young man. When he fell, they mistakenly assumed that the 4th LA was a Union regiment and opened fire. A volley was poured into the ranks of the 4th LA. According to a member of the St. Helena Rifles, "For five minutes the lead flew thick and fast." (18) Private Robertson of the Delta Rifles wrote, "The 4th TN opened up on us with terrible effect, killing and wounding 105 of the regiment, five of whom were in our Company. Col. Gibson's horse was shot under him and he fell within five feet of me." (19) Some men of the 13th ARK were also injured. The Arkansans fired back.

Balls from the Tennessee rifles killed Private Felix Hebert. He was shot in the back. Anatole Landry was wounded in the leg. Fifteen-year-old Private Pierre Emile Allain was shot in the hand. Third Lieutenant Sosthene Aillet was shot in the head and Second Lieutenant Belisaire Landry was wounded in the leg. Lieutenant Leveque was the only officer left in the company. Private Raphael Hebert Jr. was killed.

On August 8th, Alexis Hebert wrote, "Dear Papa...There was a Tennessee regiment exactly behind us. They didn't believe that they saw our flag. We were in the ravine and when they saw us they took our soldiers as Yankees and fired at us. From our camp I write you with the sadness of death. Raphael was killed by one of the Tennesseans." Alexis was to the front and was unaware of his brother's death until later that day. (20) (See Appendix G)

A stunned and demoralized 4th LA fell back to reform. While falling back they were still exposed to artillery fire. A shell fell into the ranks of Captain E. M. Dubroca's company (13th LA), killing six men, scattering their brains and blood over the Captain. (21) Dubroca had been a member of the Delta Rifles. A Bragg aide rode up and ordered Gibson to move farther to the right and into Jacob Barne's Field.

Firing had quieted down on the left as Sherman abandoned his camps at Shiloh Church, but the roar of cannon to their front intensified. Many of the Tirailleurs thought that this might be the last Federal resistance between them and the river. By this time, thousands of Yankee fugitives were at the river *hors de combat*. A Union battery was coughing loudly to the front. Unknown to the men, this battery was part of what became know as the "Hornet's Nest." Unlike the rest of the blue line, Union General Prentiss did not fall back. He offered stiff and determined resistance to the Rebel onslaught.

Gibson was in Jacob Barne's Field waiting for orders when Bragg rode up. Bragg had neglected the center of the battlefield and was frantically looking for regiments to attack Union General Prentiss. Finding Gibson unemployed, he ordered him to advance down the Eastern Corinth Road. The brigade marched by the right flank down the Hamburg-Purdy Road and then turned left down the Eastern Corinth Road. They marched 200 yards down the road then moved by the right flank into the woods and straight into the "Hornet's Nest."

It was noon. The men had been at it for six hours. The ground was uneven and had been cut-over. The new growth was thick with bull nettles, briars, and scrub oak. The Tirailleurs could feel the vibrations and breathe the smells of the battlefield, but could see nothing to their front. The 4th LA was on the left of Gibson's Brigade. To their right was the 1st ARK, then the 13th LA, and then the 19th LA on the far right.

The spinning balls set in rotation by spiral grooves in the musket barrel gave off a humming sound. Multiplied by a thousand or more, this sound made it seem as though one were in a hornet's nest.

Nineteen-year-old Private Robertson wrote, "The Federals were posted on the crest of a steep hill in an old road, which by frequent travel had become worn about three feet deep. Consequently, they could lie perfectly concealed and protected while they could see everything. Besides this, the hill was covered with the thickest undergrowth of blackjack I ever saw. It was almost impossible for a man to walk through under ordinary circumstances. On their right was a heavy, masked battery, and in the road which I have been speaking of there were twenty-seven regiments, and yet with only three regiments we charged this almost impregnable position under a terrible fire of musketry and grape." (22)

Private Landry pushed his way through the briars and tangle, no easy task with his twelve-pound Enfield rifle and bayonet snagging in vines along the way. He went up a rise, down into a gully, then up the opposing slope. Suddenly, a hurricane of rifle balls broke into the men from in front—fired from ambuscade fifty feet away. A masked cannon 150 yards to the right opened on the 4th LA. To Trasimond's left, Second Sergeant Ursin LeBlanc fell wounded. Private Landry was hit in the middle of his chest by a spent rifle ball. There was not enough energy left in it to break the skin, but it knocked him to the ground and stunned him. Before he could stand he was knocked to the ground again by the limp body of Theodore Lejeune. He had been shot through the neck. His blood covered Landry's tunic. Trasimond looked into the vacuum of Lejeune's eyes and knew he was dead.

The colonel of the 1st ARK rode up and yelled, "We are firing on our friends!" This was false, but the men did not know. This sent the men back down the hill. (23) The red-bearded Captain Pennington of the Lake Providence Cadets was wounded in this first charge. Colonel Allen rode in screaming, "Form on this line, men! Form on this line!" The men regrouped on the rise behind them. "*Fait une ligne!*" (Line Up) echoed Doc Leveque. "*Vite! Vite!*" (Quickly) The 4th LA was in woods between Duncan's field and

Davis' Wheat Field. The thick oak canopy allowed no wind into the wood, and the cannon smoke converted the field into a cloud forest.

Private Frank Richardson of the 13th LA wrote, "While we were engaged on the right center (of Gibson's Brigade), the Fourth Louisiana, under Colonel Allen, was heavily engaged on the left. They had moved up on ground more open than ours and the destruction in their ranks was very great. The enemy was entrenched on an eminence on the opposite side of a small creek (gully), a branch of Owl Creek (Briar Creek), near the Bark Road (Eastern Corinth Road)." (24) The cries of wounded horses were chilling. One horse galloped through the woods nearby, his belly ripped open and intestines trailing. He became entangled in his own guts and fell to the ground.

After a short pause the charge was repeated. The Tirailleurs rushed forward screaming their Rebel yell. "Into the jaws of death, into the mouth of hell," wrote Lieutenant Jenkins. (25) The Yankees of the 12th IOWA were poised to repel them. The enemy held its fire until the 4th LA was within twenty yards of them. The whole Yankee line opened up at once with cannon and muskets. (26) A ball ripped into Hilaire Blanchard's thigh. This second charge met the same fate as the first, but with greater loss. Trasimond felt his right arm pushed away involuntarily and looked down to see a bullet hole in his right cuff. The Yankee's cannon fire was so heavy it was clearing out the brush to their front. The noise of the battle reached a crescendo as Private Robert Lyle fell to the ground with a nasty abdominal wound. Young Lyle, greedy for life, would be taken to a hospital in Corinth.

After the second charge, there was a pause during which Colonel Gibson asked Bragg for artillery to cover his attack. Bragg refused. There was no artillery on this section of the line from noon until 2:30 P.M. During the pause, Lieutenant Leveque strained against the urge to aid the wounded. The Rebels were under strict orders never to stop in combat to aid the injured. They were to be on their own until stretcher bearers arrived.

Near Davis' Field, the 4th LA reformed. "No flinching wanted now," was the word from Bragg. This infuriated Colonel Allen. The pompous Bragg had no right to make this remark. Allen encouraged the men. The third charge into the woods and thinned-out thicket began. They were greeted with an even more galling fire from three directions. A bullet passed through Colonel Allen's cheek. Allen's clothes, cloak, and cap were riddled with shot-holes.

Private Richardson wrote, "I looked to the left and saw Colonel H. W. Allen with elevated sword urging his men to stand firm. His chin was bleeding from a wound just received. There too was my schoolmate, Captain Hilliard (Hunter Rifles B), commanding his men to rally and stand firm—when he fell dead, struck in the breast." The advance faltered. In the third charge of the brigade, Colonel Gibson had another horse shot out from under him. (27)

The ranks were totally confused at this point. The 13th LA was crouched in a ravine, but the 4th LA and the 1st ARK were greatly exposed and suffering heavy losses. Sergeant Adelarde Courtade, Private J. B. Hebert, and Private Portalis Tullier were all wounded by the same blast of canister. Under these conditions, the most solid nerves cannot resist for long; the moment arrives when the blood pounds, fever burns the body, and the urge to kill becomes overbearing.

Colonel Allen dismounted and picked up the regiment's colors from the wounded ensign, Ben Clark. He again ordered the beleaguered men forward. "This is as good a place to die as any on the field!" (28) The regiment rallied. Doc Leveque rose, shouting *"Allons-y!"* (Forward). Trasimond Landry held the company's flag as they led the advance of the Tirailleurs. Like the primeval fireball, the line burst forward for this final attack. The Tirailleurs were at a high pitch of nervous expectation and calmed their fear with a shrill Rebel yell. As Fourth Corporal Paul Babin moved forward, a Federal ball entered his left groin and passed through his hip joint. (29) Albert Doiron and Hilaire Longuepee were wounded, but kept on fighting. This final charge was made over the slippery lumps of flesh of the dead and wounded of the 4th LA. Evariste Henry, Landry Landry, and M. B. McKimmens lay wounded on the field as the Tirailleurs charged over them.

The position taken was a mere fifty feet away from the line of Yankees. The Rebel line was running parallel to the Yankee line. In a slight fold of the earth's abdomen, they lay down to fire. As Trasimond planted the flag, he could see the flame from Yankee rifle barrels reaching out to him. The volleys sounded like canvas ripping. Dense white smoke filled this small area of the battlefield as the opposing forces traded volley for volley. The powder smoke was so thick it burned the mucous membranes of the nose and throat and caused tearing in Trasimond's eyes. The frustrated Tirailleurs had no way of seeing the effect of their firing due to the thick smoke. They kept reloading and firing, reloading and firing, until their rifle barrels were too hot to touch. The excitement was extreme. Trasimond didn't notice his aches, bruises, cuts, thirst, or fatigue. As long as the cedar log in front of him held out and Colonel Allen was in charge, he felt no fear.

Twenty-two-year-old Private Samuel Leveque was wounded in the left thigh. He had been hit by the iron baseplate from a stand of grape. Rosemond Hebert lay in a heap. He held his abdomen with his hips and knees flexed. A ball had entered his left flank and exited the right flank. He lay screaming as blood, feces and enzymes scorched his abdominal lining. *"Mamman!*

Mamman!" were his last words as his life's blood drained from him. After a few moments he lapsed into deep shock and died.

Suddenly the struggle was over. Gibson had had enough. The brigade was out of ammunition and he ordered a fall back. The wounded were dragged off and out of the woods to Davis' Wheat Field. Trasimond had used all but ten of his sixty cartridges. His trousers were holed and his canteen and haversack had been shot away.

It was 4:00 P.M. (30) Lieutenant Leveque stood next to Private Landry on the edge of the field as the smoke drifted away. He asked, "*Et vous?*" (What about you?), pointing to Trasimond's tunic and right sleeve. Private Landry looked down on dried blood on his sleeve. He rolled it up and for the first time realized that he had been wounded. Private Landry heard his name called. It was a wounded Octave Dupuy calling for help. "*Vien donc m'aidez.*"

Louis Martin lay next to him. Private Landry forgot about his own slight injury. He took Louis' canteen and wet a handkerchief to wipe his forehead. *Eou ca t'fait mal?*" (Where are you hit?) Louis opened his eyes, too weak to talk.

Trasimond could find no wound on Private Martin, but he had the cold, clammy skin of someone in shock. In the hospital area, Dr. Pope found a bullet wound in Louis' left shoulder. The ball entered there and passed through his chest. Lieutenant Leveque became a doctor again. He sent the walking wounded to the rear: Prudent Daigle, Evariste Henry, Hilaire Longuepee, Theodore Doiron, Paul Babin, Landry Landry, and M. B. McKimmins would need stretchers.

In Davis' Wheat Field, the brigade was allowed to rest for a short time. The orderly sergeants went for ammunition and the men cleaned their rifles. An hour later, the advance resumed into the woods. The Tirailleurs were unaware that General Johnston was dead. Skirmishing took place, but very few Yankees were seen. The blue smoke was so thick it was hard to see any distance. It was now 5 P.M. and the men expected the Yankee rout to be pressed, but there was no order from Beauregard. In fact, there was no Yankee rout. Except for Prentiss' division, which had now surrendered, the Union troops had retreated in good order, awaiting the arrival of Union General Don Carlos Buell's army.

Moving to their right, the brigade reached an open plain (Josiah Cloud's Field), formed a line, and moved toward the river. They were now on the far right of the Rebel line. The soldiers then came under mortar fire from the gunboats. Two Union gunboats stationed themselves at the mouth of Dill Creek. Here was a gap in the high bank of the Tennessee River where their cannon could pour devastating enfilade into Beauregard's right flank.

At this time, the 4th LA was pinched out of line by an inrush of General Breckenridge's Corps. According to Private Robertson, "The shot fell around us like hail; as we could do nothing against the 'black rascals,' we retreated back about two miles. The cannonading was terrific, and yet we marched in perfect order and common time." (31)

Unexpectedly, at 6 P.M., Beauregard ordered his line rearward toward the captured Union camp grounds. It was difficult for the troops to go back over ground that had cost so many lives and wounds to win. Beauregard had little choice. The abandoned camps had the food that his exhausted and hungry men needed, and it took them out of range of the Union gunboats.

At their rendezvous at the abandoned Yankee camps, Private Landry could hear Lieutenant Leveque's voice. He was calling for men of Company H. The dirty, grimy Rebels were milling about in the near dark while captains and colonels were trying to sort out their companies and regiments.

"*Companie H! Ici!*" the lieutenant called. "Company H, Fourth Louisiana form here!" The men gathered around. He kept calling.

The dead on the field and the wounded in the rear could not hear. "*C'est tout!*" (Is this all!) His voice softened, "*C'est tout?*" He called the roll. The short line of Tirailleurs marched off to find tents for the night and clean their rifles.

Private Landry put off sleep to check on Belisaire. He feared that the surgeons may have amputated his brother's leg. Arthur Blanchard accompanied him. They tracked back in the darkness toward the 4th LA hospital area in Davis' Wheat Field. Belisaire could not be found. Private Blanchard came along to check on his sister-in-law's brother, Paul Babin. They found the surgeon, Dr. Marshall Pope.

Dr. Pope of West Baton Rouge Parish was the surgeon for the 4th LA. He was working under a tent fly. Lanterns were hanging all around, throwing a yellow pall over the gruesome sight. The surgeon's sleeves were rolled up and he was covered in blood. The two privates had their faces blackened by powder and smoke from the days fighting. Through raccoon eyes, they could see that he was busy amputating the leg of some poor Southern patriot. The sight and sounds of the wounded and dying made them both pale. They found Dr. O. P. Langworthy, but he was of no help.

It was while in the hospital area that they were approached by a tall, well-built cavalry colonel with chin whiskers. He asked them their regiment. The colonel was searching among the wounded for his fifteen-year-old son, Willie Forrest. Trasimond could be of no help. The colonel mounted his horse and rode off in the dark down the Purdy-Hamburg Road. They returned to the company.

The night was as dark as ink. The starry sky gave way to clouds and it began raining after midnight. Yankee gunboats fired eight-inch rounds every eight minutes toward the Rebel lines. Most of these shells fell on the wounded Union troops caught in the "no man's land" between the combatants. Trasimond's chest ached; his eyes burned; his throat was parched; he could smell burned flesh; and the noises of battle still groaned in his ears.

Colonel Allen passed a painful night at the hospital at Michie's farm. Not only was he painfully wounded, but he had lost Captain Hilliard of Hunter's Rifles. Hilliard was a senior class member at Centenary College less than a year before the battle. Captain J. B. Taylor of the St. Helena Rifles was wounded in the right thigh and bled to death. Captain W. F. Pennington of the Lake Providence Cadets was wounded. Captain Toorean was killed. Lieutenants Belisaire Landry and Sosthene Aillet of the Tirailleurs were lost to "fratricidal fire," and Lieutenant Oliver Perry Skolfield was shot through the hip joint. (32)

That night, Beauregard, now commanding, was not aware that Union General Don Carlos Buell had arrived to reinforce Grant. He sent off a telegram to Richmond describing the first day's fighting as a complete victory.

The first day at Shiloh was enough for Frank Hermogene. The Company H drummer walked away and was never seen again.

The next day confusion was king. Regiments, brigades, and divisions were all mixed up. At daybreak, the Tirailleurs ate Yankee bacon and drank Yankee coffee found in the abandoned camps. Before breakfast, the Tirailleurs made a gruesome discovery. They had slept next to the hospital tents of the 12th Michigan Infantry. During the first day's fighting these tents caught on fire, and in Union General Prentiss' rapid retreat, many of the sick and wounded burned to death. The Tirailleurs had spent the night next to these greasy cremations.

The Tirailleurs were amazed at how well the Yankees were supplied. They had either Sibley or Fremont tents. Each man had two uniforms, a large army overcoat, two blankets, an oil cloth, oil cloth caps, and oil cloth haversacks. They had any quantity of fresh beef, coffee, sugar, rice, flour, crackers, cornmeal, hams, cheese, apples, and candy.

Grant had been caught off guard on Sunday. He had a grand counter-attack planned for the Confederates. He now commanded forty-five thousand men. Beauregard had only twenty thousand men available. That morning, Lieutenant Colonel Hunter was placed in command of the regiment. Colonel Allen was in the hospital. Doc Leveque was the only officer remaining in the Tirailleurs.

Joe LeRay was not expecting another day of fighting and was busy loading himself down with Yankee spoils. Before the day was done he would have to part with his new overcoat, oil cloth, and haversack full of coffee. Private Landry awoke with a sore chest and a painful left shoulder. He was left-handed, and the previous day's rifle firing had left his upper left arm black and blue. Gustave Grogne had three bullet holes in his top hat. He found a sutler's wagon and was completely re-outfitted: Yankee trousers, new shoes, and a new brown derby.

Doc Leveque walked down the line of twenty-three Tirailleurs, checking their equipment. Rifle cartridges and caps were distributed. The company formed up with the remnants of the brigade. The Tirailleurs were pushed forward to the far left of the Confederate line. General Ruggles ordered Gibson's Brigade to advance to Jones' Field, where the 4th LA was ordered to attack a battery of artillery. They were marched at double-quick time through a low, swampy area and then across two open fields, all the while exposed to Federal fire.

Passing across the battlefield of the previous day was described by Private Livaudais: "Everywhere we passed, the ground was strewn with the dead; in some places, they had piled them together and then thrown blankets over them....But the most macabre spectacle was the cadavers of the preceding day; the rain had drenched them the night before and now they were totally decomposed, and so bloated that from a certain distance they appeared more like casks than men. Never before had I beheld anything such as this." (33)

Ambrose Bierce, a Union Lieutenant, described the battlefield of the previous day's fight. "Knapsacks, canteens, haversacks distended with soaked and swollen biscuits, gaping to disgorge, blankets beaten into the soil by rain, rifles with bent barrels or splintered stocks, waist-belts, hats and the omnipresent sardine box. All the wretched debris of battle still littered the spongy earth as far as one could see, in every direction. Dead horses were everywhere; a few disabled caissons, or limbers reclining on one elbow, as it were; ammunition wagons standing disconsolate behind four or six sprawling mules. Men? There were men enough—all dead." (34)

For two hours, the men huddled in a ravine created by an offshoot of Tilghman Branch. The 4th LA waited while Ketchum's Battery served the Yankees a breakfast of shell and grape. They were ordered to charge Union Lieutenant Charles Thurber's 1st Missouri Artillery, which was set up in the middle of Jones' corn field. (35)

Texas Rangers cavalry attacked the battery first and were repulsed. Gibson's Brigade, with the 4th LA, then charged from their ravine in the woods across three hundred fifty yards of open field. The guns were reached, but the Rebels were driven from the field by a galling fire from the woods coming from the 8th Wisconsin Infantry. A second charge by Gibson was brushed aside. The brigade was ordered to retire and move to the center of the Confederate line.

They rested, then stopped to draw ammunition when Beauregard rode by. A cheer rose from the soldiers. It was noon. Beauregard encouraged his commanders, when in doubt about orders, to move toward the sounds of the heaviest firing. That is where Gibson took his brigade. Gibson moved south in the direction of Shiloh Church and joined a line of resistance near Review Field and Water Oaks Pond. The Tirailleurs were in the center of the Rebel line. With a fifer playing *Dixie*, the Rebel line moved forward, driving Sherman and McClernand's divisions three hundred yards rearward. (36) For three hours, the battle raged in that spot.

Between Water Oaks Pond and Review Field, the 4th LA joined a formation of three lines of infantry stretching over three hundred yards in length. Their line pressed forward and into the Yankees. The tide of battle had swung toward the Confederates. At one point, the Yankee line was on the verge of breaking. Ambrose Bierce wrote, "As matters stood, we were very evenly matched. But all at once something appeared to have gone wrong on the enemy's (Confederate) left; our men had somewhere pierced his line." (37)

Buell's army had come up. Sheer numbers pushed the Confederates back. By 2 P.M., the Tirailleurs were in the vicinity of Shiloh Church. Alexis Hebert was wounded. Major Avegno, a refined, educated, and wealthy Creole of the 13th LA, was mortally wounded. Second Lieutenant, D. C. Jenkins was wounded and captured. Private Micajah Barrow was also captured. The 4th LA was constantly engaged until 3 P.M. Beauregard called for the troops to reform in the rear. What was left of the 4th LA filed past the little log cabin church called Shiloh. Surprisingly, the enemy did not follow.

The Tirailleurs stopped past the church to fill their canteens at Rea's Spring. Alexis Hebert, his arm bravely bandaged, asked permission from Dr. Leveque to bury his brother. The Lieutenant said no. Alexis pleaded. His brother's body was only a few hundred yards away. Leveque gave in and Privates Landry and Blanchard volunteered to go with him.

The party made their way past the gruesome battlefield to Lost Field. There were no Yankees to be seen, and the firing had died down. Alexis searched the field for his bother, but could find no bodies. Propped up under a leafless chestnut tree was a wounded Tennessee Rebel. His face was tanned by exposure and seamed by age. Next to him were three full canteens and a haversack full of crackers. He had been shot in the spine and was paralyzed. His pain was so great that he refused to be carried off the field, preferring a short trip to a Yankee hospital rather than a twenty mile jolt to Corinth. Besides, he had little hope of surviving.

"Where are the bodies, *mon ami*?" asked Trasimond.

"See 'at fresh dirt pile yonder" spoke the Reb. "They dug a hole and toted all 'em bodies in it an' covered 'em up. Too bad they didn't make room for me, cause I spec I'll give it up soon." He grimaced.

"Who dug the hole?"

"Don't know. Looked like one of 'em Roman Priests and some stragglers. Cain't understand 'em Frenchies, but he left me this water and hardtack."

"*Bon chance, vieux.*"

The three Tirailleurs caught up with the slow-moving column on the road near Seay's Field. The exhausted troops headed out toward Corinth in good order. Then the rain came down in streams.

The Tirailleurs halted in the mud at 8 P.M. and fell asleep. At 9:30 P.M. they were ordered up and the march was resumed. Limping on blistered feet, Trasimond marched with the company all night. Unknown to him, his brother had lain out all night at Michie's farm, unprotected from the rain. He was placed in a wagon loaded with wounded and was already in Corinth. The water in many streams was as high as a man's ass and the road was mired in mud.

Colonel Allen reported his losses: fifteen officers, one hundred ninety-four men killed, wounded, or missing. (38) Only one company of the 4th LA suffered more casualties than the Tirailleurs. The Hunter Rifles A had nine killed, twenty-three wounded, and three missing. One of those killed was Private Silas T. White. The Tirailleurs, being a smaller company, suffered a larger percentage of injuries, fifty percent. (six killed, twenty wounded). Five hundred dead horses from both armies were left on the battlefield.

It is impossible to know the casualties suffered on the second day at Shiloh. There were no 4th LA members captured on the first day. Sixteen men of the regiment were captured on the second day and most were also wounded. This is a good indication of the fierce fighting that occurred that day

Tirailleur Casualties at Shiloh:
Raphael Hebert, Jr., killed, shot by the 4th TN
Felix Hebert, killed, shot by the 4th TN
Theodore Lejeune, killed
Robert Lyle, died in Corinth Hospital
Felix Louis Martin, left for dead in Corinth
Rosemond Hebert, killed
Evariste Henry
Anatole Landry, shot by the 4th TN
Alexis Hebert
Hilaire Blanchard
Belisaire Landry, shot by the 4th TN
Ursin Leblanc
Landry Landry
Samuel Leveque
Hilaire Longuepee
M. B. McKimmins
Portalis Tullier

Adelarde Courtade
Sosthene Aillet, shot by the 4th TN
Louis Octave Dupuy
Leon Adolphe Dupuy
Paul P. Babin
Pierre Emile Allain, shot by the 4th TN
Jean Baptiste Hebert
Albert Doiron
Theodore Doiron
Prudent Daigle (39) (40)
The Delta Rifles had one killed and sixteen wounded.

There were hundreds of instances of personal bravery and individual suffering on the trek back to Corinth. Dr. John Montgomery tended some wounded men from the 4th LA. Waiting for ambulances, they were stranded not far from Corinth for three days without food. (41)

T. C. Robertson wrote his mother: "No one can imagine the suffering we have endured during the last week, and yet not a word of grumbling is heard. We started from Monterey yesterday (April 8th) about 12 o'clock, and arrived here (Corinth) about five. Those were twelve of the longest miles I ever traveled. The road was almost impassable, I assure you. I am not exaggerating when I inform you that all the way the mud was knee deep, and we were obliged to wade several streams which were waist deep. We have lost everything but one suit of clothes, which were badly torn by the bushes during the battle." (42)

Most of the company was back at Corinth by April 9th. The tired, wet Acadians were ordered out and into line. The gallant First Lieutenant Joseph Augustus Leveque called roll. No soldier in line would ever forget that roll call. A long pause followed each name called. When there was no answer, someone would tell the lieutenant where the man was last seen. The fate of some of the men was unknown, and would remain so forever. To the souls of the Tirailleurs, the blood of their dead comrades was still fresh. An emotional malaise and tearful melancholy overcame the men. Private Richardson of the 13th LA wrote in 1885, "The gallant Fourth Louisiana, that was camped next to us, had not more than 300 men for duty out of 900 before the battle. No richer offering has been laid on their country's alter." (43)

Lieutenant Leveque found his brother Daniel at Corinth. He was uninjured. Their stories were much the same. Because of their blue uniforms, the Guards were fired on mistakenly by Tennessee troops. They had lost ninety of their 140 men in a suicidal charge on the first day. On the second day, they turned their coats inside-out, exposing their white lining to avoid any more mishaps.

Trasimond searched the hospitals in Corinth and found Belisaire. His wound would end his military career, but he would survive. Private Landry made frequent visits to see Belisaire and arrangements were made to send him home as soon as he was able to travel. Belisaire, along with Sergeant L. O. Dupuy, Privates J. B. Hebert, Portalis Tullier, and Samuel Leveque were sent by rail to Memphis. There they boarded the steamer *Laurel Hill* for Baton Rouge. They were attended along the trip by Dr. Edward Delony and arrived home on April 16, 1862. (44)

Private Landry visited the wounded Private Lyle. The hospital had been a small college before the war. Robert was in a room with a tall ceiling. Lyle had been shot in the abdomen. A tear in his abdominal wall caused loops of small intestine to lay exposed These bowels were covered only by a wet towel. The worst of the wounded surrounded Lyle. Hospital stewards shuttled by. Some of the wounded groaned, some screamed out, and others prayed. In the still air, the smell of suppurative juices and feces mixed with the odor of sweat and sour clothes.

Poor young Lyle followed Trasimond with his eyes and made a weak attempt to talk. Sweat beaded up on his forehead. His eyes were dull and sunken in their sockets. Trasimond held a tin cup up to his dry lips and he took a small sip. The water caused Lyle to cough and grimace. With each cough, the bulge of eviscerated bowel raised the damp towel covering his wound.

Flies were landing on his loose bandages. No amount of waving or shooing could keep them away. Trasimond felt uncomfortable at Private Lyle's bedside, but could not seem to find the right words to say good-bye. Poor Lyle's skin was sweaty and greasy. He was now thin and wasted, having had no real nourishment since the battle. Here he was, dying, little more than a boy, slight and frail. Lyle lifted his head a little off his pallet. His eyes seemed to rekindle. Private Landry leaned closer. Lyle's ashen voice whispered, "Was I brave?"

"*Oui*," replied Trasimond, "the bravest." Trasimond could stand it no more. He smoothed Private Lyle's hair with a wet cloth, squeezed his hand, and left the room. Outside in the muddy street, he felt relief, but with a hollow feeling in his stomach. Private Lyle held on until late that night, then the last destitute spark of life left him.

Moving about the wounded at the hospital, Trasimond noticed a slight, frail, coarsely-clad man in a black cassock. His name was Father Isidore-Francois Turgis. There were almost twenty thousand Catholics at Shiloh. Father Turgis, along with Fathers Francis Pont (13 LA), Anthony DeChaignon, S.J., and Francois Bertaud, were the only priests. Turgis gave absolution for over eighteen hours nonstop during the battle. He was with the men of his battalion during the fighting administering last rites and helping the wounded; he narrowly escaped death while aiding a mortally wounded Yankee officer. He was bearing the wounded Yankee off the field when a grape shot passed through the man's body and killed him in the priest's arms. (45) The little French priest spent the first week after the battle at Corinth ministering to men of the 4th, 13th, 17th, 18th and 24th LA. (46)

The 4th LA was ordered to return to Monterey. This was a small village of about ten log cabins. They stayed there one miserable week. While the rain turned the roads into mush, the creeks overflowed their banks. While at Monterey, the day they were to leave for Corinth, members of the 5th Company Washington Artillery came splashing down the road. They were led by Lieutenant Joseph A. Chaleron. These wet artillerymen had returned down the path of retreat to gather up the equipment of the battery. They had salvaged a traveling forge, caissons, limbers, and intact cannon with ammunition.

Trasimond Landry found Villeneuve Allain among the artillery-men. He was from West Baton Rouge Parish and the same age as Private Landry. Trasimond called him by his nickname, "Fatty." He was five feet six inches tall and to Trasimond's view he had gained weight since he had last seen him. Fatty's brother, Alex Allain, was Trasimond's classmate at St. Joseph College. He was glad to see them both. The Allain brothers had enlisted in March.

Trasimond marched along with Fatty, who was on foot as well. The 4th LA could have sorely used the Washington Artillery at the "Hornet's Nest." They traded stories of the Battle of Shiloh Church. Private Landry showed him the shot-holes in his trousers and tunic.

It was still dark as the column neared Corinth and came upon Ten Mile Creek. The artillery was pushed across the indigent-looking bridge with considerable difficulty, wrestling cannon and caissons across. Creek water was overflowing the bridge. The 5th Company and the 4th LA camped on a hill just past the bridge at daylight. The tired Rebels made breakfast fires. By this time, the troops had learned to start a fire in all kinds of weather. They pulled Yankee coffee from their haversacks and sat around trying to dry out. Sitting there, shivering in the cold and drizzle, they waited impatiently for their fires to build up. Suddenly a squadron of cavalrymen came dashing across the bridge and through the camp of the 4th LA. A Confederate officer trailed them, trying to rally the men, but to no avail.

Instantly, there was a rush of sound like a force of wind and vibration rushing toward the Rebels. Federal cavalrymen came swooping down on to the creek. They came on in regular order with sabers at guard. Colonel Allen formed the men up into hollow squares and ordered, "Fix Bayonets!" This group of infantrymen was bait that the Federals could not resist. Not knowing that the Washington Artillery was ready with canister loaded cannon just out of view, they dashed for the bridge.

The Union cavalry charged on. Lieutenant Chalaron opened up with all his guns. The Tirailleurs emptied their Enfield rifles. The enemy vanished, leaving their dead and wounded before the creek. The battle was over in just a few moments. (47) It was a sweet victory.

The Acadians moved back into their old camp at Corinth. Private Landry's feet were sore and blistered. From then on he would take Belisaire's advice and keep a clean change of wool socks in his knapsack. He washed his socks daily. The company's time was taken up constructing abatis. The damp, the wetness, and the bad water started filling up the hospitals around Corinth. Chills, fever, dysentery, and malaria were rampant. Those houses not taken over by the quartermaster, commissary, or ordinance officers were used to house wounded or sick soldiers. You could walk down the streets of Corinth and hear the moans of the wounded. Piles of amputated arms and legs gave off an odor of purulence and despair. Hospital stewards hammered the lids on many coffins at Corinth.

Private Landry felt the need to write home, but he put it off. The Battle of Shiloh had been such a powerful and emotional experience that he knew he could not find the words to describe it. This was true of many of the participants in the battle. For several weeks following the battle, the volume of outgoing letters from camp slumped. Even active diarists tended to have gaps in their diaries for a while after Shiloh.

April 18th was Good Friday and a day of fasting for the Acadians. Colonel Allen called for Private Landry to report to his tent. Landry saluted mechanically. Allen's face was still swollen and distorted from his wound. In spite of this he was smoking a cigar. He tapped a large ash onto the plank floor of his dark tent. The end of the cigar glowed red. Trasimond tried to think of what misdeed he could possibly have done to warrant this meeting. His anxiety was calmed when Allen began to express his gratitude to Trasimond for his bravery and leadership at Shiloh. Allen had seen Private Landry take the company flag and rally the beleaguered Tirailleurs. Colonel Allen handed Private Landry a sword, and offered him the rank of brevet first lieutenant. Trasimond accepted. Doc Leveque became company surgeon of the Delta Rifles. This required his resignation, as many surgeons were not enlisted personnel.

There were thirty-five men of Company H present for duty. The Tirailleurs remained in Corinth almost one month, while the Federals slowly closed in on Corinth. Night and day, the long roll of the drum would stir the troops to the ramparts. These were all false alarms.

On April 27th, rumors circulated that Federal gunboats had broken through the forts below New Orleans. The next day, trains arriving from New Orleans were packed with soldiers and civilians fleeing that city. On May 1st, General Benjamin Butler and his troops took possession of New Orleans.

On May 2nd, the 4th LA was ordered to Edward's Station, Mississippi, to reorganize and recruit. Edward's Station was situated midway on the rail line between Vicksburg and Jackson. Reluctantly, the Tirailleurs left their rifles in Corinth, since the defenders were short of shoulder arms. Many of the Tirailleurs were suffering from flux and eager to leave their unhealthy Corinth camp ground. Even as the 4th LA was leaving Corinth, the sounds of battle could be heard from the direction of Farmington.

On May 6th, they arrived at Edward's Station and were re-armed. The companies were detailed on a rotational basis into Vicksburg to assist in mounting the big guns on the bluff overlooking the Mississippi River. One-year enlistments were up, but the Confederate Congress had passed an act conscripting everyone for the duration. The troops did have the right, however, to elect new officers.

Allen ordered an election of officers at Edward's Station for May 22nd. Since some men were at Vicksburg, they were allowed to vote by proxy. The Tirailleurs elected a recovered Sosthene Aillet as captain and Trasimond Landry as first lieutenant. H. W. Allen was elected colonel. Samuel E. Hunter, a graduate of the Western Military Institute (Frankfort, Kentucky), was elected lieutenant colonel. Thomas Vick was dropped and William Pennington, the ex-saloon keeper from Lake Providence, was elected major. Due to wounds, Belisaire Landry resigned at that time. Captain F. A. Williams was dropped from the rolls. Dr. Marshall Pope resigned on May 19, 1862. He was replaced by Dr. Charles Lewis.

One particularly interesting change was the transfer of D. B. Gorham from the Delta Rifles to the Tirailleurs as second lieutenant. This was done at the insistence of Colonel Allen. (See Appendix E) Gorham was tall and handsome with a quick laugh and a soldierly bearing. His character was a mix of boldness, sensitivity, courage, and conscience. He bravely distinguished himself at Shiloh and was bilingual. Gorham's mother was Acadian. He was warmly welcomed into the Tirailleurs and made fast friends with them. These friendships lasted well after the war. In Colonel Allen's after-action report he stated, "D. B. Gorham, color guard who amid shot and shell and in a hail storm of balls held the flag firm and erect and brought it back tattered and torn by the bullets of the enemy." (48) Lieutenant Gorham had been a student at Bardstown's St. Joseph's College from 1856–1859. While there he was captain of the college's militia company. He was also a law school graduate and an accomplished violinist.

Orderly Sergeant, five foot four inch Adelarde Courtade, was elected third lieutenant. Courtade had a French face with a sparse, well-trimmed beard and intelligent eyes. As with many people of short stature, he had developed a quick mind and sharp wit. The nineteen-year-old lieutenant was bilingual and well-educated, and on the battlefield he displayed ancient Basque fearlessness. From this time on, he was known by the nickname, "T'nant." While at Edward's Station, all three new lieutenants attended officer's schools. With the reorganization of the 4th Louisiana there was a change in the designation of the companies as follows:

Colonel: Henry Watkins Allen
Lieutenant Colonel: Samuel E. Hunter
Major: William F. Pennington

Company A (Old Co. K) Hunter Rifles A, Edward J. Pullen, Captain
Company B (Old Co. A) National Guards, Robert Pruyn, Captain
Company C (Old Co. B) Lake Providence Cadets, Charles R. Purdy, Captain
Company D (Old Co. E) West Feliciana Rifles, Reason B. Turner, Captain
Company E (Old Co. H) Lafourche Guards, Thomas E. Vick, Captain
Company F (Old Co. C) Delta Rifles, O. P. Skolfield, Captain
Company G (Old Co. I) Hunter Rifles B, Cader R. Cornelius, Captain
Company H (Old Co. D) Tirailleurs, Sosthene Aillet, Captain
Company I (Old Co. F) St. Helena Rifles, C. E. Kennon, Captain
Company K Packwood Rifles, (added May 29, 1862) George H. Packwood, Captain. This company was organized from the St. Helena and East Feliciana parishes. (49)

The Beaver Creek Rifles (Old Company G) were transferred to the 9th Battalion Partisan Rangers. Captain James Wingfield petitioned Secretary of War Seddon to allow him to use Company G as a *nidus* for the formation of a Partisan Ranger Battalion. The 9th Battalion Partisan Rangers were organized at Camp Moore on May 13, 1862. This new organization was made up of troops from Washington, Livingston, St. Helena, and East Baton Rouge parishes.

While at Edward's Station, a letter caught up with Trasimond. It was from his sister, Josephine. The first corn had been plowed and sweet potatoes planted. Union troops had started exerting control over the sugar planters around New Orleans. Their influence had not yet reached Brusly Landing, but down river the slaves were walking off the plantations. The ones that stayed would not work. Friends in New Orleans had said that the Negroes were coming into the city from all around. Patrols at Brusly Landing had placed skiffs on the Mississippi River with armed men to keep the slaves from floating down to New Orleans. Simon Alcide was riding patrols. Josephine also noted that the state capital had been moved to Opelousas. She mentioned an interesting note regarding the Police Jury. In early April, they had passed a tax levy for the appropriation of $20,000 for a war fund. Five thousand dollars was given to Monsieur B. R. Chinn to raise a new company and a $50 bounty was to be given to enrollees. In fairness, the jury decided to give $50 to those who had already volunteered. This was some news that would cheer the men of the Tirailleurs and the Delta Rifles.

Around April 15th, Governor Moore ordered all the cotton on the levee to be burned. All up and down the Mississippi, cotton fires lit up the sky. The bales burned for days. The *USS Iroquois* had landed in Baton Rouge the same day Josephine wrote her letter.

One of the great ironies of the war concerned Major General Lovell. After the fall of New Orleans, Lovell was assigned to obscurity by the Rebel High Command. Lovell had taken over the defense of New Orleans from General Twiggs. Braxton Bragg had expected to be given the command of the defense of New Orleans and protested strongly to President Davis. If Bragg had replaced Twiggs, he would have suffered the same fate as Lovell and saved the armies of the west from his bungling leadership. (50)

SHILOH BATTLEFIELD FIRST DAY

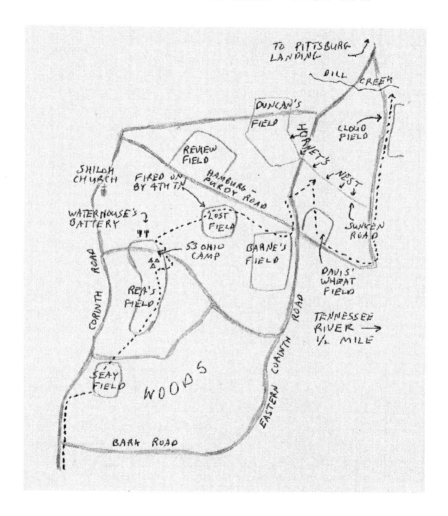

SHILOH BATTLEFIELD SECOND DAY

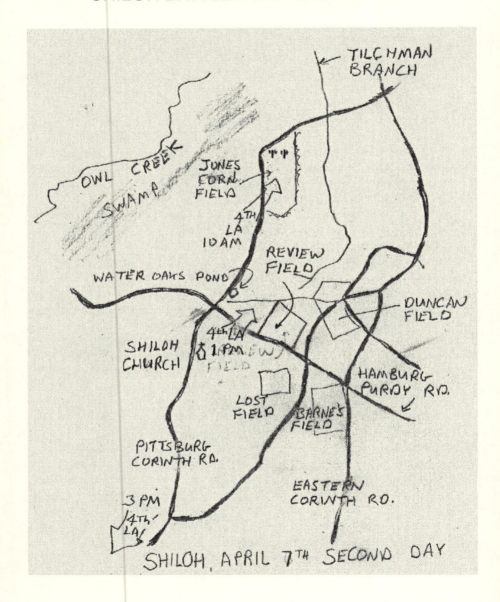

4.

First Siege of Vicksburg

Part of the 4th LA left Edward's Station in early May. They joined men of the 27th LA and the Orleans Guards in mounting eight Columbiads on the high bluffs at Vicksburg. (1) These huge cannon were put out of range of the Union fleet's guns. In June, the remainder of the 4th LA was sent to Vicksburg. They were set to work building new batteries. Long hours were spent working night after night with picks and spades mounting the heavy cannon. The Tirailleurs built the first water battery at Vicksburg. After mounting their guns they were put through artillery drill and manned the guns for a short while. (2)

The Tirailleurs had assisted in mounting heavy cannon at the small forts around Berwick City and at Ship Island. They had become familiar with artillery drill while there and found it an amusing diversion. Loading, aiming, priming, and firing the big guns was fun, for a while. Each day, the citadel at Vicksburg grew stronger.

When Colonel Allen needed special skills he always looked to the Tirailleurs. The Colonel knew that the Acadians had long been famous for their engineering skills. When the Spanish Governor of Louisiana needed colonists and militia to populate the strategic bayous along the Mississippi River, he looked to the Acadians. Their experience in dike and levee building was famous. The Spanish King sent seven ships to France in 1785 to transport Acadians to Louisiana. Fifteen hundred arrived at the expense of the Spanish Crown. Once in their new home, they were sent to strategic areas (Bayou Manchac, Bayou Lafourche, Bayou Sara) and given land grants. Here they put to use their engineering talents in building levees that tamed the Mississippi. Their skill at draining the cane fields was unsurpassed. Colonel Allen put these talents to use against the Yankees. By May 24th, there were seventeen heavy guns mounted above and below the city. The upper battery of five guns was commanded by Colonel Allen. (3)

One soldier wrote: "The water here was bad, mostly from ponds that had a green scum over them, and often we drank or sucked our water through a cloth to keep from swallowing the filth. Next to the bad water here was a number and size of mosquitoes; clothing was but little protection as they could bite through any ordinary shirting." (4)

At this time, Union General Butler was occupying New Orleans. Farragut had accepted the surrender of Natchez on May 13th. On May 18th, he had ordered the surrender of Vicksburg. Unlike Natchez, Vicksburg refused his offer. On 29th, Union General Thomas Williams arrived at Baton Rouge with 2,600 infantrymen. Memphis fell on June 6th.

The Yankee mortar boats arrived on June 20th and began shelling Vicksburg the next day. The Union fleet was divided. Some gunboats were above Vicksburg and some were below. The Acadians of Company H would first hear the deep, rich "boom" of the mortars. Soon a shell could be heard whining high up in the air. Then came the loud, shrieking noise as it sped towards its target. There was an explosion and a puff of white smoke, and then the sounds of the shards of iron humming to the ground. The mortar shells were thirteen inches in diameter and weighed 128 pounds.

John Jackman of the 9th KY regiment described it: "At night you could first see the flash, then came the report of the mortar, and almost with the thunder, came the sound of the rushing shell until it reached its zenith, then you could hear it no longer (but you could see the flight of the fuse as if it were a meteor traversing the heavens) and presently you could hear it crashing among the houses up-town." (5) The Yankees threw fifty to a hundred of these shells per day into Vicksburg.

At 7 A.M. on June 28th, Lieutenant Colonel Allen ordered the long roll. The Yankees were running the batteries and an enemy landing was suspected. While the men rushed to buckle on their belts and grab their rifles, a tragic thing happened. In the bombardment, a mother and her three daughters were rushing by the tents of the 4th LA. A shell burst overhead, mortally wounding the mother. She lived only twenty minutes. (6)

Union Admiral Porter ran the batteries past Vicksburg suffering much damage and accomplishing little. The Tirailleurs manned the water batteries during the passage and claimed several hits during the two-hour battle. Private C. J. Loe, 27th LA, wrote his sister, "Eight of their gunboats passed up by our batteries on the 28th, though they found Jordan a rough road to travel, for we sunk three of their boats and crippled all the rest besides....The shells fell pretty thick in our camps as they passed up, though hurt no one." (7)

In late June, General Butler gave instructions to dig a canal on the Louisiana side of the river to bypass Vicksburg. On June 27th, twelve hundred Negroes began digging the ditch. This activity could be seen from the river batteries, and the Tirailleurs amused themselves by taking pot shots at the laborers. Needless to say, the cutoff-canal scheme did not work, and Vicksburg would hold out for another year.

The Union troops supervising the slave labor at the canal digs had come up from Baton Rouge and were under the command of General Thomas Williams. These three thousand men spent six weeks in the hot, swampy summer of the delta, where many became ill. These same Yankees would face the 4th LA at the Battle of Baton Rouge in August. The shelling of Vicksburg continued. The mortar boats started at 10 A.M. and continued firing until noon. They took two hours off for lunch and then resumed until dark.

With the batteries finished, artillerymen from Fort Pillow arrived to take over the guns. Trasimond was quite fond of the Tirailleur's big cannon, a thirty-two-pounder Columbiad. To him it was like a sphinx guarding the river bluff. He would miss the smell of sulphur. It got into his skin and even with bathing remained for several days. The scent of sulphur was the connection between the soul of the cannon and the soul of the soldier.

On July 2nd, the Tirailleurs were on picket duty north of the city on the road to Yazoo City. At this time, Colonel Allen commanded a brigade consisting of the 4th LA, 17th LA, 27th LA, 3rd MS, and the 6th MS Battalion. (8) On July 10th, the men were paid off. They all received an extra $50 this pay period. The bounty money that Josephine Landry Rivet had written her brother about had caught up with the company. Most of this money went to mess funds, liquor merchants, or *pour des filles de joie*.

On July 10th, the Tirailleurs were awakened by ferocious cannon fire far to the north. The men heard from a courier that the ram, *CSS Arkansas*, was breaking free from its berth on the Yazoo River. The Yankees chased the ram for two hours in one of the most exciting running river battles of the war. She arrived safely under the guns at Vicksburg to rousing cheers from the soldiers and citizens.

On July 14th, the Tirailleurs struck their tents, loaded their wagons, and moved their camp to the suburbs. That day, Private Rivault raised a small French flag in front of his tent. This was Bastille Day. Camp was on a high hill one mile in the rear of the city, shaded with trees. At the base of the hill there were several fine springs. (9) For two weeks, the Tirailleurs had what all soldiers need, rest and a full belly.

The bombardment of Vicksburg continued. Most of the Yankee firing was random and poorly aimed. Little damage was done, but it was persistent. On July 16th, one shell fell in the company street, killing a mule. A favorite tactic was for a gunboat to approach Vicksburg and fire down the streets that lay perpendicular to the river. This made movement in the town difficult.

On July 22nd, the company was in town when "Whistling Dick" began firing. They went down to see what was going on. The USS *Essex*, a Union ironclad, ventured down river and gave the *CSS Arkansas* a broadside. "Whistling Dick" was an eighteen-pounder iron siege gun that had been rifled and reinforced at its breech. It got its name from the peculiar sound its shells made in flight. (10) (11)

At Vicksburg, each company had its own row of tents and a company street ran down the middle. The men formed their mess groups and ate meals together. The food was plentiful at this time, but monotonous. Spencer Talley wrote, "New Orleans having fallen, her treasure was transported to this point (Vicksburg) and consisted largely of sugar, rice, and molasses. We had become very tired of our place on account of almost a single diet of sugar and rice." (12) Occasionally the company could get figs (*figue*) and watermelons (*melon doux*). Vegetables could be purchased from local farmers. One soldier recorded in his diary some local prices: "Spring chicken, 50–75 cents; tough hens, 80 cents to $1; old roosters, $1 to $1.25; turkeys; $1.50 to $2.00; old ganders, $1.50; goose, same." (13)

There was some enmity towards the local Vicksburg merchants. Private Loe wrote, "The rascals are selling us goods so high that I don't care if the plagued Town was torn down and a few Deaths with it. They sell Tobacco @ one Dollar per plug. Shoes at from $10.00 to $18.00 per pare, other articles in perportion." (14) A few citizens of Vicksburg seemed very angry to see Rebel troops in their city. They believed their presence would only cause the Yankees to show up. (15)

The evening meal was very important to the Tirailleurs. Cooking and eating broke up an otherwise intolerable day into tolerable spans. It brought the men together, reinforcing their group identity. (16) Whenever the Acadians could supply themselves with liquor, Sam Leveque and D. B. Gorham would rosin up their bows and entertain the company. The members of a mess became a family. The other members of the company were the extended family. The evenings at Vicksburg recalled the Acadian tradition of the *Veillée*. (17) This was the time at the end of the day when the Acadian family gathered to do light household work and to talk, tell stories, and sing songs. It was a folkway that probably originated in France.

The Acadian members were having no trouble getting along with the French Creoles. They all belonged to the same affluent planter class. They messed together and were friends as well as neighbors. The natural instinct of the Acadian was to be wary of *les Américains*. Their expulsion from Acadia by the English in 1755 was still a powerful ethnic memory. Wariness by the francophones of Company H and the bigotry on the part of *les Américains* led to less than usual fraternization between the groups. The Acadians, with their easy discipline, cohesiveness, and easy-going, party-style camp life caused uneasiness among the Anglos. The Florida Parish Scots-Irish companies had a visceral dislike for Catholics.

These very different cultural groups shared the same miseries of hard labor. In spite of long spans of inactivity, broken up by occasional combat, these men performed well as a regiment. In any event, the Tirailleurs always camped next to the Lafourche Guards and Delta Rifles.

Captain Aillet was on leave in June, and Lieutenant Landry was in charge. On June 20, 1862, the Lieutenant signed "Form No. 8, Quartermaster's Department—Confederate States of America." He requested: Caps (22 at $2.00 each), Coats (7 at $10.00 each), Pants (23 at $5.00 each), Socks (23 at $.70 each), and Drawers (19 at $2.25 each). (18)

In late June 1862, mail arrived in Vicksburg. Trasimond received a letter from Belisaire and was glad go get some news from home. The family had planted more acres of sweet potatoes and more corn. He had two double plows breaking up the black clay for peas. Belisaire had planted four barrels of Irish potatoes in February and was late in getting them dug. The Yankees sent troops over the river to round up mules. There were not that many left after the Confederates had conscripted mules earlier in the war. Belisaire lamented the problem of getting in the sugar harvest in the fall without mules. He was looking for oxen to buy, since he doubted there would be any mules left for the planting season. There was a great deal of illness among the slaves.

Belisaire also wrote that he had not figured out how he was going to get his hogsheads to market. Before the war, all the sugar was sent from Brusly Landing by steamer to New Orleans. New Orleans was now occupied. Prices for sugar in Virginia were sky high, but getting the sugar there was difficult. Some thought was given to converting the molasses into rum, but not much came of the idea. He was looking into shipping sugar to Texas. Many speculators were buying sugar in West Baton Rouge and doubling their money on sales in Texas. Simon Rivet had been talking about enlisting. His job as a government clerk kept him exempt from conscription. Simon was married to Narcisse's daughter, Josephine.

On July 25, 1862, the Yankee mortar boats left the river at Vicksburg. The siege was lifted and the shelling ceased. In May, June, and July, the Yankee bombardment fleet threw fifty thousand shells into Vicksburg.

On 27th, Confederate General Van Dorn took over command of the Department of Southern Mississippi and Eastern Louisiana. He replaced General Mansfield Lovell and made his headquarters in Vicksburg. On the entire Mississippi River, only Vicksburg remained in Southern hands. Van Dorn began developing plans to direct Union attention away from Vicksburg and towards Baton Rouge.

5.

Battle of Baton Rouge

Order of Battle, Battle of Baton Rouge
    Department Commander, Major General Earl Van Dorn
        Mission Commander, General John C. Breckenridge
            Second Division, General Daniel Ruggles
                Second Brigade, Colonel H. W. Allen
                    4th LA, Lieutenant Colonel Samuel E. Hunter
                    30th LA, Colonel Gustavus Breaux
                    9th LA Infantry Battalion, Colonel Samuel Boyd
                    39th MS, Company I, Captain Randel
                    9th LA Partisan Rangers, Major James De Baun
                    Semmes' Battery (lst Regular Battery) Captain Oliver Semmes

The 4th LA was ordered back to Camp Moore as part of a force of four thousand men. Confederate "intelligence" had determined that Union forces were preparing an advance on Camp Moore from Baton Rouge. The 4th LA, under command of General Breckenridge, was hastily rushed by rail from Vicksburg to Camp Moore. The train passed farms and plantations. Cotton was blooming. Barefooted slaves behind double plows worked the ground for planting peas. The regiment arrived on July 28th.

They had to part with their baggage and equipment and traveled only with their weapons, bedrolls, and haversacks. At Camp Moore, the supposed attack never came. The 4th LA rested there for several days. Lieutenant Landry went into town to have his sword sharpened. In the summer's intense heat many men had become ill, reducing Breckenridge's force by four hundred men.

At Camp Moore, the 30th LA had been organized in May 1862. This regiment had a good many Creoles from Orleans Parish and Acadians from Iberville. They were at Camp Moore when the 4th LA arrived. The 30th LA would be paired with the 4th LA for the remainder of the war. Daniel Leveque's Orleans Guards Battalion had been disbanded. Some of the men from the Guards formed a company in the 30th LA under Captain Louis Fortin. Daniel Leveque joined this company.

Also transferring from the Orleans Guards to the 30th LA was fifty-seven-year-old Father Isidore-Francois Turgis. He was a Frenchman, and was ordained in 1846. He joined the French Corps of Military Chaplains in 1847. He served with the *Armée de l'Orient* in the Crimea at the battles of Alma, Inkerman, Balaklava, and the Siege of Sevastapol. He was also with the Franco-Piedmontese armies in Italy in 1859 at the Battles of Magenta and Solferino. The intrepid little priest was with the French army when it garrisoned Saigon in Cochinchina. He turned up in New Orleans in 1860 and became chaplain of the Orleans Guards. In July 1862, he became chaplain of the 30th LA. He served with this regiment through the end of the war and became the *de facto* priest for the Catholic members of the 4th LA.

Priests and seminarians were subject to the Confederate military draft. Many younger priests went north to avoid conscription, or their parish paid for a substitute. As a French citizen, Father Turgis was exempt. However, he saw the war as an opportunity to save souls, especially on the battlefield, and was held in high esteem by the troops of many regiments.

On Sunday morning, July 30th, Breckenridge's force numbered four thousand men, plus another thirteen hundred already at Camp Moore under General Ruggles. Under Colonel Clark, half of these men left Camp Moore for William's Bridge (Grangeville) on the Amite River. Two days later the 4th LA and the remainder of the expeditionary force under General Ruggles left camp. They joined Colonel Clark on the Amite on August 2nd. The troops camped in the open that night to the noise of thousands of locusts. From William's Bridge, they marched down the Greenwell Springs Road toward the Comite River.

Joining the march with Colonel Allen was the 1st Regular Battery, led by Captain Oliver J. Semmes. This battery evacuated New Orleans after its surrender and was sent to Camp Moore. Captain Semmes was West Point trained and the son of Admiral Raphael Semmes. They fell into line on the march to Baton Rouge.

The march resumed through the level coastal plain. The Tirailleurs were unaccustomed to the pine forests of Tangipahoa. The pines were straight and not very thick, presenting an unobstructed view deep into the forest. The air was hot and still and filled with the unfamiliar piney smell of the longleaf and the loblolly. Hardly a bird or cricket chirped. The foliage of the pines only partially obstructed the sun's oily rays. Many soldiers fell out as stragglers due to dehydration.

On August 3rd, ten miles from Baton Rouge, the force arrived at the Comite River at Corinth Bridge. Waiting at the bridge was eighteen-year-old Isidore Daigle. He had arrived to join his brother Prudent as a Tirailleur. (1)

The dusty, smelly troops halted to rest. The riflemen headed into the stream to wash and fill their canteens. Trasimond cautioned Isidore Daigle to always fill his canteen upstream from a bridge. Rebel soldiers seemed to be unable to pass a bridge without urinating (*piser*) off it. It was an unofficial marking of territory.

Lieutenant Landry was on the edge of exhaustion. He flopped down on the cool, damp sand of the riverbank. He lay back, surrounded by the fragrance of the cool water and the melody of the wind rustling in the laurel cherries. The "no-seeums" were out, as well as mosquitoes. In Vicksburg he had written to the daughters of the *Veuve* Bujol describing his adventures in that city. One of the daughters had written back. During this rest he reached into his pocket and pulled out the well-worn letter and read it over again.

Colonel Allen's Second Brigade had 1,035 men present for duty camped at the Comite River Bridge on August 3rd. (2) In the official records, General Breckenridge claimed to have 2,600 men. This error was repeated in Se De Kay's *Memphis Daily Appeal* account of the battle. The Rebel force numbered at least 3,600 men and probably more. (3) (4) The army spent one full day resting. On the 4th, General Breckenridge gave them a speech.

On the evening of August 4th, the riflemen filled their canteens. Artillerymen began bringing up water to fill their sponge buckets. The men dug into their greasy haversacks for a quick supper.

Breckenridge left the Comite River at 11 P.M., August 4th. They headed down the Greenwell Springs Road toward Baton Rouge. The column reached the bridge at Ward's Creek at 3 A.M., August 5th. They crossed the creek and bivouacked in a plowed field, "In the woods back and leftward of the residence of Captain R. W. Robinson, and about three fourths of a mile to the rear of the central portion of Baton Rouge." (5) The force was then shortly moved to a field immediately west of the Magnolia Cemetery, a little over a mile from the Mississippi River. Pickets were sent out.

The troops were split into two divisions. The second division was commanded by General Ruggles and was divided into two brigades. Colonel Allen's Second Brigade was composed of the 4th LA, 400 men; the 30th LA, 312 men; the 9th LA Battalion, 194 men; the 9th Partisan Rangers, 31 men; and Semmes' Battery, 89 men. All the men of the 9th LA were from East Baton Rouge Parish. Company I, 39th MS (Captain Randel) was attached to the 4th LA.

Breckenridge had hoped to surprise the enemy at Baton Rouge and coordinate his attack with the arrival of the powerful Confederate ram, the *CSS*

Arkansas. The *Arkansas* was to take care of the Union gunboats on the Mississippi while the land forces of Breckenridge staged a surprise attack on the garrison. The Federals were aware of the Confederate approach and were prepared for them. (6) It seems that everyone in the area knew of the attack. Isidore Daigle found out from slaves that his brother's regiment was marching to Baton Rouge. He found out in time to join them on August 4th.

Lieutenant Landry rested on his arms in the early morning of the 5th. He gave the new recruit, Isidore Daigle, instructions to stay next to him. Mosquitoes feasted on him as sleep hung on his eyelids. He thought about his brother, wounded at Shiloh and said several "Hail Marys." Trasimond stared at the I. D. bracelet on his right wrist. Remembering an Anglo in the 13th LA who had been decapitated by a cannon ball at Shiloh, he reassured himself with the thought, "*Si un boulet de canon me décapiterait, ils pourraient m'identifier*" (If my head gets blown off by a cannon ball, I can still be identified).

In the solidified darkness, Breckenridge waited anxiously for sounds of the arrival of the *Arkansas*, but none were heard. The dry crack of rifle shots rang out to the right and the Rebels could hear Yankee drummers beating the long roll. A cavalry picket had briefly engaged the enemy before daylight and returned to the Rebel lines. Mistaken for Union cavalrymen in the inky blackness, they were fired on. Brigadier General Benjamin Helm was wounded and Lieutenant A. H. Todd was killed. Both men were brothers-in-law of Abraham Lincoln. In the melee, Captian Cobb's two cannon were damaged. There would be nine Rebel cannon facing eighteen Federal pieces plus Federal gunboats.

Breckenridge knew there would be no surprise and realized he could wait no longer. A gray light filtered through the tree tops as the battle began. One company of the 30th LA (Thomas Shields) and a section of Semmes' Battery were detached from Allen's Brigade and sent to the Rebel's far right flank at Plank Road.

Captain Aillet's Tirailleurs rose with daylight. No one had slept. Lieutenant Landry went down the short line checking the men's equipment and putting them in place. From out of the milky pool of fog, dark figures moved forward. The 4th LA of Allen's brigade was on the far left of the attacking Rebel line. Ruggles, with his Santa Claus beard, rode around checking his two brigades. His division moved south, off the Greenwell Springs Road, three miles from Baton Rouge, and advanced in four lines. "The advance was made over very rough country, across ditches, through sugar cane, over fences—a very tiring and exhausting march." (7)

Across the river that night at Brusly Landing, Simon Alcide Landry was riding patrol. The small band of men had ridden around their ward all night long. Slaves in the South had an incredible "grapevine." It was easy for word to travel for miles, passed on from one plantation to the next in amazingly rapid time. The citizens of Brusly Landing knew something was going to happen on August 5th. Simon Alcide and Alexis Hebert rode up the River Road near dawn to listen.

The tense waiting ended. Colonel Allen's Brigade started off in a dense wood at the bottom of an ocean of fog. As they moved forward they came under fire from the first line of Union troops. Volleys were exchanged and the enemy fell back. Allen's troops then came out into an open field. There was fire from the right that could not be returned. The men were halted. Allen ordered the Tirailleurs out into the fog as skirmishers. Captain Aillet spread out his company and they passed on into the woods. The rest of the regiment followed. Lieutenant Landry could hear rifle fire to his right. Because of the fog, Union gunboats were quiet for the moment. The sulfurous smell of gunpowder was in the air. Trasimond Landry's heart started beating rapidly. He was sweating and already thirsty. The second line of the enemy was unmasked and the Union troops again fell back.

Allen then formed his brigade in an area of thick woods adjoining a cultivated field. The ground was broken with fields surrounded by picket fences and hedges of Cherokee rose. The brigade's left rested on a fence in the rear of Magruder's Institute. To his right was Thompson's brigade. (8) This brigade was made up of the 3rd KY, 6th KY, 7th KY, and the 35th ALA regiments. Allen advanced in a single line of battle, crossed an open field, and came under fire from snipers. The 30th LA was sent to attack these sharpshooters. The line reformed and advanced again through a small strip of woods. The enemy was driven back past another open field on the left. Two volleys of grape tore the still air wide open as the Yankee cannon added its blue smoke to the fog. The enemy was charged. They again retreated.

The 4th LA was then opened up on by cannon fire. Allen halted the men. Due to the fog, the position of the battery of cannon was well-masked. Allen dismounted. The fog had lifted several feet above the ground. Allen then crawled 150 yards in the direction of the noise of the cannon. After locating its position he crawled back. Colonel Allen called for three cheers for the Confederacy and ordered a charge. (9) The Federals again broke, taking their guns with them. Captain Chinn of the 9th LA was wounded in this charge.

As Isidore Daigle reloaded his Enfield a burst of grape passed very close, sending him sprawling to the ground. A section of a Federal battery had found them with the lifting of the fog and had their range. Allen took this to be a flanking maneuver. This was a section of Captain Ormand F. Nims' 2nd Massachusetts Battery, supported by the 6th Michigan Infantry Regiment. Nims was a forty-three-year-old Boston druggist who had drilled his men until they were equal to any of the regular army batteries. Teachers, merchants, and professionals, these Bostonians, in their red-trimmed jackets, were spoiling for a fight. They were located at the junction of Perkins and Claycut Road. Claycut road merged into and became Government Street.

The cannon of Nims' battery sent the men of Allen's battalion back into the brush. With the men laying flat, the brave Allen rode down the line forming them up for a charge on the battery and its supporting infantry. The Yankees were firing grape shot and were shooting high at that moment. Tree limbs overhead were cracking. The difference between this place and Shiloh Church is that they could now see the enemy. Nims had two bronze six-pounder field pieces. Captain Bynum summed up the situation: "We soon found ourselves upon the edge of an old field, on the opposite side which is the Benton Ferry Road (Government Street), and the enclosure of the racetrack. Square in our front was posted along the roadside a number of the enemy skirmishers and sharpshooters, and to their left a battery was planted (Nims)....A regiment supported the battery (6th Michigan) and its men were placed behind the fences, outhouses, and houses in the neighborhood of Hockney's." (10)

Colonel Allen kept Private Oscar Hebert next to him. Oscar stood nervously, with his bugle ready. His mouth was dry and his heart raced. Beads of sweat broke out on his upper lip. He began tightening his lips across his front teeth. Tightening and relaxing his lips, he was getting himself ready to signal the command he knew would soon come. Allen shouted, "Boys, we must take those guns! Fire low, men, fire low!" Allen's face was as hard as bronze. He turned to the private and calmly said, "Sound the charge, Oscar." Colonel Allen then rose in his stirrups and shouted, "Fix Bayonets! Forward, trail arms, double quick, march!"

The sun had just risen above the treetops behind the Rebels. The field was three hundred yards across. Trasimond started out in a crouch. He instinctively felt the need to make himself as small a target as possible. The grape continued. The balls, one and a half inches in diameter, were whirring overhead. Some tore into the ground, releasing the smell of earth. Trasimond's heart raced in his chest. He felt as if his stomach were spinning inside his belly. Deep within his most inner self was an unwashed fear. Not of the grape shot, but the fear of giving in to the fear. He knew he could make this assault, but he had seen brave men panic and give in to the terror of cannon fire. These thoughts flashing through his mind were suddenly drowned out by the shouting of men giving a Rebel yell.

The middle of the line advanced, looking as if they were moving forward in a rain storm: heads bowed, shoulders shrugged. (11) Lieutenant Landry could clearly hear the sickening thumping sound of grape colliding with human flesh. He could feel the vibrations of shot whirring near his head. With an iron-like will, the Tirailleurs crossed three hundred yards of open ground. The enemy was posted just beyond a shallow ravine. As the brigade passed the middle of the field the Federal artillerymen switched to canister. Pierre Hilaire Longuepee dropped to the ground, wounded. Captain Aillet fell from his horse, wounded.

A participant in the charge was A. P. Richards. "With a mad rush, and a grand yell, the men (not boys now) dashed into the opening before them, only to be met by a storm of shell, grape, and canister from the Federal battery, and a scorching fire from a strong line of infantry supporting the artillery." (12)

Canister converts a field piece into a giant shotgun. It sprays a tin can full of half inch lead balls in huge patterns into oncoming infantrymen. More men began dropping, this time in small clusters, as the canister tore through flesh. Sergeant L. O. Dupuy was wounded. It was now First Lieutenant Landry's duty to lead the Tirailleurs.

By this time, Trasimond felt numb. He was panting. Sweat was pouring down into his eyes. In the anoxic heat and sulphurous atmosphere of that field, the Acadians bravely charged forward into the smoke of the cannon. Colonel Allen rode, as always, in front of the brigade, urging them on. There were no stragglers as the brave Confederates charged forward. At one hundred yards, a wall of flame burst forth from the muskets of the 6th Michigan. The Yankees shot over the heads of the battalion, a not uncommon phenomenon in the heat of battle.

Yankee artillerymen switched to double canister at one hundred yards. Canister, with a one-pound charge attached, was rammed into the 3.64-inch cannon bore and was followed by another canister. Range was point blank. The gunner moved the handspike to aim the piece. The vent was punched, the friction primer placed in the vent hole, and the order given to "FIRE!" The lanyard was pulled. The friction primer sent a flash into the powder charge and the cannon fired, sending the two-thousand-pound gun and carriage recoiling six feet rearward. A large cloud of white smoke filled the air. The lead balls left the cannon muzzle at a speed of twelve hundred feet per second. The canister radiated its pattern wider and wider as it spread out over the field and into the advancing Rebels. This was repeated every twenty seconds. The last few frantic volleys were fired without sponging the barrel. The Rebels advanced at first in a wedge shape, slowly straightening out the line. Early in the charge, the center of the line took the worst beating. Louis Beleau was wounded.

Fifty feet from the battery a blast of double canister tore into Colonel Allen and his horse, felling them both. Lieutenant Colonel Samuel Boyd of the 9th LA also fell, wounded. The Tirailleurs and the St. Helena Rifles reached the guns.

Near the Union guns, Gustave Grogne and Prudent Daigle tangled with each other and tripped. As Gustave struggled to his feet, a Yankee lieutenant came galloping into the fray riding between the two Rebels. The Union officer raised his artillery sword and struck to his left at Gustave's head. The sword hit the side brim of Gustave's derby, sliced off his left ear, and crashed into his shoulder and the leather strap of his ration sack. At the same time, Prudent plunged his bayonet at the horse and rider. The bayonet sliced into the soft underbelly of the horse's flank. The horse's right hind leg kicked the Enfield hard from Prudent's hand, throwing the rifle high into the air. The horse turned his head and neck violently, baring his teeth, and stopped. The Yankee lieutenant was thrown forward over the horse's head and landed hard on the ground.

The screaming horse dropped back on his rump, then fell to his side kicking in circles. Gustave was seething in anger. In the dust and smoke he rushed to the Yankee officer. He stomped the Yankee's wrist and the sword fell free. He pulled the Yankee up by his hair and placed his knee in his back. Using the sword like a garrote he slit the Yankee's throat. Blood pulsed with force from the dying Federal's carotids. He breathed through his neck one time and died. The dying horse had been stolen from across the river from the Allendale Plantation.

The Acadians broke through the cannon smoke and into the Yankee artillerymen. The bayonet did its work. Their faces blackened with powder, Union artillerymen fought back with swords and rammers. The St. Helena Rifles came into the battery using their unloaded rifles as clubs. In the crush, there was the clatter of metal on metal, an oath, the quick mushy sound of rifle butts against skulls, and the grunts following bayonets to the belly. Lieutenant Landry unloaded his revolver in the hand-to-hand melee. Rather than support the battery, the 6th Michigan broke to the rear. John Gyles, regimental ensign, planted his flag among the guns. Then, someone reported that Colonel Allen was wounded. This stunned the men of the 4th LA. Their advance suddenly lost its energy. No one took charge.

It was now 9 A.M. The Federals regrouped and began firing from houses. Another section of Nims' Battery opened up from the right and enfiladed the brigade with grapeshot. The Yankees then mounted a counter-attack, sending the brigade retreating back across the open field. A few Yankee artillerymen were taken prisoner, but the enemy quickly re-acquired their cannon, and again turned them on the Confederates. Lieutenant Landry ordered the men to carry the wounded from the field. They tramped back across a field that had been ploughed up by cannon shot. The 9th LA Battalion lost their battle flag in the counter-attack.

Captain Thomas Bynum of the 9th LA wrote, "We were saved a panic, but the annoying fire from the enemy's sharpshooters left them no alternative but to fall back across the field to the shelter of the woods. (13) Colonel Gustavus Breaux of the 30th LA and Lieutenant Colonel Hunter managed to reform the men into a new line. With the help of Semmes' Battery, the Yankees were halted."

Norwich Military College graduate Colonel Breaux reported, "It now became evident that fatigue and thirst were overpowering our men."(14)

After leaving the field, a regiment of Federals in column of companies moved up Government Street. Lieutenant West of Semmes' Battery double-shotted canister and fired. "The terrible sweep of balls opened a broad avenue right through the whole column, in the path of which could be seen the mangled victims leaping, turning, and writhing about while the two halves left standing stood motionless with terror for an instant, and then turned and fled in panic." (15)

The palindromic Semmes reported five men killed and one caisson exploded by an enemy shell. His battery fired two hundred rounds of smoothbore six-pounder ammunition and one hundred rounds of six-pounder rifled ammunition. (16)

Lieutenant Colonel S. E. Hunter, 4th LA wrote, "The troops, exhausted by fatigue and crying for water, were thrown in utter confusion, and all attempts to rally them were fruitless. From this time, no more fighting was done by our brigade." (17) The brigade entered the battle with strong leadership. With Colonel Allen and Lieutenant Colonel Boyd wounded, Lieutenant Colonel Hunter and Colonel Breaux did not take control of the field. The majority of the blame for the faltering of the attack falls on Hunter, the only staff officer with battlefield experience.

"Victory was stamped upon the face of every man. But alas, for the fate of battle, soon all was in confusion and no orders came. The enemy were reforming their line, while sharp firing from houses in front became deadly. Oh, where is the commanding officer?" (18) A. P. Richards wrote this well after the war ended. Did he mean, "Where is Colonel Allen?" or did he more likely mean, "Where is Hunter?"

Lieutenant Landry, now in command of Company H, sought out Hunter and suggested taking his company and the cavalry screen around the race track to flank the Yankees from their position. Hunter would not hear of it. He was content to sit it out in the relative safety of the woods.

It was now 10 A.M., and canteens were empty. Trasimond's thoughts went back to the night of April 6th on the battlefield of Shiloh Church. His memory could call up the sounds of the wounded men between the battle lines pleading for water. These thoughts made his thirst seem less onerous. Captain Bynum of the 9th LA also noted, "Having been under arms for more than sixteen hours; having neither supper, breakfast, nor sleep; having marched over twelve miles; and having gone through four hours of heavy fighting, it is not a matter of surprise or blame that they (the men) paid but little heed to the rallying cries of their leaders." (19)

A number of factors prevail upon soldiers to advance under fire: inspiring leadership, thorough training, and tight group cohesiveness. (20) The accounts of Hunter, Breaux, and Bynum place the proximate cause of the failure of the charge on "demoralization" of the troops at the loss of their leader. In the alternative, they blamed fatigue and thirst. Despondency and thirst could have been overcome with strong leadership. After the war, Allen's biographers never challenged this absurd proposition, because it made his leadership qualities look almost omnipotent.

Colonel Allen was taken four miles back to the home of Granville Pearce. He was cared for by Breckenridge's staff surgeon, Dr. Amzi Martin. The men of the 4th LA stayed on the field inactive, thinking more of water than of the hissing shells being fired at them. More time passed. The Federals had retreated to their redoubt on the river and the gunboats opened up on Allen's Brigade. Just as at Shiloh late on the first day, the Yankees huddled under the protective umbrella of iron provided by their gunboats.

At 4 P.M., Breckenridge learned that the *Arkansas* had developed engine failure and could not support him. She was scuttled the next day. Breckenridge reported, "I saw around me not more than a 1,000 exhausted men, who had been unable to procure water since we left the Comite River. The enemy had several batteries commanding the approaches to the arsenal and the gunboats had already re-opened up on us with a direct fire. Under these circumstances, although the troops had shown the utmost indifference to danger and death, and were even reluctant to retire, I did not deem it prudent to pursue the victory further." (21)

Simon Alcide and Alexis Hebert joined many local citizens that morning on the river road. They knew a fierce battle was taking place. As the fog lifted over Baton Rouge, they watched as Yankee signal men atop the state capitol building directed the fire from Union gunboats. Simon Alcide knew that his brother was in the thick of this battle.

The citizens of Baton Rouge, surprised by the attack, fled. They passed through Catfish Town and headed south. Some found shelter in the homes on Highland Road. Many crossed the river and were sheltered at Brusly Landing. (22) Narcisse Landry opened his home to as many refugees as he could. Those citizens that did not flee came out on the battlefield during the lull in the fighting. They brought wagons and loaded up as many wounded as they could carry off. When Alcide returned home that evening, the house was full of refugees from Baton Rouge. Many had moved into the sugar house. He knew some of them, but most were strangers.

The Tirailleurs fell back quietly that evening, leaving the abandoned Federal camps and stores burning. The Acadians hopes of liberating Baton Rouge and reclaiming New Orleans had turned to dust. Their mood was one of despair. They trudged away slowly in the dirty twilight. It rained on the march from the battlefield to the Comite. William Dixon wrote, "It has always seemed to be a natural consequence for rain to come whenever we had to move, especially if it was a retrograde move." (23) That evening there was no pissing off the bridge.

Camp was made on the east bank of the Comite River, eight miles from Baton Rouge. There was no Federal counter-attack. An outpost was maintained five miles east of Baton Rouge on the Pratt farm. The next day, Lieutenant Landry spent his twenty-third birthday camped on the Comite.

Confederate losses were eighty-four killed, two hundred and ninety-five wounded, and fifty-seven captured or missing. Captain Aillet, Fourth Sergeant T. C. White, and Private Sam Leveque were listed as missing. Allen's Brigade suffered 166 casualties. Many men of Allen's Brigade were killed within walking distance of their homes. The Union forces saw eighty-four killed and total casualties of three hundred and fifty-eight men. The former Vice President of the United States, General Breckenridge, wrote after the battle, "The enemy were well clothed, and their encampments showed the presence of every comfort, and even luxury. Our men had little transportation, indifferent food, and no shelter. Half of them had no coats, and hundreds were without shoes or socks; yet no troops ever behaved with greater gallantry and even reckless audacity. What can make this difference, unless it be a sublime courage inspired by a just cause." (24)

Trasimond was leaning against the wheel of a powder wagon cleaning his finger nails with a sharpened bayonet. Lieutenants Gorham and Courtade were sitting complacently in the shade. Daniel Gorham suggested that they go down to have a look at the prisoners. At the Comite River camp, Union prisoners were kept in a roped-off area near the river. The Yankees were looking demoralized, but by no means penitent. They were sure they would be paroled soon and set free. The three approached the rope line.

Lieutenant Courtade spit tobacco juice. The dark liquid hit in the dusty ground and beaded up into a dirty brown oyster. A Yankee sergeant looked at him and said, "Hey Reb. I sure could use a chew." Adelarde tossed him half a twist.

Trasimond asked him where he was from. He replied, "I'm with the 6th Michigan. Where you from?"

Daniel Gorham answered for them, "We're from right here. What I want to know is why you 'bluebellies' are here? What de hell are you fighting for?"

The Yankee confidently replied, "We're fighting for the Union."

Daniel responded, "Well I'll jess be damned. I tought you were fightin' for de niggers."

The prisoner tilted his head slightly to one side, "'Taint so, Reb. If we thought that we'd all strike. We're fighting for the Union. Why do you fight, Reb?"

Pointing his finger, Lieutenant Gorham replied, "We fight 'cause y'all are here."

The Battle of Baton Rouge was at best a draw, but Butler's evacuation of Baton Rouge fifteen days later left it a strategic victory. Fortification of Port Hudson could proceed unchallenged. Before heading for New Orleans, the Federals looted the town of furniture and valuables of all kinds. All the houses on North Street were burned to the ground. The state capitol was looted. To the delight of local felons, the penitentiary doors were flung open. Union Colonel James McMillan wrote General Butler from Baton Rouge, "This place has been nearly completely sacked by the soldiery. Scarcely a single house has escaped, all the citizens having fled. Even officers' tents are filled with furniture from deserted houses." (25) Rather than withdrawing from Baton Rouge, Union General Butler would have been more prudent had he occupied Port Hudson. The strategic importance of these bluffs was known to the Union river fleet. Passing up this opportunity to preempt the Confederacy was a blunder.

On August 9, 1862, Union Admiral Farragut bombarded and torched Donaldsonville. This wanton destruction was done in reprisal for partisan rangers who were firing on Yankee transports with shotguns. Plantations for six miles below and nine miles above Donaldsonville were bombarded and set on fire. A citizen's committee, which included J. T. Landry, West Baton Rouge Parish Police Jury president, petitioned Governor Moore to order the rangers to cease firing. During World War II, one of the techniques used by the Nazis against partisan bands was to punish local civilians when German army targets were attacked. Americans considered this outrageous behavior when done by the Nazis.

Isaac Erwin lived on Shady Grove Plantation on Bayou Grosse Tete. He wrote in his diary on August 10th, "It is reported that the Yankees are taking all the Negroes off the plantations in West Baton Rouge Parish....Everybody, almost, are moving away from Plaquemine, deserting the town." (26)

History was repeating itself. This was not the first time the Yankee race had persecuted the Acadians. Beyond the motives of plunder and rapine was a deeper more powerful reason for their barbaric behavior. The Yankee soldier of the nineteenth century had been whipped into a state of anti-Southern fanaticism by his New England preachers and ministers. Once on Southern soil, these prejudices were acted out with predations against the civilian population. Protestant New Englanders of the seventeenth century held a deep hatred for the French in Acadia. Preachers in New England railed against France, a France which to them had become the home of Romanism and Satanism. They saw the revocation of the Edict of Nantes by the King of France as justification for crusades of destruction focused on the Acadians of Nova Scotia. (27) Unspeakable crimes committed by New Englanders against seventeenth century Acadians in the name of religion were now being repeated against nineteenth century Acadians in the name of Abolitionism.

Samuel Eugene Hunter assumed command of the 4th LA after the Battle of Baton Rouge. Hunter was not a tall leader. His features were good—straight nose, firm mouth, broad forehead. He wore a mustache and pointed beard, but no whiskers. His eyes were keen and projected the look of a man more worried about his own appearance than the Cause. He received his official commission on January 19, 1863. He commanded the 4th LA through the remainder of the regiment's existence, but was not popular among the men. (28) William Pennington became lieutenant colonel and six-foot-two-inch E. J. Pullen, Hunter Rifles A, became major.

Battle of Baton Rouge August 5, 1862

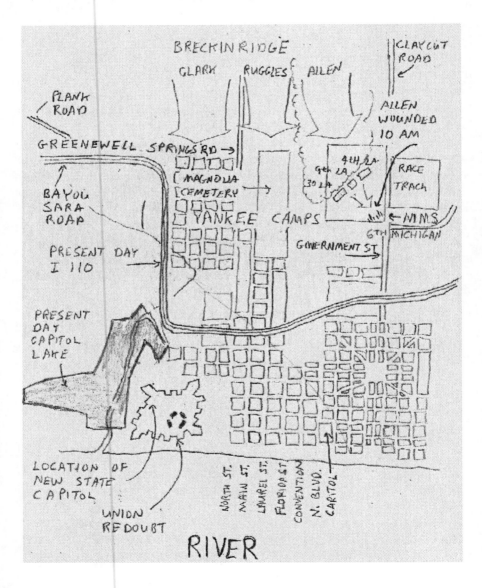

Lieutenant General P. G. T. Beauregard

Lieutenant General Joseph Johnston

Lieutenant General John B. Hood

General Henry Watkins Allen

General Gardner

Major General Samuel B. Maxey

Major General William A. Quarles

Brigadier General Randall Gibson

Major General John Breckenridge

First Lieutenant J. A. Leveque

Private Samuel Leveque

Colonel Samuel Eugene Hunter

First Lieutenant Daniel B. Gorham

Father Isidore-Francois Turgis

Gustave Grogne

Private Simon Alcide Landry
Photo courtesy of Mrs. Jane Landry Comeaux

6.

Port Hudson

Department of Mississippi and East Louisiana, Major General Van Dorn
    Corps: Major General, J. C. Breckenridge
        Division: Brigadier General, Daniel Ruggles
            Brigade, Brigadier General, Samuel B. Maxey's
                4th LA, Colonel S. E. Hunter
                30th LA, Colonel Gustavus Breaux
                42nd TN, Lieutenant Colonel Isaac Holms
                46th TN, Colonel A. J. Brown
                48thTN, Colonel William Voorhies
                49th TN, Colonel J. E. Bailey
                53rd TN, Captain H. H. Aynett
                55th TN, Colonel A. J. Brown

With the fall of Memphis and New Orleans, it became important for the Confederates to defend Port Hudson. This gave them control of the Mississippi River between Vicksburg and Port Hudson, and kept open river traffic and commerce down the Red River. Port Hudson was an ideal site for batteries to control the river. (1) It was, however, more exposed than Vicksburg on its landward side.

    On August 14th, the 4th LA and 30th LA broke camp and marched to Port Hudson. The regiments marched northwest to the Plank Road. This road was built in 1852, and stretched from Baton Rouge to Clinton. Moving north, they crossed the Redwood Bridge then turned left onto the Redwood Road. Under a yellow sun, the column crossed Doyle's Bayou and White's Bayou. They camped at the farm of a Mr. Moteguda. August 15th was a Catholic Holy Day, the Feast of the Assumption. Father Turgis celebrated Mass. The Acadians spent the rest of the day on the march. They then took the Bayou Sara Road to Plains Store and then went west down a wagon road to Port Hudson.

There were some fine farms in the Plains. Slave gangs were busy scraping cotton, double plows were laying by cane, and hands were pulling fodder for cattle. In less than a year these local planters would be ruined. Yankee thieves would steal their cotton and sugar, conscript their corn, and take their slaves.

These veterans of Shiloh, Vicksburg, and Baton Rouge were greeted all along the way by local citizens and the young ladies of the parish. These men would have been the first really battle-hardened Rebels that the locals had seen. The 4th LA was marching with only the barest necessities: blanket, musket, bayonet, and haversack. Knapsacks had been lost. Carrying extra clothing on the march was deemed useless. The men wore their clothes until they were only good to be thrown away. They depended on what they could find in enemy knapsacks or purchase for themselves—or more so, from what the folks would send them from home. They were down to one blanket. This was carried by rolling it lengthwise with the rubber cloth outside and tying the ends of the roll together. A loop was made in it and it was worn over the left shoulder with the ends fastened together under the right arm.

Many men had discarded the heavy cap boxes and cartridge boxes, carrying their caps and cartridges in their pockets. Also in their pockets were gun wipers, gun stoppers, and wrenches. Some had discarded their canteens as too cumbersome and merely carried a tin cup for use at streams or springs. Some carried new Yankee zinc canteens. These were frequently used to carry buttermilk, cider, sorghum, or liquor. Revolvers were discarded as too heavy and useless. (2) Lieutenant Landry would not part with his Navy revolver and cleaned it daily. Those Bowie knives that were not discarded were either used in lieu of machetes to clear brush or ended up with the cooks.

The 4th LA camped in a cornfield between William Slaughter's residence and Port Hudson on August 15th and 16th. At camp, on August 16, 1862, another Daigle recruit arrived. He was Private Louis Daigle. He was the twenty-five-year-old brother of Private Joseph I. Daigle and Private Prudent Daigle. He was shrewd, hard-bitten, and stood as straight as an Indian chief. Louis was very popular with the company and would be elected third lieutenant four months later. Louis had joined Company F, Orleans Cadets, April 11, 1861, and served in Virginia in Dreaux's Battalion. This group disbanded in May, 1862, and Louis returned home to join the Tirailleurs.

The regiment entered the village of Port Hudson on the 17th. Arriving at midday, the men stacked their arms and set up a tentless camp on the commons east of the Methodist Church. Several days after arriving at Port Hudson, Lieutenant Landry purchased a bar of soap (*brique de savon*) in the town. For $2 he got a $1.50 bar of soap and a fifty cent shin plaster (small paper notes issued by merchants as change; they took the place of specie during wartime, and were usually in denominations ranging from 5 cents to 50 cents). Sunday, August 19th, Trasimond and half a dozen fellow Acadians walked down to Sandy Creek. They still had the grime and crud on their bodies left over from the Battle of Baton Rouge. Although they had camped on the Comite River August 6th, they had no soap.

The Acadians splashed into the shallow creek buck naked and bathed. The men never knew they could derive such pleasure from a bath. They splashed around for several hours in the cool water. They remembered how good they had it when they were stationed on the Gulf Coast. Fed by springs and rainfall, the water in Little Sandy Creek was cool. The steep banks supported growths of water oaks, beech trees, and Carolina laurel cherry. Muscadine vines hung down from the tree tops. The sandy edges of the creek were autographed with the tracks of deer, coons, and herons, and the shallow areas were covered with rich red algae.

It was a short respite from their lousy clothes and the itch of lice crawling around on their testicles. The Tirailleurs were sure the lice had been spread by Tennessee troops. In warm months the louse was a constant aggravation. Trasimond detested these little creatures. The Anglos called them "greybacks."

Breckenridge's old Kentucky brigade arrived on August 18th. That night they received orders to return to Kentucky. Their regimental band struck up "My Old Kentucky Home" to cheers from the Kentuckians. The Daigle brothers, Daniel Gorham, and Lieutenant Landry visited with the 6th KY that night. They had many friends in that regiment, which was mostly raised from Nelson County, Kentucky, and St. Joseph's College in Bardstown. Louis Daigle was a personal friend of Major John Wickliffe. The Tirailleurs awoke the next morning to the music of "Get Out of the Wilderness". The Kentucky brigade was just leaving the camp. (3)

Captain Aillet arrived in camp along with Sam Leveque and T. C. White. Fourth Sergeant White and Private Leveque had lifted Captain Aillet off the battlefield and stayed with him while he was taken care of in a private home on the outskirts of Baton Rouge. All three were listed as "missing in action." Also arriving in camp was the regiment's baggage from Jackson. The men finally had their tents back. Gustave Grogne left for Mobile, intending to have his ear looked after by private surgeons.

Company H was under the command of General Daniel Ruggles. The Tirailleurs would to serve under General Ruggles, General Breckenridge, General Beall, and General Franklin Gardner during their nine months at Port Hudson.

The Yankee General Benjamin "Beast" Butler, feeling threatened after the attack on Baton Rouge, ordered Federal troops back to New Orleans. The Union evacuation began on August 20th. Isaac Erwin wrote in his diary August

24th, "The Federals have left Baton Rouge, having stripped the town of all pianos, iron, etc." (4) Butler initially ordered the whole city burned, but fortunately the order was not carried out.

The 4th LA was ordered to garrison Baton Rouge, and the regiment marched out of Port Hudson on August 21, 1862. They started for Baton Rouge at 3 P.M. and camped halfway there across from a Mr. Benjamin's house. The next day the march continued. They camped at the Monte Sano Bridge and entered Baton Rouge the next day. (5) The regiment boarded in the State Penitentiary. Garrison duty was fine with the Tirailleurs, since their families lived a short distance down the river. Some of the townsfolk of Baton Rouge had returned to their looted and wrecked homes. Some returned only to find their homes burned.

Several days after arriving, the Tirailleurs walked over the battlefield. Magnolia Cemetery was impressive. The place was covered with Yankee graves. Some graves were so shallow that bones were exposed. The stench was so great that the Acadians cut their visit short. For some reason, General Ruggles had left the Federal flag flying over the burned-out state capitol. (6)

On August, Hunter gave Trasimond a one-week pass. Lieutenant Landry borrowed a horse and took the ferry to San Michel. The weather that morning was cool and very pleasant. The river was low. Before college, hardly a day had passed in Lieutenant Landry's life that he had not been near the river. The powerful Mississippi, the "Father of Waters," the longest river in the world; it was a spiritual force. Part of his soul flowed in its turbulent waters. He filled his nostrils with its sustaining fragrance and relaxed in the comfort of its power.

When he arrived home he was shocked by the changes. Weeds had grown up, the house looked worn, and the turn rows were untended. Belisaire was still using a walking cane. Brother Amedee was off on Bayou Grosse Tete looking for runaways. Narcisse and Manette hugged him. To Narcisse, his third son looked much older than when he had last seen him. His skin was bronzed from the sun, his uniform was a mess, and he smelled like a saddle blanket. Alcide had been cutting and storing tobacco in the carriage house. Alcide pestered his brother for all the details of his campaigning. Trasimond was the retina through which he viewed the war and he could not see enough of his older brother.

On August 10th, the Yankees had come down the Mississippi "Coast" and taken all the old corn and most of the able-bodied slaves. Many of Narcisse's slaves were ill at the time, enabling him to salvage some of his laborers. The grinding season was approaching rapidly, and the plantation laborers that were left were busy cutting and hauling sugar wood. Belisaire had to supervise their work closely, otherwise the slaves would spend more time gathering Spanish moss than wood. There was a lively trade in moss between slaves and traders along Bayou Teche. Moss was a chief ingredient of *bousilage* (insulation made of moss and mud) and an easy way for the slaves to make money. Turnips had been planted, but the sweet potatoes were almost lost to weeds.

With the Union in control of New Orleans and Memphis, Narcisse knew that unless fortunes changed, this might be the last sugar crop he would deliver to the Confederacy. Trasimond brought with him a bolt of cloth made by men of the 4th LA at the penitentiary looms. The looms were later dismantled and taken to Clinton, Louisiana.

Unfortunately, the regiment did not stay long at Baton Rouge. Trasimond was able to visit home several times. General Ruggles was replaced by General William Beall on August 29, 1862. The irascible Ruggles could not get along with Louisiana's Governor, Thomas Moore, and was sent to Mississippi. The men were happy to see Ruggles go.

William Nelson Rector Beall was from Bardstown, Kentucky. He was a thirty-three-year-old West Point graduate. When the war started he led troops in Arkansas as a cavalry officer. He rose to the rank of brigadier general and was sent to Port Hudson. (7) By August 31st, there were over 900 men at Port Hudson under his command. On August 30th, the 30th LA supported Semmes' Battery as it fired on the *USS Anglo American*. On September 2nd, Semmes' Battery was ordered to cross the Mississippi and join General Richard Taylor's Army.

On September 17th, General Beall was ordered to concentrate his troops at Port Hudson. The 4th LA was recalled from Baton Rouge, leaving the St. Helena Rifles to garrison the city. This caused great fear and consternation among the townsfolk still living in Baton Rouge.

Homesickness had to top the list of miseries at Port Hudson. Also on this list were bad food, bad water, bad clothes, bad medical care, lice, and boredom. To combat the boredom, Daniel Gorham organized a Tirailleur football team. This was a rough sport and kept many Acadians bruised and sprained. Morale was high. By mid-September, Confederate forces held Frederick, Maryland, and were threatening Washington. Stonewall Jackson was over the Potomac, Buckner was marching on Louisville, and Kirby Smith was a few miles from Cincinnati.

The Confederates experienced difficulty in obtaining guns to mount at Port Hudson. The Federals had a large gunboat, the *Essex*, on the Mississippi above Baton Rouge, thus, the heavy guns could not be brought down by boat. The only means of acquiring them was over the narrow gauge railroad between Clinton and Port Hudson. The guns, many weighing several tons, were sent to Mississippi by rail. From Osyka, Mississippi, they were shipped overland by wagon to Clinton and from there by rail to Port Hudson.

The Clinton-Port Hudson railroad was built in 1833 and was one of the first railraods in the United States. Like most rail lines of that era it was a feeder for water traffic. The presence of this rail line enhanced the strategic value of Port Hudson. There was one engine and seven cars. Only one car was for passengers. The railroad could transfer one half of a regiment per trip. (8)

On the evening of September 24th, a dress parade was held. Many local women and young girls were in attendance. Some were on horseback and several were in carriages. One Jersey wagon, pulled by two mules, held old General Carter from Lynwood Plantation and three young ladies. One young lady, Sarah Morgan, wrote in her diary: "I think the Confederates were much the most respectable. And what a sad sight the 4th LA was, that was then parading! Men that had fought at Shiloh and Baton R., were barefooted. Rags was their only uniform, for very few possessed a complete suit, and those few wore all varieties of colors and cuts. Yet he who had no shoes, looked as happy as he who had, and he who had a cap, had something to toss up, that's all."

Sarah Morgan described the camp: "I was watching the hundreds of tents—it looked like a great many—and was wondering how men could live in such places….Altogether it was a very pretty picture; but poor men! How can they be happy in these tents?" (9)

It was September 27th, and without any warning Simon Octave Rivet walked down the Tirailleurs' company street. He stopped at Lieutenant Landry's impoverished-looking tent. Trasimond was poking the coals of a small fire with a bayonet. He looked up.

"*Que le tonnerre m'écrase en mille poussières!*" (May the thunder crush me into a thousand pieces of dust), exclaimed Trasimond.

Trasimond hugged his brother-in-law, who was decked out in the fresh new uniform of a Confederate private. Simon was a welcome addition to Lieutenant Landry's depleted company. He was accompanied by Jules Doiron, Allain Hebert, and Diogene Isaac.

Fifteen-year-old Louis Kirkland, a veteran of Shiloh, transferred from the Lake Providence Cadets. Also, new privates Louis Doiron, Edward Gibson, Dorval and Ulysse Tullier, and Ulysse Ferbos joined up in September. This infusion of late "volunteers" and conscripts would be the last meaningful addition to the Tirailleurs. With the loss of slaves along the "Coast," the economy at Brusly Landing was wrecked. With no jobs, the only recourse for many young men was to join the army. Also, with Jayhawkers, Confederate conscription gangs, and Yankees putting

Military-age men in prison, the army was probably the safest place to be. Even a physician, Doctor J. A. Landry, enrolled as a private. He was a second cousin of Lieutenant Landry and brother-in-law of Sam Leveque.

After 1863, the Confederacy would suffer continually from manpower shortages. Many companies resented the "intrusion" of conscripts. It had the effect of devaluing the battle-hardened veterans' sense of solidarity. Though these new men were not their equals, they were grudgingly absorbed into the company.

This was not so in the Tirailleurs. The new men were all relatives and were heartily welcomed into the company.

The economy in the entire state was suffering. Isaac Erwin wrote on September 13, 1863: "This cruil war still continues and what is certain, ever since the commensement it has been said that we would have peace in 30–60–90 days. But peace never comes, but constant fiteing all the time one thing certain, Louisiana will soon be in a state of starvation for Meat." (10)

Private Rivet brought news and letters. Belisaire was readying to cut the cane. What slaves were left, as well as the few mules and oxen, were pooled with neighbors. Neighbors were helping each other bring in the cane. The "Genteel Acadians" had to resort to the old Acadian tradition of the *ramasserie*—the communal harvest. The pooling of the remaining mules and oxen was an old Acadian custom known as *halarie*. Draft animals where used to assist neighbors in particularly heavy tasks. This would be followed by a party and dance. (11) Things were much better since the Yankees had left Baton Rouge. Private Rivet brought along a quantity of fresh okra and peppers. The men feasted on a kettle of gumbo that night.

Sergeant Charlie Howell of Fenner's Battery was a Bardstown classmate of Daniel Gorham. Captain Fenner was in need of improving his field of fire. The sergeant asked Daniel for help to remove some of the pecan trees near Slaughter's farm. The Tirailleurs were running low on firewood anyway. This way they could use the artillery horses to haul the wood back to camp. With all the morning's axe work, pecans began to cover the ground. Negroes with tow sacks gathered around for the easy pickings. Lieutenant Landry insisted on a share for his company. That night around the campfire, the officers of the Tirailleurs enjoyed a delicious batch of pralines cooked by Lieutenant Gorham.

On October 9th, the Federal steamer *USS Laurel Hill* came up from New Orleans for a prisoner exchange. Private Joseph Bemins and Private John Davis returned to the 4th LA. A cartel had been arranged by treaty between Union General John Dix and Confederate General D. H. Hill in July, 1862. The Dix-Hill Cartel called for the prompt exchange of prisoners at the designated points of Vicksburg, Mississippi, in the west and City Point, Virginia, in the east. (12) Rather than send all prisoners to camps, many captured soldiers were "paroled." Once paroled, they were bound to stop fighting and return home or to a parole camp. From these camps, they were "exchanged." Breaking parole was a hanging offense.

Camp was moved again on October 14th. The regiment moved two miles down river to a ridge near Gibbon's gin.

On October 24th, Hunter called the men together to announce that he was aware that some in the regiment had accused him of cowardice at Shiloh and Baton Rouge. He stood before the regiment. The men listened to his clammy words: "I have ascertained within the last few days that there have been evil reports flying around through the regiment about me, and the substance of them is that there have been certain charges brought against me of cowardice, and that I am about to be court-martialed for it." The men listened to his slippery speech. A few grunted, a few coughed an unnecessary cough. Many were amazed that it had taken him so long to find out how the soldiers felt about him.

For this reason he asked for the assembly of a Court of Inquiry. Hunter seemed somewhat paranoid at the time, stating, "A petty envy towards me causes many to slander and depreciate my command." General J. C. Gorham presided over the court and one member was Colonel William R. Miles. Robert Patrick was recorder for the "trial" and wrote, "...the trial was the rottenest thing in the way of a trial I ever saw. There was no attempt to convince the board of the guilt of Lieutenant Colonel Hunter, because all of the testimony in Christendom would fail to do that. They had evidently made up their minds that he should not be found guilty and there was no use bringing any witnesses against him. Old Miles himself would turn and twist the testimony of the witnesses to suit himself and in favor of Hunter, and whenever a witness was brought upon the stand that was not favorable to the case of the accused he was frowned down and his evidence made to read in Hunter's favor, if possible. The truth is that it was utterly impossible to bring Hunter out guilty before such a court because they were officers themselves and did not wish to set a precedent before the men. Taking it altogether, I think it's the lamest thing I ever saw." (13)

In October, Josephine Landry Rivet and Simon Alcide Landry made a visit to the camp. They took a buggy up the River Road from Brusly Landing and were rowed over to Port Hudson. They found the company street and visited with Trasimond and Private Rivet. Simon Alcide brought along a letter from one of the *Veuve* Bujol's daughters. Private Rivet and his wife wandered off to find some privacy and Lieutenant Landry showed his little brother around the camp. Simon Alcide was overwhelmed at the number of flies. They were everywhere, in swarms. The camp garbage dumps were conspicuous and filled with empty whiskey bottles and liquor jugs. Stagnant pools of water filled parts of the freshly dug trenches. Camp life didn't seem as romantic as Alcide had imagined. He stayed in camp with his brother for one week. Private Rivet accompanied Josephine back to Brusly the next day. They were late getting across the river and recovering their buggy. The two went on to Morganza and spent the night at the Grand Levee Hotel.

On October 11, 1862, Captain Reason B. Turner of the West Feliciana Rifles resigned. He wrote, "I have been raised and lived with the young men of my company in the closest intimacy. After nearly five months experience, I find that I cannot exercise that strictness necessary for good discipline." Captain Turner was a river pilot before the war and wrote, "Having a thorough knowledge of the Mississippi River, I feel that I could better serve my country onboard the new gunboat being fitted out in the Yazoo River." His resignation was accepted by Major General Beall. (14) Lieutenant Landry also felt the same pressures of leadership that Captain Turner noted. He was not only lifelong friends with the enlisted men of his company, but was related by blood or marriage to most of them.

On November 1, 1862, the weather was fair, dry, and comfortably cool. It was Indian summer. The ground was parched and dusty. That day there was a brigade inspection in camp. Hunter mustered the men. He had made it a new rule that no one should receive pay unless they answered the rolls. (15) This is an indication of the fact that many of the men were visiting families. Sunday, November 9th, was cold, with a very heavy frost. The days were getting shorter and shorter. There were now twenty-six hundred men in camp at Port Hudson. On November 11th, four gunboats came up and shelled Port Hudson for two hours without doing any damage. (16)

That Sunday, the weather warmed up and it turned into a very pleasant day. Mass was celebrated outdoors by Father John Scollard of Bayou Sara. Father Turgis had taken leave and returned to New Orleans. In the afternoon, the men of the 9th Tennessee Cavalry Battalion began taking bets on a gander pull. This battalion had arrived in late October and were initially without mounts, having been freshly released from a Union prison. Now that they were beginning to acquire horses they were eager to display their abilities. A large gander was strung up by his feet from a limb on an old leafless oak tree. His neck was greased and he hung down just barely low enough for a galloper to grab him. The goal was for the rider to reach up as he galloped by and pull the head off the goose.

Troops and visitors filled the east breastworks to watch and place bets. With each pass at the goose, cheers would erupt from the onlookers. The goose's neck stretched little by little. There were some ladies present who seemed to enjoy this blood sport as much as the men. One Tennessee cavalryman slipped from the saddle and came crashing down, apparently only lightly injured. After twenty or so passes, one Tennessee private yanked the goose's head off to cheers and hat tossing by the men. The blood from the gander stained his arm and cotton shirt.

In November, Captain Aillet resigned. His age and wounds had exhausted him. Company elections were held and Trasimond Landry was elected captain. (17) Landry was very popular among the men. He had an easy laugh. When he smiled, his whole face participated. He was respected by his comrades and had proven his courage in battle. College educated, bilingual, and tall by Acadian standards, he was the natural choice to lead his company. Aside from reputation and example, Captain Landry's most powerful leadership quality was his eyes. Although Trasimond himself was unaware of this power, he used his eyes to command respect, discipline, and courage.

The regiment was paid a visit by Colonel Allen. His military career had been put off by his severe wounds at the Battle of Baton Rouge. The men were elated to see him. They gathered round him with cheers, hugs, and even put him on their shoulders and paraded him around the camp. Colonel Allen could not have been more pleased with the new Captain Landry. After seeing his bravery and leadership at Shiloh and Baton Rouge, he knew the Tirailleurs would be ably led.

In early 1862, word had come down from a higher command that all orders would be given in English. Sosthene Aillet ignored the order. This irked Hunter, who was somewhat of a martinet. Hunter never said anything to Captain Aillet. Sosthene was five feet ten inches tall and weighed over two hundred pounds. He had jet black hair, slitted eyes, a strong jaw, and was powerfully built. He was also a Mexican War veteran and several years older than Hunter. It was clear that Captain Aillet intimidated Hunter.

After Captain Aillet resigned, Hunter reminded Captain Landry of the "order in English" edict. As a matter of company pride, Captain Landry ignored Hunter. When the Lieutenant Colonel would strut by, Captain Landry would give an absurd order in French and all the men would laugh. This enraged Hunter. "*Ne comprends pas*" (I don't understand) and "*Ne parle pas Anglais*" (I don't speak English) were common responses for Hunter.

On November 24th, the Tirailleurs moved camp next to Miles' Legion. They went from near the gin house to the woods near Slaughter's Field, and not far from Slaughter's house. They were less exposed to the north wind from the river, but their water was not as good. These breastworks were located just north of the present-day site of the National Cemetery at Port Hudson. By this time, the breastworks near the river were looking quite formidable, with a base nearly thirty feet through and a ditch about eight feet deep. (18) On November 30th, Ordinance Sergeant V. M. Purdy received one hundred new leather waist belts and one hundred new bayonet scabbards for the new recruits joining the regiment. (19)

The daily routine began with reveille at daybreak, then roll call, inspection of arms and policing of the camp, guard mounting, non-commissioned-officer drill, drill in the school of the company, dinner, skirmish drill, battalion drill, dress parade, sunset, retreat, then taps. Officers attended schools. This regimen was not nearly as informal as on the Mississippi coast or as at Berwick City. Trasimond spent evenings sitting around the campfire roasting potatoes and passing the *viellée*.

As winter came on, the men tried to make themselves as comfortable as possible. Chimneys were installed into tents. There was plenty of wood to burn since the forests were being cleared all around to make breastworks and abatis. By November, rations were slim. Many of the Negro servants had disappeared. There was nothing but meal and beef that was very inferior. The water was also very bad and had a foul smell. Many soldiers preferred locally-made corn beer, which was a cloudy concoction of corn, sugar, and water that had a vinegary taste. On December 9, 1861, Captain Landry signed "Special Requisition No. 40." He requested nine ovens, four tents, three camp kettles, one axe, and nine mess pans. (20)

December 15, 1862, the weather was crisp and clear, a cold front having passed through the previous evening. Trasimond slept late that morning. He awoke to the sound of a rooster crowing. He hadn't slept this well in months. Waking up on a soft mattress was a pleasure he had almost forgotten. There was a knock on the door and Manette entered. "*Bon matin, Trasimond*," she said, "*Ce l'heur pour te lever.*" (It's time to wake up.)

Trasimond had been home for three days. Doc Leveque was to marry December 22nd. The three banns had been published and everything was ready for the wedding. Trasimond's sister-in-law had made him a new uniform and on it proudly stitched three bars—the collar symbol of a captain. He was eager to wear his new uniform at the wedding. The wedding would be small. Most of the planters along the "Coast" had taken what slaves they had and moved off to Texas or St. Landry Parish.

Belisaire was still bothered by his leg, but was back helping with the plantation. Narcisse Landry was sixty-five-years-old and was doing his best to keep the plantation going. They had managed to get some of the cane harvested. There were four heavy frosts in the last days of October which killed the remaining cane. The Landrys sent twenty-five hogsheads of sugar by wagon to Grosse Tete. It went from there by way of Fordoche to Morganza. That year they got ten cents per pound. This was Narcisse Landry's last sugar crop for the Confederacy.

Belisaire explained to Trasimond that he might have to look for wage workers soon, but there was no certainty that there would be any money to pay the wages. There was no coffee. There had been no flour for several months and salt was $128 per barrel. Belisaire conceded that they were bound to lose all their slaves soon. He confessed to Trasimond that he thought the war would end slavery for good.

Yankee dominance and control of West Baton Rouge Parish would force the Landrys to deal with order #76. September 24, 1862, General Butler issued an order requiring those who had not taken the oath of allegiance to the Union to report to the nearest provost marshal with a descriptive list of all their property. They would then be given a certificate of registration showing them "to be an enemy of the United States." Failure to do so made them subject to a fine or imprisonment and confiscation of their property. (21)

Belisaire was a hard man and drank too much for his own good. He had a broad forehead and what hair he lacked on top of his balding head he made up for by a flourishing black beard that completely hid his mouth. He was fifteen years older than Trasimond and had always treated him like a little child. He had certainly never valued Trasimond's opinion. This visit home was different. Trasimond got the distinct feeling that his oldest brother was seeing him finally as a man and not a little boy. This was a welcomed change.

Captain Landry would spend Monday and Tuesday visiting friends. He put on his old civilian clothes and did his visiting. He had letters and messages from his men to deliver to families and parents. Simon Alcide tagged along. Trasimond was careful to leave Alcide at home when he visited the *Veuve* Bujol. She lived not far from Narcisse Landry's plantation and had four beautiful daughters. Trasimond was particularly partial to the tender charms of nineteen-year-old Marie Amelite. Trasimond had monopolized her attentions at the prior Saturday night's *bal de maison* (house dance) at the Leveque plantation. The Landry and Bujol families formed a strong bond. Trasimond's oldest sister, Marie Irma, had married Marie Amelite's uncle, Francois Joseph Bujol. The *Veuve* Bujol herself was a half-cousin of Trasimond. Her father was Joseph Emanuel Landry, half-brother of Narcisse.

Tuesday, Alcide took a rest from building a Christmas bonfire to take Trasimond to the swamp for a duck hunt. Wednesday morning, December 17th, he was awakened by Manette. She shook him rather hard and he noticed alarm in her eyes. "*Leve toi! Leve toi!*" She said, "*Il y a des bateaux d'armée sur la rivier!*" (There are warships on the river!)

Trasimond rubbed his eyes, pulling back the mosquito bar he rose. The small bedroom had a marble-top dresser with a water pitcher and bowl. He washed his face in cistern water. The only other furniture in the room was a large, comfortable chair stuffed with dried moss. He sat for a moment, thinking, then finished dressing.

From the levee in the foggy early-morning hours he could see the Yankee river fleet steaming for Baton Rouge. In the van was the *Essex,* followed by the *Genesee,* and two rams. Steamers girded by cotton bales and loaded with Yankee troops followed closely behind. He knew they must be headed for Baton Rouge.

Trasimond knew this would cut his leave short. He sent a note of regret to Doc Leveque. Louis Kirkland, Daniel Leveque (30th LA), and Samuel Leveque stayed for the wedding. He took time to pack his new uniform and some comforts for camp life and readied to return to Port Hudson. A family servant, Nonc Henry, would accompany Trasimond in Narcisse's buggy up the west bank to the level of Port Hudson. He would be able to hire a boat to take him across to the camp. Nonc Henry had been with the Landry family since 1821. He was born in Madison County, Alabama, and was sold to Narcisse for $600 by a Mr. John F. Newman. Henry was now fifty-six-years-old and white haired. His French was quite good.

The black man and the soldier traveled up the river road, watching closely for Union patrols. A cold north wind blew in their faces. They passed the plantations of Landrys, Daigles, and Heberts. Then through Brusly Landing, they passed Zephirin Blanchard's old plantation. They swung wide of San Michel, crossing in back of Dr. J. C. Patrick's plantation, and crossed the Grosse Tete railroad behind Carolina Plantation. Next they took a wagon road shortcut back to the levee. This road passed down the east boundary of the estate of Pierre Paul Babin (Babina Plantation).

Captain Landry and the old black man passed the Lobdell Store. They could see Profit Island off to the right. There were a few Federal gunboats below the island on picket duty. They rode up the levee at Babina Plantation to check the river for activity. In the sooty twilight, Trasimond could see sixteen crosses on the riverbank marking fresh Union sailor's graves. Nonc Henry explained to Trasimond that these were graves of sailors killed when a Rebel shell entered a porthole on the *Essex* and exploded. When they got to A. S. Robertson's Plantation it was dark. For $1.50, Trasimond found someone to row him over to Port Hudson.

This put an end to the captain's visits home. He wouldn't see his family again until the war's end. A few days later, Louis Kirkland arrived with the Leveque brothers. Louis brought Trasimond a forgotten blanket and stories of the wedding, the partying, and the *charivari.*

Orders were for no one to leave camp and to prepare for a fight. Outnumbered Confederate forces had withdrawn from Baton Rouge without a battle. The city was held by the Yankees without opposition until the end of the war.

By the end of December the camp had become a very lonely place. The first robins were beginning to appear. The surrounding woods were leafless and gray. V-shaped formations of geese were still honking their way southward. The bastion at Port Hudson was nearing completion. Columbiads stood at the bluffs, and the men drew confidence from their phallic hugeness. Surely, no navy could pass these monsters. Dispatches brought news of Union General Burnside's defeat at Fredericksburg.

In late December Isaac Erwin wrote in his diary, "Alf, El, Elias, Bazele, Leroy, and three others of our Negroes have gone off today. Runaway I think. I expect to start off (leave for) with some of my Negroes to Texas on Tuesday if God is willing to try to get out of the way of the Yankees, but I doubt if I will do wright or not. As I fear the Yankeys will still pursue us where ever we go. And I think they will war against the South until Slavery is entirely destroyed for ever." (22)

With the beginning of the new year, the troops were laboring under the most difficult circumstances and had very little clothing. For several months at a time there was no pork or flour issued. The men received half rations of peas and rice. Salt was scarce. Sugar and molasses were of inferior quality. Instead of issuing clothing, the Confederate army provided a bonus of $50. (23) Many of the Tirailleurs visited home with or without leave. Proof of the frequency of home visits by these Acadians is given by the fact that of the married members, nine children were born during the war.

December 17, 1862, as Yankee troops re-entered Baton Rouge, Major General Franklin Gardner, a native of New York, arrived at Port Hudson. There was no fanfare for the new commandant. Gardner had strong marriage ties to Louisiana. His sister married former Louisiana Governor Alexander Mouton. General Gardner married ex-Governor Mouton's daughter. Gardner had graduated from West Point in 1843, ranking ahead of U. S. Grant. He had led men in battle at Shiloh and Perryville.

The day before Gardner's arrival, Union General Butler was replaced by Major General Nathaniel Banks as commander of the Department of the Gulf. Confederate propagandists would miss Butler. He was a political general and before the war was a Breckenridge Democrat. Through his thievery and rude treatment of the citizens of New Orleans, he did as much as anyone to steel the resolve of Southern soldiers to fight on.

General Gardner ordered the troops into three brigades. The Tirailleurs were assigned to Brigadier General Samuel Bell Maxey's Brigade. With this brigade, the Tirailleurs and the 30th LA were put into the center of the Port Hudson defenses. They were not happy being brigaded with Tennessee regiments.

Maxey was a Kentuckian, born in 1825. He graduated from West Point in 1846, and was decorated for bravery in the Mexican War. He later became a lawyer in Paris, Texas, and organized the 9th Texas Infantry. (24)

In January, Southern newspapers printed Lincoln's Emancipation Proclamation. This weak political move brought laughs to the Southern troops. Lincoln did not free slaves in border states or in areas of the South held by Yankee troops. He only freed slaves in those areas of the South held by Confederate forces. Union Secretary Seward wrote, "We show our sympathy with slavery by emancipating slaves where we cannot reach them, and holding them in bondage where we can set them free." (25)

In West Baton Rouge Parish there was no certainty regarding emancipation, the place was being claimed by Union and Confederates alike. Planters told their slaves they did not know whether they were slaves or free men. Many slaves preferred to stay under the protection of their masters. At the same time, many more slaves were returning to the plantations from New Orleans. In the cities they were free and hungry, while back on the plantations they were worked but fed. These events gave Narcisse Landry a way to hold on to his remaining laborers. (26)

By January 1863, the Confederates had mounted seventeen heavy guns to protect the river and had constructed two and a half miles of fortifications on the landward side. Gardner imposed a rigid schedule that left little free time for the troops. Soldiers on fatigue duty labored from 7:30 A.M. to noon and from 1:00 P.M. to dark. They unloaded steamboats, herded cattle, or cared for hospital patients. Some troops performed guard, picket, and scouting duty. Soldiers not on work detail drilled.

On January 12th, there was a general review of troops by the Inspector General. There was a freeze on January 13th, which was hard on the men with no tents. During early 1863, poor food and exposure caused increased sickness. The camp had become much more crowded, with over 12,000 men present for duty on January 31, 1863. (27) Fevers, chills, diarrhea, and jaundice were common. At this time, Gardner moved the hospital to Woodville, Mississippi, so patients could travel by boat to Bayou Sara and from there by rail to Woodville. In camp each regiment had its own hospital tent. More serious problems went to the camp hospital, a larger tent. The Tirailleurs were in amazingly good health at Port Hudson. There were only three admissions to the camp hospital. (28) As the camp became more crowded, there was more illness among the companies.

The costs for local farm products were high: a turkey: $2, a goose: $1, lard: $1/pound, eggs: $1/dozen, bacon: 60 cents per pound, flour: $100 a barrel, and potatoes: $2 a bushel. (29) Homesickness increased with time, and so did desertions. The winter of 1863 was the coldest recorded for twenty-five years. The climate in North America was still in what scientists have labeled the "little ice age." A new recruit, Auguste Longuepee, arrived on February 4, 1863. Mail became more sporadic as the Union army increased its buildup in Baton Rouge and the surrounding area.

Trasimond received a letter from Belisaire. It described the heroics of Captain R. Prosper Landry of the Donaldsonville Artillery. According to Belisaire, their second cousin, Prosper, practically won the Battle of Fredricksburg. The Yankees had taken all the Negroes except Nonc Henry and a few that refused to leave. Narcisse had refused to flee to Texas, preferring the role of *les habitants* to that of a refugee. A huge crevasse had developed in the levee at Chinn's plantation, inundating thousands of acres. On the plantation, they planted two barrels of Irish potatoes and would plant corn soon.

Two ships, USS *Queen of the West* and the USS *Indianola*, had run the Confederate blockade at Vicksburg and threatened Rebel communications with the West. Confederate riverine forces captured *The Queen of the West*.

With the CSS *Queen of the West* captured and re-floated, the only ship menacing the Confederate communications with the west was the USS *Indianola*. This river ironclad, designed and built by James Buchanan Eads, was a formidable vessel. Her sides were oak, thirty-two inches thick, covered with three inches of iron plate. She had five boilers and seven engines. There were paired side-wheels as well as two screw propellers. All her machinery was in her hold below the water line. Forward casemates mounted two eleven-inch Dahlgrens, after casemates had two nine-inch guns, and there was one gun on each side.

The *Indianola* was on the river looking for the CSS *Webb*, a powerful Confederate ram, and possibly the fastest ship on the river. On discovering that the *Queen of the West* had been re-floated, she retreated up the Mississippi to Grand Gulf.

Major General Richard Taylor commanded the Western District of Louisiana. On February 19, 1863, he ordered Major J. L. Brent to command an expedition to capture the *Indianola*. His little flotilla was made up of the *Webb*, (Captain Charles Pierce) and the CSS *Queen of the West* (Captain James McCloskey).

Acting independently of General Taylor, General Gardner fitted out a rickety old steamer named the *Dr. Beaty*. She was built in Louisville, Kentucky, in 1850, and was outfitted with 900 bales of cotton armor. She sported a twenty-pounder Parrott rifle and was manned with volunteers from the 4th LA and Miles' Legion. The 250 volunteers were commanded by Lieutenant James B. Corkern, and their plan was to take the *Indianola* by surprise, by boarding her.

The *Indianola* was sighted at 9:30 P.M. on February 25, 1863. The order of approach was *Queen of the West,* followed by the *Webb,* and then the *Dr. Beaty* (Lieutenant Colonel Brand commanding). The *Dr. Beaty* was two miles back, lashed to the steamer, *Grand Era.* The *Indianola* had coal barges lashed to each of her sides for protection.

In the dark, the *Queen of the West* approached at full steam and fired its two Parrott guns at one hundred yards, then violently rammed into the coal barge protecting the *Indianola's* side. Sharpshooters from the *Queen* raked the deck of the *Indianola* with fire. The *Queen* freed herself and rounded for another ramming pass. An instant later, the *Webb* dashed by the *Queen* and rammed the *Indianola* in her rear, disabling her port-side engine. The *Indianola* opened up with her two eleven-inch Dahlgrens. The *Indianola* was now stripped of her two protecting coal barges.

The *Queen* then rammed again, and in turning away took two blasts at very close range from the *Indianola's* nine-inch rear guns, killing two men and wounding four. The *Queen* then rounded and rammed a third time, followed rapidly by a second ram from the *Webb.*

By this time the *Indianola* was taking on water. The *Queen of the West* was listing to port and the *Webb* had her bow knocked off to within fourteen inches of the water line. The *Webb* was rounding for her third ram when she was hailed from the *Indianola.* Her Captain requested surrender. The *Dr. Beaty* was cast off the *Grand Era* and was closing in on the action when the surrender occurred.

The *Grand Era* steamed alongside the *Indianola* after her surrender and took her crew prisoner. The *Indianola* was taking on water fast and Major Brent wanted her to come aground on the east bank of the river. He took her in tow to the eastern bank, where she sank on the sand bar in water up to her gun deck. She went aground in front of Joe Davis' home. One hundred prisoners and their liquor stores were captured. (30) (31)

Union General Nathaniel P. Banks was a political general, the former Governor of Massachusetts and speaker of the U.S. House of Representatives. He had been thoroughly whipped by Stonewall Jackson in the Valley Campaign in Virginia earlier in the year. Banks was under pressure from Lincoln to "do something," so he increased activity around Baton Rouge. In late February, Federal forces advanced from Indian Village toward Morganza. Indian Village was a ferry landing on Bayou Grosse Tete.

Two days after Mardi Gras, February 26, 1863, the steamer *Red Chief* rounded to at Port Hudson. The 4th LA, Miles' Legion, and Fenner's Battery were ordered up to Morganza to fight the Yankees. Whistles were blowing and bells were tolling on the boat. The camp band played the *Marseillase.* The day was gloomy and threatened storms. The boats landed the troops at the

Hermitage Landing, about three miles above Port Hudson. They marched ten miles up False River, the last three miles in a heavy rain. They camped near the carriage way of the widow Parlange's plantation, five miles south of New Roads. Fenner's artillerymen watered their horses in False River. Beautiful gardens surrounded the French Colonial plantation house. No Yankees were found and the Confederates returned the next day. (32) Before the war ended, Yankee horses would eat the entire garden.

On March 12, 1863, General Gardner telegraphed Lieutenant General Pemberton at Vicksburg, "The enemy appear to be advancing slowly on three roads. I have three day's corn and thirty day's meat." (33) The next day, Private A. H. Beauchamp, Company F, 1st ALA, wrote his wife: "Three large steamboats have arrived loaded with corn which will do us until we thrash Banks....The Yankees have raised a flag on the point just below here on this side of the river. I recon before another day we will be hard at it." (34) Union infantry was edging closer to Port Hudson.

March 14th was a big day at Port Hudson. Farragut had decided to run the bluffs with his fleet. He had basically said "to hell" with Bank's land force and decided to proceed without a land attack. He felt it imperative to shut down Rebel traffic on the Mississippi at all costs. After his success at running the batteries of Fort St. Phillip and Fort Jackson below New Orleans, he felt certain he could run past Port Hudson. After all, his fleet was capable of throwing four tons of iron per minute.

That Saturday, March 14th, 1863, Farragut ordered his river fleet forward. It was 11:20 P.M. The USS *Hartford,* lashed to the *Albatross,* led off. She was followed by the *Richmond,* lashed to the *Genessee*; the *Monongehela,* lashed to the *Kineo*; and the *Mississippi.* The *Hartford* made it past the Rebel batteries unharmed. The *Richmond* was devastated by the Confederate batteries and drifted back down the river. The *Monngehala* met a similar fate, luckily reaching safety below the batteries.

The *Mississippi,* the oldest and slowest of Farragut's river fleet, followed last. She grounded on a sandbar before the Rebel batteries and was their only target for thirty minutes. Union Navy Lieutenant George Dewey, future hero of the Spanish American War, was aboard the Mississippi. The order was given to abandon ship as flames engulfed the doomed vessel. Around 3 A.M. she slipped off the bar and floated downstream. At five minutes past 5 A.M. the ship's magazine blew. She was five miles above Baton Rouge when the magazine exploded.

That night, at 11 P.M., Narcisse was awakened by Manette. There was a low, rumbling thunder and an uncertain glow in the sky to the north of Brusly Landing. The family gathered on the *galerie* and listened. Josephine was there.

All knew their loved ones were engaged in a battle. The thunder died down at 2 A.M. Narcisse went back to his bed. He was shaken awake around 5 A.M. by the explosion of the *Mississippi*.

This grand river battle did no damage to the Port Hudson batteries but casualties included three men killed and nineteen wounded. Farragut's casualties were: six killed, thirty-six wounded, and sixty-four killed or missing off the *Mississippi*.

Private Robert Patrick, an eyewitness to the battle wrote: "About eleven o'clock we heard a heavy gun, and then the shell, then another, and another, and finally the whole of the fleet let loose on us, though our batteries did not answer for some time. It was not long however, before every one of our batteries cut loose and of all the noises that ever I heard, this beat all. The very earth trembled. It waked everybody up in Clinton, and was heard very distinctly high up on the Jackson Railroad. This was kept up without the slightest intermission, until near 2 A.M., when they drew off, with the loss of one of their finest vessels, the USS *Mississippi*. She took fire and floated away down the river. It was a grand sight to see her, as she drifted slowly down, lighting up the neighboring shores and the turbid tide of the Mississippi with a lurid glare, and the shells on her decks were exploding constantly. After she drifted below Prophet (sic) Island her magazine exploded with a tremendous roar." There were sixteen thousand Rebels present to witness the most famous Mississippi River battle of all time. (35)

Mrs. Ramey Delatt wrote her sister March 20th, "On the night of the 14th, at half past eleven, a terrific bombardment commenced at the Port, which continued without cessation until two o'clock—It was awfully grand. We could see the signal rockets ascending and the west seemed in a continual blaze—At five o'clock the *Mississippi* (which our guns had fired) exploded, and you may form some idea of the report by what sister Mary wrote, 'that it almost blew her out of bed,' a distance of twenty-five miles—old Bleak House rocked to its foundation, as if by an earthquake." (36)

The Tirailleurs got no sleep on the night of the 14th. As the river battle raged, shells were falling thicker and thicker. The night was lit up all around. Fires were lighted by Gardner's men on the west bank of the river to aid the batteries on the Bluffs of Port Hudson. Also, a number of locomotive headlights were turned on the river, which threw a glare over the water enabling the shore gunners to aim their pieces.

The Tirailleurs had hurried to their section of the breastworks. There was fear that the naval attack would coincide with a land attack by General Bank's army. Unknown to the Confederates, the noise of the river battle sent the Union troops scurrying back to Baton Rouge. The Tirailleurs were exposed to firing of the thirteen-inch mortars from the river, but there were no injuries. There was panic in the camp among the Negroes and civilians. One woman who had come to camp to visit her husband fled in panic into Little Sandy Creek, where she and her child drowned.

During their return to Baton Rouge, Yankee thieves plundered $300,000 worth of cotton and sugar. On March 18th, the Tirailleurs were sent out as part of Maxey's Brigade to disrupt the plundering Yankees. They marched out on the Springfield road. The Rebels expected a fight, but none took place. The Yankee's fled, leaving the Confederates with fifteen wagon loads of abandoned plunder. (37)

These invading Yankee troops had been raised to believe that Southerners were lazy, ignorant, and cruel slave masters. They believed that they were merely making war on an inferior culture. German troops in France during World War II had much more respect for civilians and private property than the Union army. During the first occupation of Baton Rouge, Union Brigadier General Thomas Williams wrote, on May 27, 1862, "These regiments, officers and men, with rare exceptions, appear to be wholly destitute of the moral sense. They regard pillaging not only as a right in itself, but a soldierly accomplishment." (38)

On March 19th, the repaired *Monogehela, Essex,* and *Genessee* shelled the bluffs from about a mile down river. Due to the constant shelling, Gardner moved his landing to Thompson's Creek. He ordered each brigade to send its smallest regiment to help unload the steamers. This meant the 4th LA and the Tirailleurs. These military stevedores worked around the clock to unload the transports. By April 1st, there were over 20,000 men under the command of General Gardner. (39)

Morale at Port Hudson was running very high after the successful repelling of the Federal fleet. Trees were greening and dogwoods and silver bells were in bloom. Writing to his sister on March 30th, John Morgan wrote, "It is believed here that they (the Yankees) are all leaving Baton Rouge, as they have given up all hope of taking this place." (40)

After the threat of siege was ended, General Gardner changed the daily rations, doubling the rice, tripling the peas, and increasing the meat. The quality of the beef had improved as well. Gardner also moved the hospital from Woodville back to Clinton and Jackson.

Private Beauchamp wrote, "We catch as many fish now as we want with dip nets, yet when the current runs fast near the shore and dips downstream sometimes we catch buffalo weighing twenty-five or thirty pounds, but mostly hickory shad, the boniest things I ever saw, but very sweet fish." (41)

Private Beauchamp wrote his wife April 13th: "About six thousand troops have left here to go somewhere else about Jackson, Mississippi....I hear the enemy's guns away down river shelling some gin or sugar house. They fired a dwelling some miles below here a few days ago—that seems to be the height of their ambition—poor miserable creatures—I should not be a Yankee for all the world and I am damn glad I have no relations that are." (42)

On a scout in late April, a platoon of Tirailleurs shot up a small Yankee outpost, raided it of everything that wasn't nailed down, then returned to the ditches of Port Hudson. Louis Daigle returned with an Enfield rifle with a telescopic sight. He lovingly cleaned it and the next day zeroed it in.

In March 1863, Grant was ready to make his flanking move against Vicksburg and wanted a diversion. He ordered Ben Grierson, with the 6th and 7th Illinois Cavalry and the 2nd Iowa Cavalry, to make a raid on Mississippi. On April 17th, Grierson led 1700 officers and men with two cannon from La Grange, Mississippi. At the same time, Colonel Abel Streight led a similar raid into Alabama, but his opponent was General Nathan Bedford Forrest. His whole force was captured by Forrest. This group of Yankees would be paroled and face the Tirailleurs later in the war.

Grierson's raid trailed down through Mississippi; being cut off from Port Gibson, Mississippi, he headed for Baton Rouge. Traveling through Osyka, Mississippi, with Rebel cavalrymen hot on his tail, he crossed the Tickfaw River on May 1, 1863, at Wall's Bridge. Passing next through Greensburg, he headed for William's Bridge over the Amite River at present-day Grangeville. The small bridge guard was captured and the 6th and 7th Illinois clattered over the 200-yard span at midnight. They were thirty miles from Baton Rouge.

General Gardner ordered Colonel A. J. Brown to seize William's Bridge over the Amite. The 4th LA and the 55th TN, with Fenner's Battery, left Port Hudson at 3 P.M. on May 1st with three days rations, cooked. They marched from Port Hudson down Plains-Port Hudson Road to Thompson's Road. Then down present-day LA Highway 412 to Olive Branch. The men rested that night for two hours at Olive Branch. William Dixon wrote, "At an early hour we resumed the march, passed Pleasant Hill Plantation (the residence of Miss Julia Muse on present-day Blairstown Road) and about 10 A.M. arrived at William's Bridge." (43) They were ten hours too late to catch Grierson. The 4th LA camped at William's Bridge for four days, expecting to be ordered back to Port Hudson. (44)

Grierson entered Baton Rouge May 2nd. He was hailed as a hero by Northern newspapers and promoted to general. Later in the war, he was thoroughly whipped by General N. B. Forrest at the Battle of Okalona and at Brice's Crossroads. He finished out his career as a loser.

The 4th LA had to march thirty-five miles to get to William's Bridge. The average marching speed of the 4th LA over Louisiana and Mississippi roads was two miles per hour. The 4th LA would have had to leave Port Hudson at 5 A.M. and march at three miles per hour to get to William's Bridge in time to deploy with some daylight left. By the time Gardner made the decision to send the 4th LA, it was already too late. Here again, the factor of leadership entered the equation. A delay in the march arose due to an argument between Colonel Hunter and Colonel Brown over who would command. This delayed their leaving by five hours. Private William Dixon put the blame on General Gardner. Gardner knew of Grierson's likely crossing at William's Bridge well before May 1st. (45)

On Wednesday, May 6th, Captain Landry woke up tired and stiff from sleeping on the ground. The 4th LA received orders to hurry northward and join Joe Johnston's army at Jackson, Mississippi. They were to cooperate in the efforts to relieve Vicksburg. The Lake Providence Cadets, led by Captain Charles Purdy, remained behind when the 4th LA left for Mississippi. This company had been on provost duty at Jackson, Louisiana. The following members of the Tirailleurs were left at Port Hudson: (46)

Ulysse Ferbos	Sick in hospital
August Gassie, 4th Corpl.	Sick in hospital
Allain Hebert	Sick in hospital
Charles Hebert	Captured July 9th
Jean Baptiste Hebert	Captured July 9th
Oscar Hebert	Detached duty, captured July 9th
Theodore Hebert	Sick in hospital
Louis Kirkland	Sick, captured at home, May 13th
Theodule Lejeune	Deserted in May
Theogene Lejeune	Captured in May
Samuel Leveque	Detached duty, captured July 9th
L. A. Longuepee	Sick in hospital
Charles Rivault	Detached duty for removal of looms from State Penitentiary to Clinton
Charles Scoval	Captured July 9th
Thomas Sherron	Deserted May 14th
Dorval Tullier	Sick in hospital

In May of 1863, with Union troops threatening to envelop Port Hudson, three Tirailleurs deserted. Soldiers from East Baton Rouge and West Baton

Rouge parishes found it very tempting to call it quits and go home. Besides the Tirailleur desertions, many of the 9th LA battalion deserted. These men were all from East Baton Rouge Parish. The high command was aware of this temptation, and for this reason few troops from Louisiana were used in the defense of Port Hudson.

Charles Hebert, J. B. Hebert, and Charles Scoval were left behind to collect and transport the company's baggage. Samuel Leveque was left behind for another reason. (47) Captain Pruyn and Samuel Leveque were part of the small group that was manufacturing a torpedo. Their work was not completed until May 12th, too late for Private Leveque to make the march to Osyka. The torpedo attempt deserved merit for its audacity, but it failed to destroy any Union ships. After the failed torpedo attempt, Private Leveque was ordered by General Gardner into the "Secret Service." He was sent to West Baton Rouge as a spy. (48)

On May 8th, mortar barges were brought up on the river and the fort was attacked by thirteen-inch projectiles for forty-eight days. General Gardner had been ordered to abandon Port Hudson and come to the support of General Johnston outside Vicksburg. Before he could start his move, Port Hudson was surrounded and the siege began. Historian Lawrence Hewitt contends that had Port Hudson been abandoned, the "political general" Banks would have been free to march to Vicksburg. Once there, as senior officer, he would have replaced Grant. With a victory at Vicksburg, Banks could possibly have ended the career of Grant and robbed Lincoln of his best general. (49)

At Brusly Landing everyone had heard the news of Grierson's arrival in Baton Rouge. Yankee patrols were seen daily on the River Road. Yankee thieves had taken off most of the livestock and poultry. Louis Kirkland was recovering from illness at home when Yankee cavalry surrounded the plantation house. They had been informed by a Negro servant that a soldier was inside. The house was searched and young Louis was taken off as a prisoner. Belisaire sent Simon Alcide off to campout in the swamp until things cooled off.

Port Hudson was enveloped on May 21, 1863. The men left behind from Company H were assigned to Miles' Legion. Private Theogene Lejeune was captured in the Battle of Plain's Store. There were 6,500 defenders of Port Hudson facing over 30,000 Union attackers. The small platoon of stranded Tirailleurs were on the extreme left of the right flank of the breastworks. To the platoon's left was a regiment straddling a sally port. This opened on the road leading eastward from Port Hudson and out across Slaughter's Field.

On May 25th, an alarm was sounded and signal guns fired. Yankees were seen marching toward the ramparts. It turned out to be Captain Purdy and his company, the Lake Providence Cadets. They were left at Jackson alone and with no orders. Purdy boldly marched his company in the moonlight past thousands of Yankee soldiers—unchallenged. They entered the sally port on the Jackson road. (50)

Jean Baptiste Hebert was in the breastworks on May 27th. He had just finished a meal of horsemeat and peas. This was the hot, dusty day that Union General Banks had decided to attack Port Hudson. Private Hebert looked out over the 2000-yard-wide field of short grass and saw it filled back to the woods with Yankees. Captain Charles Purdy was in command of the eighty or so men of the 4th LA that day.

The Union troops advanced toward the breastworks in fine style. Little geysers of dust popped up on the dry breastworks as Minnie balls landed. At 150 yards the Confederates opened with canister. The riflemen of Company H were each supplied with a rifle and a shotgun. The Zoauves of the 165th NY made their way through the abatis in front of the 4th LA. The men of the 4th LA opened fire. They were reinforced by men of the 23rd ARK. At seventy yards the Yankee Zoauves wavered. Their colonel, Abel Smith, Jr., was killed. Their major, Gouverneur Carr, mounted a pecan tree stump and with his sword, waved the Yankees on. Every rifle of the Tirailleurs took aim at Major Carr. He finally went down, but a few of the Zouaves made it to the parapet. (51)

Private J. B. Hebert was reloading when a Federal Zouave climbed up the parapet. He was killed by a shotgun blast from Private Charles Hebert. The enemy broke.Later they made one more advance, then fell back for good. Matt Howley of the Lake Providence Cadets bounded over the breastworks and retrieved the colors of the 165th NY. (52)

The siege had begun. The little group of Tirailleurs was subjected to constant sniping and artillery fire. The remnants of the 4th LA were then ordered to the northern extremity of the works, where they remained for three days. From there they went to the southern end of the line commanded by Colonel Miles. They were in the trenches continually from May 27th until the surrender. June 14th brought on another grand assault by the Union Army. It also failed.

News reached General Gardner of the fall of Vicksburg. He gave up on July 9, 1863, ending the longest siege in the history of the United States Army—forty-eight days.

Of the 4th LA, ninety-three men were captured at Port Hudson. Among the four killed was Captain Purdy. Two were wounded in the fighting. After the surrender, the members of the Tirailleurs were immediately paroled, except for Louis Kirkland, who was sent to Grant's Island. They all returned to West Baton Rouge with their parole papers. Of the sixteen men left at Port Hudson, only Jean Baptiste Hebert and Louis Kirkland rejoined the company. Leaving Samuel Leveque behind left the Tirailleurs with only one fiddle player, Daniel Gorham.

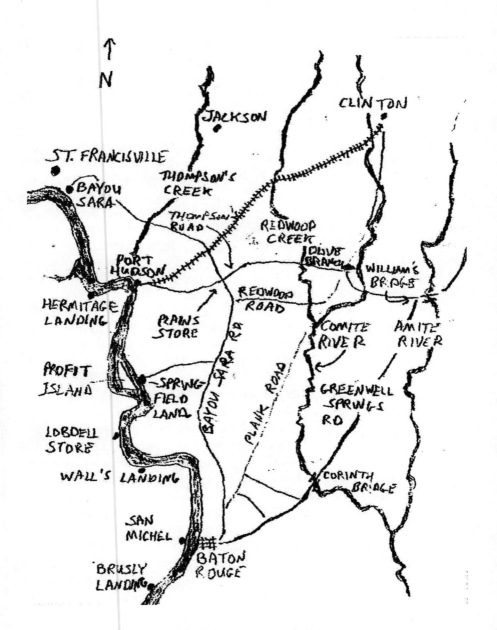

The Port Hudson Area

7.

Siege of Jackson

Order of Battle
Army of Mississippi, Lieutenant General Joe Johnston
    Division: Major General Loring
        Brigade: Brigadier General Maxey
            4th LA, Colonel S. E. Hunter
            30th LA, Lieutenant Colonel Thomas Shields
            46th TN, Colonel Robert A. Owens
            55th TN, Colonel Robert A. Owens
            48th TN, Colonel William M. Voorhies
            49th TN, Colonel William F. Young
            53rd TN, Colonel John R. White

From William's Bridge on the Amite, the Tirailleurs marched toward Osyka, Mississippi, on May 7th. All their baggage was left at Port Hudson. They camped that night on the Greensburg Camp ground (a religious revival camp). On May 8th, they passed through Greensburg. On the 9th, the 4th LA arrived at Osyka Station. The Acadians swam in the Tangipahoa River and washed their clothes.

    The Tirailleurs were now reduced to forty-one men. The brigade was split up with the left wing of the 4th LA (Company G, Company H, Company I, Company K, the 48th TN, and Fenner's Battery) and ordered to march to Jackson on foot. The rest of the brigade and the right wing of the regiment entrained. The Tirailleurs tramped up the railroad tracks. General Maxey traveled with the men on this march. For ten days this battalion of the 4th LA had no cooking utensils. The company lived off ashcakes. The shuck of an ear of corn was parted and the cob removed. The husk was filled with a batter of corn meal, salt, and pork grease. This "vessel" was buried in hot ashes for half an hour.

The 30th LA arrived outside Magnolia after a four-day march from Port Hudson. They shared their pots and pans with the Tirailleurs. This itinerary was recorded by Private William Dixon:

May 10, Marched to Magnolia. (16 miles)
May 11, Passed through Summit. (17 miles)
May 12, Passed the Bogue Chitto, camped two miles below Brookhaven. (16 miles)
May 13, Passed Bahala Station, camped near Hazelhurst. (10 miles)
May 14, Passed Hazelhurst, marched back to Brookhaven. (20 Miles, rained)
May 15, Camped at Brookhaven.
May 17, Marched to Monticello, crossed the Pearl River. (16 miles)
May 18, Camped three miles east of the Pearl River. (9 miles)
May 19, Marched 20 miles northeast.
May 20, Marched 20 miles to Westville.
May 21, Marched to within 12 miles of Brandon. (20 miles)
May 22, Passed Brandon. (17 miles)
May 23, Crossed the Pearl River, arrived in Jackson. (9 miles) (1)

The right wing of the 4th LA arrived at Jackson on May 14th. They joined General Joseph Johnston's army of 6,000 men and met General Grant's army of 40,000 strong in the first Battle of Jackson. Despite heavy skirmishing, the 4th LA had no casualties, and on May 15th, they were retreating toward Canton, Mississippi.

On May 27th, the 4th LA was in camp two miles from Jackson. Rumor in camp was that Port Hudson had been given up by the generals. Little did they know that on this day Gardner was under strong attack by General Banks.

From Jackson, the troops were ordered to harass the rear of Grant's army, which now surrounded Vicksburg. The next few weeks were spent marching and counter-marching in the rear of Grant's army. At about this time, the men's spirits were lifted on news of General Robert E. Lee's victory at Chancellorsville.

The 4th LA was under the command of General Joseph Eggleston Johnston. A Virginian, born in 1807, and a West Point classmate of Robert E. Lee, he served with great distinction in the Mexican War. He was a hero of first Manassas in 1861, and was wounded at Seven Pines. Commanding the Department of the West, he was trying desperately to save General Pemberton at Vicksburg. The men of the 4th LA greatly respected General Johnston. (2)

Grant was entrenched on the west side of the Big Black Swamp, and his position was considered impregnable, at least by Johnston's small force. It was thought that Vicksburg could hold out until September. This would give the heat and bad water a chance to weaken Grant's forces and work to the Rebel's advantage.

On May 31st, the Tirailleurs marched five miles up the railroad and took cars for Canton. They camped two miles west of the town. Captain Kilbourne paid off the troops the next day—two month's pay.

According to William Dixon:
March 31: Marched 5 miles to Canton, Mississippi.
June 2nd: Marched 2 miles north of Canton.
June 3rd: Crossed the Big Black River, marched 10 miles to White Church.
June 6th: Marched to Benton.
June 10th: Marched back to White Church, rained at night. (8 miles)
June 11th: Marched 5 miles to the Big Black River, crossed to the east bank and marched 10 miles south and camped.

This part of Mississippi was dry, with no running streams between the Big Black and Canton. The local planters used cistern water. Field hands were busy with hoes, scraping cotton. On the 13th, there was a parade and a general review of the brigade by General Maxey. Afterward, the Tirailleurs picked blackberries.

On June 14th, the Tirailleurs marched about ten miles down the road, camping on the bank of the Big Black River. General Maxey gave a speech that night. The next day the Tirailleurs went swimming. Maxey's Brigade was transferred from Loring's Division to French's Division at this time. The soldiers were not happy with this transfer. Major General French was a commander that the brigade greatly disliked. The troops had had enough of high-ranking officers of Northern birth.

General French was born in New Jersey in 1818 and was an artillery officer in the Mexican War. He was in the same West Point class as U. S. Grant and Franklin Gardner. He became a planter in Mississippi in 1856 and resigned from the U. S. Army. After service in the East, he was assigned to Joe Johnston's Army of Mississippi. (3) There were twenty-six Northern born generals in the Confederate States Army, and the 4th LA served under four of them (Lovell, Ruggles, Gardner, and French). Joe Leray purchased two gallons of cherry bounce from a slave that day. That night the tired Tirailleurs made multiple toasts to the Confederate high command.

The next day the brigade moved six miles west of Livingston, near the farm of Mrs. Carraway. On the march, the men got their water from horse ponds or mudholes. When they halted at night, fires were lighted. Bread was baked and meat boiled. Breakfast was cornbread and beef cooked in water (no grease)—the same for dinner, the same for supper. The troops were out of tobacco and were irritable as a result.

On the 22nd, they marched ten miles to Livingston and camped. It rained hard on June 23rd. By this time there were only two tents in the brigade. General Maxey had one and Colonel Hunter had the other. They both leaked. (4) The 4th LA was camped for six days one half mile from Mrs. Andrew's plantation in a fine, shady grove with excellent spring water. Cotton was blooming. Summer flies kept the cow's tails swinging. Africans, with their shiny black skin, bare to the waist, were pulling late corn. The women slaves carried the corn in baskets on their heads to turnrows, where it was dumped into wagons. There was a general inspection and muster, June 30th. French had the men standing in line under a pitiless sun from 8 A.M. until 3 P.M.

Colonel Hunter reported, "We have marched in every direction through Hinds, Madison, and Yazoo counties. Have accomplished in all a distance of 300 miles from May 1st to June 30th, 1863." (5)

On July 1st, the Acadians awoke to the clanging noises of Fenner's blacksmith shoeing artillery horses. At noon, the 4th LA left from Mrs. Cannaway's farm. A great many soldiers were overcome by the heat and fainted by the wayside. Local citizens stood at the roadside with buckets and dippers, a sight the Acadians welcomed. It was a juiceless heat. The roads also suffered from the heat, and the dust was shoe-mouth deep. This was by far the hardest march the troops had made yet. The next day they resumed the march through Brownsville and bivouacked at Birdsong's Pond. Birdsong's plantation was four miles from the Big Black River and ten miles from Edward's Depot.

The men thought that at any moment, General Johnston would order them to attack Grant's army. They were kept in a suspense of uncertainty. On July 3rd, there was a downpour. That night they could easily hear the heavy cannon at Vicksburg. Instead of attacking on July 4th, they were preached to by a missionary and given a speech by Chaplain James A. Godfrey.

That morning, Captain Landry was standing under a tree shaving. A messenger arrived—"Report to Colonel Hunter's Headquarters." There he was told to have his men ready to move at 2 A.M. He was cautioned to allow no straggling and to have two days rations cooked. Artillery horses were harnessed up to the guns and caissons. Was Johnston ready to attack Grant? The men were ready at 2 A.M. and rested on their arms until daylight. They were making their mental preparations to fight. The sun rose, promising another scorching July day.

Suddenly, the officers were told that they were in imminent danger of being captured. The wagon train began stealing to the rear along with the artillery.

Many men could not understand why they were headed east. They marched nearly all day before they were told of the fall of Vicksburg.

The column was dogged all the way to Jackson by sections of Sherman's mounted artillery. Lionel Levy wrote, "For the first time we came in contact with mounted artillery, which followed us up quite actively, taking advantage of every favorable elevation to send a shell or solid shot as an accelerator of our retreat." (6) Bursting shells made the legs grow longer, and the men raced with their shadows.

With the fall of Vicksburg, Grant was determined to maintain his momentum. He immediately sent Sherman with 46,000 Union troops to attack Johnston and destroy the railroad. Joe Johnston's force could not stand up to the legions of General Sherman. French's Division, with Maxey's Brigade and the Tirailleurs, began the arduous trek back to Jackson. July 5th, they camped six miles west of Clinton, Mississippi. The next morning, the retreat was resumed. Sappers and miners followed the army, draining ponds, backfilling cisterns, and burning bridges.

The march to Jackson was dry and dusty. Artillery and wagons raised clouds of dust, and the men's tongues cracked for lack of water. Their nostrils filled with dust, becoming dry and parched. Grit was felt between their teeth and dust collected in their eyes and hair. There were no citizens offering water on this march. Along the roadside, hundreds of men lay exhausted and worn out, unable to march. Thirst and fatigue had become their masters. Along the way, past cotton fields and stands of corn, more than one Rebel soldier lay dead on the roadside of sunstroke. The poor dead soldiers, lying there, becoming stiff, had had no one to hear their last parched words. On the march, the commissary drove cattle along with the regiment. When water was found, the cattle would make for it ahead of the troops or arrive to muddy it up while they were filling canteens.

"On hearing of the fall of Vicksburg, we left Birdsong's, July 5th, and arrived at Jackson, 6th of July," wrote Hunter. (7) The 4th LA camped on the lower side of town close to the Great Northern Railroad, with the Pearl River to their left. The men were sleeping on the ground when a heavy rain almost washed them away. The rain started at 10 P.M. On July 8th, near dark, Sherman's troops made contact with the Rebel picket. Seven days of continuous contact and fighting followed.

Confederate breastworks around Jackson were unimpressive but strong enough to keep the Yankees at bay. Hunter reported, "The regiment was detached as sharpshooters and sent out in front to skirmish with the enemy, which we did successfully from 2 P.M. on the 9th till 5 P.M. on the 10th of July, when we were relieved by another regiment" (8) The skirmishers were to keep the Yankees back until Johnston's cannon could be put in place. Late in the evening of the 9th, the skirmishers (1st ARK, 4th LA) advanced on the Federal pickets and drove them back. Houses that had sheltered the Yankee snipers were burned. The men came under fire by Union artillery and several men were injured. Theodore Doiron was wounded in the skirmishing. Hunter was ill at the time. The attack was led by Lieutenant Colonel Pennington. (9)

Louis Daigle was energized. This was his chance. He had carried his sniper rifle around for months. From his fresh rifle pit he scanned the Yankee front. Sherman's over-confident troops would make easy targets. The barrel of his Enfield protruded through his fence rail barricade and he scanned the horizon. "*Voilà!*" his brain called out. A "bluebelly" lieutenant was encouraging his men forward—500 yards. Louis followed him in his crosshairs.

Deep in Louis' hypothalamus, the most primitive part of his brain, chemicals poured out into his body. His breathing picked up, his heart thumped, he felt the unknowable tightness deep in his abdomen. He took a deep breath. The front of his brain planned his next move. Like his rifle, his motor cortex was cocked to send the impulse that would bring this drama to climax.

Louis waited until the officer faced him. The air was still. Louis blocked out the sounds of war. All his senses were focused on his quarry. His index finger flexed. The Yankee lieutenant never heard the shot that killed him. A fine reddish mist surrounded his head, which seemed to explode. That evening, the 4th LA was relieved by the 49th TN.

On Sunday, July 12th, Sherman brought up his artillery and the bombardment of Jackson began. He fired 3,000 rounds into the city that day. The 4th LA was in the line with General Breckenridge's troops. Strangely, the Tirailleurs could clearly hear the crisp notes of piano music as firing broke out. "*Tonnerre m'écrase!*" At 2 P.M., the Yankees attacked. They swarmed out of the woods 400 yards to the front "like a dark cloud of blackbirds." (10)

The first sounds were the spitting noises as riflemen bit off their paper cartridges. The ditches hummed as ramrods scratched in musket barrels. There was the "coo cluck" of hammers cocking and the crash and flame of Rebel rifles firing. The Federals were slaughtered that morning. The Tirailleurs, protected by breastworks, opened on the enemy at 300 yards. The Yankees began dropping. The first volley staggered the "bluebellies," but they pressed forward. Captain Landry ordered his men to lower their sights as the thinned-out Yankee line came closer to the breastworks. The 5th Company Washington Artillery and Cobb's Battery decimated the Federals. The 5th Company had just received four new Napoleons and two new James rifles. (11) These cannon sealed the fate of Sherman's frontal assault. Suddenly, what was left of the blue line turned and limped back into the woods.

Trasimond saw their colonel at one hundred yards take a grape shot to the head. He fell dead with his scalp torn from his skull. There were plenty of volleys exchanged. In spite of all the firing, there was only one death, Corporal W. D. Lea, Hunter Rifles A. Willie Lea volunteered to help at a heavy gun on the breast works, and while there he exposed himself unnecessarily and was shot through the top of the brain. He never knew what hit him, though he breathed for several hours after he was wounded.

In the attack on Johnston's left, the Yankees lost two hundred and fifty captured, three battle flags, a large amount of small arms, and some five hundred men dead or wounded who had been left on the field. On the 14th, an attack was made on the right of the breastworks and was repulsed. Major E. P. Pullen had a horse shot out from under him that day. He sent the Confederacy a bill for the cost of the horse, $1,200. (12) It was about this time that news of Lee's retreat from Pennsylvania reached the men.

For two days, the rotting bodies of the Federal invaders lay out on the battlefield. The sun beat down, heating up the earth and bloating up the now-black remains. Their bodies were swollen and the gases in their dead bellies made hissing and belching noises. Their blue skin seemed to pullulate from the swarms of flies covering them. The smell of dead flesh floated over the field, flowing into the Rebel ramparts. Johnny Reb took shots at hungry turkey buzzards.

On July 14th, a truce was called in order to bury the dead. One member of the 4th LA wrote: "During the existence of the truce, curiosity led us to pass over the ground where the Federals had fallen in their charge upon our works, on the morning of the 11th (12th). A detail from both armies was busily engaged in the burial of their putrid remains. The civilian, who has never passed over a battlefield, where the dead have been exposed to the scorching sun for over forty-eight hours, cannot picture its horrors. The mother would utterly fail in the recognition of the son, to whom she had given birth, and over whom she had watched so long and devotedly. Swelled to double their natural proportion, and changed to the hue of the African, recognition would be impossible. The mode by which these bodies were interred was sufficient in itself to sicken the stoutest heart. Into a shallow pit, the mangled remains, which almost fell to pieces at the touch, were heaped, and a little dirt thrown upon them. This was the glory they achieved!" (13)

Private Levy wrote, "It was a July day and there lay between 500 and 600 stalwart men, literally festering in the scorching sun, their condition so sickening and appalling that many of the burial squads were unable to stand the work; and the burying was accomplished in many instances by pulling or pushing the swollen and discolored corpses into the (burial) trenches with the aid of long hooked poles." (14)

Confederate General Johnston had both his flanks resting on the Pearl River. The Yankees began crossing the river above the town with the aim of getting into Johnston's rear. This forced the Confederates to abandon Jackson. At 10 P.M., on the night of July 16th, the Tirailleurs crossed the Pearl River on a rickety pontoon bridge and left Jackson behind them. They camped four miles east of Brandon the next day.

Samuel Lambert, Hunter Rifles B, wrote: "After falling back from Big Black Swamp, General Johnston was fully aware that to subject Jackson to a siege would be to leave his rear exposed and endanger the safety of his army. To meet them in an open field, his command was entirely too small to warrant anything but defeat against the heavy columns of Sherman. Consequently, he wisely decided to evacuate this weak position, and save his army by retreat." (15)

On July 17th, they marched before daylight and camped at Brandon. Here the 4th LA learned that French had become ill and was granted an extended leave of absence. (16) This was good.

Captain Landry awoke on July 18th to a commotion. One whole "mess" had disappeared during the night. Louis Beleau, Ebenezer Girffin, Oscar Peyronin, and Hilaire Blanchard deserted. They were taken prisoners. From Camp Morton, Indiana, Hilaire Blanchard had enlisted in the U.S. Army, March 24, 1865. Louis Beleau enlisted in the 12th Michigan Battalion in August 1863. Peyronin and Griffin were sent to Camp Morton Prison Camp. Griffen died there. Adamis Hebert and Doctor Landry also failed to answer roll call. Adamis Alexandrie was gone. He was taken prisoner and sent to Camp Morton. There he took the Yankee oath and was released.

There were desertions from all the companies of the 4th LA. The Delta Rifles lost a sergeant and nine privates. Bernard Moses was the regiment's chief musician. He was a Bavarian cornetist and saloon keeper before the war. He was bewildered. Five band members had deserted.

Desertion at this time in the war is easy to understand if you put yourself in the soldier's position. Vicksburg and Port Hudson had fallen, the whole of the Trans-Mississippi Department was lost, and Robert E. Lee was defeated in Pennsylvania. It was ninety degrees in the shade, the Union army was in front in huge numbers, and you were the target of a continuous artillery bombardment. To most, the war would seem almost over and the urge would be overwhelming to take oneself out of danger. To the faint of heart, especially the conscripts, this made perfect sense. The faithless act of desertion in this case only heaped more glory on the steadfast and courageous Acadians who continued the fight.

On July 18th, the 4th LA marched thirteen miles to a mill pond, nineteen miles east of Brandon. On July 19th an unsympathetic thunderhead soaked the

Tirailleurs. With the energy of despair, another fourteen miles was made in the rain and mud. In some places the road filled with water high enough to almost reach the limber chests of Fenner's caissons. The wet column halted at a creek to allow the troops to wash their clothes and cook rations.

The journey resumed July 20th, and would be burned into the Tirailleur's memories. The heat and the thirst were unbearable. A greasy sun burned its light down on the sweaty column. Wet shirts stuck to their skin. The road was full of wagon trains and artillery. Men and horses were breaking down all along the way. By this time the soldiers were deserting Johnston's army by the hundreds. (17)

On the trek, Francois Turgis walked most of the way, giving his horse to exhausted privates. With Napoleon III's armies, he had never experienced a retreat. William Dixon wrote, "We camped that night in a dreary wilderness-looking place on the banks of the Strong River." (18) At this place the Strong River was nothing more than a ditch. That night a scout rode up to the Tirailleurs' campfire. He was looking for General Johnston's headquarters with news that Sherman was burning Jackson.

July 21st, the 4th LA rested at Strong River. There was a brigade inspection on July 23rd. That morning they drew rations—crackers. On the 24th, they marched fifteen miles down the Meridian Road. They were now forty-five miles from Jackson and Sherman's army. That evening they camped in the rain, twelve miles south of the railroad. All the men had to eat that day was raw sweet potatoes. That night's camp was noticeable for unprecedented flatulence. On August 1st, they were paid—two month's wages. (19)

Desertions continued. A. P. Richards wrote, "The boys, for the first time, became gloomy and despondent....The campaign was against us, with gloomy prospects before us. Some of our boys had families behind, others sweethearts, many loved parents, and to turn our back upon them perhaps forever, must indeed have been trying to this brave, true, and patriotic band....In due time, many of these men returned to duty." (20)

August 7th was Captain Landry's birthday. The company was lounging around in the shade laughing and taking sips from a jug of pine-top whiskey. Lieutenant Pennington joined them. The lieutenant colonel felt a warm complacence at the respect paid him. The Acadians dropped their French and all spoke English in his presence. Pennington took a little silver demitasse cup from his coat and poured himself a drink. He notified the men that they would be moving soon.

Pennington also had some news. Captain Oliver J. Semmes had been with the 4th LA at Ship Island and had saved the brigade at Baton Rouge. He had been captured April 14th at the Battle of Fort Bisland and sent north to prison.

While aboard the transport *Mapleleaf* on June 10th, he organized a daring escape. The Rebel prisoners overpowered their guard and took control of the ship. They landed on the Virginia Shore and made their way safely back to Rebel lines.

On August 8th, they packed up and moved to Forrest Station. The next morning they took cars for Meridian. During the trip, the Tirailleurs were fascinated when they passed through a tunnel a quarter of a mile long. At Meridian they changed cars for Enterprise, Mississippi, and arrived there late that evening. The regiment slept in the open near the depot.

August 10th, camp was put up one mile from town on the Chickasaha River. The Tirailleurs took a bath and washed their clothes. They spent twenty days at Enterprise waiting for orders. While there, they drilled to the sound of the bugle, heard speeches, and enjoyed an occasional concert. "We get many good rations with plenty of vegetables and fruit." wrote Lieutenant J. B. Corkern. "We have nothing to complain of except the high price of clothing and shoes." (21) On August 29th, the 4th LA took the "down train" on the Mobile and Ohio Railroad. They left Enterprise at noon and arrived in Mobile the next day at 8 A.M.—a trip of 125 miles.

In the official regimental "Record of Events" for July and August, 1863, Captain Landry dryly summed up the activity of the Tirailleurs: "On the morning of the 5th July the company fell back with the regiment from its camp on the Big Black towards Jackson, Miss., where it arrived on the evening of the 6th. On the 9th, the enemy having invested the place, the regiment moved out of the works to engage him. In the engagement the company lost one man, slightly wounded (Theodore Doiron). On the 16th, when the place was evacuated, the brigade fell back to Brandon, subsequently to Morton, Miss., from there to Enterprise, where it was encamped...." (22)

Corporal Theodore Doiron was sent to a hospital at Lauderdale Springs, Mississippi. This place, with its mineral springs, had been a resort before the war. It was now a Rebel hospital town. The resort's two-story inn had been converted into a hospital and was now always full. Next to the hospital was the "death house," where soldiers *in extremis* lived out their last hours. On a hill up from the "death house" was a cemetery that would eventually hold over 1,200 Confederate patriots.

Theodore Doiron had blue eyes, black curly hair and a nose for good food, good wine, and soft jobs. On arriving there he found his cousin, Louis Doiron, desperately ill. Louis had been a Tirailleur for less than a year and was only fifteen years old. Theodore hardly recognized him. Disease had its grip on him; fever, jaundice, and diarrhea were his only military experience. Theodore was at his bedside when he passed.

The Tirailleurs had by now given up the concept of a "camp chest." Their baggage had been lost twice since the war started and now they traveled everywhere with their necessities. There was one kettle for the entire company. It passed from mess to mess at mealtime. Each mess owned a frying pan. They used an oil cloth to prepare their dough. They carried their water for cooking in a leather bucket. The frying pan was generally carried by sticking the handle in the barrel of a musket.

Their greasy haversacks contained a minimum of supplies. It most frequently held salt pork, corn meal, and whatever fruit that could be found: persimmons (*plaquemines*), black berries (*mûre d'éronce*), apples (*pommes*). In hot weather the grease from the pork seeped through the sack and coated their left hip. One veteran wrote after the war, "Reduced to the minimum, the private soldier consisted of one man, one hat, one jacket, one shirt, one pair of pants, one pair of drawers, one pair of shoes, and one pair of socks. His baggage was one blanket, one rubber blanket, and one haversack." (23)

At Brusly Landing the spring corn crop was left in the field to dry. In June, Simon Alcide spent exhausting hours bending corn stalks. Belisaire decided to leave as much corn in the field as possible to keep the Yankees from taking it. After Port Hudson fell and Banks moved his armies away, Belisaire started bringing corn into his cribs. Farm work did not suit young Alcide. In August he would turn eighteen and join the Confederate army.

By late July, Belisaire's thumb and first two fingers were green from suckering tobacco. He didn't trust the care of the tobacco to anyone but himself. Landry family members and field hands together started pulling corn. July 29th, Alcide was sitting on the bench of a corn wagon heading to the barn. His thoughts were on the army. As he headed toward the barn he peeled corn off a cob and tossed the dried kernels onto the old mare's shiny back, watching them fall off. Directly, the old mare raised her tail. The mare's anus gapped wide as she expelled gas. This happened a little more than a few feet in front of Alcide's face. Near the barn, the old mare raised her tail once more, her anus gaped open, and a sudden, unexplainable impulse overcame Alcide. He shoved a corn cob up her ass.

Suddenly the horse stalled in her traces. "*Tonnerre m'écrase!*" All Alcide could see was the white belly of the horse as her back legs crashed into the corn wagon and Alcide's rib cage. Alcide's corn wagon injury delayed his enlistment by two months.

After the grueling campaign around Jackson, the men were spent. Many became ill. Third Lieutenant Adelarde Courtade developed diarrhea as a result of drinking contaminated water. On September 5th, he joined other members of the 4th LA at Ross Hospital in Mobile.

On September 1st, the regiment transferred to the steamer *Dixie* and headed south down the bay. Some of the men took baths in the steamer's wheelhouse, a delightfully dangerous undertaking. They sailed up the Dog River for a few miles, landed, and camped for the night.

The next day, they marched five miles up river on an oyster shell road and camped at Hall's Mill. Camp Hall was a training camp used for Alabama troops all during the war. The Tirailleurs didn't care for the place, but the water was good, with a mill stream and natural springs. (24) Colonel Hunter and Quartermaster Captain Kilbourne went on leave September 9th. On September 12th, the 4th LA began a cheerful march to Mobile. They took off in a line of march, keeping time to the "Delta Quickstep." This tune had been composed and arranged by Private William Keppler of the Delta Rifles. (25) That evening they marched into Mobile with their brass band playing the "Parade Polka." Pavements and balconies were lined with ladies waving handkerchiefs and Confederate flags as the 4th LA paraded by in their ragged uniforms. (26)

On September 13th, the 4th LA was paid a visit by their old beloved commander. He was now Brigadier General Henry Watkins Allen. He made them a speech, shook hands, and said a tearful farewell. His last words to the men were, "May God bless and keep you all." There was a bond between Allen and his men that could only be broken by death.

Before leaving, Allen requested the transfer of D. B. Gorham to his staff. The Tirailleurs were not pleased with his leaving. Lieutenant Gorham would later become Captain of Company A, 3rd State Guards Battalion of Cavalry. The Tirailleurs were now without a fiddler.

General Maxey was transferred to the Trans-Mississippi District and his place was taken by General Quarles. Maxey was dearly respected by the 4th LA. Samuel Lambert recalled, "Often during a long and dusty march, have we seen this true soldier dismount and tender his horse to a private. Such courtesies are but common, however, among the Texians." (27)

General Quarles was a Virginian lawyer who practiced in Clarksville, Tennessee. Before the war he was an active politician, judge, banker, and railroad executive. He organized the 42nd TN regiment and became its colonel. He was captured at Fort Donelson and paroled. The Tirailleurs knew him from Port Hudson. (28)

Beady-eyed, balding, and with chin whiskers, the thirty-eight-year-old Quarles was popular with the men. Okra was plentiful in Mobile and large kettles of gumbo were frequently prepared. One evening in camp, General Quarles stopped by the company street. The Tirailleurs invited him to dine with them. After this first dose of gumbo he made many trips by the tents of the Tirailleurs at meal time. Needless to say, the Tirailleurs became a favorite of the general. General Quarles always spoke highly of the 4th LA, sparing no praise on them. It was as if he was doing penance for the deaths of Felix and Raphael Hebert at Shiloh. He always marched the 4th and 30th LA in the rear of the brigade.

From this camp, on September 15th, Orderly Sergeant Numa Hebert sent in a fuel requisition. He listed the company's complement as one captain, three subalterns, twenty-six NCOs and privates, and four laundresses and servants. They were due forty-nine cords of wood. (29) From fuel records the other companies listed the following complements: West Feliciana Rifles, 58; Hunter Rifles A, 45; National Guards, 18; St. Helena Rifles, 36; Delta Rifles, 42; Hunter Rifles B, 37; Lafourche Guards, 45; and the Packwood Rifles, 43. There was a total regimental strength of 354 men, plus staff. The loss of the Lake Providence Cadets at Port Hudson was never replaced.

On September 16th, headquarters was moved to Camp Cummings, about five miles from the city of Mobile. The regiment camped near redoubt No. 9, between Dauphin and Government Streets, about one mile from the bay. There they did provost duty.

Suddenly, the 4th LA was ordered back to Mississippi. They were rushed by rail to Meridian. Grant had organized a cavalry raid moving toward Morton. General Polk sent the regiment to occupy Palmetto Station. The 4th LA marched from Enterprise, forty-two miles in twenty-four hours. They arrived at Palmetto Station before the Federals and thwarted their raid. Footsore and exhausted, they returned to Mobile. (30) (31)

The Tirailleurs then moved to a new camp on Government Street Road. The 4th LA took over a position at No. 12 Redoubt Street on the line of defense. There they went into winter quarters. On September 19th, Adelarde Courtade became first lieutenant, Louis Daigle was elected second lieutenant, and Numa Hebert became third lieutenant. (32) Gustave Grogne returned to the Tirailleurs. Many thought the loss of his ear would damage his love life. Instead, Gustave's war wound attracted the ladies like flies. He boarded at the home of a widow woman, who provided more than just meals.

Regimental headquarters remained at Camp Cummings. (33) Mail arrived from Josephine. The letter was delivered by Dr. Lewis, returning from furlough. All she wanted to write about was the jayhawker activity in West Baton Rouge Parish. These scoundrels would strike suddenly and rob the plantations of what they could carry off, then disappear into the swamp. She also complained that Belisaire had caught some fugitive slaves in the swamp. They were cutting down huge cypress trees just to strip them of moss. If it were not for the blockade, he would have shipped the lot of the contrabands off to Cuba. Belisaire was walking with hardly any limp.

The Confederate States Postal Service was probably the most efficient department in all of the new Southern government. Ninety percent of the Southern soldiers were literate, and the war spawned a renaissance in letter writing. Thousands of letters were written by members of the 4th LA during the war. There was no official mail service to areas occupied by Federal forces, and this especially applied to members of the 4th LA from Iberville and West Baton Rouge parishes.

After the fall of Port Hudson an ersatz postal service developed. No matter where the regiment was located, there was constant contact with folks back home. These contacts were by men traveling home on leave, Negro servants going home, relatives visiting the camp, or hometown preachers doing missionary work. There also developed a certain type of entrepreneur who traveled regular routes, crossing and recrossing the Mississippi River with letters and packages for the troops. These men were, of course, paid for their risky efforts. In the 4th LA there was a lot of inactivity among the doctors of the regiment, and they made frequent visits home. This was also true of the commissary and quartermaster officers of the 4th LA. Anytime anyone was leaving camp for home, he was weighted down with mail from all the companies. Mail usually flowed to Brusly Landing by way of Clinton. This *ad hoc* mail service was amazingly efficient.

Mobile was a strategic Confederate port. It was a destination for blockade runners and a major east-west rail connection. The Union navy had it surrounded, but the Federals, in 1863, were unable to mount a land attack. Aside from breastworks and fortifications, the war had scarcely touched Mobile. The city was bustling with activity and social functions. The city of 30,000 civilians had changed in the two years since the Tirailleurs had visited it on leave from East Pascagoula. There were now sandbagged ramparts thrown all around. Hotels had turned into hospitals and warehouses were packed with war materiel.

There were many locally-sponsored women's groups established to aid the soldiers. Soon after arriving, the ragged Tirailleurs met Mrs. Ellen Walker of the Mobile Military Aid Society. She was very gracious and made arrangements for the officers of the company to be measured for new uniforms. (34)

On September 20th, Sergeant Bibe Hebert filled out another "Form No. 8." By this time in the war there were no more pre-printed forms and requisitions were being written out by hand. He requested the following items: Forty pairs of pants, eighty-one drawers, seventy-five shoes, two caps, fifty-eight shirts, thirteen jackets, nineteen blankets, eight camp kettles, and one axe. (35) On September 22nd, dispatches arrived with news of Bragg's victory at Chickamauga.

With replacements and returnees, there were now thirty-six officers, NCOs, and privates in Company H. The sergeant ordered two pairs of shoes for each member. The quartermaster department probably laughed at this request. A few weeks later, Captain Landry signed "Special Requisition No. 40," requesting twenty-seven pairs of pants, four jackets, nine pairs of drawers, twenty-six pairs of shoes, six hats, two camp kettles, twenty-four tin cups, and two buckets. (36)

The citizens of Mobile were very welcoming to the Acadians of Company H. There were so many exiles from New Orleans that the French language was spoken almost everywhere. These people opened up their homes to the Tirailleurs. John Doyle wrote, "The whole regiment either boards or have their cooking done by some private home." (37)

Back at Brusly Landing, the two Landry brothers were alone in the stables. By the inconstant light of a burning pine knot they saddled up Narcisse's horse. Belisaire Landry hugged his baby brother with tears in his eyes. Simon Alcide's ribs were healed and he was eager to enter the fight for Southern rights.

Jean Baptiste Hebert had been captured at Port Hudson and paroled. He joined Simon Alcide and they rode off on September 25, 1863, heading north. Nearing Morganza after dark, they were ferried across to Bayou Sara. The Yankees had garrisoned Port Hudson and would arrest them on sight if they caught them. That night they got a pass from a Rebel provost martial. Even with papers, they were careful to avoid Home Guards and Confederate conscription gangs. Early on the 26th, they traveled to near Osyka, Mississippi. Next day they crossed the New Orleans and Jackson Railroad, passing through Osyka. That night they camped on the Bogue Chitto River. On September 28th, they crossed the Pearl River at Clark's Ferry, making forty-five miles that day. The next day they passed Mississippi City and stayed overnight in the home of a Confederate deserter. They crossed the Pascagoula River and camped near Mobile on September 30th.

On September 25th, the 4th LA was sent to briefly garrison Fort Morgan. The commandant at the fort, Colonel William Powell, had died, and the garrison accompanied his remains to Mobile as an escort of honor. They left on the steamer *Dick Keys*, sailing that day and night toward the Gulf. There were twenty-five Yankee gunboats in sight of the fort's seventy-two cannon. At 7 A.M., September 27th, they boarded the *Flying Cloud* and were back in camp in Mobile that night. (38) Back in Mobile they learned that Father Turgis had returned. He had been to Richmond, Charleston, and Augusta visiting all the garrisons. Priest missionaries were scarce in the Confederacy and the soldiers of the 4th and 30th LA were glad to see him return. (39)

Captain Landry had to add a new mess-mate, October 1, 1863. Simon Alcide had arrived and enrolled for the duration. Young Private Landry was the last soldier to join the company. He came equipped with a Bowie knife and Belisaire's pistol. Company H, 4th LA, had two members named Alcide Landry. This thirty-year-old Alcide had enrolled at Mississippi City, July 25, 1861. The men of the Tirailleurs had their way, poking fun at the new private.

Theodore Doiron arrived back with the company on October 5th. He had been hospitalized at Lauderdale Springs. He was promoted to fourth sergeant on October 14th. In mid-October, 1863, Private Louis Kirkland rejoined the company. The Yankees had sent Louis to Grant's Island near Mobile. From there he had gone to a parole camp at Demopolis, Alabama, and then back to the Tirailleurs.

Captain Landry and Lieutenant Courtade took advantage of their status as officers and made many trips to Crisp's Theater and the Battle House Hotel. (40) The hotel was noted for its fresh oysters (*huître*), whiskey (*boisson*), music (*musique*), and women (*putain*). Another favorite diversion of Captain Landry and Lieutenant Courtade was the Mobile cock pits. On Saturday afternoons, the two officers went to the cock fights (*bataille de guime*), which were held in a local livery stable.

There were men and boys there of all ages and colors. Smells of body odor, whiskey, and cigar smoke filled the small stadium. The cocks were brought in in sacks, each one trimmed and gaffed. Their attendants then held them up to each other and then let them go. The cock's hackles were flared out, making them look like their heads were poking through little umbrellas. There was a fury of feathers flying and spurs lashing out at each cock's head. The crowd got into the spirit and bets were laid down. Cheers and encouragement were flowing for each man's favorite cock. The bloody spectacle continued, with attack after attack, until one cock lay dead.

Lieutenant Colonel Pennington supplied some excitement in September. According to John I. Kendall, Pennington was a brave man, "though small in size and with a hand like a woman and a foot which would fit comfortably into a No. 4 shoe. He was able to knock out a man twice his size with his bare fists." He was a brawler, and at the Battle House Hotel he picked a fight with a boastful Confederate spy. He was challenged the next day to a duel. (41)

The officers of the 4th LA were present for the excitement. Pennington chose pistols—Navy sixes at ten paces. Louis Daigle figured they would both be killed. The Confederate spy turned and fired first. Incredibly, the shot kicked up dust in front of Pennington's left boot. Pennington coolly fired his pistol into the air, sparing the spy.

Lieutenant Daigle came down with dysentery on October 25th. While recuperating, he spent a lot of time at the Soldier's Library on Water Street. Post Chaplain Reverend B. M. Miller had created a library for soldiers in Mobile. (42) Louis read a serialized version of Charles Dickens' *Great Expectations* in the 1861 issues of *Harper's Weekly* newspaper. Many Yankee newspapers were available thanks to blockade runners. On *Le Jour des Morts*, November 2nd, the Acadians attended Mass with the 30th LA.

While in Mobile, the Tirailleurs did guard duty and mounted patrols. Dress parade was held regularly and was well-attended by the townsfolk. Mainly for this reason, the Confederate government supplied new uniforms for the 4th LA while they were in Mobile. The government did not want their army dressed in rags while marching on parade in front of Southern taxpayers.

Order of Battle, First Georgia Campaign
Army of Tennessee, Lieutenant General Braxton Bragg
    Corps, Major General John C. Breckenridge
        Division, Brigadier General William Bate
            Brigade, Brigadier General William A. Quarles
                4th LA, Colonel S. E. Hunter
                30th LA, Lieutenant Colonel Thomas Shields
                46th TN, Colonel Robert A. Owens
                55th TN, Colonel Robert A. Owens
                48th TN, Colonel William M. Voorhies
                49th TN, Colonel William F. Young
                53rdTN, Colonel John R. White
                Fenner's Battery

In late November, the regiment was suddenly ordered to Georgia. At this time, General Leonidus Polk considered Quarles' brigade part of his command. Due to Bragg's emergency situation (Missionary Ridge), Richmond ordered them to Georgia. The Tirailleurs were marched down to the Government Street wharf and from there they boarded the steamer *Natchez*. They made the twenty-two mile trip to Tensas Landing and to the depot of the Mobile and Montgomery Railroad in three hours.

The men prepared for a hard campaign, bringing most of their possessions with them. Colonel Hunter wrote, "Took cars and got to Montgomery on the 23rd at five o'clock, P.M. Changed cars and left that place. Arrived at West Point the same day at seven o'clock P.M., and spent the night there. November 24th at four o'clock, A.M., arrived at Atlanta, Ga. The same day we changed cars and at one o'clock, left Atlanta, Ga. Arrived Dalton, Ga., Nov. 26th about four o'clock, P.M." (43) At 3 A.M., November 25th, there was a total lunar eclipse. Many in the Tirailleurs took this as an omen.

Sergeant Lambert wrote from Atlanta on November 24th: "Trains began to pour in from above loaded with wounded soldiers, which told the tale too truly that a war of carnage had been going on between the forces of Bragg and Grant. 'How do things stand above,' inquired a friend near us. 'Whipped, badly whipped,' answered several voices, which told us that the engagement at Missionary Ridge had resulted in the rout of our army from one of the strongest natural defenses that the eye of an engineer could have selected within the Southern states." (44)

Hunter's official report continued, "Bragg's army being there falling back, we were ordered to remain at Dalton waiting for orders. The same day we were ordered to picket four miles from Dalton, Ga. On the 27th, we were ordered back to Dalton." William Dixon wrote, "We returned to Dalton. There we stopped on the summit of a very high hill from which we could look over and see some of the snow-covered mountains in Tennessee. The scenery presented by the surrounding country was beautiful." (45) Colonel Hunter continued, "On the 28th, at two o'clock, we were ordered to picket the outskirts of town to support a battery and were relieved the same day." On November 30th, the 4th LA moved one mile north of Dalton, into a valley near a small stream, and encamped. (46) The days were spent gathering wood for camp fires. The local citizens claimed that it was the coldest winter they had ever experienced. On waking in the morning the edges of their blankets would be frozen to the ground.

The campfire smoke and cold air brought on a melancholy among the men. These were the smells and the feel of the grinding season. Bringing in the cane was the most exciting season of the year. Even the slaves enjoyed this time. After the first cold snap the cane would become sweet and the race to bring it in would begin. The Acadian Coast sprang to life. The sugar-house boilers were fired up and the sweet juice was refined. Coopers, engineers, mechanics, teamsters, and shopkeepers were kept busy. If the weather permitted, the work was done by Christmas and parties were held in the "Big House" and in the slave quarters. These pleasant memories of the good times and the grinding seasons before the war weighed heavily on the men when held in stark contrast to the gloomy Georgia winter.

The Tirailleurs spent two miserable months in the red dirt of Dalton, Georgia. The camp was surrounded by lonely, gloomy hills. The scenery was framed by a sea of half-frozen mud. The time was spent on guard duty and generally freezing, since most of the men were without winter clothes. Drill continued and was bearable for men who expected nothing better. General

Leonidus Polk sent a demand for the return of the 4th LA. The matter was referred to the War Department and the men anxiously awaited a reply. Private Camille Hebert had become ill on the trip to Georgia and was sent to a hospital in Marietta. The men made up a purse of $50 for his aid. *Pérè* Turgis celebrated Mass every Sunday in the cold, open air of Georgia.

Lieutenant Charlie Howell and all the men of Fenner's Battery had begun the war in April, 1861, as part of Dreaux's Battalion. They spent one year in Virginia. Captain Fenner then organized some of the men at Jackson, Mississippi, into an artillery company. Louis Daigle had been a member of this battalion and knew Charlie Howell and Captain Fenner. Lieutenant Howell invited the officers of the 4th LA to a vacant storehouse in Dalton. The event was an opera put on by the battery: *Pirate of the Aegean Sea,* written by Private John Augustin. A stage of rough planks had been built and artillery tarpaulins hung and decorated with chalk and charcoal. A regimental band from Kentucky provided orchestral music for the play, which was a huge success." (47)

Private Simon Rivet, Trasimond's brother-in-law, received word that his three-year-old daughter was ill. He left for home in December, without leave. Little Marie Josephine Rivet died two months later at Brusly Landing.

Union General Thomas' army was not far away, but no fighting was done by the regiment. Private Oscar Contini became ill and was sent to a hospital in Macon, Georgia. In mid-December, the Tirailleurs made log houses in their camp, thinking they would spend the rest of the winter in Dalton. Their only building tools were an axe and a froe.

Rations were poor. Private Levy wrote, "The day's rations had gotten down to one third of a pound of wretched bulk pork or bacon and three fourths of a pound of meal, with a substitute occasionally for the former of a large spoonful of sour molasses." (48)

Letters home and reports were written in pencil. Ink could not be used because it would freeze in the ink wells. A cold Christmas Eve was passed off by the members of the 4th LA as merrily as circumstances would permit. The men relieved the commissary department and Dr. Craig of all the whiskey on hand. (49)

On New Years Eve it rained all day and on January 1st it snowed. The Tirailleurs had not seen snow since Jackson, Tennessee. The heavy snows at Dalton led to huge snowball fights. One company snowballed another, then regiments, then brigades took part. Private Levy wrote, "The sham battles that were fought here during the heavy snows, with snowballs, assumed large proportions....Colors, and quarters, and camps were captured, and the greatest enthusiasm and excitement prevailed. It resulted, however, in producing a great deal of sickness and was subsequently prohibited." (50)

A few weeks after Christmas, word was received that an attack was to be made by Sherman on Meridian, Mississippi, and possibly on Mobile or Selma, Alabama. An infantry force out of Vicksburg and a cavalry force from Memphis were to strike for Meridian. Confederate Lieutenant General Polk ordered the 4th LA back to reinforce Mobile.

The men of the 4th LA were "wild with delight and congratulated each other upon the happy prospect of leaving this dismal place (Dalton)," wrote Robert Patrick (51). On January 21st, the men were at the depot before sunrise. They left Dalton that night and loaded into impoverished-looking boxcars. It rained that night. It was a cold bone-chilling rain. When the train reached Atlanta there was sleet. William Dixon wrote, "A great many of the soldiers were drunk." (52) On the ride from Atlanta, a drunken brawl broke out among some Florida troops. The unfortunate Lieutenant William Ramsey of the St. Helena Rifles was stabbed. The regiment spent the night in Atlanta in terrible weather. The next day they were in West Point and stopped for the night. They crowded into the depot, sleeping on floors, counters, and in doorways. At Greenville, Alabama, the train ran off the tracks and the regiment remained there all night. On the morning of January 25th, the train left for Tensas Landing and arrived at 10 P.M. They took the steamer *St. Charles* over to Mobile, arriving exactly two months after leaving.

The "Louisiana Hospital" had been set up at Mobile and was staffed by the Sisters of Charity. Many men of the 4th LA left the train and went straight to this place. At Mobile, Dr. Hereford left the 4th LA to become medical director of the district of East Louisiana. This left Dr. Charles D. Lewis, Dr. J. M. Craig, and Dr. J. A. Leveque as surgeons.

Camille Hebert died on February 14, 1864, at Academy Hospital in Marietta, Georgia. His name is listed on the hospital's rolls for "Deaths During the Month of February." Private Hebert and five others died of chronic diarrhea, four from pneumonia, two from typhoid, one from dysentery, and one due to pyuria. (53) During the war, twenty-one Heberts served in Company H. There were now five.

The brigade marched from Mobile to Dog River Factory and encamped along with the 30th LA and Fenner's Battery. In January, 1864, after returning to Mobile, Orderly Sergeant Bibe Hebert sent in "Special Requisition No. 40": twenty-seven pairs of pants, four jackets, nine drawers, eight shirts, six blankets, twenty-six pairs of shoes, six hats, two camp kettles, twenty-five tin cups, and two buckets. On January 25th, 1864, the quartermaster filled the order in full. (54) On February 1st, a dress parade was held for the presentation of a new flag prepared by the kind ladies of Mobile. On February 4th, the 4th LA was ordered to Mississippi. (55)

Order of Battle: Second Mississippi Campaign
Department of Mississippi and East Louisiana, Lieutenant General Leonidus Polk
   Division: Major General Loring
      Brigade: Brigadier General Quarles
         4th LA, Colonel Samuel E. Hunter
         30th LA, Lieutenant Colonel Thomas Shields
         46th TN, Colonel Robert A. Owens
         55th TN, Colonel Robert A. Owens
         48th TN, Colonel William Voorhies
         49th TN, Colonel William Young
         53rd TN, Colonel John White

In January, 1864, General Sherman's preparations for an expedition against Meridian, Mississippi, were nearing readiness. His large land force was to leave Vicksburg and coordinate their attack with a large cavalry force from Memphis, led by General Sooey Smith. The focus of this pincer movement was Meridian. A goal of the attack was to lay waste to the rich farmlands of central Mississippi and destroy the railroad. Sherman left Vicksburg with twenty day's provisions, requiring a thousand wagons to haul his supplies.

The Tirailleurs took cars on the evening of February 4th, on the Mobile and Ohio Railroad. According to Samuel Lambert, Lieutenant Colonel Pennington was in command. (56) The regiment arrived in Meridian and took the night train for Brandon. At Brandon they were assigned to General Loring's Division. General William Loring was a forty-six-year-old North Carolinian. As a youth he fought in the Seminole Wars. He served as a cavalry captain under General Persifor F. Smith in the Mexican War, and lost an arm at Chapultepec. In 1861, he became a brigadier general in the Confederate Army. He commanded with Thomas Jackson in Virginia, and with Pemberton in Mississippi, then joined Polk's Corps. (57)

Simon Alcide sat cramped on the train next to Joe LeRay and Louis Kirkland. The talk went back to Shiloh. Louis had enrolled when he was fourteen years old, and to Alcide's view lorded his veteran status over him. Louis was with the Lake Providence Cadets and was wounded at Shiloh. After the Battle of Baton Rouge, he transferred to the Tirailleurs. Alcide wanted to hear the story of Shiloh.

Joe LeRay was twenty-seven-years old. He had a face of the soil and to Alcide he was an old man. He had big, thick fingers from picking cotton all his youth. He told Alcide the story of the Tirailleurs. He could see how big Alcide's eyes were and may have embellished the story a little. He described the last charge at the "Hornet's Nest" when his brother and Dr. Leveque led the men up the hill. Trasimond was holding the company flag and Doc Leveque was waving the men on with his sword. Alcide hung on every word. Joe cautioned Alcide that if he was as brave as his brother, he probably would not last long in this war.

General Loring was in retreat on February 7th, and was at Morton. Sherman's force passed Brandon, Mississippi, heading east. The 4th LA joined Loring's Division on the Brandon to Morton road. A fight was expected. An infirmary corps was appointed and litters distributed. The division headed west at 8 A.M., moving toward Sherman. After three miles, the division about faced and headed back toward Morton. Loring stopped on a long ridge, faced the division west, and deployed. They were one mile west of Morton Station. General S. D. Lee's Rebel cavalry fell back through the Confederate line of battle. Although Sherman was only a mile from the thin line of Confederates, he did not desire to bring on an engagement at that moment. At the time, Grant's forces were divided, each half of the army taking a separate road toward Meridian.

The men knew they were outnumbered by Sherman four to one. The Tirailleurs were in high spirits and ready for a fight. They were sent out as skirmishers. The bands were playing *Dixie* when the first Yankees appeared through leafless woods. The Tirailleurs held their fire until the Federals were within one hundred yards. With a cheer, a volley was sent into the advancing Federals. The 4th LA stood its ground until after sunset.

The one-armed Loring had all his regimental bands blaring and kettle drums booming. This gave Grant a false impression of his numbers. When it was apparent that Grant had the capability of getting in their rear, Loring lit huge camp fires and retired during the night. Sherman reached Morton on February 9th.

The regiment arrived at Hillsboro, Mississippi (fifteen miles) the next morning. They marched another fifteen miles that day. After resting for two hours, they marched at 9 P.M. for Newton. There was no moon. Torches were lit at the head of the column.

According to Samuel Lambert, "In forty-eight hours, we had passed over fifty-six miles, and subsisted on a half pound of bacon and a pound and a half of bread. Yet there was no grumbling or straggling." (58)

John Doyle wrote, "The Yanks were after us and were three times our number. We marched two nights and one day without sleeping and made fifty miles." (59)

Grant spread the rumor that he was heading for Mobile. General Leonidus Polk then ordered French, with Quarles and three other brigades, to Newton Station. The regiment arrived at the station at 4 A.M. By sunrise, they were on board trains for Meridian. They arrived there before dark. From there they were to move to defend Mobile. The 4th LA, with Quarles' Brigade and NcNair's Brigade, found trains for Mobile.

Sherman reached Meridian on February 14th. General Polk had evacuated the city and moved twelve million dollars worth of supplies out of the depots and on to Selma and Mobile. Grant's plans were rudely dashed when General Nathan Bedford Forrest's Cavalry soundly whipped Sooey Smith at Okolona, Mississippi.

Without cavalry, Sherman satisfied himself with burning Meridian. He then retired toward Vicksburg. Sherman wrote, "I began systematic and thorough destruction. For five days, 10,000 men worked hard and with a will with axes, crowbars, sledges, clawbars, and with fire, and I have no hesitation in pronouncing the work well done. Meridian, with its depots, store-houses, arsenal, hospital, offices, hotels, and cantonments, no longer exists. (60)

The Tirailleurs slept on the train from Meridian. On arriving at Mobile on Mardi Gras day, February 16th, they were marched thirty miles below the city. There were rumors that the Yankees were preparing to land troops. It was a tiresome march through the sand. No invasion took place. They camped there. Once during their stay, the Tirailleurs went out on the beach to gather oysters and were shelled by Yankee gunboats. March 4th, they returned to Hall's Mill on foot.

The 30th LA moved on to garrison Fort Gains and later the Bon Secours salt works. The Tirailleurs became members of the parish of Father Hubert and Father DeChaignon. They were Jesuit faculty members from Springhill College. Anthony DeChaignon had been a priest in Baton Rouge before the war and spoke very little English.

Father Turgis was destitute. The Louisiana Relief Association in Mobile raised $300. He only took enough of the money to buy a new blanket and insisted that the rest go to needy soldiers. While away from Mobile, he had B. M. Miller sell the articles in his trunk to pay for medicines for the soldiers. (61)

On March 5th, the regiment returned to Camp Cummings as a part of General Cantey's Division, Polk's Corps. They moved into musty huts previously constructed at the old training camp. They had the smell of mouse urine and better times. This was a good time for the Tirailleurs. They did plenty of courting and general dissipation.

In late March there was an outbreak of smallpox in the city. One private in Company F died of the disease. Captain Landry called the men out for formation and inspected them, one by one, for small pox vaccination scars. He found about a half dozen of the company unvaccinated. With Dr. Lewis' blessing, he marched them down to Jackson Street to the office of Dr. Kratz, where they were all inoculated. (62)

On March 17th, the Tirailleurs re-enlisted for the duration. The War Department granted four furloughs to any company that re-enlisted. The men rolled dice to see who would get the furloughs. Louis Kirkland won one. He gave it to Prudent Crochet. Prudent would see his two-year-old daughter for the first time since April, 1863. This would be the last time he would ever see his wife and daughter.

On March 18th, the regiment was called out. Company G was detailed for an execution. Three Confederate soldiers had been condemned to die. There were over a thousand soldiers ranked around. There were also some ladies in attendance. The three condemned soldiers were marched out with fife and drums playing and beating the dead march. The three were ordered to sit on their coffins. An officer placed a bandage over their eyes. One was ordered to stand. A captain stepped forward and read off the crimes of the condemned man. It was his fourth offense of desertion. "Make Ready! Aim! Fire!." Suddenly a rider galloped up. The other two condemned were granted a reprieve and sentenced to hard labor. (63)

Gustave Grogne was visiting friends in the Lafourche Guards. They were boarded up well. Captain Vick arrived to roust out stragglers for the execution. Gustave remained to finish a meal he had been offered. Admiring their very comfortable quarters, he discovered a "laundress" in one bedroom. Seeing that she had already been paid and was willing, Gustave indulged himself.

In early April the regiment received news of General Richard Taylor's great victory over the Yankees at the Battle of Mansfield. All the Louisiana troops had their spirits lifted on this news. Major General Franklin Gardner's brother-in-law, General Alfred Mouton, was killed in this campaign. Colonel Hunter was on leave all of April and Lieutenant Colonel Pennington was in command.

Part of the 4th LA was detailed to Fort Morgan. The men left at 8 A.M., April 7th, and arrived at 4 P.M. (64) Sergeant Samuel Lambert made an interesting comment regarding the discipline on garrison duty compared to field duty. "Short as our stay was, it was sufficient to displease us. The difference between the discipline here (in garrison), and what we had become accustomed to, was wide indeed. If we saluted our officers it was through courtesy; the soldiers at the fort, however were compelled to do this. This difference was owing to the duty performed on the field. This will bring about a feeling of equality between officers and soldiers; full rations, no marching, and no fighting, will serve to draw a line of distinction between the man who wears a sword, and the one carrying a knapsack and gun. This truth defies denial." (65)

April 10th, the company was transferred to the Bon Secours Peninsula at the mouth of Mobile Bay. They were transported by the steamer, *Junior*, the twenty-three miles from Fort Morgan. They were to relieve the 30th LA and guard the extensive Confederate salt works located there. Salt was manufactured from sea water by evaporation. The troops were quartered on the peninsula overlooking Bon Secours Bay. The 4th LA left the landing and marched two miles southwest to Camp Anderson. This place was nothing more than a thin sand dune stretching ten miles from east to west. There was a regular ferry to Mobile and passes were easy to get. The same day, the Lafourche Guards, West Feliciana Rifles, and Hunter Rifles B returned from Biloxi, where they had been stationed for several weeks.

A private's pay was $11 per month. First lieutenants were paid $90 per month and second lieutenants were paid $80 per month. Captain Landry's pay was $120 per month. Officers were required to pay for their own uniforms. During the war, no adjustments were made in the soldier's pay scale to account for rampant inflation. The men were paid every two months if they were lucky. Third Lieutenant Numa Hebert's pay was $70 per month. Proud of his new status as an officer, Lieutenant Hebert spent two month's salary on a new coat. It was manufactured locally of recycled cotton and doe hair, and it was said to be waterproof. The coat had the correct gold spaghetti braid signifying a third lieutenant. This earned him many jests from his comrades. The gold braid was called "chicken guts" by the privates. (66)

Bon Secours was a pleasant stay. Tents were erected and a dry campground was constructed. The spirits of the soldiers continued to improve. This stay was reminiscent of the Mississippi Coast of 1861. The Tirailleurs went fishing and boating, and enjoyed inexpensive oysters. Their stay on the Alabama beaches would be the prelude to their most serious and arduous campaign yet.

Hunter received a letter from the Medical Department of Georgia. Private Oscar Contini had died of his illness. He was thirty-two years old and left a widow and one son.

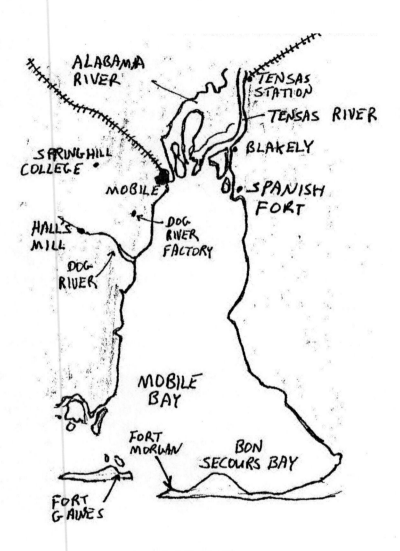

MOBILE BAY

8.

Battles for Atlanta

Order of Battle, New Hope Church
Army of Tennessee, Lieutenant General Joseph Johnston
   Corps, Lieutenant General Leonidus Polk (Army of Mississippi)
     Division, Brigadier General James Cantey
       Brigade, General William Quarles
         1st ALA, Major Samuel E. Knox
         4th LA, Colonel S. E. Hunter
         30th LA, Lieutenant Colonel Thomas Shields
         46th TN, Colonel Robert A. Owens
         55th TN, Colonel Robert A. Owens
         48th TN, Lt. Colonel Aaron S. Goodwin
         49th TN, Colonel William Young
         53rd TN, Colonel John White

After Shiloh, Baton Rouge, and Jackson, it would not have bothered the Tirailleurs if they had spent the rest of the war at Bon Secours. The men felt that they had been used more as a pioneer or engineering battalion than soldiers anyway.

Except for Colonel Allen, the 4th LA's leadership had been uninspiring up until now. The men of the 4th LA had not seen anything yet. Their leadership would get steadily worse, and there would be much more sweating, digging, chopping, and fortifying. On May 23, 1864, Polk's Corps and Quarles' Brigade (4th LA) were ordered back to Georgia. Joe Johnston had replaced the blundering Braxton Bragg as leader of the Army of Tennessee

The company was small but the men were healthy and well fed at this time. They all had shoes. On May 22nd, a steamer pulled up to Bon Secour Landing and loaded the 4th LA and their baggage. Then they were back to Blakely's Wharf. They arrived at the landing at sunset, but the river boat failed to arrive.

They spent another cold and rainy night in the open. The steamer arrived the next evening. Three hours later they were at Tensas Landing. Packed into boxcars, they were quickly on their way toward Pollard, Alabama, fifty-two miles away.

At one place in Alabama, a troupe of school girls threw their dinners into the cars. Some of the bundles were accompanied by notes signed by the girls. They changed cars at Pollard and again at West Point and Atlanta. The regiment arrived at Newton, Georgia, at daylight, May 26th. There they detrained for four hours on rumors of an expected Yankee raid. Trains arrived at Atlanta at 2 P.M. and the men drew rations. Their next stop was Marietta, Georgia. They arrived there at 5 P.M. There they began the eighteen-mile march to New Hope Church. (1)

In the fighting around Atlanta, both sides depended on railroads to move and sustain their forces. From start to finish the battle was a railroad campaign. The prize was the major transportation center of Atlanta. Union General Sherman, trying to flank Joe Johnston's Army of Tennessee, found himself blocked along an extended front centered on New Hope Church. The Tirailleurs had no familiarity with the area, no maps, no news, and no idea what they were marching into. All they knew was that they were to be part of General Leonidus Polk's Corps, and that Joe Johnston needed them.

On May 26, 1864, the evening was calm. The trees were green and the air was fragrant with wild flowers. The mixed pine and oak woods were filled with honeysuckle, which in these parts was a rich crimson color. The Tirailleurs had been raised in the vast, monotonous flatness of the Mississippi Delta (*la terre plonge*), and marching up a hill was somewhat novel to them. Streams in West Baton Rouge were slow-moving, black, and overgrown on their banks. Streams in Georgia were fast-running, noisy, and rocky. To a man, the Tirailleurs would have swapped the beauty of this place for their pre-war flatness and peace.

The Acadians proceeded in a column of fours through the heavily wooded Georgia hills. The all-night hike to New Hope Church was made without stopping for food or rest. The officers of the Tirailleurs encouraged the men onward. The sharp sounds of musketry became louder. The hollow, bass symphony of cannon firing in woods came closer. Bernard Moses struck up his brass band. The music helped the footsore Tirailleurs make another mile. The wind began to whip up.

Three hundred and sixty officers and men of the 4th LA joined the rear of the battle line at dawn. The 4th LA arrived in time to be drenched by a sudden downpour. The noise of Rebel cannon was mixed with a background of lightning and thunder. The 4th LA was moved forward to a position at the rear of New Hope Church (present-day Georgia Highway 381) and each man was issued forty rounds of ammunition. Third Lieutenant Numa Hebert was shot by a sharpshooter the same day. He was wounded in the left hand.

On their second day in Georgia, General Polk sent General Quarles' 1,500 troops to reinforce the Confederate right being held by Major General Patrick Cleburne. Cleburne was an Irishman who had taken the Queen's shilling and spent time in the British army. He migrated to Arkansas from Ireland in 1849 and became a pharmacist in Helena, Arkansas. He organized the 15th Arkansas Infantry regiment and was elected colonel. After Shiloh, he was promoted to brigadier general, and fought at Perryville, Murfreesboro, and Chickamauga. He was known as the "Stonewall of the West" and outshined all of the West Point generals in the Army of Tennessee. (2)

In what was to be called the Battle of Pickett's Mill, the 4th LA played a critical role. Sherman was trying to pass Johnston's right flank, being held by General Cleburne. Cleburne had been borrowed from Hardee's Corps on the far left to bolster the Confederate right, being held by Hood's Corps. Cleyburn moved rapidly to his right to parry Sherman's moves and found himself in need of help. Quarle's Brigade (4th LA) was sent in rapidly to add to the Rebel line. The 4th LA was supposed to be in a second line behind Lowrey's Brigade. That day the 4th LA plugged a gap in the Rebel line, throwing back a strong Yankee attack. Cleburne praised the 4th LA after the day's fighting. "The 4th LA, Col. Samuel E. Hunter, finding itself opposite an interval between two regiments of Lowrey's Brigade (8th and 19th Arkansas from Govan's Brigade and Lowrey's Brigade), advanced with great spirit into the field, halted and delivered a very effective fire upon the enemy in his front. After some minutes Quarles withdrew the 4th LA and formed it behind the field, where they continued their fire across it. General Quarles and his brigade have my thanks." (3)

Private Richards described the charge that saved Cleburne's flank. "We were rapidly moved to the right of the army, marching about seven miles by dusk (by way of Mount Tabor Road). We could hear low, sharp firing, away to our left. At the order, 'By the left flank, march,' we struck out in the woods and tangle in line of battle; nearer the firing; sharper the firing of rifles. The occasional order of Colonel Hunter could be heard, 'Steady men; guide center.' On we went, and soon we came to a line of troops." (4)

James Marston wrote, "(We) advanced slowly across a strip of woods about 200 yards in width....We came to the edge of an old (corn) field. We were ordered to charge when we raised a yell and rushed forward, driving the enemy before us." (5)

During the charge, Colonel Hunter stopped to assist the wounded Corporal William McAdams. While attending McAdams, the regiment advanced another hundred yards, leaving their leader well to the rear.

To the Scots-Irish, battle was a group phenomenon. To the French it was more of an individual event. This was especially true for Simon Alcide Landry. The eighteen-year-old private pressed ahead of his brother and into the Yankees. A Yankee lieutenant stumbled, then raised his hands. He held a revolver. "*Sacré Tonnerre!*" Does he mean to shoot? Louis Daigle shot him—graveyard dead. A terrified Yankee private next to him turned to flee as Arthur Blanchard sent his tri-corned bayonet into his back. In this violent instant the bayonet snapped off. Some Yankees stopped and organized a weak resistance. Fierce hand-to-hand combat sent them reeling back. General Quarles, who happened to be with the 4th LA at the time, realized that the flanks of the 4th LA were wide open and ordered them to fall back to the high ground between Granbury and Lowrey's Brigades.

The men of the 4th LA could hear the uproar when the troopers of Granbury's Texans made a night charge on the Yankee pickets at 10 P.M. The 4th LA was in this charge. They crossed a cornfield and crashed into Yankee General Scribner's Brigade.

Private "Dick" Richards described the night charge at Pickett's Mill: "With a long crash-fire and that terrible yell, we dashed forward and soon broke into an opening. By the dim light of the stars we saw a perfect sea of glittering bayonets moving on before us. The open ground enabled us to increase our speed, and we dashed after the fleeing enemy until the order came, 'Halt.' The enemy had taken cover under brush in a ravine before us." (6) They remained until 2 A.M., when they moved back into the woods. (7)

In spite of what Cleburne wrote in the official record, his praise of Hunter was overstated. When the 4th LA reached the battle line at Pickett's Mill, the soldiers were ordered into the second line of defense. The entire area was a dense thicket and visibility was low. A gap had developed between two of Lowrey's regiments. Hunter left the road with the 4th LA and passed ahead of the other regiments of Quarles' Brigade by mistake. Seeing no one in his front, Hunter mistakenly, but fortuitously, entered the gap in the Rebel line. The Yankees were smashed into by accident. The Federals were driven from near the fresh Rebel line and back across the field.

If the Yankees of Union General Wood's division had been able to enter the gap plugged by the 4th LA, it is possible that they could have turned Cleburne's flank. General Wood's three brigades could have easily poured into Cleburne's rear. It is unlikely that Sherman would have exploited the victory, but it could have been a serious blow to General Johnston's Army of Tennessee. Colonel Hunter, the lawyer and politician, exploited his brief moment of glory. To the folks back home, he lawyered the truth and offered this victory as proof that he was not a coward and a weak leader. After the Battle of Pickett's Mill, he felt vindicated. This victory did, in fact, lead to a more favorable attitude of the homefolk toward him. Of course, Landry, Courtade, and Daigle knew what had happened. The officers of the Tirailleurs were so energized by the victory that they were willing to give Hunter the benefit of the doubt and did not object to his brief moment of glory.

This sharp little engagement cost the 4th LA three killed and seventeen wounded. (8) Private Leon Isaac of the Tirailleurs was wounded. There were ten thousand Rebels involved all along the line. It was a rare event to be able to get at Yankees in the open and that night the Tirailleurs could hear the familiar racket of Yankee axes.

The men stood in their line all night, holding their rifles. They watched as a brilliant Venus rose in the east. It was only at sunrise that they noticed they were standing among dead Yankees. These Yanks were immediately stripped of everything useful. Around their breakfast fire, Portalis Tullier admired a picture of a young woman he had taken from a dead Union soldier. There was also an unfinished letter. He opened it and handed it to Lieutenant Louis Daigle. He could not read English. Louis took the letter. It was from a young private in Union General William Hazen's brigade to his wife in Ohio.

> Dearest Darling, Alice, 27th May, 1864: I take this time to write on a rest. We are marching hard to flank the rebels from Atlanta. I know not where we are in this harsh country. The inhabitants are very poor and ignorant creatures. We expect a fight soon. I suspect we will teach the secesh a lesson. If my life should end, my only wish is that I not be buried in this traitorous land....

On May 28th, the regiment collected two thousand stands of small arms, giving them a good idea of the size of the force encountered at Pickett's Mill. Quarles' Brigade moved back to their original position at New Hope Church. At 4 P.M. they marched back to the Pickett's Mill battlefield and their first good night's sleep since leaving Bon Secours. On May 29th, they moved to a position to the right of New Hope Church, near the center of Johnston's defenses. They were in reserve and entered the front-line trenches two days later.

No man values the earth more than a cane farmer, except maybe a soldier. In the face of the brute force of artillery the earth is a sustaining force. The report of cannon and the dry cracking sounds of broken tree limbs overhead create an urge in the soldier. It is an immediate urge to press himself deeply into the earth. They had experienced shelling in the first morning at Shiloh, at Vicksburg, in the woods at Baton Rouge, on the night of the great river battle at Port Hudson, and at Jackson. No one ever got used to being shelled, although this day was not as terrifying as that first day at Shiloh. Nevertheless, no one had to order Tirailleurs to dig a trench. When they halted more than thirty minutes, they began throwing up earthworks. At one place outside Atlanta, the troops used roof shingles as spades and bayonets as picks to dig down into the welcoming depths of the earth. These trenches were called "ditches" by the Rebels.

By this time, the war had become "professional." Each soldier was his own engineer, and given two days he could produce ditches that were almost impenetrable. A log was cut and placed on the ground. After the ground was broken up, dirt was thrown over the log. The covered log was to prevent artillery shells from passing through the dirt revetment. A headlog was placed lengthwise across the top of this dirt mound. The headlog rested on poles which extended to the rear of the trench. This was done to ensure that if an artillery shell should dislodge the headlog, it would not crush the defenders. The Rebels fired through a slit beneath the headlog as it rested on these skid poles. Other trees were felled in front of the works, with the limbs facing forward as an abatis. The branches of these trees were sharpened. Sharp stakes were driven into the ground and slanted forward. Behind these works were *chevaux-de-frise*. Rebels called them "sheep racks." They were poles bristling with sharp stakes and were designed to impale attackers. (9)

One Rebel soldier of the 4th LA was heard to say that after the war, he would never have an overseer to superintend his Negroes while ditching, but would instead simply put a twelve-pounder in position and shoot over their heads once or twice, telling them at the same time, "Dig damn you, dig." This process got more work out of him in eight days than he thought he could do in eight months.

James Marsten wrote on May 31st, "Skirmishing going on continuously since we arrived being not a moment during the day when you cannot hear the crack of the rifle, booming of cannon, the whizzing of minnie balls, and the bursting and buzzing of shells, and even at this moment that I write it is going on." (10) At this time Sherman was trying to withdraw back to the railroad. Johnston ordered a series of nigh attacks which made the Yankee withdrawal very difficult.

On June 1st, the regiment moved from reserve trenches into the front-line trenches. On June 2nd, there was fierce fighting to their right. Cleburn attacked and captured 750 Yankee prisoners. At night, one third of the men were up on guard, with one sergeant and officer from each company. Also, one field officer was present "to see that the men did their duty." (11)

In this part of Georgia water was scarce. The Tirailleurs spent ten thirsty days in these fortifications. It was a rude, sudden change from their comfortable winter quarters in Mobile. New Hope Church was one of the most arduous periods of the history of Company H. Even Sherman's men referred to New Hope Church as "The Battle of the Hell Hole"

June 2nd, a thunderstorm began that afternoon. The ditches filled up with water. Captain Landry slept in water up to his knees. On June 3rd, there was another heavy thunderstorm. The Tirailleurs were sure it was the incessant artillery fire that brought on the rain. It rained again on the morning of the 4th. It rained again that night. Royal Collins, Company A, was killed in the ditches that day.

Quarles called for Colonel Hunter. He wanted to know what troops he faced and ordered him to bring in some prisoners. Hunter called for Captain Landry and sent the Tirailleurs into the rifle pits, June 4th.

The Acadians slipped into the muddy rifle pits after dark. Captain Landry had borrowed revolvers from the men of the regiment and wrapped them to keep them dry. A dozen Acadians crouched in the rain. With the rain drowning out the sound of their movement, they slithered toward the Yankee outposts. Simon Alcide fumed at his brother, who made him stay behind. With a crash, the Acadians bound over the parapet and into the Yankee rifle pit. They took a half dozen startled Yankees prisoner. It was easy. No shots were fired. The rifle pits were thoroughly looted and the prisoners were taken back to General Quarles' marquee. The men rolled dice for their rubber coats.

Yankee snipers were industrious, producing "the never-ceasing hideous sounds of balls." (12). Leaving the trenches in daylight was certain death. (13) New Hope Church was the beginning of ninety-eight straight days of almost continuous fighting for the Tirailleurs. Nights were spent rotating on picket duty. There was rain, heat, constant alarms, continuous sniping, the stench of the dead, screams of the wounded, shortages of food, clouds of green flies, and thirst. To compound all this misery, the "graybacks" reappeared and the men had not been paid in five months. Pipe smoking was not allowed on picket. Captain Landry resorted to chewing tobacco.

There was constant flanking activity by Sherman and soon the men were ordered to move. The New Hope line was left for the Lost Mountain-Brushy Mountain Line on the night of June 5th, at 1 A.M. The Tirailleurs hiked off in the darkness and rain. Teamster's whips were cracking and wagon wheels creaked and groaned as the men heard the familiar noises of retreat. They halted at the foot of Lost Mountain, nine miles west of Marietta. In spite of the hardships at this time, one soldier of the 4th LA wrote home, "The morale of the army was never better than it is now and the men are sanguine of success and their confidence in Joe Johnston is undiminished. There is less straggling than ever known before." (14) It rained every day from June 2nd to June 13th.

On June 5th, at dark, they climbed to the top of the mountain, arriving at 11 P.M. The Tirailleurs slept on rocks that night. The ground "was so steep we had to sleep with our backs against trees to keep from sliding down." (15) On June 6th, Quarle's Brigade (4th LA) was transferred to Walthall's Division, Polk's Corps.

At Lost Mountain, there was good protection from the enemy guns, but life was miserable. Digging ditches in the rocky ground was exhausting. The Tirailleurs, protected only by the meanest of shelter, fought either the heat and thirst or the rain and mud. The noise never ceased. Yankee cannon kept pounding an irregular rhythm. They were frequently sent out on picket duty or as videttes, night and day. (16) On June 9th, just after finishing their trenches, they were ordered five miles to the right. Picks and shovels were issued and digging began again. General Polk rode by and received a cheer from the 4th LA. On June 10th at 1 P.M., a violent thunderstorm struck. It rained until dark. At night it was cold enough for fires and overcoats. On June 12th, it rained all day, slacking up some at night and not ceasing until noon the next day. There were no rations issued that day. (17) The Acadians could hear locomotives whistling at Big Shanty. Sherman had repaired the railroad bridge over the Etowah River and was reinforcing his army.

On June 13th, the wind came in from the northeast and was cold for that time of year. Wagons with rations arrived and a jigger of whiskey was issued to each man. That day, a shell exploded over the Tirailleurs. Shrapnel threw up rocks and mud. "*Sacré Merde! Quoi c'est ça!*" (Holy Shit! What was that?) The stunned Acadians stood in the smoke shaking off the dirt and gravel. Gustave Grogne lay quietly. He appeared unconscious. His friend, Bibe Hebert, gently lifted him. The spoon salesman from New Orleans was dead. That day the men were briefly relieved to bury their comrade on Lost Mountain. In a coffin-less hole they placed his derby across his face, folded his arms across his chest, and threw red dirt over him. It rained all day.

On June l4th, the rain had ceased, but the sky was overcast and gray. Around 11 A.M., General Sherman arrived to make a personal reconnaissance of the Pine Mountain area. Through glasses he observed a group of Confederates standing near a battery on the crest of the mountain in plain view. Turning to General Howard, he said, "How saucy they are!" Sherman ordered a nearby battery to fire a volley at the bold Confederates and then rode off.

Unknowingly, the target Sherman picked happened to be Generals Johnston, Hardee, and Polk, also out to observe the battle-field. General Howard gave the fire order to Captain Peter Simonsen of the 5th Indiana Battery. He ordered several shots to establish range. Aiming their Parrott ten-pounder rifled cannons at the group of Confederate generals, the first round went a little high. The second round passed through General Polk's arm, through is chest, ripping out his heart and lungs, and then out the other arm. Range, 650 yards. (18)

Suddenly, Confederate wigwag signalmen started passing messages to the rear. The Federals noticed the Pine Mountain crest buzzing with activity. Sensing something important, the Union batteries began a ferocious barrage of the mountain. Fatty Allain was on the mountain on June 13th and had witnessed Corps Commander Polk being killed. The 5th Company Washington Artillery was in a terrible position. It was excellent for observation, but terribly exposed to the Yankee's rifled pieces.

Le diable s'en a mêlé. (All hell broke loose). The Federals decided to fire all their guns at one time, at one target—the 5th Company Washington Artillery. Imagine one hundred guns arranged in a semi-circle going off at once. The solitary booming of cannon suddenly dissolved into one prolonged deafening roar. The sides of the mountain trembled. The members of 5th Company stood by their guns. The Tirailleurs had never experienced anything like it. The Yankees unleashed everything. The cannon roared, with the vibrations echoing up from the valley below and radiating out to Kennesaw Mountain on the right and Lost Mountain on the left. It reminded Captain Landry of the explosion of the USS *Mississippi* back at Port Hudson. The earth called out to the Acadians and they pressed themselves down into its bosom. As the shells passed over, they seemed to be saying, "*Eou est vous? Eou est vous? Eou est vous?*" Miraculously, only one man was killed. The next day, the 5th Company moved off Pine Mountain. General Loring took over command of Polk's Corps.

This artillery tactic of firing all guns at once on one target is known as "time on target" and was used with devastating effect during WWII. Federal artillery was able to produce this effect due to a telegraph wire Sherman had strung between his artillery batteries. This was the first time electricity was used on the battlefield to co-ordinate artillery. Most artillery tactics used by the United States army in later wars were developed and proved during the War Between the States.

On June 15th, the ditches at Lost Mountain were evacuated for a new line called the Mud Creek Line. The Tirailleurs were the last to leave that night, as they were on picket duty. At dusk, the company made its way toward their rifle pits. Smoke and mist hovered breast-high over the field. The pale hour made their faces look gray. A voice called out, "Halt." The countersign was given and the Acadians manned the pits, relieving men of the 49th TN. The night now belonged to the locusts. The pines stood like blurred ghosts in the fog and dark. The occasional red glow of cannon fire flickered in the shadows. It revealed too much and too little. With cocked rifles and big eyes, the Tirailleurs stared into the darkness. Thumbs toyed with the hammers of the rifled muskets. The remainder of the regiment moved off the mountain, leaving them there alone.

The front was restless that night. At midnight firing broke out between pickets. There was a yell from Union troops to the right of the Tirailleurs and the clash of metal on metal could be heard. Union soldiers had come up in the fog and attacked the Rebel pickets. The commotion soon died down. Five men of the West Feliciana Rifles were captured. Yankee pickets got into their rear after a portion of the line gave way on the right. As the darkness dissolved into dawn, the men moved off to a new set of ditches. The Mud Creek Line had been marked off by Confederate engineers and dug by slave labor.

On June 16th the Mud Creek Line was abandoned for the Kennesaw Line. The move to Kennesaw Mountain was not completed until June 18th. The mountain is about four miles northwest of Marietta, Georgia. It is over two and one half miles in length, and rises abruptly from the plain to a height of 600 feet. Sherman, with reinforcements, now had 100,000 men and unleashed a continual bombardment on the Confederates.

The two-week Battle of Kennesaw Mountain began as Sherman slowly closed up on Johnston. There was fighting every day as well as work strengthening fortifications. The Tirailleurs were about 500 yards from the Union trenches. On June 16th, they could hear the bands playing in the Union rear. From their post on the summit of Kennesaw Mountain they could see the entire battlefield. On one side of their position was Lost Mountain and Pine Mountain. They could walk thirty yards to the east and see Marietta. On a clear day they could see Stone Mountain twenty-eight miles to the southeast. When the Yankee batteries would make a good shot they would send up a cheer and the Rebels would do the same. The 4th LA was on picket duty or sent out as skirmishers five nights in June. On June 22nd, the Federals opened up a violent artillery attack on the 4th LA. One shell hit the headlog of the Hunter Rifles A. The log slammed back and hit Captain Fiester in the head, knocking him unconscious. Feister, a bricklayer from Clinton, recovered. Thanks to the skid poles, no one else was injured. (19)

Union artillerymen constantly harassed the Confederate lines. Hunter called for Captain Landry.The colonel was lying on a plank stretcheHis arms were folded behind his head. Trasimond arrived, neglecting to salute. This always irked Hunter. With a smile, he informed Captain Landry that he had a job for him. Trasimond spit. General Johnston had asked for companies to mount heavy Parrott rifles on the summit of Kennesaw and Hunter was sending the Tirailleurs. The Acadians, with 100 men from the 1st ALA, went to the summit of Big Kennesaw Mountain. They spent several days placing heavy Parrott guns into position. (20)

From the mountain, the Rebels could view the enemy in the valley below. Yankee trenches spread out before them like the leading edge of a skin fungus. The Federal wagon trains were clearly visible from atop Kennesaw. They stretched out behind the Yankee trenches for miles. Every two or three hundred yards the enemy batteries could be seen. A blue-white cloud of smoke would appear from a battery, then a report would be heard. An instant later a cloud of smoke would puff over the Rebel trenches, followed by another report. At night, batteries could be located by the tongues of fire spit out by the enemy cannon.

On the night of June 17th, Trasimond Landry was bone tired. The intermittent red glow from the forest plain below gave him a feeling of peace. It was really more a feeling of *schadenfreude*. He knew the Rebel ditches were receiving these shells—the peace came from knowing he was not in them. Between the reddish cannon flashes, lightening bugs gave off little green dots of light. He lay back. Starlight filtered through the night's luminiferous ether. Antares, the eye of the Scorpion, looked down on the Captain from the southern sky. He closed his eyes. His memories took him back to a summer evening. He was slowly rocking on the *galerie* of his father's home. There was no one there but himself. He could hear a steamboat's whistle in the distance and the sounds of banjo music from the nearby slave quarters. The warm sun magnified the deep green leaves of the jujube tree, planted years before by his mother. It was a gift from Sosthene Allain. Suddenly, softly, everything became calm and quiet.

Sunday morning, June 19th, the entire mountain was in a cloud. As the sun lifted the mist, a lone crow flew across the valley. He kept an uncertain course as a mockingbird attacked him. By size, it seemed an uneven match. The little gray and white bird was a better flier than the powerful crow. Repeatedly, the smaller bird dove at the crow, the goal: to peck out the crow's eyes. With luck and skill, the little mockingbird could take down the crow. These two natural enemies flew off into the glare of the sun and disappeared.

Sherman kept thrusting his armies forward, grinding them against the Rebels. The arms of Atlanta kept clawing and scratching, trying to push him away. The Federals inched closer and closer to Johnston's lines until they practically embraced each other. There were attacks and counter-attacks, mining and counter-mining, and constant artillery duels. The noise was mind-numbing.

Living on the margins of death, life was reduced to its primitive and most destitute form. Trench life meant constant thirst. Food was cooked in the rear, but could only be brought up at night. There was no bathing. Finger nails were sore from crushing "greybacks." The trenches had a smell of urine, and flies were everywhere in swarms. *Regulations for the Army of the Confederate States, 1863*, No. 92. "Where conveniences for bathing are to be had, the men should bathe once a week. The feet to be washed at least twice a week. The hair kept short, and beards neatly trimmed." Trench life made Regulation No. 92 a farce. (21) There were only four clear days in the first three weeks of June. June 22nd was the first full day to pass that month that Captain Landry was dry.

The Tirailleurs didn't spend all their time on the mountain dodging artillery shells. Every fifth night was spent on picket duty. A lot of fraternizing went on in these dark nights of close contact with the enemy. (22) On June 23rd, the Tirailleurs were on picket. The next day they were back on the mountain. Captain Landry awoke to the sounds of enemy shells still pounding in his brain. He smelled the aroma of coffee brewing. Investigation revealed Portalis Tullier supervising a small fire and his mess mates enjoying a fresh cup of real coffee, not the ersatz Confederate kind.

"*D'accord, Tullier. Le café est d'ou?*" (Hey Tullier, Where did you get the coffee?) asked Trasimond.

Edmund Longuepee spoke up. "*Il avait échanger avec les Yankees, le tobac pour le café, mon Capitain.*" (He's been trading with the Yankees, coffee for tobacco.)

"*Vous ne pouvez pas parler Anglais, Tullier. Comment le faits-vous?*" (You can't speak English Tullier. How do you do it?) asked Trasimond.

"*Il y a Alsacien dans leur fossé. Il est tres sympathetique,*" (There's an Alscacian immigrant in their trenches. He's very friendly) Portalis replied as he handed his captain a fresh cup of coffee.

Captain Packwood returned from furlough with thirty-nine pairs of shoes. He sold a pair to Captain Landry and Lieutenant Daigle at his costs. General Johnston was now able to supply the men in the ditches with sugar, tobacco, and whiskey. The Tirailleurs were in good spirits. There were a few cases of scurvy in the regiment. General Johnston had his commissary department ship in carloads of tomatoes from Florida and Alabama.

Late in the day, artillery fire would taper off and the bands on both sides would strike up. Occasionally, the Rebel bands would play the "Marsiellaise," getting a rousing cheer from the French-speaking troops. June 26th was a gloomy, rainy Sunday. A shell struck in a redoubt of the 5th Company Washington Artillery. It hit the axle of piece four, exploded, and knocked down all the crew. Gunner Alex Allain was injured in the arm and Fatty was also wounded. Private John Jackman of the 9th KY was wounded in the same bombardment. (23)

Thousands of Parrott shells were sent at the Kennesaw line by the Federals. Due to the height of the mountain, most overshot and exploded harmlessly at high elevations. Many of the afterparts of the shells (sabots) came down in the Rebel ditches. The afterpart of the ordinance rifle's Hotchkiss shells were heavy and could easily kill a man if he was hit by one of them.

The morning of June 27th, the sun rose as a great ball of red. It was one of those mornings when the fog was just the right density to allow a soldier to stare directly into it. The fog quickly burned off and the same sun poured its heat onto the battlefield. The sounds of bickering skirmishers opened up the morning. On this day, the fighting around Kennesaw Mountain climaxed. The combat was ferocious. At about 8 A.M., the enemy charged the Confederate right where the 4th LA was posted. Their advance was repulsed by General Quarles' Louisiana and Tennessee regiments. The enemy in front of Quarles' pickets was caught in crossfire. A platoon of Union troops was driven into Quarles' line and captured. (24) The attack against Quarles and the Confederate right was only a demonstration. The main attack came at Little Kennesaw, where the fighting was vicious and bloody, and where the "bluebellies" were decimated. The sun set that evening in a red sky over almost three thousand dead and wounded Union soldiers.

The 1st ARK had been brigaded with the 4th LA at Shiloh. They were in Cleburne's Division in this battle. During the fighting, the woods caught fire in front of their regiment and began burning wounded Union troops alive. Colonel W. H. Martin, 1st ARK, tied a handkerchief to a ramrod and shouted to the enemy, "Come and remove your wounded; they are burning to death. We won't fire a gun until you get them away. Be quick!" His men leaped over their works and helped the Federals remove their wounded. The brief truce ended; the Arkansans returned to their works and the battle resumed. (25)

On the flowerless hillsides lay the Union dead. There was a nauseating smell of necrotic flesh and a busy humming of swarms of flies. What were once men with breath and pulse and thought were now blue melting hulks of *rigor mortis*: death, willing or not, for the Union and Abolition. The night of June 29th was still. Yankee cannon were quiet. They were still carrying off their dead. Many of the pickets had negotiated an *ad hoc* armistice, agreeing not to shoot at one another unless there was a charge.

After Kennesaw Mountain, Sherman never again used a frontal attack on the Confederates. The irony of it is that the Rebels would soon switch to this failed tactic. Sherman moved to his left and flanked Johnston off the mountain. Orders came to withdraw from the mountain on July 2nd. The Tirailleurs moved out at midnight. With a noiseless step they moved through the cool night air. Trasimond led his men down the newly-pioneered roads through the

Georgia piney woods. "*Allon nous, mes amis, allon nous. Doucement, Doucement.*" (Let's go, quiet.)

Company H fell back to Marietta, passing through at daylight. They camped a mile from the Chattahoochee River, where the men were set to digging new entrenchments (Smyrna Line). On July 4th, the Tirailleurs tramped eight miles to Vining's Station on the Western and Atlanta Railroad. They were "severely shelled by the enemy on that day." (26)

The Tirailleurs left Vining's Station on the night of the 4th and made their way to a point on the railroad on the Chattahoochee River. Sherman kept up his flanking movements in his effort to get across the Chattahoochee. On July 7th, Polk's old corps was assigned to Major General Alexander P. Stewart. On July 8th, Arthur Blanchard was slightly wounded by shrapnel. That night, under a full moon, the Acadians crossed the Chattahoochee on a pontoon bridge, heading closer to Atlanta. The regiment then camped south of the river for several days, taking a much needed rest. This was the first time in forty-one days that these Acadians could actually walk around upright without worrying about snipers. The woods below the Chattahoochee were infested with red bugs and ticks.

The regiment then moved "to the extreme right of the infantry line north of Peach Tree Creek on the Pace Ferry Road." (27) At this time, in spite of constant retreat, the morale of the men was quite high. They had great confidence in Joe Johnston. On July 9th, the predawn sky north of Atlanta was aglow. The bridges over the Chattahoochee were burning.

On the morning of the 11th, the Tirailleurs returned from the right and went on picket duty. The 4th LA advanced as skirmishers and drove the Federals back. Rifle pits were dug and served as their home for two days. On the 13th, they were in the Atlanta ditches. On July 14th, there was partying among the French troops of the 30th LA. Many men in the 30th LA were born in France and they were celebrating Bastille Day. By this time in the war, booze was scarce. Nevertheless, there was plenty in the ditches that day, and their little band struck up the "Marseillaise." Little French flags popped up along the red dirt ramparts.

Two days earlier, Hood telegraphed Bragg requesting the transfer of General Quarles' two Louisiana regiments to General Gibson. (28) On July 17th, the 4th LA officially became part of Randall Lee Gibson's Louisiana Brigade in Clayton's Division of Hood's Corps. This created dissatisfaction within the 4th LA, but all Louisiana troops in the Army of Tennessee were put under General Gibson's command. (29) The 4th LA and the 30th LA had been with Quarles' Tennessee regiments for so long they had made many friends in their ranks. Officers and privates drew up a petition and asked officials in

Richmond to cancel the transfer. The real reason for objection to this transfer was probably General Hood's reputation. That day it rained.

On July 18th, Joe Johnston was relieved of command and replaced with the one-legged General John Bell Hood. The unprepossessing Hood was from Kentucky, and after graduating from West Point in 1853, he served in California and Texas. He had fought in many battles in the Army of Northern Virginia. A severe wound at Gettysburg left him with a gimpy arm, and after Chickamauga, he ended up with a cork leg. His wounds left him with chronic pain and with an opium habit. He became a Lieutenant General in early 1864, and commanded a corps under General Joe Johnston. He was thirty-three years old when he took over the Army of Tennessee. (30) Hood's old corps was now commanded by Major General Cheatham. He would be replaced nine days later by Lieutenant General Stephen Lee. Cheatham would later command Hardee's Corps.

News of Johnson's dismissal shocked the Army of Tennessee. The troops mulled around in small groups, grumbling about the loss of their leader. For the first time, men started openly talking about going home. Some deserted. Their anger slowly passed. By now, the men in the ranks were bonded more to each other than to their generals.

The three corps commanders of the Army of Tennessee were now Hardee, A. P. Stewart (Polk's old corps, the Army of Mississippi), and Cheatham (Hood's old corps). On July 20th, Sherman was crossing the Chattahoochee. Hood intended to strike him during this move. The attack was delivered at Peach Tree Creek, but due to Hood's tardiness, the Union troops had plenty of time to throw up breastworks. Hardee's Corps attacked the Yankees. He called for reinforcements and Gibson's Louisiana Brigade (with the 4th LA and the Tirailleurs) was sent forward from the Atlanta breastworks. They came into action at dusk. "We were outside the works to protect Stewart's right flank in his attack on the enemy that day." (31) The men were pushed forward, and as they came into enemy artillery range, the order came to fall back. Several men were hurt, even though the 4th LA never saw the enemy. The Tirailleurs again fell back to the ditches around Atlanta. The Army of Tennessee could only hope that this was not "the last ditch."

July 22nd, the Battle of Atlanta (Battle of Bald Hill) was fought to the right of the 4th LA. Hardee's Corps made a night march around Sherman's left flank, separating himself from the rest of the army. The idea was to catch Union General McPherson's corps by surprise and attack him from front and rear. At 4 P.M., Clayton's Division of Cheatham's Corps, with Gibson's Brigade and the 4th LA, crossed their works and advanced north of and parallel to the Decatur Wagon Road (present-day DeKalb Avenue).

Samuel Lambert described what happened next: "At four o'clock, P.M., our brigade and corps crossed our works, moved some half-mile to the right, and near the Augusta Rail Road, and advanced through an open field to attack the enemy. Our Division (Clayton's) was divided into three lines, Stovall's brigade forming the first, Baker's the second, and Gibson's the last. In this order, the enemy's works were reached by the foremost line, the third following some 200 yards in the rear, and the enemy forced from his position. Troops, however, giving way on our right, we were ordered back to our defenses." (32)

Clayton's brigades became separated and the attempt to attack Bald Hill from the North petered out. Private Christophe Hebert was injured in the foot by shrapnel. The regiment was ordered back into their works inside the Atlanta defenses. (33) Hardee's Corps inflicted some losses, but to no real gain. Union General McPherson was killed. Two thousand Union prisoners and eight guns were captured.

Sunday, July 24th was unseasonably cold. The men had on their coats and were huddled around breakfast fires. That Sunday, Private Robert Patrick, Hunter Rifles A, wrote in his diary: "This morning I passed the grave of a Yankee who died yesterday, and I just thought to myself, now, old fellow, you have traveled a long ways to secure a very small spot of earth. When you might have purchased 10,000 times as much nearer home and much cheaper than you got this. You were not satisfied to remain at home and let us alone; you must come to the South to murder our citizens, burn our houses, desolate our homes and lay waste to our country; to make war on women and children, turning them out to die of cold and want without the slightest compunction of conscience. You for one have met your just reward, which is a grant of land from the Confederates of three feet by six feet." (34) The next four days were quiet, except for the activity of Federal siege artillery.

Sherman's maneuvering north of Atlanta had led part of his army to Ezra Church, a few miles west of Atlanta. Lieutenant General Stephen D. Lee took command of Hood's old corps on July 27, 1864. He was greedy for glory. The thirty-year-old prodigy was the youngest lieutenant general in the Confederacy. An 1854 graduate of West Point, he joined General Beauregard's staff as an artillerist. He took command of Pemberton's artillery at Vicksburg and was captured there and paroled. Subsequently, he became commander of cavalry in the West. Later, he presided over the debacle of the Battle of Harrisburg before taking command of Hood's old corps. (35) It only took him one day as a corps commander to screw up again.

Lee had been instructed by Hood to hold the Lick Skillet Road west of Atlanta against any Union advances. Union General Howard and S. D. Lee's troops came into contact on July 28th. The impetuous Lee decided to attack

Union General Howard. He assumed Howard was on the move, when in fact he was entrenched.

Order of Battle, Ezra Church (The Battle of the Poor House)
    Army of the Tennessee, Lieutenant General J. B. Hood
        Corps, Lieutenant General Stephen D. Lee
            Division, Major General Henry D. Clayton
                Brigade, Brigadier General Randall L. Gibson
                    4th LA, Colonel Samuel Eugene Hunter
                    30th LA, Major Arthur Picolet
                    13th LA, Lieutenant Colonel Francis L. Campbell
                    16th LA, Lieutenant Colonel Robert H. Lindsay
                    19th LA, Major Camp Flournoy
                    20th LA, Captain Alexander Dresel
                    25th LA, Colonel Francis C. Zacharie
                    4th LA Battalion, Captain T. A. Bisland
                    14th LA Battalion Sharpshooters, Lieutenant A. T. Martin

    This order of battle remained as such for the remainder of the war.
    French language chatter rose from the Tirailleurs. They joked and laughed, walking along with their shirts off. The Acadians had left the breastworks and were snailing lazily toward the picket line. A rider approached. They were suddenly ordered into line and told to advance. They were totally unaware that they were about to enter into a big battle. "On the 28th, we marched through town and arrived on the Lick Skillet Road (present-day Gordon Road) near the 'Poor House,' four and one half miles southwest of Atlanta." (36)
    The brigades were kept close together. They then marched out on the road toward the enemy's position (the present-day name of this road is Martin Luther King Jr. Drive). The Tirailleurs were posted among the scrub oak and pines that skirted the north side of the road. The general advance had a crunchy, metallic sound: canteens clinking against metal, hammers cocking, and sabers rattling. They made their way through 500 yards of thick woods "when we came upon the enemy in heavy force. We halted and began to fire for half an hour." (37)
    "The thick undergrowth through which we were forced to pass afforded enemy sharpshooters an excellent opportunity of concealing themselves, pouring a galling fire into our crowded line." (38) The Tirailleurs on the left of the 4th LA line looked across a road to a gentle slope. The menacing crest of the rise was filled with Union troops protected behind fence rails and church pews. At noon, the Rebel line was marched up and ordered to attack. The Tirailleurs

advanced in front of a storm of fire with no cover. Theodore Martin fell wounded. The men lay down and began returning fire. "Thump.... Thump.... Thump...." bullets hit the ground in front of the Tirailleurs as powder smoke filled the battle lines.

No one could withstand the fire for long in the open. The men continued returning fire, but slowly drifted back into the cover of the trees. Prudent Crochet was reloading when a ball smashed into his left eye, passed through his brain, and exploded out of the back of his skull. Ten feet away, T. C. White was hit in the left arm and spun around by the force of the blow. His arm hung limp. The bullet had passed through his arm and ripped his axillary vein and artery. He dragged himself rearward, leaving a trail of blood in the pine needles in his path. He quickly bled to death. The Mexican War veteran died fighting against an army for which he once fought. All around, bodies lay in scarlet puddles as the sounds of death echoed through the scrub oaks.

Alcide Landry the elder was injured by a ball in the left foot. He had been lying on the ground, firing into the Union line. The Yankee ball first hit the ground, then ricocheted into Private Landry's bare foot, fracturing a bone.

The Rebel line slowly drifted deeper into cover, continuing to return fire. Until this time, all injuries were from rifle fire. The Tirailleurs then came under an enfilade fire by a battery of Federal Parrott rifles. A shell exploded in the trees, sending shards of iron and large splinters of pine into the men. One ten-pound shell whistled through, cracking tree branches, and spun off its brass sabot. This three-inch circle of death ricocheted off the side of Private Arthur Blanchard's skull, taking a full thickness of skin and hair and leaving a fully-exposed depressed skull fracture. He was standing next to Edward Longuepee when he slumped to the ground. The Tirailleurs had had enough and began dragging their wounded to the rear.

Prudent Daigle held a rag over his bleeding scalp. Corporal John Renaud held his bleeding left side as he strained to leave the field. Bibe Hebert was hanging on to Louis Kirkland, holding his wounded flank. In this brief clash with the Federals, the Tirailleurs were shot up even quicker than at Shiloh.

Diogene Isaac's shoulders struggled with the weight of his wounded brother. With each rearward step, Leon groaned. Diogene fell in with the stream of wounded as his brother's groans ceased. He found Dr. Craig and gently lay Leon on the ground. "Sorry soldier, but this man is dead." The words stabbed like a bayonet to his heart. Diogene dropped to his knees, sobbing and clutching his limp brother's dead body.

This contest lasted less than an hour. The battle line was thoroughly used up and slowly retired. General Gibson wrote later, "Striking an overwhelming force in a position splendidly adapted for defense and difficult to assault, the brigade fought with much energy and obstinacy, but failed to dislodge the enemy. The 4th LA moved back 400 yards to the crest of a hill." (39) Two thirds of the brigade's left wing were used up completely. The 30th LA had been ground up like sugar cane, losing three-fourths of their strength among the killed and wounded. Lieutenant Colonel Thomas Shields and Major C. J. Bell of the 30th LA were killed. Father Turgis was busy administering last rites and aiding the wounded. At Gibson's behest, Clayton sent in Baker's Brigade.

John Doyle of Hunter Rifles B wrote home, "We were ordered back under a perfect storm of lead. We fell back about 200 yards and joined the reserves (Baker's Brigade). These men were ordered forward and could only stand the withering fire of the enemy for but a few minutes, when they came rushing back in great confusion, not even halting at our line. That was a desperate little fight. The enemy, having been three or four times our number, besides having the advantage of position, they being behind logs and rail piles (sic)." (40) John Doyle was killed five days after writing this account.

Prudent Crochet and T. C. White were left on the field. The intensity of the battle had moved to the left as the wounded began streaming to the rear. Surgeons J. M. Craig and Charles D. Lewis were overwhelmed by the sudden deluge of wounded. The unconscious Private Blanchard was placed gently on a soft carpet of pine needles. Hospital steward Joe Whitehead removed the bloody rag from his wound. Flies covered the wound as it was redressed.

"*In nomine Patris, et Filii, et Spritus Sancti. Amen,*" ended Father Turgis' prayer over a shallow grave. The Tirailleurs buried Leon Isaac near the Poor House. Father Turgis had been wounded himself in the battle. His head was wrapped in a bloody bandage. (41)

One of the wounded was Samuel Lambert. He was helped to the rear by Major Pullen, who was also wounded. He wrote, "After reaching the road a few hundred yards in the rear...the road was lined with wounded and bleeding soldiers. Some had lost an arm, another a leg, an eye, a finger, or been wounded in the body. Beneath the shade of every tree, our surgeons were at work. With coats off and sleeves rolled up, they were passing from soldier to soldier, extracting a ball, amputating a limb, or dressing a wound." A temporary hospital was established.

S. D. Lee got a message from Hood, to "hold the enemy, but not to do more fighting then necessary, unless you should get a decided advantage." For the Confederates, the battle was over. (42) Union losses were 632 killed, wounded, and missing. Gibson's Brigade of Louisianans had 150 casualties. Of two hundred and forty men present for duty in the 4th LA, eighty-two were casualties. (43) John I. Kendall claimed that Gibson entered the battle with 900 men and lost 540. (44) Total Confederate loses came to 3,000. Lieutenant William Jeter,

Delta Rifles, had been captured at Port Hudson. He was on his way under guard to a Union prison camp in Florida when his group of Confederate officers overpowered their guard and escaped. Jeter was killed at Ezra Church.

Surgeon's report of July 28, 1864 listed:
A. Hebert, wounded right side
Arthur Blanchard, head wound
L. Isaac, killed
Prudent Crochet, killed
T. C. White, killed
John Renaud, wounded left side
P. Daigle, severe head wound (sent to hospital in Forsythe, GA)
Alcide Landry (the elder), left foot severe
P. Martin, wounded (45)

The men of the Tirailleurs blamed Hood for the slaughter. The true culprit was Stephen D. Lee. Disregarding Hood's instructions, he attempted to crush Sherman's right flank with piecemeal attacks that stood no chance of success. This was the same conduct that Lee had demonstrated at the disaster of the Battle of Harrisburg two weeks earlier. Lee's attack should not have been made. This battle swept away any trace of confidence in General Hood. Hardee was sent to evaluate the scene, and afterwards declared, "No action of the campaign probably did so much to demoralize and dishearten the troops engaged in it." (46)

Samuel Lambert was treated for his leg wound in the rear and late that night was put into a wagon, along with Arthur Blanchard. The teamster cracked his whip and the mules started forward with a jolt. They made it to Atlanta by morning. Arthur Blanchard was transferred to a hospital in Forsythe, Georgia. Sergeant Lambert spent a week in the hospital and then went to a private home near Macon, Georgia. He developed gangrene in his leg. After his wound doubled in size, he underwent the pain of having it burnt with a piece of red hot iron. Doctors ended up saving his leg.

Captain Landry felt ashamed at the thought that he had left his friend, Prudent Crochet, on the field at Ezra Church. The Captain's thoughts of Prudent caused a feeling of heaviness in his stomach that dropped as if it had weight. He thought of what he would say to Prudent's wife, Adolphine. How would she cope with her two small children and now her husband killed, buried somewhere in the red Georgia clay? The next spring, his shallow grave would be marked only by a patch of dark green grass.

Trasimond couldn't know, but Arthur Blanchard, another friend, would also die. He passed in the hospital at Forsythe, Georgia, August 24, 1864. Unlike Private Crochet, Jean Baptiste Arthur Blanchard had no parents, wife, or children to grieve for him. He was a true hero to the Cause and died bravely. Two generations later, not even a family expert would have any memory of the glory Arthur Blanchard won for his family's name.

After Ezra Church, the regiment fell back to the Sandtown Road, east of Utoy Creek, eight miles from Atlanta. Sandtown Road (present-day Cascade Road) separated Gibson's Brigade from the 2nd Brigade Georgia Militia. The Acadians stayed in these breastworks from July 29th until August 30th. On Sunday, July 31st, all was quiet. Church services were held all along the front, and many soldiers were baptized that day. A spiritual awakening was taking hold of the Southern soldier.

On August 5th, the National Guards and the Packwood Rifles were captured while on picket duty. They were sent to man unfinished redoubts on the skirmish line. Men from the 16th and 25th LA were to their left. Yankees from Union General Reilly's Brigade had crept up through their abatis during the night and attacked around 10 A.M. Troops to the left of the 4th LA gave way and the Yankees got in the rear of the 4th, 16th, and 25th LA.

In this unnamed battle, a total of twenty-four men of the 4th LA were lost in hand-to-hand combat. Captain Packwood was wounded and captured. He was sent to Johnson's Island prison camp for the remainder of the war. Part of the drama of this scrimmage was the fact that it took place in the plain view of the regiment and there was nothing they could do to help. That same day, to the left of the 4th LA, the drama of an artillery duel unfolded. The Washington Artillery silenced a Yankee battery.

The National Guards were left with five men on its rolls. Fifty-men remained in the National Guards, Delta Rifles, and Packwood Rifles. These three companies were consolidated into one company under Captain David Devall. (47) The company of Delta Rifles had become so small that Dr. Leveque resigned. He accompanied his ill brother, Daniel, to Iberville Parish. He later became Major Leveque, surgeon of the 8th LA Cavalry. By the end of August, the entire 4th LA could field only 144 men.

The Battle of Utoy Creek was fought on August 6th. Sherman's goal was to put pressure on Hood's southern flank and gain control of railroads below Atlanta. During the battle, the 4th LA manned their ditches, holding the Confederate right flank. The main force of this Union attack came at the Rebel's exposed left flank, and fierce fighting occurred there. On August 7th, Hood gave up his salient and pulled back to prepared positions. (48) Thomas Jefferson Sparkman, Hunter Rifles A, was killed in the Battle of Utoy Creek.

On the Sandtown Road, the men were exposed to Union artillery fire and were confined to the ditches. Artillery firing was continuous. The men dug traverses for protection and burrowed into the red clay. On August 7th, a shell exploded in the trenches. Sixteen men of the West Feliciana Rifles were hit: two were killed outright, four died later, two had leg amputations, and ten others were wounded. This was a testament to the devastating potential of an exploding twenty-pound Parrott shell. Another shell killed seven men in the Lafourche Guards. (49) Trasimond's birthday passed without him even realizing it.

Every morning, the men were awaked by the crowing of roosters. Cockfighting had become very popular in the Army of Tennessee and many Rebs kept roosters. Atlanta was a great place to fight chickens, and it became a Tirailleur pastime.

On August 15th, the Tirailleurs attended Mass on the Feast Day of the Assumption at the Immaculate Conception Church in Atlanta. They walked the eight miles into the center of Atlanta. Mass was said by Father Thomas O'Reilly and the men all took Communion. The church was cool and dark. Occasionally, a shell from Sherman's siege guns would land nearby. The vibrations would send down fine showers of plaster dust from the vaulted ceiling. Sunlight shining through the stained glass windows highlighted bars of dust that stood out like swords. The next Sunday was spent in the trenches.

The routine in the ditches at this time had the Tirailleurs in a camp near Atlanta. The men went on duty in the trenches every three days. They marched twelve miles from camp to the works. These dusty rifle pits, which held four to eight men, were connected with trenches and low earthworks. These trenches stretched over low hills for miles and were fronted by abatis. Sharpshooting and sniping were the main activities. S. D. Lee could not hold his line of videttes against the enemy, which was putting pressure on his picket line. This failure put combatants within rifle range of each other. (50)

On August 16th, the Tirailleurs were in rifle pits on picket. There was a new moon. The only lights were from the starry sky and red flashes from Yankee cannon. The open ground in front of their abatis was as black as an Egyptian plague. Lieutenant Daigle and Captain Landry were talking in low tones and swatting mosquitoes. The cannon firing became desultory, and then stopped. Yankees fired off a signal rocket, interrupting the night's opaqueness. There was only a quiet breeze from the west, cooling the gray faces that stared into the darkness.

Tu sent ail? (Do you smell garlic?) asked Louis. All at once, a silhouette rose in front of Captain Landry. His first thought was that a Rebel was making his way back to Confederate lines. Trasimond reached out over the headlog and grabbed him forcefully by the coat, throwing him into the rifle pit. The black figure hit his head on a rock and Landry realized he was a Yankee.

Attaque!! (Trench Raid!!) Louis Daigle fired his rifle into another Yankee climbing into the rifle pit. Alcide, startled awake by the commotion, reached for his Bowie knife. He looked up to see a Yankee lieutenant with his saber blade crashing toward his head. He raised his arm to protect himself, his knife deflecting the saber stroke into the dirt. The Yankee officer, aimed a pistol in his left hand at the young Rebel private. Alcide swung the Bowie knife and crushed the Yankee's left hand. He then pulled back the knife and plunged it into the Yankee's belly. The knife stuck into the Federal's vertebra, and he slumped forward, dead. The alarm spread. In the darkness, none dared to shoot, as blue and gray grappled in a vicious hand-to-hand contest. Suddenly, it was over. The Yankees backed off, scurrying like startled cockroaches through the abatis and back into the night.

Alcide stood panting and pale. Sweat poured into his eyes. This was his birthday. He was nineteen years old, and still alive. Trasimond could hear a mushing thud, like a deer stomping on a watermelon. Louis Daigle was smashing his rifle butt into a Yankee corporal's skull. The next morning there were three dead Yankees in the pit and one on the ground in front. It took two people to pull Alcide's knife out of the Yankee lieutenant's spine. Alcide had "met the elephant." He was no longer a new recruit. From then on, he was a Tirailleur.

That morning, for the longest time, Alcide stared at the Union officer's dead face. He wondered why this poor dead Yankee would want to kill him. This thought hung up in Alcide's brain. He felt saddened and guilty over the man's death. There was a hollow feeling in his gut, an emptiness that filled him. He reached down and pulled the dead lieutenant's forage cap over his eyes. With the stiff Yankee's face hidden, he thought, "*Meilleur vous que moi.*" (Better you than me.)

Alcide kept the officer's sword. He later traded it for a gallon of molasses. The men found $75 in greenback currency as they stripped the Yankees of valuables. That night, they dragged the swollen bodies back behind their pits, out of their range of scent, and threw dirt over them.

The blundering Hood sent 6,000 Rebel cavalrymen off into East Tennessee with General Joe Wheeler. What the cavalry was doing, no one really cared, but with no cavalry, Hood's left flank south of Atlanta was soft. Sherman sent cavalry Colonel Kilpatrick on a raid to destroy the Atlanta to Macon railroad on August 18th. Kilpatrick's force did little damage and was almost captured by the Confederates. The 4th LA was moved rapidly to the far left of the Rebel lines during all this commotion.

As Sherman moved off from the Atlanta front, Hood needed information on Federal movements. With no cavalry, volunteers were called for to form fifteen to twenty-man "reconnoiter" squads. (51)

Major Pullen asked for scout volunteers. Twenty men from the Tirailleurs and the Lafourche Guards traveled down the Atlanta to Macon railroad to just above Rough and Ready. It was dawn when they marched off westward to make contact with the Federals. Pullen spread the men out twenty yards apart and they picked their way through the woods and briars for several miles. As they moved closer to where they thought the Yankees would be, their movement slowed. The men went from tree to tree, trying to keep their skirmish line straight. A noisy Georgia rabbit rustled the dry brush in front of Captain Landry and sent a burst of adrenalin into his gut. Louis Daigle stopped. He could smell Yankees. A rifle shot cracked in the dry Georgia air. Then another, and another. The Rebels returned the fire, aiming at the white puffs of smoke in front of them. Rifle balls zipped through the branches and peeled bark off the tree trunks. No one was injured, and nothing was gained. Major Pullen withdrew the men.

By now, Second Lieutenant Louis Daigle was a master sharpshooter. Louis had been a skilled hunter prior to the war. He would sit in front of a loophole in the entrenchments for hours, watching and waiting. He had gotten good use from his Yankee Enfield rifle, with its telescopic sight. His younger brother, Isidore, was his spotter. Few men in the Tirailleurs thought much of the honor involved in sniping, but all had respect for Louis' abilities. Louis was five feet eight inches tall. He had black hair and green, piercing eyes. When he was stalking a Yankee sniper his composure became intense. To look at him, you would never know he had a college education and could read and write in Greek and Latin. Louis had five sniper kills during the activity around Atlanta. After a hit, Louis would try to pick off the Yankee stretcher bearers. Occasionally, a Yankee would be seen answering a call of nature and Louis would pick him off. Louis relished these shots. His nickname was "*Veuve Faiseur*" (Widow Maker). He was a natural killer.

In late August, news of Arthur Blanchard's death was sorrowfully received. The word was delivered by Father Turgis. He had been at Arthur's bedside when he died. The news left the captain with a deep, incomprehensible melancholy that bored into his soul. The two had grown up together. He remembered Arthur's father, the old, crusty Zephirin Blanchard, and had fond memories of Arthur's mother, Eliza. Anatole Blanchard was Arthur's twin brother. He remembered the hurt and pain Arthur had gone through when his brother died, at age fourteen. It was the first funeral Trasimond had ever attended where he cried. Arthur was there at St. John the Baptist cemetery after the death of Trasimond's mother, Marie Carmelite, and they both cried. Their tears were mixed again two years later, when Eliza died.

Other than the war, Arthur Blanchard had no history. He went from youth and college to soldiering. Like Captain Landry and most of the Tirailleurs, he had taken no root. For the older soldiers, the war was an interruption. They had wives and children and a life. For Arthur Blanchard, life had taken no form. War had become life for Arthur and his contemporaries, and beyond the war, life did not extend. Now that tenuous hold on life was lost. Trasimond Landry felt the weakness of this hold.

Diogene Isaac had been despondent since his brother's death. He mistakenly blamed Colonel Hunter. He transferred at the first opportunity to Alcide Bouanchaud's Battery (Company A, Pointe Coupee Artillery Battalion).

The men missed Sergeant White. They knew him well. They knew him to be a good citizen, an excellent father, and a soldier who brought honor to the Southern armies.

The Yankees broke contact with the Confederates August 26th and started a general flanking movement to their right (south). The next five days were peace and quiet for the Tirailleurs. In the field between picket lines, little Negro boys were busy picking up spent lead balls fired by pickets during the siege. In one field, the little Negroes picked up 5,000 pounds of lead balls to sell to the Confederate Ordinance Department. (52)

KENNESAW MOUNTAIN AREA

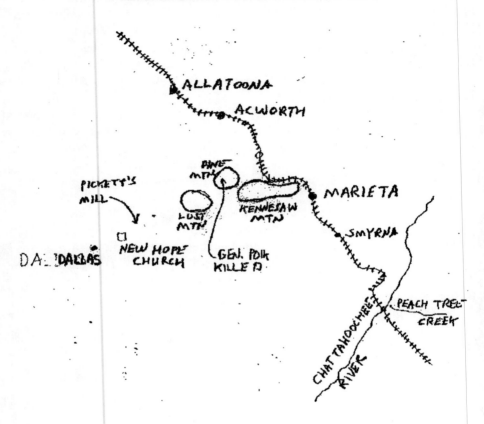

9.

Jonesboro

On August 30th, Hardee's Corps was sent to Jonesboro, Georgia, in an effort to keep the Federals from cutting the Macon to Atlanta rail line. They were faced by Union General Howard. Howard didn't feel strong enough to attack, but was hoping that the Rebels would attack his strong position.

On August 31st, the Tirailleurs of the 4th LA regiment of S. D. Lee's Corps were rushed from Atlanta in the early morning to assist Hardee. At 1:30 P.M., the last of S. D. Lee's units reached Jonesboro. His troops had had little sleep for two nights. They had marched fifteen miles over rough roads, and many were shoeless, with swollen, bleeding feet. All were exhausted and hungry. Of S. D. Lee's Corps, hundreds had dropped out along the way, unable to keep going. Never had there been so much straggling. Half of the remaining Tirailleurs dropped out from exhaustion on the march.

The amount of time required to produce combat exhaustion varies. It depends on the intensity of combat and the duration of exposure. It takes several weeks of combat for the soldier to become "battle wise." Then comes a variable period of combat efficiency. After thirty or forty days of continuous combat, a period of exhaustion sets in. This is heralded by a short period of overconfidence. Then comes a stage of over-reaction and over-caution, followed by emotional exhaustion, and then a vegetative state. (1)

The Army of Tennessee had not been in continuous combat as, for example, a World War II soldier in the Bocage area of Normandy would later be, but the Tirailleurs had been at it off and on for almost ninety-eight days straight. Hardee's, Stewart's, and most of S. D. Lee's Corps had been at it since November and before. The surprise is that this barefooted, half-starved, and poorly-led army could perform as well as it did by the time they formed up on the battlefield at Jonesboro. Sam Watkins, 1st TN wrote: "(The soldiers) were broken down with their long day's hard marching—were almost dead with hunger and fatigue......Each one prayed that all this foolishness might end one way or the other. It was too much for human endurance." (2)

Hardee planned to attack the entrenched Federals. The old guard of West Point-trained officers could not give up the idea of the bayonet charge. In the Mexican War, this tactic worked, but in that war the charging bayonets faced defenders with smooth bore muskets. These muskets were only accurate for short distances and only effective when massed. These West Point generals and Mexican War veterans failed to account for the rifled musket. These weapons were accurate at up to 400 yards. Bayonet wielding attackers could be wiped out long before reaching enemy ramparts. Braxton Bragg's faith in the bayonet had sent many men to an early grave at Shiloh.

Hardee's front extended about one and a half miles. Lee's Corps composed the north wing, or right flank, of the battle line. According to the Army of Tennessee's official returns for August 31st, Hardee's and Lee's Corps totaled close to 26,000 men "present for duty." Because of straggling, no more than 20,000 of them were in the line that afternoon. S. D. Lee, when he heard the sound of battle on the left, would join in the assault, with the object of shattering the Union left flank. Lee formed the corps into two lines of battle. The Tirailleurs, with the 4th LA, were in the first line.

Captain Landry sent Lieutenant Daigle to see if there were any Tennessee regiments in their rear. The Tirailleurs had been in eleven frontal assaults. Each time, Captain Landry never imagined himself being killed. He always saw himself after the battle helping to bury the dead. For some strange, icy reason, he felt differently this time, as if some *gris-gris* or *conjo* ruled him. He prayed. He wondered if God was getting weary hearing his pleas for life. He wondered if God listened at all. He wrote his name on a small piece of paper and pinned it to his shirt. Sweating, scared, and hungry, the Tirailleurs waited to be killed.

Lieutenant General William Hardee, prior to the war, had written the book on infantry tactics. He was well aware of the concept that any force attacking defensive works should be three times the size of the defenders. The Yankee commander, Howard, had available a force that was at least equal in size to Hardee's and was strongly-fortified, well-fed, rested, and confident. At 3 P.M., Hardee's artillery opened fire, and after ten minutes or so, Cleburne's skirmishers started forward on the left. Lee, displaying the same impetuosity that he revealed at Harrisburg and Ezra Church, mistook their fire for the beginning of Cleburne's assault. At once, he commanded his corps to charge. (3)

The advance was across open country, with the 4th LA getting the worst of it. The Tirailleurs were on the right of the brigade advance and were exposed to enemy firing from the front and enfilade fire from the right. The red clay fortifications facing the 4th LA were jutted out from the main line of breastworks.

The Yankee line was marked with hundreds of puffs of smoke. Federal rifle pits were fifty feet in front of their works. One member of the St. Helena Rifles remembered the order, "Forward, double quick, march!" and described a mad rush and yell across 300 yards to the rifle pits. The St. Helena Rifles had twenty-one men in that charge. Nineteen were killed or wounded. That day, the St. Helena Rifles ceased to exist. (4) This was one charge that Colonel Hunter led.

The 104 men left in the 4th LA would be decimated. The Tirailleurs boldly advanced on the right of the brigade. The line advanced briskly and in good order, driving the Federal pickets from their rail barricades. Private Auguste Longuepee died for his country, shot through the chest.

The Acadians chased Yankees from their rifle pits and leaping the pits ran into a galling fire. Smoke was everywhere. Rifle balls clipped through Trasimond's ragged trousers. Joinville Doiron was wounded. Alphonse Aillet lay dead. Missiles vibrated around their heads like swarming bees. Captain Landry turned. The rifle pits welcomed him. He grasped them with his eyes. With a noiseless leap he was sucked into the temporary safety of the earth. The rest of the Tirailleurs dove into the abandoned Yankee rifle pits with what was left of the 4th LA. Sergeant Theodore Doiron lay there, holding a bleeding left hand. A ball had passed through it. Pinned down, cut up, and unable to return fire, Colonel Hunter ordered the colors raised, and the Tirailleurs passed back across the battlefield. (5)

Battle inertia gripped the second line of attack. Generals and officers desperately endeavored to rally their men for another charge, but they would not budge. Union troops continued to pour on fire. It was less a battle than an execution. Military theorists have described a concept known as "the well of courage." You can only make so many trips to the well before it runs dry. Meanwhile, Cleburne's attack got underway and almost immediately degenerated into chaos. No new attack took place.

Hardee's attempt to fling the Yankees back across the Flint River had failed. This was the end of the Tirailleurs' share of the fighting at Jonesboro. Union casualties came to 172. Hardee's total casualties were 2,000, of whom about 1,400 were of Lee's Corps. Hood, in his memoirs, and Lee, in his report, characterized the Confederate attack as "feeble." This was a terrible memorial to brave troops squandered by "feeble" leadership. The men were physically unfit for the heroic exertion demanded of them. In spite of everything against them, the men of the 4th LA did their duty.

Gibson's Louisianans suffered fifty percent casualties. (6) The Tirailleurs went into the fight with twelve men and lost five—two killed and three wounded. In the 4th LA, of one hundred and four men present, sixty-seven men were lost. (7) The regiment lost twenty-three killed, thirty-five wounded, and seventeen missing. Those wounded and left on the field were taken off by the Yankees. Those taken off by the Rebels were captured the next day when General Hardee abandoned Jonesboro. Only five wounded men were saved from capture. Captain Feister of Hunter Rifles A was shot in the neck and left on the field at Jonesboro. He died six weeks later in a Federal field hospital. Also, the wounded Private Joinville Doiron was left on the field and captured. The last of the battles around Atlanta was over.

Hardee's Corps was left at Jonesboro to face an even larger Union force the next day. Outnumbered six to one, Hardee's men fought the Union troops to a standstill on the 1st of September. This saved Hood's Army, which was then evacuating Atlanta. S. D. Lee's Corps left Jonesboro at 1 A.M., September 1st. Stomachs ached for food and tongues were cracked as the Tirailleurs made a night march back to the outskirts of Atlanta. They were then ordered to fall back, along with Stewart's Corps, to Lovejoy Station, forty miles south of Atlanta. The Tirailleurs had raced to Jonesboro at breakneck speed, engaged the enemy in a ferocious losing battle, and then raced back to Atlanta. They had not slept or eaten in two days when they were told to head south again to Lovejoy Station, thirty miles away. This required marching south in a wide arc to avoid Sherman's army at Jonesboro. Along the road was the litter of a retreating army: broken-down wagons, abandoned artillery ammunition, knapsacks, bayonets. On the march south, Gibson's Brigade protected the rear of S. D. Lee's Corps.

On September 2nd, Hardee's Corps was alone at Lovejoy Station, fending off most of Sherman's army. Stewart's fresh corps passed S. D. Lee's Corps on the road at Rough and Ready, and made it to Lovejoy Station September 3rd. Lee's ragged corps arrived near Lovejoy Station on September 5th. Hood collected his three corps and entrenched.

Regimental surgeon J. M. Craig wrote in his diary this itinerary:

Sept. 1st, 1864.—Left the bloody field at Jonesboro, under a severe shelling from the enemy. Marched back to within 7 miles of Atlanta, 14 miles.

Sept. 2nd, 1864.—Left camp at daylight, marched all day, 15 miles.

Sept. 3rd, 1864.—Rained. Marched all day, halted at McDonough at dark, 14 miles.

Sept, 4th, 1864.—Left McDonough at sunrise and marched to Mt. Carmel Church, 5 miles.

Sept. 6th, 1864.—Moved into a good camp at Steven's Mill, 2 miles, remained here until the 17th. (8)

With the arrival of stragglers, by September 5th there were eighty men in the 4th LA. The once-splendid 4th LA regiment that had paraded in their handsome uniforms and fine regimental band at Corinth was now reduced to the size of a small company. It was spring when the regiment came up to Georgia. Everything was fresh and green. Now it was autumn, and things would soon turn brown and die.

Starving, bone tired, shoeless, and out of heart, the Tirailleurs took their positions in the breastworks at Steven's Mill near the railroad to Macon, forty miles below Atlanta. The water had a bad smell.

Orion, the hunter, and his dog were making their appearance in the night sky. Sherman was also the hunter and pressed in on Hood. The two armies faced each other until September 6th, with continuous skirmishing and sniping. Suddenly Sherman withdrew back to Atlanta to start his march to the sea. Sherman boasted that he would "make Georgia howl!"

Sherman sent a message to Hood regarding the civilians in Atlanta. He was ordering them all to leave the city. This created 18,000 refugees, who mostly headed south. It was a pitiful sight. The black nebula of Sherman's soul worked its evil on civilians and even his own men. Sherman also offered to exchange prisoners, provided he only received men who had two more years to serve in the Union army. Prisoners who had served out their period of enlistment or who had only a short time to serve would not be received. (9)

Jefferson Davis' move to fire Joe Johnston and replace him with Hood resulted in the devastation of the Army of Tennessee. Under Hood's command, the army had engaged in five great battles, endured a siege of one month, and seen Atlanta burned. Immense quantities of government stores were lost as well as over 20,000 battle-hardened Southern patriots. The loss of the rail center of Atlanta had a profound psychological impact on the South and its armies. It also did as much as anything in aiding the re-election of Abraham Lincoln.

S. D. Lee regarded the morale of the army greatly impaired after the fall of Atlanta. Combat exhaustion and Lee's blundering were large parts of the reason for the troops' low morale.

On September 17th, the Tirailleurs marched seven miles to Lovejoy Station. Captain Landry developed diarrhea and was burning up with fever. Alcide found an old, sore-back horse for his brother, who had been on foot. The next day was spent filling Trasimond's canteen and keeping him as dry as possible. Tenesmus, weakness, and fever made it hard for Trasimond to stay on horseback. Alcide walked alongside him to keep him from falling off. The Acadians then marched to Fayetteville, another eight miles.

Lieutenant Courtade called for Surgeon Craig to examine the captain. He ordered him to an ambulance and started treating him with paregoric. The next day they traveled in the rain to Palmetto, twelve miles down the road. They arrived in Petersburg, two miles further, and stayed there for nine days.

The weather was quite cool. On September 22nd there was a general exchange of prisoners during an arranged armistice. The 4th LA received eight men in the exchange. On September 25th, General Gibson sent Colonel Hunter to Mobile. His purpose was to get shoes for the men of the brigade. Hunter met with General Richard Taylor, who promised that 500 pairs would be shipped immediately.

The one week of rest at Petersburg probably saved Captain Landry's life. Weak and feverish, he was able to recover. They stayed at Petersburg from September 20th until September 29th. Trasimond was too weak to attend the parade in honor of the visiting Jefferson Davis. The weather was quite cool in Petersburg. He did not go to a hospital, and was nursed by his brother, Alcide. There was great fear of hospitals in the Southern army.

Simon Alcide found a kindly old Irish lady named Rayburn with a spare room. Dr. Craig visited twice a day. On June 23rd, Trasimond's fever raged. Alcide brewed a tea from red oak bark and fed it to his brother. Trasimond slept, but got no rest. During his illness his brain strained for quietness and calm. The incessant drone of cannon fire was gone, but he could still hear it. His mind brushed the cob webs off his memories and took him back to Brusly Landing. He could see himself perched on a kneeler next to his mother. He could barely peer over the pew in front of him as their Spanish priest, Father Paul Jordan, celebrated Mass. The words of the Latin Mass were strangely similar to his native French, but still unknown and mysterious. The church still had the smell of newness and the awe of hugeness. The Stations hung on the unplastered walls. His memories went forward to his First Communion. He could see his mother's proud smile. Suddenly a shaking rigor brought him back to Georgia.

Simon Alcide was unhappy about his brother's progress. He found a *traiteur* (healer) in the 30th LA. After his visit, the flux began improving rapidly. On June 25th, Captain Landry was cleaning his revolver. Simon Alcide knew he was recovering. Captain Landry sat on his bed, wiping down the revolver. He held the gun out at arm's length and looked down the barrel at the sight. He aimed the gun at a Georgia cockroach (*ravet*) scurrying across the plank floor. The Georgia roaches were puny. Cockroaches in Mobile were more respectable, but nowhere in his travels had he seen roaches to beat those from Brusly Landing for size.

Word arrived from home in a letter from Josephine. She was still grieving over the death of her daughter. Private Rivette was too ill to return to the army. The new priest, Father Theophile Blancgarin, was attacked by jayhawkers. He was beaten and had his horse stolen. A visiting priest, Father Gioacchino Manoritta, was on his way to administer the Last Sacrament to a dying parishioner and was shot by a Federal soldier.

Hardee and Hood had become like matter and antimatter. Hardee met with Jefferson Davis on his visit and made it clear that either he or Hood must go. Hardee was transferred to the Department of South Carolina. The 4th LA and the 30th LA were combined at Petersburg. Consolidation of regiments was frequently a demoralizing event. It was seen as a loss of identity and a devaluation of the glory the unit had achieved.

The 30th LA was not really a regiment, but had become a battalion after the Battle of Baton Rouge. The 4th LA and 30th LA had been brigaded together since 1862, and the men were not strangers to one another. The 30th LA began the war with over one hundred Acadians, and many were from Iberville Parish. There were ten Landrys in the 30th LA and other surnames such as Blanchard, Hebert, Rivet, Breaux, Martin, and Babin.

Their colonel, Gustavus Breaux, had resigned in early 1863. He returned to New Orleans and took the U.S. Oath of Allegiance on June 16, 1863. He was replaced by Lieutenant Colonel Thomas Shields and then by Major Arthur Picolet. Consolidation was welcomed by Father Turgis. He had as many parishioners in the 4th LA as he had in the 30th LA.

On September 30th, the Tirailleurs left camp after a sparse breakfast of bacon and cornbread. They marched from camp, near the Chattahoochee River, for fourteen miles to Dark Corner. They camped in the open on rocky ground. Trasimond was fully recovered from his diarrhea. By October 2nd, the remnants of the Army of Tennessee were within a dozen miles of Marietta, Georgia. Hood issued a circular stating that he intended to strike the railroad. The men would have to live on parched corn and beef without salt. Foraging parties were taking all the cattle and flour from farms along the route. On October 3rd, they marched until about noon (about eight miles), stopping at Lost Mountain. There were no bread rations. "We listened to cannonading in the direction of Marietta and commenced digging rifle pits." (10)

That night the mist was cold. Lost Mountain renewed memories of Arthur Blanchard, Prudent Crochet, Thomas White, and Leon Isaac. A tired melancholy flowed in Trasimond's blood. It brought a restlessness into his thoughts that slashed like a machete. He had led these men, and he felt a guilty mourning at their loss. The night's mist seemed to creep up out of the ground, releasing the souls of his lost comrades. His hands grew cold. He moved closer to the campfire.

On October 4th, it rained, miring up the roads. While Lee's and Cheatham's Corps were at Lost Mountain, Stewart's Corps was at Big Shanty tearing up the railroad. On October 5th, French's Division fought the Battle of Allatoona. The Tirailleurs left Lost Mountain on October 5th at 8 A.M., and made a twelve-mile mud march to Dallas in the rain.

Portalis Tullier was a small, undersized fellow. He was skilled in the art of profanity and all of its various branches. During this march he sunk into mud over his knees. "*Sacré fils de putain!*" (Holy son of a bitch) When he pulled himself out, both his shoes were sucked off, leaving him sockfooted. His face revealed a comically pained look, as if he had a *pet accrochet*. He entertained his comrades with a string of rude and profane remarks.

The men were without coats and winter clothing. What clothes they had were wet and covered in mud. Colonel Hunter arrived in camp. He had returned from his trip to Mobile and made the last fifty-five miles of the journey on foot.

On October 6th, it rained all day and flooded the roads. The harsh, cold rains soaked the men to the skin. The Tirailleurs camped that night in a Yankee graveyard after passing through the New Hope Church battlefield. Most of the trees had been killed by the bullets—even huge trees were cut down by artillery. Human bones were bleaching in the sun. Feral hogs in the Georgia piney woods had rooted up the bodies of some of the dead Yankees and vultures had picked their bones clean. October 7th was a beautiful day. The Tirailleurs were at Van Wert, about thirty miles from Rome, Georgia. The next day they marched into a cold north wind for eighteen miles toward Blue Mountain.

When the men awoke on October 9th, the ground was white and crunchy from a heavy frost. They were about twenty-five miles from Rome, Georgia, in a place called Cedartown. They left there at 9 A.M. and passed through Cave Springs. At this place a huge spring flowed out of the mountain and the soldiers filled their canteens. They camped two miles from the Coosa River. The next day, Trasimond washed his feet in the Coosa River. Hood's army flanked Rome and swung eastward toward the railroad, which it struck at Resaca on October 12th.

"All along the road near Rome the citizens had been robbed of everything. Bureaus broken, women's clothing torn to pieces, children left in rags, mirrors broken, books torn, featherbeds emptied in the road, stock driven off, and no effort left untried to distress families." (11) In camp there was only beef and bread to eat, and not much of that. Persimmons, chestnuts, and apples were plentiful, and were used to fill the Tirailleurs' ration sacks.

The 4th/30th LA was ordered away from the column to strike the station at Calhoun, Georgia, eight miles south of Dalton on the Western and Atlanta Railroad. (12) Men from Captain Devall's company were sent off to the south of the station to cut the telegraph wires. Captain Landry was sent north of Calhoun to seize a block-house guarding a trestle on the railroad. Meanwhile, the main body of troops surrounded Calhoun. The town was occupied by several companies of Federal cavalry and was well-stocked with large stores of arms and a well-supplied warehouse. (13)

The troops arrived outside Calhoun at 4 P.M. Colonel Hunter agreed to delay his attack on the station until he heard firing from the blockhouse attack. Captain Landry, with twenty men, marched up the track, taking care to remove anything that might tinkle or make racket. They found the blockhouse with no pickets. Their sally port was wide open and lanterns and a fire lit up the place. There were about thirty Negro troopers occupying the little fort.

Outnumbered, and with no artillery and very little time, Captain Landry decided on a daring plan. Half the men were stationed outside the blockhouse in view of the sally port. With reckless audacity, Captain Landry marched his men up to the blockhouse and through the sally port. With the men at attention and their arms shouldered, he asked to speak to the commanding officer.

A scruffy, intoxicated German NCO struggled to his feet. The captain announced, in his best English, that the blockhouse was completely surrounded by Confederates and Confederate artillery and invited him to surrender. The Negroes, with rifles stacked, raised their arms over their heads. The little German screamed at his men. Trasimond put his revolver to the Yankee's temple and he became quiet. The men leveled their arms and marched the Yankees out into the fresh air. The blockhouse was relieved of its abundant supplies. A wagon was called for and loaded down with hams, bread, tinned meats, coffee, and all sorts of luxuries the troops had not seen in months. Their eyes were already feasting on their plunder. The Tirailleurs burned the blockhouse, then marched off with their captives. Before leaving, Captain Landry had kegs of gunpowder placed under the trusses on the railroad bridge and lit a slow fuse.

The men could see the glare of the railroad depot burning and hurried back to the regiment. The town of Calhoun was also well-stocked with a generous supply of tents, foodstuffs, arms, and commissary stores. What the men could not carry with them was turned over to the townsfolk, and the rest was burned. Each soldier was loaded down to the limit with goodies. A few miles out from the station a huge explosion was heard from the direction of the railroad.

Captain C. R. Cornelius of the Hunter Rifles B wrote, "This was indeed a lucky day for the 4th. Tired and jaded as they were, the boys seemed to have regained new life and vigor at the sight of hams, bacon, crackers, cheese, etc., of which there was any quantity." (14)

Those Tirailleurs who were without shoes took them off the Negro soldiers. It is interesting to note that the Southern soldier would wear the shoes of the Negro troops, but they would not wear their caps or clothes. There was more than one instance of reports of Union officers finding their dead white troops naked on the battlefield with fully clothed but shoeless dead Negroes nearby.

On the 13th of October they caught up with the column near Resaca. The 4th/30th was now outfitted with warm Yankee coats and new blankets. On the 13th, they left camp at 8 A.M. and halted four miles ahead near Snake Creek Gap. Sherman sent troops from Rome toward Resaca. Hood's army then moved to avoid a confrontation. A large Union force dogged Hood after he left Dalton. The next day they marched to Snake Creek Gap and rested until sunset. Then they resumed the march, moving near the mouth of the gap, and camped. The enemy moved with a large force to the gap, and on the 15th several severe skirmishes took place.

The next day they debouched from the gap at sunrise and marched fifteen miles. The regiment made three miles the next day. The tired faces of the Tirailleurs filed past Pigeon Mountain. The scenery was beautiful, but the Acadians were too weary to appreciate it. On October 17th they were on the road at 4 A.M., and marched until 3 P.M. The Acadians passed through Summerville after crossing the Chattooga River, eighteen miles. (15) The river was about twenty-five yards wide with a rocky bottom. There were some good farms on this river.

In Hood's zigzag march into Alabama each corps would take separate roads. Pioneers would precede the corps and make a peculiar "blaze" on the trees along the route. This was a great help to the columns and especially to the stragglers. For Hardee's old corps, it was "two blazes and a notch"; for Stewart's Corps, "two notches and a blaze"; and for Lee's Corps, a "blaze, notch, and blaze." (16)

On October 18th, the company crossed the Alabama line, marching twelve miles over bad roads. They were now in the Alabama highlands, a cultural wasteland. They traveled fifteen miles to Blue Pond, then to within eight miles of Gadsden. On October 21st, the column marched past Gadsden. The 4th LA was marching along at route step, arms-at-will. That day the men were in fine spirits. They were singing, laughing, and joking as they trekked onward. Suddenly a loud cheer was heard from ahead of them. It propagated and passed on toward the Tirailleurs. Soon the men found the reason. Beauregard was with them. That night the General was in camp. The bands played in his honor and speeches were made. This was the first hint to the army that they were bound for Tennessee. The Tennessee regiments were ecstatic, raising cheers and tossing hats.

At Gadsden, clothing and shoes were issued to the troops. On October 23rd, the men were called up and marched sixteen miles to Lick Skillet Crossroads and bivouacked on Sand Mountain. They stopped occasionally to fill their pockets with chinkapins. At cook fires they pulled out their ubiquitous tin cups, dropped in a chunk of salt port and crushed hardtack, and had their supper.

On October 24th, they left at sunrise and passed through Brookeville and Summit on Raccoon Mountain, twenty miles. They camped at the base of the mountain the next day. The 4th LA was traveling through the mountainous parts of Northeast Alabama. This was a section of the South that tolerated neither Yankee nor Rebel. This was "bushwhack country" and it was dangerous to stray from the column.

On October 26th, the Tirailleurs left at sunrise, marching in the rain and mud until dark. They camped two miles north of Somerville, sixteen miles. Cook fires were doused by the rain. The men ate their salt pork raw, sandwiched between slices of hardtack.

The counties of North Alabama had been very prosperous before the war. The men now saw ghostly bare chimneys, blackened walls, and burned-out gin houses as they passed through this once rich land. October 27th was the hardest marching of the trip. Breaking camp at 6 A.M., they marched nineteen miles in the mud and rain until 4 P.M. The soldiers were well ahead of their commissary wagons, and food was scarce.

They marched another nineteen miles on the 28th with only raw sweet potatoes to eat. They laughed and farted all the way into Courtlandt, Alabama. On the 29th, they halted at Leighton in the Tennessee Valley, a march of fifteen miles. At this time, Stewart's and Cheatham's Corps (Hardee's old corps) were in front of Decatur, Alabama. (17)

They could see the church steeples of the town of Florence, Alabama, across the Tennessee River. The river was about 250 yards wide and placed under the cover of Confederate artillery. Gibson's Louisiana Brigade was ordered to cross at Florence. The enemy occupied the town with a thousand cavalrymen and had a strong picket at the railroad bridge. Twenty or so men with Captain Landry shouldered a pontoon boat and on a signal rushed with it into the river. This was the Tirailleurs' first amphibious landing. The men rowed quickly across the wide river. The Tirailleurs' boat was the first to reach the far side and opened a covering fire on the Yankee garrison to protect the boats following.

After enough boats had landed, the town was rushed with a cheer. The Yankee garrison fled. The townsfolk were overjoyed to see the Yankees leave. A big fat lady rushed up to Captain Landry and hugged him. Trasimond pushed her back, knowing how wet and dirty he was, but then he thought *"Que diable,"* (Oh, what the hell) and accepted the corpulent lady's hugs with relish. The women of this town poured out into the streets to greet their Rebel heroes. The ladies literally danced in the streets while others wept tears of joy.

That night they slept on soft pallets in the homes of the townsfolk. Captain Landry was able to get a bath and get his clothes washed. Trasimond warmed himself in front of a big, friendly fireplace in the home of a family named Baggett. Mrs. Baggett had just finished sewing buttons on a new butternut coat just before receiving news that her son had been killed. Holding back tears, she gave the coat to Captain Landry, knowing that he had many more freezing nights ahead of him. The men of the Tirailleurs had found that life in the open had hardened them to the cold, and most refused to lug around heavy overcoats. Trasimond's illness had scared him, and he knew that if he got sick again he would need a warm coat. By this time in the war, nearly every overcoat in the army was captured from the Yankees.

Things were looking up. The twenty days spent in Florence were a welcome rest for the Tirailleurs after their 400-mile march from Jonesboro. Surgeon Craig wrote, "We received a very cordial welcome at Florence and from the 30th of October until the 20th of November, were encamped in and about Florence, and among other amusements threw up a line of works all around the town." (18) Florence once again became a festive town. On November 1st, there were four regimental bands serenading the town. On the evening of November 2nd, the bands gave a concert that wound up in a dance. On the 3rd, there was a slow drizzling rain.

The town was buzzing with news. General Forrest had arrived with his 3,500 cavalrymen. On November 15th, the Tirailleurs wanted to get a look at him. That evening he was serenaded by Tennessee troops and gave the men a speech. Trasimond couldn't help but think that he had seen him someplace before.

There was uncertainty about invading Tennessee. Lee's Corps was the only one across the Tennessee River, and there were rumors that they would recross this river and head to Corinth. Stewart's and Cheatham's Corps were still at Tuscambia.

The Acadians were in good spirits. Beauregard was in camp, and the men felt confident that with his presence, Hood would do nothing rash to endanger the army. They were wrong.

While at Florence, Hunter began making efforts to get out of field service. He wrote a letter to General Franklin Gardner seeking a transfer to his service. General Gibson gladly gave his approval. The men of the 4th LA never knew that Hunter was trying to get transferred. On November 19th, orders were given to be ready to move in the morning.

After the war, Grant wrote: "The blindness of the enemy, however, in ignoring the movement (Sherman's march to the sea) and sending Hood's army, the only considerable force east of the Mississippi River, northward on an offensive campaign, left the whole country open and Sherman's route of his own choice….Hood, instead of following Sherman, continued his movement northward, which seemed to me to be leading to certain doom." (19)

ATLANTA AND JONESBORO

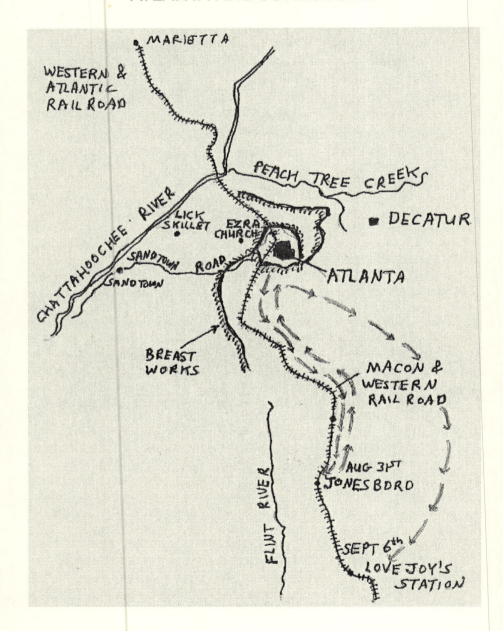

THE LONG MARCH

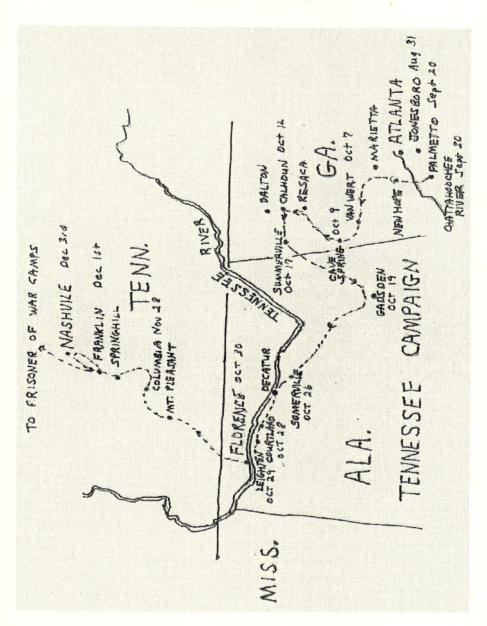

10.

Nashville

Hood's incredible scheme was taking shape. He was moving his army, now 30,000 men, against Nashville. Sherman sent General Thomas to defend Nashville and concentrate Union troops there. George C. Thomas was a Virginian and classmate of Joe Johnston at West Point. He had applied for the position of Major General in the Confederate army and was turned down by Jefferson Davis. When offered a position by Lincoln, he went North.

On November 20th, the 4th/30th was ordered to march.

"Orders to move!" "Fall in!" The men thought, *This must be another exercise in counter-marching. It is much too close to winter to start a major campaign.* Carleton McCarthy wrote, "One fellow picks up the skillet, holds it awhile, mentally determining how much it weighs, and what will be the weight of it after carrying it five miles, and reluctantly, with a half-ashamed, sly look, drops it and takes his place in ranks. Another, having added to his store of blankets too freely, now has to decide which of the two or three he will leave."

"This is the time to say farewell to the bread tray, farewell to the little piles of clean straw laid between two logs, where it was so easy to sleep; farewell to those piles of wood, cut with so much labor; farewell to the girls in the neighborhood." (1) The men were convinced that they were off to demonstrate against the Federal troops in Tennessee and then move to Corinth, Mississippi, or off to Virginia to save General Robert E. Lee. The orderly sergeant was shouting "Fall in!" The Acadians were off.

They left by the Lawrenceburg and Waynesboro road in mud and snow. The weather was bitterly cold. Surgeon Craig wrote this of their itinerary:

Nov. 20th, 1864.—Left Florence at 7 A.M., marched 12 miles.
Nov, 21st, 1864.—Marched to Sugar Creek, 10 miles.
Nov. 22nd, 1864.—Marched to West Point; had some snow, 8 miles.
Nov. 23rd, 1864.—More snow; weather bitter cold, marched 10 miles.

Nov. 24th, 1864.—Camped 3 miles north of Haneyville, 16 miles.
Nov. 25th, 1864.—Marched to Mt. Pleasant; our regiment was left as provost guard, marched 12 miles.
Nov. 26th, 1864.—Rain; marched to near Columbia Tenn., 8 miles.
Nov. 28th, 1864.—Marched to Columbia; remained on provost guard, marched 2 miles. (2)

Through the cold and rain they reached Columbia, Tennessee, November 28, 1864. The Acadians slept in the town that night, warm and dry for a change. The next morning pontoons were let out on the Duck River. The Army of Tennessee crossed and headed to Franklin. The 4th/30th was kept on provost duty at Columbia and the artillery of Hood's army was kept there as well. This was a dumb move on Hood's part. Hood felt that the artillery would delay the march.

The 4th/30th LA was kept in reserve at the Battle of Franklin. This battle was nothing more than an arranged slaughter for the Confederates. (3) Aristotle's concept of a tragedy was the story of a hero (Hood) whose downfall is brought about by some flaw in his character. Literary theorists describe the three unities of a tragedy: one plot, occurring at one spot, on one day. All the ingredients were present at Franklin for a tragedy except for one thing. The hero, General Hood, suffered no downfall, only his army did.

The defenses at Franklin were formidable. The Federals were dug in on the Harpeth River with an abundance of artillery. The entrenchments could be approached only by an advance of nearly two miles across an open, slightly rolling plain. General Nathan Bedford Forrest pleaded with Hood to give him one strong division of infantry, with which he would flank the Federals from their works. The blundering Hood could not see the realities of the situation. Lieutenant General Forrest, the greatest natural military genius of the war, was ignored by the West Point-trained Hood.

Captain Landry's men of Gibson's Brigade of S. D. Lee's Corps came up to Franklin from Columbia with most of Hood's artillery, too late to be engaged in the battle. The Battle of Franklin lasted two hours. It was fought on November 30th, two hours before dark. The Confederate losses were sickening. Of the 16,000 men engaged, 4,000 were killed, wounded, or captured. Among the dead lay General Patrick Cleburne, General Hiram Granbury, and General States Rights Gist. General William Quarles was wounded. Total losses were two major generals, ten brigadier generals, and fifty-three regimental commanders. At midnight, the Yankees abandoned Franklin for the safety of Nashville, eighteen miles away.

The morning after the battle, the 4th/30th LA came up the road to Franklin. Just over a rise, a panoramic view of the battlefield spread out before them. The awful evidence of carnage lay everywhere. A chorus of "*tonnerres,*" "*quel malheurs,*" and "*mon Dieus,*" rumbled through the men. Between the dead men and the dead horses the battlefield was a mulch of dirt, blood, and lead. Ambulances moved about, flying their yellow flags. Empty ammunition boxes, bayonet scabbards, hats, tin cups, and playing cards littered the battlefield. It was disgusting.

The worn and tired Acadians made camp in the court house square at Franklin, December 1st. Three inches of sleet fell during the day, froze, and formed a solid coating of ice over the ground. It was bitterly cold. Tentage was woefully inadequate and exposure devastating in spite of what help the townspeople could contribute. (4) Doctors Lewis and Craig spent forty-eight sleepless hours in a temporary hospital in Franklin treating the wounded.

That night at their campfire, the images of the dead at Franklin sank down inside Trasimond. These dark thoughts did not linger. He had seen many mangled bodies. They were now mere shadows and memories. He no longer saw himself as a corpse. Trasimond knew the army was on the move to sustain itself. Peace had to come soon, and with it this part of his life would pass.

There were seventeen officers and one hundred and thirty men fit for duty in the 4th LA. On December 1st, the 4th/30th LA marched three miles outside of Franklin and camped. The following day, Captain Landry marched with his men twelve miles toward Nashville. During the march to Nashville, troops were halted every hour for roll call and absentees were reported. Wounds that did not actually interfere with marching were not considered reasons to excuse duty. On arrival at Nashville, the higher-up officers thought that the troops were too used up to make an instant attack, the preferred tactic. (5) The brigade arrived near Nashville about 2 P.M., December 2nd. Lee's Corps, with the Tirailleurs, was in the center of the Confederate line with Cheatham's Corps on the right and Stewart's Corps on the left.

At sunset, rations were issued: one pound of barbecued meat, one pound of corn meal, and three ready-made corn dodgers (corn meal, flour, and water in a batter fried in pork grease).

The company was so small at this time that the men all messed together. For shelter, a blanket was pegged down at one end and elevated on slanting sticks. An oil cloth or rubber blanket was placed on the ground. Two men usually slept together, covering themselves with their blankets and putting a second rubber cloth on top of all this. A fire was built in front of this rude shelter. The Tirailleurs gave up on their skillet and fried their salt pork in one half of a

Federal-issue smooth-sided canteen. It was light to carry and could also be used to dig ditches.

On arriving at Nashville, Captain Landry and his men were exhausted. They immediately began digging into the frozen ground. They fortified high ground between Brown's Creek and the Granny White Pike, near present-day Leeland Lane. Hood was laying siege to Nashville, his 23,000 men facing General George Thomas' Union army of 60,000 men. It was insanity.

On December 4th, Private James Chaney, Hunter Rifles A, was struck on the picket line by shrapnel and killed instantly. That night the men made hoe cakes. A spade was held on the fire to sterilize it. A batter of cornmeal, salt, pork grease, and water was boiled in a tin cup and made into a patty. This was placed on a greased-up spade and cooked over the camp fire.

December 6th was a cold, dreary day. That day, the losses at Franklin were made known to the troops: 3,800 men killed, wounded or missing. The men of the Tirailleurs figured Yankee losses must have been just as bad, since they abandoned Franklin after the battle. They were wrong.

December 8th was the Feast of the Immaculate Conception. Father Turgis celebrated Mass. A makeshift alter had been made of a plank stretched over two empty mess-pork barrels. Father Turgis stood before the alter. Thoughts and memories of the terrible winter during the Siege of Sevastapol filled his head. Before him stood Tirailleurs in their aged slouch hats, their faded breeches, their greasy left hips, their ragged jackets, dented canteens, muddy brogans, and bright muskets. Everyone took Communion. The Battle of Franklin had again renewed the soldier's faith in the frailty of the human body. The spiritual revival among the troops, which had begun in Atlanta, waxed.

In 1864, there was no city in America, except Washington and Richmond, more strongly fortified than Nashville. Hood was a great Southern patriot, but to the misfortune of his troops he had been promoted far above his maximum level of competence. Nashville was the triumph of hope over reason. Hood's opium-soaked brain placed too much reliance on his fantasy that he would receive large numbers of Texas troops from Kirby Smith's Trans-Mississippi District. Entrenching continued.

On December 10th, a terrible storm began. It was the wind of the centuries. With the wind came freezing rain and sleet. The storm lasted four days. When the weather lifted, the battle began.

On the 15th, the Tirailleurs were up with the first cyanotic blush of the morning sky. The Union army began shelling. The left of the Rebel line was pounded and gave way. (6) During the night, they were ordered back three miles. The 4th LA never really did any fighting that day. Hood had ordered his lines rearranged and shortened from six miles to two miles. Cheatam was moved to the left, Stuart to the center, and S. D. Lee to the right. Troops worked all night on the new line of entrenchments. The night of December 15th was unusually warm and windy. A low pressure system had pulled warm air with low clouds up from the Gulf.

Lee's Corps dug into Overton's Hill (Peach Orchard Hill). On the 16th, the Battle of Nashville continued. That morning a heavy mist hung over the battlefield. Lee's Corps, being on the right, was ordered to cover and hold the Franklin Pike. Lee's forces were arranged with Clayton's Division (Gibson's Brigade with the 4th/30th and the Tirailleurs) on the right, Stevenson's Division in the center, and Johnson's Division on the left.

Except for cannon fire to the left, the morning was quiet. Fog lay thick across the valley. The Tirailleurs had dug fifty feet of trenches during the night. Private D. J. Cater wrote, "Our brigade was behind a rock fence, which made us feel pretty safe, but we worked all night to make it stronger." (7) That night they had cut abatis to put before the wall.

Overton's Hill rose up out of the plain below to 300 feet. The crest of the hill was 800 feet to the Acadian's right. Entrenched on the east and north face of this hill was Stovall's Brigade. Dug in between Stovall's Georgians and Gibson's Brigade was Holzclaw's Brigade. Holzclaw's Alabama troops straddled the Franklin Pike. Gibson, with the Tirailleurs, was to the left of Holzclaw's Yellow Hammers and about 300 feet west of the pike, the only good road they could use if they needed to escape. At this time in the war, most brigades had between 500 to 1,000 men, about the size of a regiment at Shiloh.

As the fog lifted, the Tirailleurs could look out over a large cornfield to their front. It stretched downward toward the level plain. A wooded area began 350 yards to their front. The corn stalks were brown and still standing. The field was sloppy wet and the mud was thick.

Digging continued until about midday. Then Union artillery began a merciless two-hour bombardment. The Yankee gunners cut their fuses well that cool December day. Captain Landry, his men, and even General Hood felt sure the main Union advance was intended for this part of the line. The faces of the Tirailleurs were a little different that day. Another artillery bombardment, the vibrating, shuddering air had made their eyes a little wider, their lips thinner, their neck veins visible. Six Union batteries (thirty-six guns) firing from less than a thousand yards created a sooty cloud of powder smoke over the Rebel lines.

As Trasimond crouched in the hastily-dug entrenchments, he could feel his heart start the thumping that he had experienced many times before. Next came the sinking feeling in his stomach. A shell exploded overhead and fragments howled and droned. In a spasm of terror he flinched, then shook. All he could do was groan and clench his teeth and pray.

Standing alone against shellfire is like a crapshoot. Take your pick: life, death, or perhaps a war-ending wound. The Tirailleurs pressed themselves against the stone wall. In the bombardment, shards of shrapnel kicked up rocks and dirt. Their ditch vibrated and the noon sky roared and flashed.

Simon Alcide punched his brother with his elbow and motioned to William Blaire. Through the sulfurous haze, Captain Landry focused on the private. Blair's eyes bulged from his pale, sweating face. He was grinding his teeth, opening and closing his fists. Trasimond quickly moved next to Private Blaire. "Steady, Bill. Steady." Captain Landry, using only his eyes, told Louis Kirkland to watch Blaire. Nearby, a scream rang out. Tom Hudson of Hunter Rifles A was mortally wounded in the leg by a shell fragment.

The shells continued, spreading terror among the Acadians. The captain set the men to work digging into the earth. "*Beche! Merde! Beche!*" (Dig, damn you, dig!) They worked, their skin nothing more than a thin membrane stretched over a corpus of fear. Working took their minds off the fear and calmed the Tirailleurs. After two hours, the shelling stopped.

At 2:45 P.M. the Yankee buglers sounded the charge. Flags were unfurled and drums rolled. The Rebels were in their muddy trenches standing about five feet apart and surprisingly intact. After a two-hour bombardment, with all its howling fury, imagine the Yankees' surprise when Rebel slouch hats appeared over fresh earthworks. Union Colonel Thompson's men of the 12th and 100th U.S.C.T. (United States Colored Troops) started across the cornfield and up the slope of Overton's Hill. A battery of Rebel cannon sent volleys of canister into the advancing Negro troops.

The Tirailleurs could hear Rebel yells and taunts from their own lines to their right, but could not see the main attack. Some white troops from Union General Streight's Brigade moved forward. The first and second line of Streight's advance spent itself in front of Holzclaw's Brigade. The third line of Streight's troops neared the stone fence in front of the Tirailleurs.

The straining troops rushing toward the Tirailleurs were the same Yankees whipped by Nathan Bedford Forrest in the spring of 1863. Streight's Union troops were stunned by the Rebel rifles, but pressed forward. They were seeking redemption. To Simon Alcide Landry, these Yankees represented Death with bayonets. He fired and reloaded.

Alcide's eye, looking down the smooth, black barrel of his Enfield, made contact with a Yankee. Between a blue kepi and a black beard, two Yankee eyes fastened on the nineteen-year-old private. For one insane nanosecond a thousand thoughts passed through Simon Alcide's brain. The noise, the smells, the screaming, and an erythematous terror swirled like a tornado of madness in

Alcide's head as he squeezed off the round. The Yankee's eyes became motionless as the ball tore through his pelvis.

For those brief, primitive moments, the Tirailleurs became like animals. In their greed for life and revenge, they poured lead into the wavering Federal line. This line of Yankees broke about 100 feet from the Acadians. General Gibson estimated Union losses in his front to be 200 killed and 700 to 900 wounded. (8)

The 13th U.S.C.T. was the last regiment to attack Overton's Hill. These Negro troops veered to the right and came into range of the Tirailleurs' rifles. The Acadians poured an enfilading fire into their ranks.

To the attacking ex-slaves the headlogs of the freshly dug Rebel trenches seemed to burst into flame. The Confederate line opened up on the Negro troops at 200 feet. They were felled in clumps as if by an invisible sickle. The white officers leading the Negroes were singled out for special annihilation. Two volleys were all they could stand. A member of Company B, 4th LA recalled: "The Negroes broke and fled. I remember one huge color-bearer who stood erect among his falling companions. His terror was apparently too great to allow him to move. He stood clinging to the flagstaff, while a hundred men on our side tried in vain to hit him. The bullets whistled around him by scores. Finally, one struck him and he fell. I felt a sudden compassion. He was a big, fine-looking chap. It seemed a pity." (9)

Colonel R. H. Lindsay, 16th LA, sent a detail out to capture the colors of the 13th U.S.C.T. They returned with a handsome flag inscribed, "Presented by the Colored Ladies of Murfreesboro, Tenn." Three cheers went up down the line of Gibson's Louisiana Brigade. (10)

The 4th/30th LA remained in their works quietly after the repulse of the Federal attack until about 3 o'clock in the afternoon. They could hear the anxious sounds of the battle raging to their far left. Then news was received of the disaster. The Yankees had gotten in behind the left of the Rebel line. The Confederate army was in panic. The rout began, the only rout of a major Confederate force during the entire war. There is only so much water in the "well of courage."

Surgeon Craig, 4th LA, summed up the battle in his diary entry of December 16, 1864: "The enemy attacked early on the morning before we had our works completed. Fighting was constant all day, the right (S. D. Lee) and center [Stewart], where we were, repulsed every attack with ease; but the left (Cheatam) broke again about 3 P.M., allowing the enemy to flank our position, when we had to retire in the utmost confusion. The rout was complete; all organization for the time being lost; Maj. Pullen, Lieutenant Giles (Gyles), and Quicksell, and a few privates (about twenty), were captured at the works." (11)

Private Phillip Dangerfield Stephenson, who was on the left of the Rebel lines, provided an eloquent summary: "It is difficult to assess whether it bears harder on Hood for allowing us to get into such a fix or on (Union General) Thomas for allowing a single man of us to escape! Throughout the whole of that terrible day, a spell seemed to be on the whole army, officers and men, a palsy not of fear, but of despair. All movements were mechanical, in a spirit of passive indifference, like condemned criminals waiting the hour of execution. I never saw men behave more like dumb, driven cattle than on that fatal day. Ordinary precautions were left neglected, the 'what's the use' spirit dominated every mind. The machinery, in a word, was rotted. It required but the impending blow of the enemy to make it fall to pieces." (12)

The Tirailleurs made for the woods to their rear and the Franklin Pike. The 4th/30th LA managed to stay together loosely. Lieutenant Colonel Pennington was hollering for the men to form up. General Clayton kept control of his brigades and in the woods along the Franklin Pike organized a resistance. S. D. Lee rallied Stevenson's Division, along with a few pieces of artillery, and the Yankees stalled.

S. D. Lee's Corps was ordered by Hood to cover the retreat. Lee put Gibson's Brigade in the rear. General Gibson struggled to establish order among the regiments of his brigade. As dark came on the army continued southward. The Yankees halted their pursuit during the night.

As they pressed on toward Franklin on the dark, crowded pike, there was the usual garbage of a retreating army: discarded muskets, broken-down wagons, wrecked artillery caissons, abandoned ammunition, and even thrown-away blankets. The corps stopped for the night in the rain and mud at a place called Hollow Tree Gap. This was the only defensible position on the pike from which to protect the Harpeth River crossing, about four miles to the south.

S. D. Lee gave special credit in his report to General Gibson. "The enemy force was checked by Brigadier Gibson, with his brigade and a regiment of Buford's Cavalry under Colonel Shanklet, allowing me to withdraw to Franklin." (13) The 4th/30th LA was then directed to return some half a mile north and picket the Gap, about three and a half miles south of Brentwood. (14)

On December 17th, the men awoke in a heavy fog. They began building fires and cooking breakfast when the enemy's cavalry surprised them. Advanced elements of General Wilson's Union cavalry were the attackers. This cavalry division had over 9,000 men mounted. In the fog the horsemen rode right into the camp before they were recognized as Yankees. With their arms stacked, there was nothing to do but surrender.

At this time in the winter war in Tennessee, Rebel cavalrymen were mostly wearing Yankee long coats. It was difficult to tell friend from foe until they were on you. Stephen Lee reported that at daylight on December 17th, the Federal cavalry resumed a "most vigorous pursuit, charging at every opportunity and in the most daring manner." (15)

"General (Randal Lee) Gibson, of whom we were always proud, was not to blame for the capture of the fourth and thirtieth LA regiments of our brigade. The enemy's cavalry had gotten in our rear and the capture was unavoidable." Douglas John Cater. (16)

The Tirailleur's capture at Hollow Tree Gap spared him from the most desperate and painful retreat of the war. Barefooted men with little or no rations retreated over 127 miles through freezing rain, snow, and sleet, over rutted, icy roads. The day after Christmas, 1864, what was left of Hood's Army of Tennessee crossed the Tennessee River to safety.

"The officers of the Fourth Louisiana, who were captured in the engagements of the 15th and 16th of December, 1864, and held prisoners of war, were the following:

Col. S. E. Hunter	Lieutenant Peter E. Brewer
Lieut. Colonel W. F. Pennington	Lieutenant Wm. Quicksell
Major E. J. Pullen	Lieutenant T. H. D'Armond
Captain C. R. Cornelius	Lieutenant John B. Giles
Captain David Devall	Lieutenant John I. Kendall
Captain Charles E. Kennon	Lieutenant Martin Landry
Captain T. Landry	Lieutenant L. A. Courtade
Captain James F. Reid	Lieutenant R. T. Duncan
	Lieutenant Louis Daigle" (17)

The Nashville campaign virtually ended the existence of the 4th LA and the Tirailleurs. From May 25, 1864, to the end of the campaign in Tennessee, December 17, 1864, the killed and wounded of the 4th LA were 233. (18)

After Nashville, remnants of the 4th LA that were on detached duty or recovering from illness and wounds drifted into Tupelo, Mississippi. There were two officers and eighteen enlisted men. Gibson's Louisiana Brigade slowly reformed and was ordered to Mobile. Isidore Daigle, Emile Hebert, Jean Baptiste Hebert, and Amedee Templet entered the redoubts at Spanish Fort, March 15, 1865. They were commanded by Captain P. E. Lorio of the Lafourche Guards, and reformed as "New Company E."

Somehow, J. B. Hebert had evaded capture at Hollow Tree Gap and had made the march south with Father Turgis. On that terrible march the little priest walked most of the way. He loaned his horse to the barefooted privates.

At the fort on the northeast corner of Mobile Bay, the work continued on entrenchments and bombproofs. Torpedoes (land mines) were planted around the fort's perimeter and rifle pits were dug and supplied with hand grenades. Union General Canby's 30,000 men slowly surrounded the fort and planted their siege guns. A new weapon was introduced to the defenders, the coehorn mortar. Both sides employed this weapon. From a stubby fifteen-inch barrel it fired a twelve-pound ball high into the air and could easily clear out enemy trenches. At night, the Rebels shot fireballs from them to illuminate the battlefield.

Yankee sharpshooters with Whitworth rifles kept up a well-aimed fusillade on the Rebels. Never had Tirailleurs seen such a wicked bombardment as on April 4th. Muskets, coehorns, siege guns, field pieces, and fifteen-inch siege mortars fired from their front and Farragut's gunboats fired into them from the rear

On April 8th, another devastating artillery attack began, followed by an infantry attack that broke through on the Rebel's left. At dark, Gibson ordered the fort abandoned. Of the 2,300 defenders, 650 were captured. The men escaped across a trundle bridge over the marsh and made their way back to Mobile. Father Turgis and Father Andrew Cornette made their way back with the men of the Louisiana Brigade. Six veterans of the 4th LA were captured and one was wounded in the siege. One of those captured was Bernard Moses, who had become General Gibson's band leader. (19) Shortly after the fall of Mobile, the remainder of the 4th LA surrendered at Meridian, Mississippi.

During the War Between the States over 1600 men served in the 4th LA. One hundred twenty died in battle, three hundred and thirty-three were wounded, two died in accidents, one was shot by an officer, two drowned, and one was run over by a train. Twelve legs and ten arms were amputated. Sixty men died of disease. Twelve of these deaths occurred in Yankee prison camps. Two women served in the 4th LA. Jane Heywood and Betsy Patrick enrolled for twelve months at Camp Lovell as "matrons."

The Tirailleurs started the war with seventy-nine officers and men, enrolled on May 25, 1861, at Camp Moore. In December 1861, there were seventy-one men present at Berwick City. The company was joined during the war by fifty-five recruits or transfers. The Tirailleurs were in over twelve frontal assaults and received four assaults from defensive works. Thirteen were killed, twenty-eight wounded, six died of disease, and two drowned; roughly, a thirty percent casualty rate for the war. In comparison, the Delta Rifles had six killed and four die of disease out of a total membership of 218 men. Fourteen Deltas were captured at Nashville.

From May 25, 1861, to December 17, 1864, eight men passed through the entire war and were in every engagement: Trasimond Landry, Adelarde

Courtade, William Gibson, Edward Longuepee, Albert Hebert, John Renaud, Joseph Leray, and Portalis Tullier.

"We are emaciated and starved, dysentery dissolves our bowels. Our artillery is fired out, it has too few shells and the barrels are so worn they shoot uncertainly. We have too few horses. Our fresh troops are anemic boys in need of rest. For our one hungry soldier, come five of the enemy, fresh and fit. For our one loaf of bread there are fifty cans of tinned beef over there. We are not beaten, for as soldiers we are better and more experienced; we are simply crushed and driven back by overwhelmingly superior forces." (20)

This was not written by a Southern patriot, but by an author writing of the Imperial German Army in the summer of 1918. The fate of the Southern armies was uncannily parallel with the Kaiser's army of 1918. Both countries were effectively blockaded, their navies limited to sporadic commerce raiding; both were starved, civilians as well as soldiers; both armies started out maneuvering, but ended up in trench warfare. Both won their first battles with splendid victories. They both coped with a two-front war. Toward the end, the Germans faced fresh American troops just as the Confederates faced large masses of foreign immigrants and Negro troops. In the end, enemy technology overcame both armies. For the Germans it was tanks, for the Confederates, it was the Yankee's artillery and repeating breech-loading rifles.

There was one huge difference between the Imperial German Army and the Confederate States Army. The Kaiser's armies started with a huge military-industrial-complex and a large standing army. The South started with nothing, save patriotism.

11.

Prison Camps

Except for a few men on detached duty or sick and excused, the entire force of Company H was captured. There were fifteen Tirailleurs captured at Hollow Tree Gap:

Trasimond Landry, Captain	Johnson's Island
Adelarde Courtade, First Lieutenant	Johnson's Island
Louis Daigle, Second Lieutenant	Johnson's Island
John Renaud, Corporal	Camp Douglas
Alcide Landry (the elder)	Camp Douglas
W. Blaire	Camp Douglas
Jules Doiron	Camp Douglas
William Gibson	Camp Douglas
Joseph Leray	Camp Douglas
Portalis Tullier	Camp Douglas
Andrew Allain	Camp Douglas
Simon Alcide Joseph Landry	Camp Douglas
Louis Kirkland	Camp Chase
Edmund Longuepee	Camp Chase
Albert Hebert, First Sergeant	Camp Chase

Three Tirailleurs were sent to Camp Chase. They were the most fortunate. Edmund Longuepee was paroled at Camp Chase in February, 1865, and was captured a second time, April 5, 1865. Louis Kirkland was captured three times during the war. He was captured at home, May 13, 1863, at Hollow Tree Gap, December 17, 1864, and at the mouth of the Red River, April 5, 1865. Sergeant Albert Hebert was paroled and went home. The men sent to Johnson's Island and Camp Douglas and Camp Chase were in for six months of misery.

The two Alcide Landrys, Corporal John Renaud, Sergeant Theodore Doiron, and Privates Joseph Leray, William Gibson, Andrew Allain, W. Blaire, and Portalis Tullier were sent to Camp Douglas. This camp was established in Chicago in the Spring of 1862 to house the thousands of Rebel prisoners from Fort Donelson. The prison site was built on lands previously owned by Stephen A. Douglas. It was 400 yards from Lake Michigan and four miles from downtown Chicago (between 32nd Street and 33rd Street in modern-day Chicago). The camp was constructed on low ground, which flooded. In winter it became a sea of frozen mud. (1)

The death and illness rates were very high. In late 1863, the Sanitary Commission's investigation concluded, "We have never witnessed so painful a spectacle as that presented by the wretched inmates. The ground at Camp Douglas is most unsuitable, being wet and without drainage. We think it ought to be abandoned." (2)

Private Simon Alcide Landry suffered through the raw winter weather at Camp Douglas. Freezing winter winds howled in off Lake Michigan. In January 1865, a Union inspector of prisons wrote: "Very objectionable as a depot for troops. Privies removed and sinks imperfectly covered, so that the filth is seeping into the ground. When there is rain, the grounds are flooded with an infusion of this poisonous matter....Prisoners too much crowded." (3)

Simon Alcide arrived at Camp Douglas scarcely a month after an attempted prison break. Camp commander General Sweet and his henchmen were now under the command of General Joe Hooker. Hooker had recently been removed by General Grant for his incompetence shown at Missionary Ridge. He was in no mood for prison reform at Camp Douglas, so the squalid conditions persisted. On January 15, 1865, there were over 11,000 prisoners at Camp Douglas. The level of cruelty to prisoners had increased in the winter of 1865. The camp guards were men who had been ruled unfit for combat duty, usually for reasons of physical, moral, or mental disability, and it showed in their cruel treatment of Rebel prisoners.

The Tirailleurs arrived by train at Camp Douglas Christmas Eve, 1864. They detrained from cold boxcars, hungry and thirsty. Many of the men were so frostbitten they had to be taken from the train to the prison by ambulance. They were then rushed into the unfriendly confines of the camp. Yankee guards stripped the prisoners outside the gates and searched them for valuables and weapons. The prisoners stood there in the snow and cold while the guards robbed them. The hydrants were frozen and there was no water. The "deadline" of the camp ground was eighteen feet from the prison fence. The deadline was clearly marked on the camp side by mud and slush. Across the line was fresh snow. The thirsty Alcide walked toward the snow and was grabbed by a camp veteran and warned to stay clear. Even reaching over the line could get you shot.

This group of Nashville prisoners swelled the prison by over 3,000 men. By December 1864, the camp, designed for 8,000 men, now held over 12,000 prisoners. The new arrivals had a good deal of "new issue" Confederate currency on them and were hence nicknamed the "New Issue." (4) A smallpox epidemic had raged in camp in November and December of 1864, but was waning at the time of the Tirailleurs' arrival.

After taps, there was no talking or lights allowed. To enforce this rule, guards would simply fire their rifles randomly through the thin barracks walls. Many prisoners put boards up around their bunks and for protection against these depredations.

On February 20, 1865, General William Beall arrived with clothes, shoes, blankets, jackets, shirts, socks, and tobacco. General Beall had been captured at Port Hudson, and in late 1864 he was released to head a cartel for the relief of Southern prisoners. He was allowed to travel in the North and broker Southern cotton to New York factors. Profits were used to purchase supplies and clothing for the inmates at Camp Douglas. (5)

In March, the over-crowding was lessened by a temporary re-opening of the exchange program. The military yielded to pressure by Northern families trying to get their kin out of the Rebel prison camps. Those prisoners in camp since 1862 and 1863 were exchanged. An observation tower was constructed near the prison walls, and for a ten-cent admission insensitive Chicagoans could gawk at the Rebel prisoners. Many Rebels saluted these gawkers with their middle finger. The January and February death toll was 551 men. (6)

On many winter days the Acadians were confined to the barracks. The hours dragged on. There were card games, checkers, and chess. There was no camp library. Some lapsed into a deep state of despair, many huddling in corners staring blankly into space. The imprisoned Tirailleurs performed the usual activities that men in captivity do to occupy their minds and to maintain hope.

After Captain Landry's capture he was marched to the Yankee rear. He was treated well by Wilson's troopers. The few remaining Tirailleurs were fed the same food as the Union troops. The further to the rear the worse the treatment became. The men were marched to Nashville, where they entrained into box cars for Louisville, Kentucky. They arrived in Louisville, December 20, 1864.

There, they were kept in a prison compound for several days. They then went by train to Sandusky, Ohio, December 22, 1864. Lake Erie was frozen this time of the year. The prisoners were marched over the ice to Johnson's Island prison camp. All the remnants of the Tirailleurs spent Christmas in prison. The men sang Christmas carols that night. Trasimond's thoughts drifted off to home. He wondered how many more Christmas nights would pass before this profitless war would end.

Johnson's Island is a half mile wide and a mile long and located in Sandusky Bay south of Marble Head Peninsula. During the war, fifteen thousand men passed through the prison gates. There were twenty-five Confederate generals that called the place home for various lengths of time. Many of its former inmates would become Congressmen, governors, ambassadors, authors, and physicians. One private incarcerated there would one day sit on the Supreme Court. (7) Edward Douglas White of Thibodeaux became Chief Justice of the U.S. Supreme Court in 1910.

Johnson's Island was not so bad in summer months as prisons go, but was terrible in winter. The Acadians could not have arrived at a worse time of year. The winter winds blew in off Lake Erie and howled through the planks in the prison quarters. Existence was hard, but the death rate was less than at any other prison camp. Despite a twelve-foot plank fence, armed guards, and the fact that the prison camp was an island, twelve men did manage to escape.

At Johnson's Island, the prison stockade was sixteen acres squared. At the base of the fence was a ditch dug down to the base limestone to prevent tunneling. Inside the stockade were thirteen two-story blocks, each twenty-five feet by one hundred twenty-five feet. Twelve were used as barracks and the thirteenth was designated as a hospital. There was a prison yard down the center of the barracks and latrines at the rear. (8)

The structures were built of green timber which quickly shrank, leaving large gaps in the boards incapable of keeping out the cold Lake Erie winds. Each barracks had a kitchen at one end with a small cooking stove. Here prisoners cooked their food and washed their clothes. Details were formed and each man on a rotating basis cooked for a week. Others washed dishes. The generals took their turns, along with the lieutenants. Each man washed his own clothes. When Trasimond arrived in mid-January the pumps were frozen. An unappetizing mess of salted fish or pickled beef in a stew with rice was standard fare. It was Yankee policy to keep the prisoners half-starved in retaliation for treatment of their soldiers in Confederate prison camps.

Each day followed another with excruciating sameness. The only change seemed to be the newspapers brought in each day by the sutlers. The Northern newspapers carried little good news from the South. Captain Landry remembered the homesickness he had felt at Camp Moore, but the feeling was almost unbearable on the Island. At least he was in prison with friends. Adelarde Courtade and Louis Daigle, as well as many other acquaintances from the 4th LA and the 30th LA, were also prisoners. To bear the boredom, there were debating clubs, baseball games, theatricals, relief work, reading, chess, and music. Nothing at camp gave Trasimond more joy than a letter from Marie Amelie.

The drum beat every morning at 8 A.M. The prisoners were required to go to the yard for roll call. A Union army sergeant would then count off the men. Rations were issued every seven days, but the men had to attend roll call to get their daily rations of meat and bread. This meant standing outside in any kind of weather for over an hour each morning.

By mid-February, Captain Landry felt like he had been on Johnson's Island for a year. The month of March passed by at glacial speed. News arrived in April of Lee's surrender. The officers of the Tirailleurs knew the war would soon be over. A speech was made by the post commandant offering release to any man that would take the Oath of Allegiance to the United States. Trasimond refused. No Acadians took the oath. There was a special resistance to the oath from the Louisiana Acadians. In these Southern patriots flowed the blood of their ancestors. Their Celtic-French origins had bred in them a stubbornness and independence that forced them to mimic their ancestors in Acadia who had refused to take the oath of allegiance to the English Crown.

There was plenty time for writing letters. Writing materials were furnished by the Union authorities. Trasimond took time to write Marie Amelie and his brother. This letter was sent from Johnson's Island, January 10, 1865:

"Dear Brother, I wrote to you earlier informing you of my capture and imprisonment on Johnson's Island. My health remains very good, and I am very comfortably situated. I have become reconciled to prison life, though it is very confining. The prisoners enjoy good health generally. The weather still remains quite cold, although very pleasant in doors. If an opportunity presents, please send me a small sum of green backs, as I am entirely without. In writing to me—write only one page and avoid all contraband news. My clothes are rather thin for the climate. If you should see an opportunity, send me some woolen goods. There is still much talk in the papers of a general exchange of prisoners. Give my love to all the family." (9)

On March 1, 1865, a letter and package came addressed to Captain Landry. It was from Josephine. She had enclosed some green back currency. Union troops were occupying West Baton Rouge Parish, but were not much protection from jayhawkers. These predators added to the hardships of the Landrys and their neighbors. Captain Ratliff, C.S.A., was operating in Grosse Tete and had done his best to clear out the Jay Hawkers. At the request of parishioners, Father Francis Follot at Plaquemine had said a High Mass for friends in the 30th LA. Hearing this, the Yankees banned Follot from celebrating Mass and even took the keys to the church from him. The package Josephine sent contained flannel shirts, socks, and drawers.

In June, the last armed Confederate resistance ended and there was no longer any reason to refuse the Oath. Trasimond took the Oath on June 16, 1865. The prisoners were then dismissed according to their date of capture. The last sentence on the parole read,"The Quartermaster Department will furnish transportation to the point nearest accessible to his home by rail or steamboat." (10) Trasimond Landry, Adelarde Courtade, and Louis Daigle were ferried to Sandusky and entrained for Cincinnati and the Ohio River. Before Trasimond was allowed on the steamboat, he was required to remove the buttons from his coat. All symbols of the Confederacy were outlawed.

The river stretched out in front. It was low from bank to bank. The July low water would make for a slow run to Brusly Landing. Trasimond arrived home in late July 1865.

Enfin, la guerre est fini.
Finally, the war was over.

Epilogue

Slavery had been practiced since the dawn of time, but it took the Portuguese to develop modern agricultural slavery. Portuguese-style slavery was developed in the Canary Islands and transported to the New World by the Spanish. The "Peculiar Institution" blossomed in the Virginia Colony under the guidance of the English Cavalier upper classes. At first, the slaves were used to grow rice and tobacco. Later, large-scale agricultural slavery exploded with the invention of the cotton gin. The seductive profits from slavery caused the French in Louisiana to ape the practice and style of the Virginians.

The generation of young boys born in the South in the 1830s and 1840s were handed a culture that had taken over 400 years to develop. This same generation would have to live through the sudden dismantling of their culture and their "Peculiar Institution." This generation of men would do penance for their ancestors. They would be raised at the warm hearth of the plantation system and then face a terrible four years of war to preserve it—in a Lost Cause. After the war and the annexation of the Southern states, they would spend the rest of their lives in a wrecked and ruined South.

The life of Captain Trasimond Landry was typical of his generation. At home after the war he tried farming. The parish was devastated in 1865, 1866, and 1867 by floods. The crevasses in the levees had never been repaired following the war. It would take twenty years for the sugar industry to recover. In 1867, Trasimond Landry married Marie Amelie Bujol and started a family. Unable to pay the exorbitant reconstruction-era taxes, he gave up farming and became a school teacher and later a minor government official.

In 1878 the last great yellow fever epidemic spread through Mobile, New Orleans, and up the Mississippi River Valley to Memphis. Twenty thousand people died. On February 18, 1879, the tail end of the epidemic took the life of Captain Landry. Captain Sosthene Aillet, First Lieutenant L. A. Courtade, and Second Lieutenant Louis Daigle all died in the same epidemic. A victim of scalawag and carpetbagger reconstruction, Captain Landry's passing left his wife and five children destitute. With his death at the age of thirty-nine, Trasimond had paid the price.

Appendices

APPENDIX A

MUSTER ROLL OF THE TIRRAILLEURS (sic)
(May 25, 1861)
As it appeared in the *Sugar Planter*

Francis A. Williams, Captain
J. A. Levesque, 1st Lieutenant
Bird, 2nd Lieutenant
Belisaire Landry, 3rd Lieutenant
Sosthene Aillet, 1st Sergeant
Tras. Landry, 2nd Sergeant
Aug. Buquoi, 3rd Sergeant
Amedee Landry, 4th Sergeant
Emile Allain, 1st Corporal
T. C. White, 2nd Corporal
Leon Dupuy, 3rd Corporal
Oscar Hebert, 4th Corporal
Alphonse Aillet
D. Alexandrie
P. P. Babin
G. (James?) Bennett
Aurhur Blanchard
G. Benham
J. Benham
J. J. Benham
O. Contini
Courtade
P. Crochet
A. Clifton
P. Daigle
A. Doiron
S. Gibson
E. Griffin
Alex Hebert
Amedee Hebert
C. V. Hebert
Felix Hebert
Louis Hebert
Numa Hebert
Ed Hebert
J. B. Hebert
Chas. Hebert
Ros'd Hebert
Albert Hebert
Hubert Hebert
Raph. Hebert, Jr.
H. Henri
Leon Isaac
J. N. Landry
Louis Leveque
H. Longuepee
Theojene Lejeune
John Peyronnin
John Reynaud
Thomas Sherrau
Gustave Serrett
Portalis Tuillier

O. Dupuy
T. Doiron
J. Garantyne
A. Gassie
Wm. Gasie
Wm. Gibson

Amadee Templet
Isham Woods
William Wagner

In the muster roll published in the *Gazette and Comet* of East Baton Rouge Parish, May 25, 1861, U. Leblanc was listed as 4th Corpl. and Oscar Hebert was listed as "ensign."

This roster was published by Samuel Lambert in the *East Feliciana Democrat* shortly after the war. He states that it is the roster at the time of the first payroll. (July 5, 1861)

F. A. Williams, Captain
J. A. Leveque, 1st Lt.
B. Landry, 2nd Lt.
S. Aillet, 3rd Lt.
Buquoi, A., 1st Sgt.
Courtade, A., 2nd Sgt
LeBlanc, W, 3rd Sgt.
Dupuy, O, 4th Sgt.
White, T. C., 1st Corpl.
Dupuy, Leon, 2nd Corpl.
Hebert, Oscar, 3rd Corpl.
Gassie, A., 4th Corpl.
Aillet, Alphonse, Private
Allain, Emile
Alexandrie, A.
Babin, P. P.
Belieu, Lewis
Bennett, James
Bernard, Felix
Blanchard, Arthur
Blanchard, H.
Bryant, J. W.
Clifton, Alfred
Contini, Oscar
Crochet, Prudent

Hebert, A.
Hebert, Camille
Hebert, Charles
Hebert, Christophe
Hebert, Felix
Hebert, Lewis
Hebert, N
Hebert, Oscar
Hebert, J. B.
Hebert, Raphael, Jr.
Hebert, Rosemond
Henri, Evariste
Isaac, Leon
Landry, Anatole
Landry, T.
Ledieu, R.
Lejeune, Theodore
Lejeune, T.
Lejeune, Theogene
Leray, Joseph
Leveque, Louis
Leveque, Samuel
Libby, Jackson
Longuepee, H.
Martin, Lewis

Daigle, Prudent
Doiron, Albert
Doiron, J.
Doiron, Theodore
Garantine, John
Gassie, Wm.
Gibson, Edward
Gibson, William
Gibson, Sylvanie
Gilbert, H.
Griffin, Ebeneezer
Garantyne, John
Peyronin, John
_____, John
Hebert, Albert
Hebert, Alexis

Martin, Theodore
McKimmons, M.B.
Garrett, Wm.
Guidry, V.
Serret, Gustave
Sherron, Thomas
Templet, Amadee
Tullier, P.
Waggoner, Wm.
Landry, A
Longuepee, Edmond
Longuepee, L. A.
Hermogene, Frank
Johnson, Harry
Woods, L. E.
Scoval, Charlie
Wolf, G
_____, W. A.
Woods, Isham

APPENDIX B

MUSTER-ROLL OF CAPTAIN F. S. WILLIAM'S COMPANY "D"
The West Baton Rouge Tirailleurs

Williams, Francis A.	Captain
Leveque, J. A.	1st Lieut.
Landry, Belisaire	2nd Lieut.
Aillet, Sosthene	3rd Lieut.
Courtade, Adelarde	Orderly Sergt.
Leblanc, Ursin	Second Sergt.
Dupuy, Octave	3rd Sergt.
White, T. C.	4th Sergt.
Dupuy, Leon	1st Corp.
Hebert, Albert	2nd Corp.
Gassie, Auguste	3rd Corp.
Babin, Paul P.	4th Corp.

Privates:

Aillet, Alphonse
Allain, Emile
Alexandry, A. D.
Beleau, Louis
Bennett, James
Bernard, Felix
Blanchard, Arthur
Blanchard, Hilaire
Contini, Oscar
Crochet, Prudent
Daigle, Prudent
Doiron, Joinville
Doiron, Theodore
Doiron, Albert
Garantyne, John
Gipson, Edward
Gipson, William
Gipson, Sylvanie
Griffin, Ebenezar
Peyronin, John

Hebert, Alexis
Hebert, Amedee
Hebert, Camille
Hebert, Chas
Hebert, Christophe
Hebert, Felix
Hebert, Numa
Hebert, Oscar
Hebert, John Baptiste
Hebert, Raphael, Jr.
Hebert, Rosemond
Hebert, Louis
Henry, Evariste
Isaac, Leon
Landry, Anatole
Landry, Trasimond
Ledieu, Romauld
Lejeune, Theodore
Lejeune, Theodule
Lejeune, Theogene
Leray, Joseph
Leveque, Samuel
Longuepee, Hilaire
Martin, Louis
Martin, Theodore
McKimmins, M. B.
O'Bryan, J. J.
Serret, Gustave
Templet, Amades
Tullier, Portalis
Wagner, Wm.
Landry, Alcide
Garrett, Wm.
Guidry, Villeneuve
Longuepee, Edmond
Longuepee, L. A.
Hermogene, Frank
Scoval, Chas.
Wood, Isham

Buquoi, A   Discharged on account of physical disability
Hebert, Hubert   Discharged on account of physical disability
Bryant, J. W.   Joined Scott's Battalion
Leveque, Louis   On sick furlough for 6 months
Libby, F. Jackson   On sick furlough for 20 days—since Oct. 5th
Sherron, Thomas   On sick furlough for 20 days—since Oct. 5th
Johnston, J. H.   Sutler Aug. 1st Ship Island
Woods, L. E.   Sutler Aug. 1st Ship Island

Camp Lovell, Berwick City, Nov. 26th, 1861
J. A. Leveque, Lieut. Commanding

Louisiana Historical Quarterly, Vol. 30, No. 2, April 1947.

APPENDIX C

The 1841 Constitution of the Tirailleurs

Preamble: Whereas the Condition of our local police affords insufficient protection; we, the undersigned, do form ourselves into a "Volunteer Rifle Company", for the purpose of protection against the objects and influences which tend to endanger our property and our peace; and do pledge ourselves to abide by following rules and laws;

Section l: This Company shall be named the "Tirailleurs d'Iberville."

Section 2: The officers of this Company shall be elected by a majority of its members present at a meeting; provided it shall require a majority of the members of the Company to constitute a quorum,

Section 3: And shall consist of a Captain, three Lieutenants, one Orderly Sergeant, three sergeants, and four corporals.

Section 4. The Captain and other officers shall hold office for a term of one year; but subject to a removal by a two thirds vote of the members present, or may resign at any time without calling upon the Company to accept his resignation; provided his resignation shall not go into effect until his successor is elected.

Section 5: The Company shall assemble every Sunday at two o'clock in the afternoon and will exercise at handling the arms and all military exercises. This assembly is mandatory.

Section 6: The absence without reason of a member of the company at these mandatory assemblies will be punished by a fine of $1.00 each time.

Section 7: Commands in the company will be made principally in the French language.

Section 8: All members of the company who would present themselves to be drunk will be considered absent, and will pay the fine imposed by Section 6.

Section 9: All members who by ridiculous situations or actions the captain will have the right to impose fines on him as he believes proper.

Section 10: It is expressly forbidden to smoke or chew tobacco in the ranks without permission of the officers.

Section 11. After the Company shall be organized by the election of all its officers, any member may propose the names or name of persons who may desire to join. The names proposed shall be given to the Orderly Sergeant who shall report the same at the first monthly meeting. The members present at such a meeting shall vote upon all applications for membership with white or black balls; three black balls shall reject any candidate.

Section 12. The Captain shall have the right to order out the Company for active service in the parish whenever he may deem it necessary; and in all cases when the Captain shall be absent from the parish or from any cause unable to act, the next in rank shall perform his duties.

Section 13: The officers shall be armed with a side sword.

Section 14: All members of this Company shall sign this Constitution.

APPENDIX D

The *Sugar Planter* of August 24, 1861, went through a list of military terms for their readership:

Company—A body of soldiers in the regular service. A company is composed of 64 men. The companies of volunteers now called into service are not organized according to the army standard. Some contain not more than forty men, while others contain 100.

Platoon—Half a company.

Section—Sub-division of platoons. If a company is large it is usually divided into eight sections; if small into four.

Regiment—A collection of companies. In the regular service ten companies form a Regiment.

Brigade—Two or more Regiments.

Division—Two or more Brigades.

Battalion—A body of infantry of two or more companies under one commander. A Regiment, or portion of it, may be a Battalion. A colonel may divide his regiment into several parts assigning separate commands to sub-ordinate officers, and each part would be a Battalion.

Army Corps—A division of the army organized for the campaign, composed of Infantry, Cavalry, and Artillery. The back bone of an army is the infantry which is sometimes divided into "light" and "heavy" infantry. Four fifths of an army should be composed of infantry.

Flank—The right and left of a body of troops. Flankers are detailed bodies of men sent out on either hand of an army in motion or at rest, to guard against attack.

Skirmishers—Bodies of men sent out to engage the attention of the enemy, a duty usually assigned to Zouaves, Light Infantry, and Riflemen.

Vidette—An advance sentry or scout who observes enemy movements, thrown out in front of pickets.

Enfilade—being fired on from the side.

APPENDIX E

Mobile, Ala., Aug. 5th, 1863

To The
    Hon. James A. Seddon
        Sectry. Of War
            Richmond, Va.

Sir,
    In the month of July, 1862, the 4th LA., Regt. Col. H. W. Allen commanding, was sent from Corinth by order of Genl. Beauregard to Vicksburg, Miss., with orders to report to me for the defense of that place. This regiment was enlisted for twelve months, while in Vicksburg their time of service expired. Under the Act of Congress I ordered elections to be held in said Regiment to reorganize the same as the law directed. After the elections were held, all the officers elected were examined by a competent board appointed for the purpose, some of said officers failed to pass their examinations, and of course vacancies were thereby created. In this dilemma, Col. Allen called on me to know how those vacancies were to be filled—upon reflection it was decided on the necessity for officers was pressing, that the several companies had exhausted their right to elect, that is they chose to elect incompetent men, some of whom knowing their own incompetency refused to go before the committee and voluntarily went back to the ranks, it was their fault, therefore for the benefit of the service, I ordered Col. Allen to fill all vacancies in his regiment by appointment, said appointments to be confirmed at Richmond; he complied with my order, and the appointed names were duly forwarded and approved. These appointments, I am advised, have all proven to be good. For twelve months, these officers thus appointed have served most faithfully, have participated in the defense of Vicksburg, Port Hudson, and Jackson. I therefore respectfully request that they be confirmed and their commissions issued as their loss at present would be serious to the service, and a great drawback to the efficiency of the regiment, besides, I deem it would be unjust to these now to force them back into the ranks. I am very Respectfully,

                                  Your Obedient Servant
                                    M. L. Smith
                                    Maj. Genl. Commd.

Letter from Col H. W. Allen:

Below are the names of the officers.... I can safely say that these officers are the elite of this regiment and have all distinguished themselves in battle.

	H. W. Allen	
J. B. Corkern	Co. B	2nd Lt.
A. W. Roberts	Co. C	Jr. 2nd Lt.
James Reid	Co. D	1st Lt.
Daniel McCarthy	Co. D	2nd Lt.
W. T. McJilton	Co. E	2nd Lt.
E. A. Carmouche	Co. F	Jr. 2nd Lt.
D. B. Gorham	Co. H	2nd Lt.

All of the 4th La. Vol.

APPENDIX F

PROSPECTUS

PROSPECTUS

OF

ST. JOSEPH'S COLLEGE, KENTUCKY.

This Institution, situated in the suburbs of Bardstown, Nelson county, was founded by the Right Reverend BISHOP FLAGET, with a view of affording to Catholic Parents and Guardians the most effectual means of imparting to their sons and wards a thorough religious and literary Education. Agreeably to the design of its VENERABLE FOUNDER, St. Joseph's College is conducted on Catholic principles, by Professors and Tutors of the Catholic Clergy, who being wholly devoted to the important work of public Instruction, spare no pains to improve the hearts of their pupils in virtue and store their minds with useful knowledge. In 1824, the College was incorporated by an act of the Legislature and empowered to confer the usual Academic Honors. The liberal patronage which the Institution has enjoyed, ever since its commencement, is the best proof of the confidence reposed in the Faculty by Parents and Guardians. The site is beautiful and healthy. The buildings are stately and very extensive. The Refectory and Dormitories are large and well ventilated. The Wardrobe is kept in the neatest possible manner, and changes are given twice a week. In the Infirmary the sick are nursed with the greatest care and attention. The diet is wholesome and abundant. The Play-grounds are very spacious and handsomely set with trees. The Students boarding in College are, at all times, under the superintendence of one or more of the Tutors or Prefects. The Discipline of the Institution is strict but paternal.

SYSTEM OF INSTRUCTION.

Besides the MERCANTILE and CLASSICAL courses, there is, at the College, a PREPARATORY DEPARTMENT, in which are taught: *Reading, Writing, Arithmetic, the Elements of English Grammar, History* and *Geography*.

THE MERCANTILE COURSE,

Besides *English Grammar, Poetry, Rhetoric, History, Geography, Penmanship, Book-Keeping, Mathematics, Chemistry, Natural, Mental* and *Moral Philosophy*, includes the study of *French, Spanish, German* and *Italian Languages*.

THE CLASSICAL COURSE,

Besides the above named branches, embraces the *Greek* and *Latin* tongues; the study of both being invariably required.

Tirailleur alumni of St. Joseph's College: A. J. Bird, Joachim Daigle, Isidore Daigle, Louis Daigle, Prudent Daigle, Daniel B. Gorham, Alfred Landry, Trasimond Landry, and Isham Wood.

APPENDIX G

April 8th, 1962
Corinth, Mississippi

Dear Papa,

It is with much pleasure that I take a minute to give you some news. From our camp at Corinth, we marched to Monterey, Tennessee. Beauregard was there and we stayed several days. We marched thirty or forty miles before the battle on Sunday. We found the Yankees and the battle began.

We first arrived at their abandoned camp. We were in a ravine when a regiment of Tennesseans came up on our rear. They took us for Yankees and fired. I write you with the sad news of Raphael's death. He was killed by a Tennessee rifle. Like myself you must resolve yourself to the fact that it is a beautiful thing to die for your country.

Raphael was shot in the head. I didn't see him when it happened. He was to the rear and I was to the front. I only learned about his death later. In the same fire from the Tennessee regiment, Felix Hebert was killed. Anatole Landry got a ball in the left leg, but I don't think they'll have to amputate. Emile Allain got a ball in the hand. Sosthene Aillet got one in the head, but it wasn't bad. Belisaire Landry got one in the thigh.

We fought them bravely and forced them to retreat. By the afternoon we had driven them back to the Tennessee River. We then moved back to their abandoned camps for the night. We slept in their tents. Sunday morning we attacked again. The Yankees to our front had 40,000 fresh troops and were waiting for us....

Alexis Hebert

The final page is missing.
The original of this letter
is on file in the West Baton
Rouge Parish Museum.
Translated by Johnnie Ruth Richey

APPENDIX H

While on the Mississippi Coast, the West Baton Rouge Police Jury met and offered a resolution of monthly aid to volunteers of the Tirailleurs "requiring pecuniary assistance."

Thomas Sherron	Wife	$8
Ebenezer Griffin	Mother	$8
William Waggoner	Wife, 1 child	$12
Thomas C. White	Wife, 2 children	$16
J. M. Bennett	Wife, 2 children	$16
Auguste Buquoi	Wife	$8
Ed Hebert	Wife, 2 children	$28
Amedee Hebert	Wife, 1 child	$20
Felix Hebert	Wife, 3 children	$20
Prudent Crochet	Wife	$8
Lami Doiron	Mother, 3 children	$20
Romeuel Ledieu	Wife, 1 child	$12
John Garrentyne	Wife, 2 children	$16
Oscar Contini	Wife	$8
Adolphe Dupuy	Mother	$8
J. L. Peyronin	Mother	$8
S. Longuepee	Mother	$8

Roster
for The West Baton Rouge Tirailleurs

The following are limited biographies of members of the Tirailleurs. The information included came from the WBR Chronicles, Internet genealogy data banks, St. John the Baptist Church Cemetery records, West Baton Rouge marriage records, Booth's Books, the 1911 Louisiana Confederate Veterans census, and the 1870 WBR census. Special help was received from Mrs. Iris Lejeune.

It is important to note that when a soldier was listed as "deserter" by the CSA it does not necessarily mean that he was unfaithful to his duties. Many CSA soldiers left their units for good reasons and returned later. Their records, however, continued to reflect desertion. Since WBR Parish was occupied by Federal troops, many men were captured and paroled and stayed at home for the remainder of the war. They were not at risk of being conscripted by roving bands of Confederate impressment officers.

These biographies will show that at least forty-four of the Tirailleurs had brothers serving with them. Many more were first and second cousins or related by marriage. They were also close neighbors and, of course, French-speaking Catholics.

Analysis of the members of the Tirailleurs with Anglo names will also show a definite trend of attrition. At least twelve members of Co. H, 4th LA, with Anglo names had disappeared from the roster before December, 1861. All but two of the new recruits that showed up after the Battle of Shiloh were Acadians and were usually related to acting members.

There was much more visiting home than can be appreciated by the military records. Four married members of the Tirailleurs that were in every campaign managed to increase the size of their families: Prudent Crochet, 2 children; T. C. White, 2 children; Romauld Ledieu, 2 children; and Amedee Hebert, 3 children.

AILLET, ASPHONSE Corporal

Born WBR Sept. l, 1842. His parents were Augustin Aillet and Apolline _____. Enrolled May 1861. On furlough in July and Aug., 1863, at WBR. Promoted from 4th corpl. to 2nd corpl., Oct. 14, 1863. Killed at Jonesboro. First cousin of Sosthene Aillet.

AILLET, SOSTHENE Captain

Born in 1822, WBR. His parents were Louis Aillet Jr. and Marie Lejeune. Louis Aillet Jr. was a member of the first WBR Police Jury in 1821. His grandfather, Louis Aillet (b 1779), had come to Louisiana on the ship *La Ville d'Archangel*, in 1785. His mother's father had come to Louisiana in 1785, on the ship *Le Bon Papa*. He was Pvt. Theodule Lejeune's uncle. He fought in the Mexican War in Captain Russeau's Company of Tirailleurs, 2nd LA Volunteers. He was elected 1st sergeant when the Tirailleurs mustered into the Confederate service in May, 186l. He was promoted to 3rd lieutenant with the drowning death of A. J. Bird, on June 18th, 1861. He went on furlough, Dec. 19, 1861. He was wounded at Shiloh, shot in the head by Tennessee troops. On May 19, 1862, was elected captain. He was wounded again at Baton Rouge and was listed as "missing." Due to disability from wounds, he resigned, Nov., 1862. He sent in his resignation from home in WBR. He was listed on the WBR 1870 census as a 45-year-old store clerk. His wife was listed as Zulma, and his children: Eliza 15, Numa 13, and Louis 4. He died in 1879, and his wife, Zulma Landry, applied for his pension. She was the daughter of Elie Onesime Landry (Narcisse Landry's brother) and Jeanne Zerbine Dupuy. She was a first cousin of Lt. Adelarde Courtade's wife. Zulma was also a first cousin of Capt. Trasimond Landry. Zulma listed $125 in real assets on the pension application. Zulma also applied for his Mexican War pension, March 1888. She listed as comrades, A. V. Dubroca and Louis Kirkland. Zulma spoke only French and could read and write. There were only two Aillets serving in the armies from Louisiana.

ALEXANDRIE, ADAMIS D. 2nd Corporal

Born in 1844, in WBR. His parents were Jean Alexandros (Greece) and Marguerite Armelande Foret (Pierre Moise Foret and Biblique Allain). He had a dark complexioned, dark hair, grey eyes, and was 5' 8" tall. Enrolled in the Tirailleurs in May 1861. He was as musician. He fought in the battles of Shiloh and Baton Rouge. He was captured near Jackson, Miss., July 17, 1863. Sent from there to Camp Morton, where he took the Oath, May 18, 1863, and was sent to New Orleans. On the 1870 WBR census he is listed as a 25-year-old farmer, wife Zeolide, 24, child Martine, age 2. He married Zeolide Lejeune (Severin Lejeune and Seraphine Aillet). He was brother-in-law of Pvt. Theodule Lejeune. Adamis Alexandry died Oct. 8, 1886, and was buried at St. John the Baptist Cemetery.

ALLAIN, ANDREW Private

Enrolled at Port Hudson, Sept. 29, 1863. In Dec. 1863, he was sick at Dalton, Ga. He was captured, Dec. 17, 1864, at Hollow Tree Gap, Tenn., and sent to Camp Douglas. Sent home June 18, 1865.

ALLAIN, PIERRE EMILE Private

Born, April 12, 1847, in WBR. His parents were Francois Ricard Allain and Pauline Lafiton. At the age of fifteen, he enrolled, May 25, 1861, at Camp Moore. Before enrollment he was listed as 1st corpl., but resigned in June, becoming a private. He was wounded at Shiloh, shot in the hand by Tennessee troops. He was at the 1st Miss. CSA Hospital, June 6, 1863. Sent to General Hospital, June 9th, 1863, at Enterprise, Miss. In Feb. 1865, he was on detached duty, clerking in the Commissary Department, Montgomery, Ala. He ended up in the 2nd LA Cav., Capt. Ratliffe. He was paroled at Natchitoches, La., June 6, 1865. He is found on the 1870 WBR census as a 23-year-old clerk in a store. He married Marie Louise Brouilhet. He died in 1935 and is buried in St. John the Baptist Cemetery, Brusly. He was the last surviving Tirailleur.

AUGERON, LOUIS Private

Enrolled, Dec. 26, 1861, Berwick City. He was in the hospital at Clinton, La., Dec. 1862, the hospital in Canton, Miss., June,1863, sick at Mobile, Dec. 1863, sick at Macon, Georgia, Sept. 1864, and finished the war on sick furlough at home.

BABIN, PAUL P. Private

Born, October 4, 1838, in Iberville Parish. He was 5' 9" tall, light-complexioned, brown hair, dark gray eyes, and before the war was employed as a cooper. His parents were Pierre Paul Babin and Euphemie Leblanc. His Acadian great grandfather had been deported to Maryland in 1755. His great grandfather on his mother's side was a militia man who served under Galvez when the Spanish took Baton Rouge from the English. He enrolled in the Tirailleurs in May, 1861, at Camp Moore for a period of twelve months. He was wounded at the Battle of Shiloh, April 6th, 1862. "I was shot through the ball joint of the hip by a musket ball coming through my left groin." He was discharged on surgeon's certificate and sent home, Nov. 29, 1862. Paid off $141.92, Jan. 12, 1863. In 1864, Federal soldiers came to Brusly Landing and took forty-three prisoners, Paul Babin included, and conveyed them to Plaquemine, La. The whole number of them were compelled to take the oath before they were returned to their homes. He may have served in Stewart's Cavalry late in the war. After the war he lived in Cinclare, Louisiana. He married Rosalie Emilisaire Doiron, April 11, 1864. He was listed on the 1870 WBR census as Paul Babin, 30, carpenter, Wife Amelina, 25, Robert, 4 M, and Lucile, 2 F. His family was living with Josephine Doiron, 48 F. Paul Babin died, Sept. 28, 1928. He listed as comrades on his pension application as J. O. Hebert (Cinclare) and Theodule Lejeune (Cinclare). He is buried at St. John the Baptist cemetery.

BELEAU, LOUIS Private

Enrolled in the Tirailleurs, May 1861, Camp Moore. He was wounded at Baton Rouge. He was captured near Jackson, Mississippi, July 1863. He was sent to Camp Morton, Indiana. From there he enlisted in the 12th Michigan Battalion (August 1863). He was listed as a deserter by the CSA.

BENHAM (BERHAM), G. Private

Enrolled May 25, 1861. No other information.

BENNETT, JAMES Private

Enrolled, May 1861 at Camp Moore. On rolls until Dec. 1861. No other information. On furlough, Jan. 29, 1862. Apparently never returned. The WBR Police Jury paid his wife and two children $16 per month subsistence.

BERNARD, FELIX EDGAR Private

He was probably born in 1830 in WBR. He enrolled in the Tirailleurs in May 1961, at Camp Moore. He was the son of Onisphor Bernard and Irene Hebert. His grandfather was Felix Bernard du Montier, who came to Louisiana in 1785 on the *La Ville d'Archangel*. He was second cousin of Arthur Blanchard. He deserted, January 20th, 1863.

BIRD, ABRAHAM JOHN 2nd Lieutenant

Born In WBR in 1837. His parents were Thompson W. Bird (Abraham Bird and Mary Bowie) and Arthenise Esnard. Thompson Bird purchased Benoit Plantation in 1840. Enrolled in St. Joseph's College, Bardstown, Kentucky, Feb. 20, 1851, in the mercantile course. He was captain of the color guard of the college's militia company in 1853. Lt. Bird married Marie Eliza Dupuy (of Iberville Parish), April 18, 1860. They had a son, Abraham John Jr., who died at a young age (in 1866). A. J. Bird enrolled, May 1861, in the Tirailleurs at Camp Moore, as 2nd Lieut. He fell overboard on the trip to the Mississippi Coast and drowned, June 9, 1861. He was replaced by Belisaire Landry. His grandfather, Abraham Bird, was born in Virginia in 1784. He died in 1860 at Hollywood Plantation in EBR. Abraham Bird was the wealthiest man in Louisiana at the time of his death. Lt. Bird's great grandfather was Capt. Abraham Bird of Virginia, who fought in the Revolutionary War. He died in Louisiana in 1820, at Hollywood Plantation in EBR.

BLAIRE W. Private

Enrolled, Sept. 1863 by Capt. Aillet in Baton Rouge. He was probably a conscript. He became a prisoner of war, Dec. 17, 1864. Last paid, May 1, 1864.

BLANCHARD, (JACQUES) HILAIRE Private

Born, Jan. 14, 1834, in Breaux Bridge. His parents were Joachim Blanchard and Emelie Arceneaux. His great grandparents came to Louisiana on the *LaVille d'Archangel*. He was the nephew of Arthur Blanchard. He enrolled in the Tirailleurs on June 5, 1861, at Camp Moore. He became a member of the musician company of the 4th LA, Oct. l, 1862. At Shiloh he received a wound in the left hip. He was short and of a slight build. He was captured, July 17, 1863, outside Jackson, Mississippi. He was sent to Snyder's Bluff and then on to Camp Chase, Ohio. On March 24, 1865, he enrolled in the U. S. Army. The CSA had him listed as a deserter. He married Azelima Patin, February 3, 1876. He had eight children and made a living at farming around Breaux Bridge. He made two applications for a pension after the war and was turned down both times. Hilaire claimed on his pension application that he was captured at Hollow Tree Gap and immediately paroled and sent to New Orleans. These facts were attested to by comrades, Joseph Leray, Philogene Babin, Christophe Hebert, and P. P. Babin. Joseph Leray was at Hollow Tree Gap and knew this pension application was fraudulent. He is listed on the 1911 Confederate Veterans census as 75-years-old, and living in St. Mary Parish. Died in 1918.

BLANCHARD, JEAN BAPTISTE ARTHUR Private

He was born in WBR in 1840. His twin brother died at the age of 14. His father was Zephirin Blanchard and his mother was Lize Levert. His mother and father had died before the war, and at age of 18 he was emancipated. He was raised on a plantation of great wealth. His paternal grandparents were Jacques Blanchard and Modest Aimee Bourg. They came to Louisiana on the *LaVille d'Archangel*. His father, Zephirin Blanchard (1792-1852), fought in the War of 1812. Zephirin cultivated sugar cane on 1,040 arpents fronting the Mississippi River between Joseph Landry and Terance Derichebourg. He died in 1852, leaving a plantation home, 68 slaves, 24 mules, 11 horse carts, 3,000 gallons of molasses, 151 bbls. of sugar, furniture, and equipment, all worth $92,887. The Antonio Plantation was purchased by the Levert family after the death of Zephirin's widow in 1858. Arthur Blanchard's brother, Theodore Elie, married Emma Babin, sister of Pvt. P. P. Babin. His brother, J. Villeneuve Blanchard, was WBR sheriff from 1843–1849. Theodore Elie Blanchard, his oldest brother, served in the Tirailleurs in the Mexican War (Capt. Russeau's Company, 2nd LA Volunteers). Arthur enrolled in the Tirailleurs in May 1861, at Camp Moore. He was wounded, July 8th, 1864, and was wounded again in the battle of Ezra Church, July 28, 1864. Official records state that he died, Aug. 24, 1864, Gilmer Hospital, Forsythe, Ga., with $34 in his pocket.

BRYANT, J. W. Private

Enrolled in the Delta Rifles in May, 1861. Transferred to Co. H, June 6, 1861. He resigned and joined Scott's Battalion. (Capt. Keep's Co.)

BUQUOI, AUGUSTE 3rd Sergeant

Born Sept. 9, 1834, in Ascension Parish. He was the son of Jean Buquoi and Delphine Buquoi. He enrolled in the Tirailleurs in May 1861. He married Marie Odile Hebert (Cramas Hebert and Hortense Babin) April 10, 1861. His wife was the recipient of subsistence relief of $8 per month from the WBR Parish Police Jury. He was the brother-in-law of Pvt. Charles Hebert and Pvt. Oscar Hebert. He was discharged in 1861 "on account of physical disability." He returned to WBR Parish and ran for the office of Coroner in 1862.

CLIFTON, ALFRED Private

Enrolled at Camp Moore, May 25, 1861. He married Josephine Legendre, February 5, 1870. She was the widow of George Clifton. He is listed in the WBR

1870 census as a farm laborer born in England. He was living with Josephine, 34 F, and Alfred 12 M, and Julia 17 F. He was listed as a member of the Tirailleurs, but never enrolled in the CSA. He was allowed to resign due to a protest lodged by the English Government. Deserted, Sept. 1, 1861, East Pascagoula.

COMEAUX, SEVERIN VICTOR Private

Born Oct. 1839, His parents were Jean Baptiste V. Comeaux and Azema Trahan. Enrolled at Camp Moore, May 25, 1861. Admitted to Camp Hospital Oct. 3, 1862, returned to duty Oct. 20th. Was sick in the hospital in Clinton. Deserted, August 7th, 1863. He is listed by Samuel Lambert as being a member of the National Guards.

CONTINI, OSCAR Private

Born Jan. 14, 1840, his parents were Daniel Contini and Marceline Bergeron (Valery Bergeron and Marie Prosper). Oscar married Anathalie Traca, July 5, 1859. She was the daughter of George Traca. He enrolled in the Tirailleurs in May, 1861, at Camp Moore. He fought in the battles of Shiloh and Baton Rouge. He became ill at Port Hudson and was sent home on sick furlough. While the 4th LA was at Mobile he was listed as sick in a hospital in Macon, Ga. His wife stated that he died in a hospital in Montgomery, Ala., of dropsy. The WBR Police Jury sent his wife, Nathalie, a sum of $8 per month subsistence during the war. She never remarried. After she moved from WBR to EBR Parish, she did not receive any Baltimore Ladies Fund monies. Nathalie survived as a seamstress. Her pension application witnesses were Charles Bergeron and Fred D. Tunnard. Nathalie died Nov. 16, 1915.

COURTADE, LOUIS ADELARDE 1st Lieutenant

Born June 20, 1845 (?), in WBR. His father was Jean Dominique Courtade (a school teacher). He was well-educated and bilingual. He had a dark complexion, dark hair, gray eyes, and was 5' 4" tall. He enrolled as a private in the Tirailleurs in May 1861, at Camp Moore. He became 2nd sgt. in June 1861, and an orderly sgt. in Nov. 1861. He was elected 3rd lt., May 1862. He became 1st lt. in August 1863, on the promotion of D. B. Gorham to Captain. He fought at Shiloh, Baton Rouge, Siege of Jackson, New Hope Church, Ezra Church, Jonesboro, and Nashville. He was wounded at the Battle of Shiloh. He was sick with diarrhea, Sept. 5–Sept. 9, 1863, at Ross Hospital, Mobile, Ala. He was captured at Hollow Tree Gap, outside Franklin, Tenn., Dec. 17, 1864. From there he was sent to Johnson's Island Prison. He was released from there on June 16, 1865. He married Marcelite Louise Comeaux in May, 1877, at St. John the Baptist Church, Brusly. He died Sept. 15, 1879. Louise applied for widow's pension in Sept., 1912, while living in Iberville Parish.

CROCHET, PRUDENT Private

He was born in WBR, March 24, 1839. His parents were Hermogene Crochet and Marie Carmelite Daigre. He married Adolphine Dupuy, Jan. 22, 1861 (Adolph Dupuy and Eleanor Babin). He was brother-in-law of Pvt. Leon Adolphe Dupuy. He enrolled in the Tirailleurs in May 1861, at Camp Moore. He was killed on July 28, 1864, at Ezra Church and left on the field. His wife received $8 per month subsistence money from the WBR Police Jury, and she received money from the Baltimore Ladies Fund after the war. She had two children. She is listed in the WBR census for 1870 as Delphine Crochet, 28 F (with Theodule Hebert), Olymph 8 F, and Ouida (?) 5 F. Prudent Crochet was obviously home in the spring of 1864 to have fathered his second child, Ouida. Prudent never saw this child. Adolphine remarried, Oct. 1, 1867, to Theodule Hebert (Elie Hebert and Gertrude Babin). Theodule was the brother of Corpl. Amadee Hebert.

DAIGLE, JOAICHIM, JR. Private

Born in WBR Parish, Jan. 4, 1833. His parents were Francois Joachim Daigle (died 1855) and Dorthilde Dupuy. His great grandfather was Francois Marie Daigle, born in Acadia and deported to France, who came to Louisiana on *le Beaumont* in 1785. He was the brother of Pvt. Joseph I. Daigle, Lt. Louis Daigle, and Pvt. Prudent Daigle. His sister married Arthur Blanchard's brother, Villeneuve Blanchard. He was descended from an original Acadian settler, Olivier Daigle. Was enrolled in St. Joseph's College, Bardstown, Ky., 1851. Enrolled in the 4th LA, May 25, 1861. Left sick in New Orleans. He died in 1862, at home.

DAIGLE, JOSEPH ISIDORE Private

Born, Feb. 16, 1844, in WBR Parish. His father was Francois Joachim Daigle (1804–1855) and his mother was Dorthilde Dupuy. Francois Daigle had thirteen children and owned Stonewall Plantation. His grandparents were Louis Francois Daigle and Marie Rose Moulaison. Private Daigle was the brother of Pvt. Prudent Daigle, Pvt. Joachim Daigle, and Lt. Louis Daigle. Isidore's sister, Estelle, married Arthur Blanchard's brother, Villeneuve. Isidore Daigle was a 16-

year-old student at St. Joseph's college, Bardstown, Kentucky in 1859. Private Daigle enrolled in the Tirailleurs, August 5, 1862, on the eve of the Battle of Baton Rouge. He was 18-years-old. He was at Port Hudson, the Siege of Jackson, Mobile, New Hope Church, Ezra Church, Atlanta, and Jonesboro. He became ill on the march from Jonesboro and was sent to a hospital at Calhoun Station, Loundes County, Ala. He did not participate in the Nashville campaign. He was on the rolls of "New Company E" for April, 1865, and was paroled at Meridian, Miss., on May 14, 1865. He was married after the war and had seven children. His wife was Martha Adonia Doiron (Jean Baptiste Doiron and Coralie Lejeune). He became the brother-in-law of Pvt. Jules Doiron and Sgt. Theodore Doiron. He married, June 18, 1867, at St. John the Baptist Church. He is listed on the 1870 WBR census at a 26-year-old farmer, W Andonia 25, Rosalie 2, Carola 9/12. His brother Prudent Daigle was living with him at that time. His wife died Aug. 23, 1903. He worked in the Clerk of Court's office in WBR and died in 1910. He listed comrades on his pension application as David Devall (Chamberlin), Louis Kirkland (Brusly Landing), and F. L. Hebert (Mark, La.). He is listed on the 1911 Confederate veterans census as 67-years-old, living in WBR, Ward 3. He died, Dec. 30, 1920, and was buried in St. John the Baptist Cemetery next to his brothers, Louis and Prudent.

DAIGLE, LOUIS 2nd Lieutenant

He was born in Brusly Landing, Nov. 8, 1836. He had a dark complexion, dark hair, hazel eyes, and was 5' 8" tall. He was the brother of Pvt. Joachim Daigle Jr., Pvt. Joseph Isidore, and Pvt. Prudent Daigle. His parents were Francois Joachim Daigle and Dorthilde Dupuy. His grandfather, Louis Francois, was very wealthy, leaving an estate worth $38,000 in 1848. He was enrolled at St. Joseph's College, Bardstown, Kentucky, 1851, at age 15. In 1856, Louis Daigle was 2nd Lt. in the Company of Cadets at St. Joseph's College. He had been a member of the Orleans Cadets (Co. F, Dreaux's Battalion). This battalion ceased to exist May 1, 1862. He enrolled in the Tirailleurs, Aug. 16, 1862, at Port Hudson, La. He was elected Jr. 2nd lieut. in November, 1862. He was at Port Hudson, and fought at the Siege of Jackson, New Hope Church, Ezra Church, Atlanta, Jonesboro, and Nashville. He was sick at Ross Hospital Mobile, Ala., with dysentery, Oct. 23, 1863. He signed a receipt for clothing in Mobile, Ala., Jan 25, 1864. He was captured at Hollow Tree Gap near Franklin, Tenn., Dec. 17, 1864. He was sent to Johnson's Island. He married Corinne Magnon, Dec. 17, 1870, at St. Anne's Church, New Orleans. He died of yellow fever, Dec. 9, 1878, and was buried at St. John the Baptist Church, Brusly, La. Corinne Magnon died Dec. 12, 1937, in New Orleans.

DAIGLE, PRUDENT Private

Born, Sept. 17, 1839, in WBR Parish. His parents were Francois Joachim Daigle and Dorthilde Dupuy. He was enrolled in St. Joseph's College, Bardstown, Ky., in 1855. He was the brother of Pvt. Isidore Daigle, Pvt. Joachim Daigle, and Lt. Louis Daigle. He enrolled in the 4th LA in May 1861. He went on furlough, Dec. 28, 1861, for seven days. He was wounded at Shiloh, April 6, 1862. He was wounded, July 28, 1864, at Ezra Church. He was sent to a hospital in Forsythe, Ga., with a "severe head wound." From there he was sent home, where he was paroled, June 21, 1865. He made no pension application. In 1870 he was living with his brother, Isidore Daigle. He married Ourelia Babin. He died Oct. 26, 1885. He was buried in St. John the Baptist Church Cemetery.

DAVID, LAWRENCE Private

No information

DOIRON, (JOSEPH) ALBERT Private

Born in WBR Parish, Nov. 20, 1844. His parents were Joseph Doiron and Rosalie Bourg. He was the brother of Pvt. Louis Oscar Doiron. Enrolled in the Tirailleurs in May 1861. He was wounded at Shiloh. While at home he was captured, December 11, 1864. He was sent to a prison camp on Ship Island. He made no pension application. He was brother-in-law of Corp. Paul Babin.

DOIRON, (JOSEPH) JOINVILLE 3rd Corporal

Born WBR Parish, Jan. 27, 1846. He was baptized at St. Joseph's Church, EBR. His parents were Valentine Onizime Doiron and Marie Seraphine Lejeune. His great grandparents Alexandre Doiron and Ursule Hebert came to Louisiana in 1785, on the *Le Bon Papa*. He was a cousin of Pvt. Charles Rivault. Enrolled, May 1861. Fought at Shiloh and Baton Rouge. Appointed 3rd corpl., October 14, 1863. He fought in all the battles around Atlanta and was wounded at Jonesboro and left on the field. He was captured by the 15th Army Corps, USA. He was taken to a general field hospital and treated for his injuries by Union doctors. He was forwarded to Chattanooga, Tenn., on Sept. 20th, 1864. He was hospitalized with typhoid fever. Nov. 4, 1964, he was admitted to the hospital with an ulcer in the right groin. He was sent back to prison, Feb. 21, 1864. From there he was sent to a military prison in Louisville, Ky., and to Camp Chase, March 3, 1865. He was transferred to Point Lookout, Md., on

March 26, 1865, and took the Oath, June 6, 1865. He married, April 30, 1866, to Zenobia (Zenothine) Trichard (Jules Trichard and Hermance Rivault). He was married at St. John the Baptist Church, Brusly, La. Witnesses at his marriage were P. P. Doiron, V. Ferbos, and P. O. Dupuy. He died Jan. 29, 1888, of wounds he received at Jonesboro. He is buried in the tomb of the Association of the Army of Tennessee, Metairie Cemetery, New Orleans. Zenobie collected his widow's pension of $24 per month.

DOIRON, JULES Private

Born in EBR Parish in July 1838. His parents were Jean Baptiste Doiron and Rosalie Lejeune. He was the brother of Sgt. Theodore Doiron and second cousin of Corpl. Joinville Doiron. He was the brother-in-law of Pvt. Joseph Isidore Daigle. His grandfather was Jean Baptiste Doiron, born in 1753 in France. (He came to Louisiana on the *Le Bon Papa* at the age of two.) Jules enrolled, September 27, 1862, at Port Hudson. He fought in the Siege of Jackson, New Hope Church, Ezra Church, Jonesboro, and Nashville. He was issued one cap and one bayonet in Dec. 1863. He was captured at Hollow Tree Gap, Dec. 17, 1864, and sent to Camp Douglas prison camp. He was discharged from there, June 19, 1865. He married Laure Bernard (1846–1941) on February 26, 1870, at St. John the Baptist Church, Brusly, La. (Oniziphore Bernard and Zelamie Blanchard). He is listed on the 1870 WBR census as a 32-year-old overseer. His wife Laura was 26. He died in 1896 and was buried at St. John the Baptist Church cemetery.

DOIRON, LOUIS Private

Born in West Baton Rouge April 10, 1848. His parents were Joseph Doiron and Rosalie Bourg. He was brother-in-law of Pvt. Albert Doiron. Enrolled, Sept. 21, 1862, at Baton Rouge. Sick in April 1863. Died at Lauderdale Springs Hospital, July 1863.

DOIRON, THEODORE 4th Sergeant

Born in WBR Parish, Sept. 9, 1842. His parents were Jean Baptiste Doiron and Rosalie Lejeune. He was the brother of Pvt. Jules Doiron and second cousin of Pvt. Joinville Doiron. He enrolled in the Tirailleurs, May 1861, at Camp Moore. He was wounded three times during the war. He fought at the Battle of Shiloh, and was wounded. He fought at Battle of Baton Rouge and the Siege of Jackson. At Jackson, July 9, 1863, he was wounded and sent to a hospital in Lauderdale Springs. He was in French's Division Hospital as a corpl., July

13, 1863, to Aug. 31, 1863. He was in Breckenridge's Division Hospital, Sept, 1863, to Oct., 1863 (Marion, Miss.). He was promoted from 2nd corpl. to 4th sergeant in October 1863. He fought in the battles of New Hope Church, Ezra Church, and Atlanta, and was wounded at the Battle of Jonesboro. He was at Way Hospital in Meridian, Miss., on Jan. 26, 1865. He had a severe wound of the left hand and was discharged on surgeon's certificate. He was listed on the 1870 WBR census as a 27-year-old farmer. He married Olivia Lebauve (Jean Baptiste Labauve and Marie Daigle), September 15, 1870, at St. John the Baptist Church, Brusly. They had eight children. He was buried in St. John the Baptist Cemetery, Brusly, La. His grave marker reads, "Sgt. Theodore Doiron, Co. H., 4th LA Inf., CSA." Olivia was alive in 1911.

DUPUY, LEON ADOLPH 4th Sergeant

Born in WBR Parish, May 17, 1837. He was the son of Adolph Dupuy, a carpenter and Mexican War veteran of Capt. Robertson's company. His grandparents were Joseph Adolphe Dupuy and Uranie Dometille Rills. He enrolled, May 1861, at Camp Moore. On furlough, Oct. 21, 1861, for fifteen days. He was promoted to 2nd corpl. June, 1861, to 1st corpl. in Nov. 1861, and later to 4th sgt. He was wounded at Shiloh. While serving, the WBR Police Jury paid his mother $8 per month subsistence. He died in 1862. He is buried in St. John the Baptist Church cemetery.

DUPUY, LOUIS OCTAVE 3rd Sergeant

Born in WBR Parish, June 24, 1838. His parents were Balthazar Dupuy and Doralise Marioneaux. He was a cousin of Ulysse Ferbos. He enrolled in the Tirailleurs, May 1861. He was wounded in the Battle of Shiloh. He returned home on sick leave, April 16, 1862, aboard the *Laurel Hill*. He was promoted from private to 4th sergeant in June, 1861, and to 3rd sgt. in Nov. 1861. He was on furlough, Dec. 21, 1861, for 15 days. He was wounded at Baton Rouge and discharged, Aug. 11, 1862. He is listed on the 1870 WBR census as L. O. Dupuy, 33 M, Grocer. On July 20, 1871, he married Marie Clara Ferbos (Paul Ferbos and Pamelia Marson). Listed on the 1911 Confederate veterans census as 73-years-old, living in Iberville Parish. Died July 8, 1916, New Orleans.

FERBOS, (FRANCIS) ULYSSE Private

Born in WBR, 1839. His parents were Paul Ferbos and Sidolis Landry. He was a cousin of L. O. Dupuy and brother-in-law of Pvt. Charles Rivault and Sgt. Louis Hebert. He married, Jan. 27, 1862, to Marie Nathalie Hebert (Eugene

Hebert and Seraphine Landry). He was enrolled in the 4th LA, Co. H, Sept. 27, 1862, by Capt. Aillet. He was next listed sick at Clinton. He was left sick at Port Hudson. On WBR 1870 census as 27 M laborer, Nina (?) 24 F, Mary LaBauve 17F. He died in 1872.

GARANTYNE, JOHN Private

Enrolled, May 1861, at Camp Moore. The WBR Police Jury gave $16 per month to his wife and two children. No information after December 1861.

GARRETT, WILLIAM Private

Enrolled, July 4, 1861, at Mississippi City. He may have been married to Tabitha Louis. No other information.

GASSIE, AUGUSTE 3rd Corporal

Born Jan. 15, 1831. His parents were Pierre Gassie and Marie Elmire Marson. His maternal grandparents were William Marson and Julie Brunteau. He was the brother of Pvt. William Gassie. He was on ten-day furlough, Oct. 14, 1861. He was appointed 4th corpl. in June 1861, and 3rd corporal in November 1861. He fought at Shiloh and Baton Rouge. He was taken prisoner after the siege of Port Hudson. After the war he married Marceline Lefebvre (Emile Mames Lefebvre and Marseline Bossier). They had two children. He died Nov. 26, 1873. He was buried in St. John the Baptist Church cemetery in Brusly, La.

GASSIE, WILLIAM Private

Born on May 10, 1835, in WBR Parish. He was 5' 6" tall, blue eyes, light complexion, brown hair and was a butcher. His father was Pierre Gassie and his mother was Elmire Marson. He was the brother of Pvt. Auguste Gassie. William's sister, Adele, married Pvt. Arthur Blanchard's brother, Pierre. He enrolled in the Tirailleurs in May 1861. He was 4th sgt. from May 25, 1861, to June 29, 1861. Demoted to private at his own request. He was discharged on surgeon's certificate in late 1861: "After a march he is unable to void his urine. The same thing occurs to him after fatigue of any kind. He contracted the gonorrhea of which it is the result, some time the year (before)." He had a urethral stricture. He married Pauline (Appoline) Hebert in 1864 (Rosemond Hebert and Pauline Marson). She died Christmas day, 1887. He was the brother-in-law of Pvt. Rosemond Hebert Jr. and Pvt. Edward Hebert. He married a second time to Eda Schexnyder on February 25, 1892 (Numa Schexnyder and d'Eugenie Levert). There was a son born in 1893, named Edward, and another in 1898, named Julien. William Gassie was appointed Inspector of Roads and Levees for the 5-ward district in June 1868. He died April 30, 1908, as a result of a surgical operation. Eda applied for his pension, May 4, 1931. He was buried in St. John the Baptist Cemetery.

GIBSON, EDWARD 4th Corporal (?)

Born, June 3, 1839, in EBR Parish, Baptized at St. Joseph's Church in Baton Rouge. His parents were William Gibson and Zepheline Hebert. He was brother of William Gibson. He was conscripted at Baton Rouge, La., Sept. 21, 1862. He deserted near Jackson, Mississippi, July 18, 1863. He was sent to Camp Morton, Indianapolis, Ind. From there he joined the U.S. Army on March 24, 1865. He was a private in Co. G, U.S. Volunteer Infantry, was appointed corpl., March 24, 1865, and sgt., Aug. 18, 1865. He was demoted to private at his own request, Aug. 22, 1866, and discharged Oct. 10, 1866, at Fort Kearney, Neb. On his pension application, Gibson claimed he only enlisted in this U.S. Army after the war ended and then only to fight Comanche Indians. Pension was denied. He married Odelia Templet (Valery Templet and Eliza Reboul). Witnesses to the marriage were J. B. Tullier, Xavier Raffray, and Cecilia Raffray. They were married, April 26, 1869, in St. John's Church, Plaquemine. Odelia applied for widow's benefits, Sept. 21, 1931, in Iberville Parish, Plaquemine, La. Her husband had died of bronchitis, October 1, 1909. Her pension applications were denied twice.

GIBSON, SYLVANIE Private

Born Feb. 3, 1833, WBR. Parents were Isaac Gibson and Euphrosine Templet. In 1850, Euphrasine re-married to William Wagoner. He enrolled, May, 1863. He was probably an overseer and with the collapse of the plantation economy along the Coast, he joined the army. He walked away from the Tirailleurs, Aug. 7, 1863, and joined the 1st Brigade, 2nd Calvary Divison, Macon, Georgia. He probably found Georgia relatives in this brigade and preferred riding to marching. He was captured in April, 1865.

GIBSON, WILLIAM Private

Born April 26, 1837, WBR. His parents were William Gibson and Zepheline Hebert. He was brother of Edward Gibson. Enrolled in May, 186l. He passed through the entire war. He was in the battles of Shiloh, Baton Rouge, Siege of Jackson, New Hope Church, Ezra Church, Atlanta, Jonesboro, and Nashville.

On Oct. 8, 1863, he was issued a receipt for the following items: Bayonet scabbard $8, 1 cap box $8, 1 bayonet $57. He was captured at Hollow Tree Gap, December 17, 1864. From there he was sent to Camp Douglas, Chicago, Ill. After his release he returned to his residence at Brusly Landing. He had a light complexion, dark hair, blue eyes, and was 5' 4" tall. He signed his name with a mark.

GILBERT, CHARLES H. Private

Enrolled, June 5, 1861, at Camp Moore. Transferred to Scott's battalion in Dec. 1861, and joined Keep's cavalry.

GORHAM, DANIEL BARLOW (AUGUSTA) Captain

He was born Feb. 15, 1838. His mother was Helen Elimire LeBlanc. He was Catholic. He was nine years old when his father died. His uncle, Dr. Daniel Barlow Gorham, had a great influence on him, and out of respect for his uncle, he changed his name to Daniel BARLOW Gorham. He attended St. Joseph's College, Bardstown, Ky, 1856–1859. In 1855, he attended St. Louis University. He then entered the College of Law in New Orleans and received his J. D. He enrolled in the Delta Rifles as a private. His father was John Lyon Gorham. He sold his plantation, Homestead, to Alexander Barrow in 1839, for $40,000. Homestead was located on the north outskirts of present-day Port Allen. He distinguished himself at Shiloh and was individually mentioned in Col. H. W. Allen's after-action report. "D. B. Gorham, color guard who amid shot and shell and in a hail storm of balls held the flag firm and erect and brought it back tattered and torn by the bullets of the enemy." After Shiloh, Allen transferred him to Co. H., 4th LA, as 2nd lieut., Belisaire Landry's former position. He was held in high esteem by Lt. L. A. Courtade, who quoted the above testament of Allen's in his own will. In Nov. 1862, D. B. Gorham took Trasimond Landry's position as 1st lieut. and his position was filled by Adelarde Courtade. While at Mobile in the Fall of 1863, Col. Allen convinced him to join his staff. He was promoted to captain and went to Shreveport, La., with H. W. Allen. He later became captain of Co. A, 3rd State Guards Cavalry, in June 1864. This company was raised in West Feliciana Parish and originally was called the "West Feliciana Home Scouts." This unit served with Col. John Scott's cavalry brigade near Clinton. After the war he practiced law in Harrisonburg, La., and farmed. He married Zoe Lombard in 1874. She was 14 years old. They had eight children together. In 1870, he became District Attorney and later, District Judge. His farm was washed away in 1885 and he moved to Calcasieu Parish, where he farmed and practiced law with Col. A. R. Mitchel. D. B. Gorham died

March 19, 1916, in Lake Charles due to apoplexy. A report from the Adjutant General's office, May 19, 1914, claimed that D. B. Gorham was AWOL after 1863. This was not true, as he had assumed a staff position with Gen. Allen. (O.R., Ser. I, Vol. LIII, p. 1003) However, this record made it difficult for his wife, Zoe, to claim his pension. F. L. Reynaud of the Delta Rifles became a physician after the war and attested to his record in an affidavit restoring his honor. Zoe died Aug. 23, 1929.

GRIFFIN, (JOSEPH) EBENEZER (EBENEZZER) Private

Born Nov. 15, 1832, WBR. His father was Ebenezer Griffin, Sr. and his mother was Poalite Daigre. Enrolled, May 1861. He fought in the battles of Shiloh and Baton Rouge. He was captured near Jackson, Miss., in July, 1863, and sent to Camp Morton, Ind. He died in prison on Oct. 13, 1863. He was carried on the Confederate books as a deserter. The WBR Police Jury allotted his mother $8 per month subsistence pay. His brother married Portalis Tullier's sister.

GROGNE, GUSTAVE Unenrolled Private

Unenrolled. No military record.

GUIDRY, VILLENEUVE LOUIS Private

Born May 17, 1823, in WBR Parish. He was a 26-year-old planter in 1850. He enrolled at Mississippi City, July 4, 1861. Present on rolls until Dec. 1, 1861. His parents were Firmin Guidry and Azelia Leblanc. Married Feb. 28, 1848, to Rose Dulcinoe Broussard (Dominique Broussard and Elanore Tullier). They had eight children. Farmer in WBR in 1870 census (Ward l).

HEBERT, ADAMIS Private

Born Dec. 29, 1825. Parents were Valentin Hebert and Elize Hebert. Deserted at Siege of Jackson. On the 1870 census he was a 45-year-old farmer, wife Rosalie.

HEBERT (BIBE) ALBERT 1st Sergeant

Born Oct. 18, 1840, in WBR. His parents were Janvier Hebert and Ameline Commeaux. He was the brother of Pvt. Allain Hebert and Corpl. Hubert Hebert. He enrolled as a private in May 1861, at Camp Moore. He fought at Shiloh, Baton Rouge, Siege of Jackson, New Hope Church, Ezra Church,

Jonesboro, and Nashville. Promoted from 2nd sgt. to 1st sgt., Oct. 14, 1863. He was wounded at Ezra Church. He was captured at Hollow Tree Gap. From there he became a prisoner of war and was sent to Camp Chase, Ohio. He was paroled, February 17, 1865. He married Elvina Tullier, Dec. 13, 1869 (Adolphe Tullier and Euphemie Malanson). His wife died at the age of twenty-eight after they had had one child. In 1870 he was listed as a farm laborer. He never remarried. When he applied for his pension he listed as his comrades: Louis Kirkland, Joe Leray, Joseph I. Daigle, and P. P. Babin, all of Cinclare, La., and F. L Hebert of Mark, La. (Addis). "I was taken prisoner on the 16th of Dec., 1864. I was called out at Camp Chase on the evening of the 17th Feb., at four o'clock 1865, arrived at Akin Landing on the James River at ten o'clock, arrived Richmond, Va., at five o'clock on the twenty-five instant. Arrived at home on the 10th of April, 1865." He was paroled from Camp Chase along with Ed Longuepee and Louis Kirkland. He died in 1904, and was buried at St. John the Baptist cemetery, Brusly, La.

HEBERT, ALEXIS Private

Born Jan. 13, 1839, WBR. Enrolled on May 25, 1861. His parents were Raphael Hebert and Odille Landry. He was the brother of Raphael Hebert Jr. He was brother-in-law of Pvt. Jean Baptiste Hebert. Before the war he was overseer on Mrs. ___ Landry's Plantation. Was on furlough, Dec. 29, 1861, for one week. He was wounded at Shiloh. No further military information. The drowned Lt. A. J. Bird's brother (William C. Bird) would marry Alexis' sister (Marie Jeanne) in 1868. Many of his letters home were donated to the WBR Parish Museum by Miss Marguerite Hebert and translated by Jack Pastorek. Alexis messed with Gustave Grogne, Raphael Hebert (his brother), Camille Hebert, Rosemond Hebert, and "the Judge." There were eight others in his mess in 1861. A reference to Alexis Hebert is made in the diary of Ernest Gourrier, Feb. 17, 1864. A squad of Federal cavalry (Craig's Co.) came by, arresting all the Vicksburg and Port Hudson paroled prisoners. Alex Hebert was in a group arrested and jailed in Baton Rouge. They were sent to New Orleans on board the U.S. transport *John Walker*. They were released several weeks later.

HEBERT, (PIERRE) ALFRED Private

Born May 15, 1829, WBR. His parents were Jean Baptiste Hebert and Amaranthe Landry. His grandfather had been an Acadian exile and was born in Maryland. At age thirty he enrolled in the Tirailleurs, May 1861, at Camp Moore. He was detailed to take charge of his plantation and the estate of N. S.

Landry in WBR Parish. Another record lists Landry Hebert, enrolled Sept. 29, 1862, discharged to take care of the plantation of W. S. Landry. (Possibly the same person.) Married Elvina Landry (b. June 2, 1833). Alfred died May 3, 1900. He is buried at St. John the Baptist Cemetery.

HEBERT, ALLAIN Private

Born in 1845, WBR. Parents were Janvier Hebert (Etienne Hebert and Emily Daigre) and Armeline Comeaux (Henri Comeaux and Marguerite Hebert). He was brother of Sgt. Albert Hebert and Corp. Hubert Hebert. Enrolled, September 26, 1862, in Port Hudson by Capt. Aillet. In May 1863 he was sick in Port Hudson. He died of disease around Sept. 1864. At the time of his death he had $12 in his personal effects.

HEBERT, AMEDEE 1st Corporal

Born in WBR, Dec. 28, 1832. His parents were Hilaire Hebert and Clarisse Templet. He married Zulma Hebert (Elie Hebert and Gertrude Babin), June 1, 1857. He was brother-in-law of Corp. Hubert and Pvt. Theodore Hebert. He enrolled as a private in the Tirailleurs, May 1861. Promoted to 3rd corpl., June, 1861. In Nov. 1861 he was sick at home in WBR. In June 1863 he was again sick in the hospital at Canton, Miss. In June 1863 he was attached to hospital duty as a nurse. In Aug. 1863 he was transferred to Lauderdale Springs Hospital. He was promoted to 1st corpl., Oct. 16, 1863. He fought at New Hope Church and Ezra Church and Jonesboro. He was paroled in Baton Rouge, May 18, 1865. He was busted to private in 1864 after being AWOL at Dalton, Ga. "I obtained a furlough of 30 days from my command in January 1865, and at the expiration of my furlough I could not report due to sickness." He suffered from rheumatism. He surrendered at home in WBR. He had a wife and seven children. He listed his comrades as F. L. Hebert and Simon Octave Rivet. Dr. T. P. Vaughn attested to his disabilities. He was married before the war with one child. WBR Parish subsistence pay of $12 per month was given to his family during the war. His first child was born in 1857. He fathered three children during the war. His last two children were born in 1874 and 1875. Amadee's brother-in-law, Theodule Hebert (Elie Hebert and Gertrude Babin) married Pvt. Prudent Crochet's widow.

HEBERT, CAMILLE Private

Born Dec. 11, 1841. Parents were Eli Hebert and Gertrude Babin. Enrolled as private in the Tirailleurs, May 1861. He was the brother of Pvt. Felix Hebert and Pvt. Theodore Hebert and brother-in-law of Corpl. Amedee Hebert. He was faithfully present on all rolls. He died at Academy Hospital in Marietta, Ga., of chronic diarrhea, on Feb. 13, 1864, with $50 in his pocket. He was not married.

HEBERT, CHARLES CROMAS Private

He was born in WBR, Oct. 26, 1839. His parents were Cramas Hebert and Eurenie Doiron. He was the brother of Pvt. Oscar Hebert. He was the brother-in-law of Sgt. Auguste Buquoi. He enrolled, May 25, 1861, at Camp Moore. He went on furlough, Dec. 15, 1861. He was sick in the latter part of 1861 with a leg injury. He was left at Port Hudson and was captured. He asked to be exchanged to Co. K, 2nd La Cav. Sept. 15, 1866, he married Olesida Templet (Marcelin Templet and Clementine Guidry).

HEBERT, CHRISTOPHE Private

Born Dec. 7, 1844, at Brusly Landing. His father was Adolphe Hebert (Jean Baptiste Hebert and Amaranthe LeBlanc). Adolphe was second sergeant in Capt. Robertson's company in the Mexican War. He had one brother, Pvt. Jean Baptiste Hebert. He enrolled in the Tirailleurs at Camp Moore, May 1861. He was wounded near Atlanta in a skirmish line, July 22, 1864 (Battle of Atlanta). "The bullet or shrapnel landed in my left foot, the piece of shell penetrating through the foot, and entering in the hollow (plantar surface) of my foot." He was taken to Gibson's Brigade Hospital in Florence, Ala. He was unable to move and applied for an extension of his sick furlough. His furlough was extended until after the Battle of Nashville. Christophe returned home to recover. He was paroled in Baton Rouge. He suffered from this wound for the rest of his life. He married Odalie Hebert (Gilbert Hebert and Celise LaBauve). She was the widow of Ernest Hebert. He was first cousin of Pvt. Louis Kirkland. He applied for his pension, Dec. 7, 1899, and his comrades were listed as Louis Kirkland and Joseph I. Daigle. Christophe died Oct. 3, 1911. He was listed on the 1911 Confederate veterans census as 63-years-old, living in WBR, Ward 2.

HEBERT, (JEAN BAPTISTE) EDGARD Private

Born in WBR in 1844. His parents were Valentin Hebert (b. 1787) and Euphrasine LaBauve. The WBR Police Jury set aside $28 per month for his wife and two children. He enrolled, May 1861, at Camp Moore and was discharged one month later at Mississippi City. He married Marie Cecelia Aillet, Dec. 28, 1871.

HEBERT, (FRANCOISE) EDWARD Private

Born Aug 21, 1836. His parents were Rosemond Hebert and Pauline Marson. He was brother of Pvt. Rosemond Hebert and brother-in-law of Pvt. William Gassie. Enrolled, May 25, 1861, at Camp Moore. Discharged, June 25, 1861, at Mississippi City. He married Nov. 30, 1865, to Arthemise LaBauve (Pierre LaBauve and Coralie Dupuy). He died Oct. 15, 1907. He is buried in St. John the Baptiste cemetery, Brusly.

HEBERT, EMILE Private

He was born in 1844 in WBR. Parents were Camille Hebert (b. 1822) and Ann Elizabeth _____. Enrolled Sept., 27, 1862, Port Hudson by Capt. Aillet. Present on all rolls to April, 1865. In 1870, he was twenty-six and living with his parents.

HEBERT, F. LOUIS 2nd Sergeant

He was born in WBR in 1839. His parents were Eugene Hebert and Seraphine Landry. He was the brother-in-law of Ulysse Ferbos. Enrolled May, 1861, at Camp Moore. He fought at Shiloh and Baton Rouge. He was in the hospital at Osyka, Miss., on May 9, 1863. He became ill in the march to stop Grierson's Raid. He became 2nd sgt., Oct. 14, 1863. He fought at New Hope Church, Ezra Church, Atlanta, and Jonesboro. He was sick on furlough in late 1864, and missed the Battle of Nashville. After the war he resided in Mark, La. (Addis). He married Celina Aline Bergeron, (Hilaire Bergeron and Amelina Landry), June 5, 1865. In 1870 he was farming. He applied for pension, Sept. 6, 1905. He had seven children. He listed his occupation after the war as "Journeyman." He suffered from rheumatism. He listed his comrades as Theodore Doiron, Jules Doiron, and F. L. Hebert(?) He is listed on the 1911 Confederate veterans census as 73-years-old, living in WBR, Ward 2. He died Sept. 11, 1913. He is buried in St. John the Baptist Church Cemetery, Brusly, La.

HEBERT, (FELIX) LOUIS Private

Born June 19, 1825. Parents were Elie Hebert and Gertrude Babin. He married June 8, 1848, to Virginia Comeaux (Vitale Comaux and Celeste Prosper). WBR Police Jury gave $20 per month subsistence to his wife and children. The Baltimore Ladies Fund gave $50 per month. He is listed as "killed" in the lists of killed, wounded, and missing of the 2nd Corps, Army of Mississippi, at the

Battle of Shiloh, April 6th and 7th, 1862. He was shot in the back by troops of the 4th TN regiment. Buried somewhere in Lost Field.

HEBERT, HUBERT 3rd Corporal

Born in WBR on June 1, 1839. His parents were Janvier Hebert and Marie Armeline Comeaux. He was brother to Sgt. Albert Hebert and Pvt. Allain Hebert. They lived in Iberville Parish on the left bank of the Grand River. Enrolled in Tirailleurs, May 1861. Elected 3rd corpl. in June, 1861. He was discharged on surgeon's certificate, September 7, 1861, East Pascagoula, Miss. He married April 4, 1872, to Philomene Dupuy (Adrian Dupuy and Eloise Daigle). They had eleven children. He applied for a pension, Sept. 1913. He died Jan. 21, 1927, and was buried in Plaquemine. He listed comrades as P. P. Babin and Joseph Leray. In 1920 he was living with his daughter, Philomene Hebert Grandeury, in Iberville. His obituary states that he was in a charge in which his brother Albert was wounded (Ezra Church?) alongside him, but he was unable to stop and render assistance.

HEBERT, JEAN BAPTISTE Private

Born Oct. 28, 1839, in WBR Parish at Brusly Landing. His parents were Adolphe Hebert and Rosalie Traca. He was the brother of Christophe Hebert. Enrolled May 1861. He was wounded at Shiloh. He arrived home after Shiloh on the steamer *Laurel Hill*. He was left at Port Hudson and taken prisoner. He was paroled. He was present on the rolls from May 1864, until Feb. 1865. In May 1864, his $50 bounty from the WBR Parish police jury had not caught up with him. He was listed on the rolls of POWs (May 14, 1865) of the 4th LA Vols. CSA, commanded by Capt. P. E. Lorio, surrendered at Citronelle, Ala., by Lt. Gen. Richard Taylor, CSA, to Maj. Gen. E. R. Canby, USA, May 4, 1865, and paroled at Meridian, Miss., May 14, 1865. He claimed that he was taken prisoner at Hollow Tree Gap on the retreat from Nashville. He claimed to have escaped and gone to Tupelo, Miss. There he was assigned to an "outfit" and went to Spanish Fort. He didn't remember the company or regiment. He listed no comrades. After the war he married Celestine Hebert (Raphael Hebert and Odile Landry), Feb. 3, 1866. In 1870 he was farming. He became brother-in-law of Pvt. Alexis Hebert. His pension application was denied. He is listed as 72-years-old in the 1911 Confederate veterans census, WBR, Ward 2. He was buried in St. John the Baptist Cemetery.

HEBERT, NUMA 3rd Lieutenant

Born in WBR in 1838 (?). His parents were Hippolite Hebert and Celeste Doiron. He was the brother-in-law of Pvt. Romauld LeDieu. Enrolled May, 1861, as a private. He was elected 3rd lieut., Sept. 1863. He was wounded (in the hand) at New Hope Church, May 27, 1864, and was sent on sick furlough to Mobile. He was captured by Capt. Brown of the 118th Illinois Infantry, Jan. 18, 1865, at home. He was then sent to New Orleans and exchanged, May 12, 1865 (four months in prison). He married, March 4, 1867, to Marie Leontine Lejeune (Elie Lejeune and Eleonore Aillet). They lived in WBR, Ward 2. She died Oct. 9, 1912. On the 1880 WBR census he was a 39-year-old Barkeeper. He is buried in St. John the Baptist Cemetery, Brusly, Louisiana.

HEBERT, (JEAN BAPTISTE) OSCAR Private

Born Jan. 10, 1835. Parents were Cromas Hebert and Marguerite Uranie Doiron. He was the brother of Charles Hebert. He was listed on the rolls prior to May 25, 1861, as ensign. Enrolled May 1861. He fought at Shiloh and Baton Rouge. He was detailed as a teamster, Nov. 1862, and sent later on detached service to Clinton, La. He was detached at one time on orders of Gen. Beall to attend his plantation. He was taken prisoner at Port Hudson. He was wounded somewhere after Port Hudson. He was captured again at Fort Adams, La., October 6, 1863, and sent to Camp Morton. Released on Oath, May 22, 1865. His complexion was florid, hair dark, eyes gray, 5' 10" tall. After the war he resided at Cinclare, La.

HEBERT, RAPHAEL, JR Private

Born in WBR, July 26, 1836. His parents were Raphael Hebert Sr. (son of Alexis Hebert and Marguerite Chaisson) and Odille Landry (daughter of Simon Landry and Manon Hebert). He was Pvt. Alexis Hebert's brother. He attended college in Florence, Ala. (LaGrange College) prior to the war. Enrolled May 1861, at Camp Moore. On furlough, Dec. 29, 1861. Present on rolls until December 1861. He was last paid Aug. 1861. He was killed at Shiloh. He was shot in the back by troops of the 4th TN regiment. Buried somewhere in Lost Field.

HEBERT, ROSEMOND, JR. Private

Enrolled, May 1961. His parents were Rosemond Hebert and Pauline Marson. He was the brother of Pvt. Edward Hebert and the brother-in-law of

Pvt. William Gassie. He was a clerk in a store prior to the war. He went on furlough, Dec. 29, 1861, for seven days. He was killed at Shiloh.

HEBERT, THEODORE Private

Born in 1846, WBR Parish. His parents were Elie Hebert and Gertrude Babin. He was the brother of Pvt. Camille Hebert and Pvt. Felix Hebert. Enrolled, Dec. 13, 1861, at Berwick City, Louisiana. Sick at Port Hudson and taken prisoner. No record after Port Hudson. In 1870 he was a farmer and neighbor of Raphael Hebert Sr. He is listed on the 1911 Confederate veterans census as 67-years-old, living in WBR, Ward 2. He married Odile Lejeune, Nov. 17, 1868 (Jean Baptiste Lejeune and Roselean Allain). She was the widow of Edward Bourg.

HENRY, EVARIST Private

Born Dec. 28, 1838, WBR. His parents were Francois Henri and Oreline Lejeune. Enrolled at Camp Moore, May 1861. He was wounded at Shiloh. He married, Jan. 16, 1865, to Marie Eleonore Lemoine (Andre Lemoine and Virginie Daigre). His brother, Richard Henry, enrolled at St. Joseph's College in 1851. He signed the Father Vaudry petition, Dec. 1878. On the 1880 WBR census he was a store clerk.

HERMOGENE, FRANK Private

Enrolled, May 22, 1861, at Camp Moore in Capt. H. A. Rauhman's Co, 4th LA. He transferred, July 1, 1861, to the Tirailleurs. In Dec. 1861, he was on special duty as a drummer (bass drum). Was AWOL after the first day at Shiloh. Listed as "deserted," April 9, 1862.

ISAAC, DIOGENE Private

Enrolled Sept. 15, 1862, at Baton Rouge by Capt. Aillet. He was present in all battles around Atlanta and at Jonesboro. He transferred to Bouanchard's Battery (Company A, Pointe Coupee Artillery) Sept. 11, 1864. This battery was captured at Nashville.

ISAAC, LEON Private

Enrolled May 1861. His parents may have been Emanuel Isaac and Basilide Traca. He fought in the battles of Shiloh, Baton Rouge, Siege of Jackson, and New Hope Church. He was wounded at New Hope Church. He was admitted to Ocmulgee Hospital, Macon, Ga. It was a minor wound, in the thigh. He was killed at Ezra Church, June 28, 1864.

JOHNSON, HARRY J. Private

Enrolled in Co. H, 4th LA, May 25, 1861, at Camp Moore. Absent on detached duty as "sutler of the Regiment."

KIRKLAND, LOUIS RICHARD VINCENT Private

Born, Aug. 21, 1847, on the Kirkland Plantation at Brusly Landing. His grandfather, Richard H. Kirkland (born in Georgia and married to Levicy Williams), migrated to St. Helena Parish. He fought in the War of 1812, 2nd division, 1st Regiment, Louisiana Militia. Richard H. Kirkland was a civil engineer. He was clerk of Court for WBR for fourteen years, and later was state engineer under Governor Paul Hebert. Louis Kirkland's father, Richard Vincent Kirkland (b. 1804, Augusta, Ga.), married Appoline (Pauline) Hebert in 1836, at St. Joseph's Church, Baton Rouge. Pvt. Louis Kirkland was the first cousin of Lt. Adelarde Courtade, Pvt. Felix Bernard, Pvt. Anatole Landry, Pvt. Jean Baptiste Hebert, and Pvt. Christophe Hebert. He was educated in WBR schools and attended Magruder's Institute in EBR. He enrolled as a private in the Lake Providence Cadets and fought at the Battle of Shiloh, where he was wounded. He transferred to the Tirailleurs at Port Hudson in late 1862. He was fifteen years old when he fought at Shiloh. Louis was a tall, handsome young man. He became ill and was hospitalized in the Fort and did not leave with the 4th LA on their March to Jackson. He was captured at home, May 13, 1863. He was then sent to Grant's Island near Mobile and from there to a parole camp at Demopolis, Ala. He was paroled and returned to the 4th LA while at Mobile.He fought at New Hope Church, Ezra church, Atlanta, Jonesboro, and Nashville. He was wounded, July 28, 1864. He was captured again at Hollow Tree Gap, Dec. 17, 1864, and sent to Camp Chase, Ohio. He was paroled again, Feb. 17, 1865, and captured a third time at the mouth of the Red River on April 5, 1865, with Scott's cavalry. At his last capture he was accompanied by Edmond Longuepee. He was taken to Waterproof Louisiana, by way of the gunboat *Lafayette*. After the war, in 1866, Louis married Marie Mirza Hebert, his third cousin (Lovinski Hebert and Adeline Orellie Daigle). In 1868, he served on the WBR Parish Police Jury, second ward. He was Sheriff from 1878 until 1894. Louis died, September 11, 1915, in New York City after surgery. He was buried in St. John the Baptist Church cemetery.

LANDRY, ALCIDE (THE ELDER) Private

Enrolled in the Tirailleurs, July 25, 1861, at Mississippi City. (Pass Christian according to him). He fought at Shiloh and was wounded. Afterwards, he was sick in the hospital at Canton, Miss. He was transferred from the hospital in Canton directly to Port Hudson in Jan. 1863. He was wounded in the foot at Ezra Church, July 28, 1864. He recovered and was captured at Hollow Tree Gap, December 17, 1864. He was sent to Camp Douglas, Chicago, Ill. He applied for a pension in 1898. At that time he ran a small grocery store in Plaquemine, La. He listed comrades as Theodore Doiron and Paul P. Babin.

LANDRY, (JOSEPH) ALCIDE Private

Born, Aug. 16, 1845, in WBR at Brusly Landing. His parents were Narcisse Landry and Marie Carmelite Hebert. He was the brother of Lt. Belisaire Landry, Capt. Trasimond Landry, and Sgt. Amedee Landry. He enrolled, Oct. 1, 1863, at Mobile, Ala., and fought the remainder of the war. He fought at New Hope Church, Ezra Church, the battles around Atlanta, Jonesboro, and the Battle of Nashville. He was captured at Hollow Tree Gap, Dec. 17, 1864. He was sent to Camp Douglas, Ill. After the war he married Marie Celeste Leveque. (Joseph Auguste Leveque and Marguerite Basalite Landry). He was the brother-in-law of Lt. J. A. Leveque, Pvt. Louis Leveque, and Pvt. Samuel Leveque. In the 1870 census he was farming in WBR and living between Simon Rivet and Trasimond Landry. He later moved his family to Calcasieu Parish and lived in Lake Charles, working for the railroad. Listed on the 1911 Confederate veterans census as 66-years-old, living in Calcasieu Parish, Ward 4. He applied for his pension, March 1911, at the age of 66. He gave as references, D. B. Gorham of Lake Charles and Louis Kirkland of Cinclare, La.

LANDRY, AMEDEE 4th Sergeant

Born Dec. 31, 1828. Parents were Narcisse Landry and Marie Carmelite Hebert. He resigned when the regiment reached Camp Moore in May 1861. He was discharged the same day. He was appointed Road and Levee Inspector for Ward 5, WBR Parish, June 3, 1861. He died Dec., 1901.

LANDRY, ANATOLE Private

His parents were Ursin Landry and Amaranthe Hebert. He was eight years old in the 1850 census. His brother, Alfred, was a student at Bardstown. He was second cousin of Trasimond Landry. He was first cousin to Louis Kirkland,

Felix Bernard, Christophe Hebert, and J. B. Hebert. Enrolled in the Tirailleurs in May 1861. He was wounded in the leg by Tennessee troops at Shiloh and sent home.

LANDRY, (PIERRE) BELISAIRE 1st Lieutenant

Born, June 29, 1824, at Brusly Landing. His father was Narcisse Landry and his mother was Marie Carmelite Hebert. He was a veteran of the Mexican War and was married to Marguerite Gatton Manuelite "Lise" Leveque, May 1851, (Joseph Augustus Leveque Sr. and Clarisse Doralisse Landry). Belisaire's father and his wife's grandfather were half-brothers. He was the brother of Sgt. Amedee Landry, Capt. Trasimond Landry, and Pvt. Alcide Landry. He was the brother-in-law of Lt. J. A. Leveque, Pvt. Louis Leveque, Pvt. Samuel Leveque and Pvt. Alfred Landry. He was parish assessor from 1849 to 1851, and was on the Police Jury in WBR Parish from 1857 to 1861. He enrolled in the Tirailleurs May 1861, as 3rd lieut. He became 2nd lieut. When A. J. Bird drowned. At Shiloh he was wounded in the leg by Tennessee troops and returned home on sick leave, April 16, 1862, aboard the *Laurel Hill*. He resigned, May 19, 1862. On the 1870 census he is listed as a farmer, with assets of $2000 and living next to Sam Leveque. Note: All contemporary records spell Belisaire with and "s" rather than a "z."

LANDRY, JOSEPH E. Private

Born 1840. No information.

LANDRY, J. A. (Joseph Alfred) Private

He was born Sept. 5, 1832, in WBR Parish. His parents were Ursin Landry and Amaranthe Hebert. He was the brother of Anatole Landry and second cousin of Capt. Trasimond Landry. He attended St. Joseph's College in Bardstown, Ky. He married Alozia Leveque, Oct. 8, 1856, and became the brother-in-law of lst Lt. J. A. Leveque. Enrolled in Co. H, 4th LA, Sept. 27, 1862, at Baton Rouge, probably as a conscript. Deserted, July 16, 1863 (?) Listed on the 1911 Confederate veterans census as seventy-one years old, living in WBR, Ward 2. On the 1870 census, he was listed as a 38-year-old physician, wife's name Eloise. He was buried in the St. John the Baptist Cemetery, Brusly.

LANDRY, J. N. Private

Enrolled in the Tirailleurs, Sept. 27, 1862, at Port Hudson. He is also reported to have enrolled, May 25, 1861, at Camp Moore. Present on the rolls until May

1863. He was a member before the war, but did not go to Camp Moore in May 1861. He was probably a conscript. He deserted, July 17, 1863, at Jackson, Miss. No other information. Signed the Father Vaudry petition, Dec. 1875.

LANDRY, L. (LANDRY) Private

Enrolled Co. H, Dec. 11, 1861, at Berwick City. Wounded at Shiloh. On the 1870 census he was a 30-year-old farm laborer, wife Letitia.

LANDRY, TRASIMOND Captain

Born August 7, 1839, in WBR (Addis). His parents were Narcisse Landry and Marie Carmelite Hebert. He was the brother of Lt. Belisaire Landry, 4th Sgt. Amedee Landry, and Pvt. Simon Alcide Landry. He was second cousin of Pvt. Anatole Landry and Pvt. J. A. Landry. He studied at St. Joseph's College, Classical curriculum, 1859–1861. He enrolled, May 1861, in the Tirailleurs as 2nd Sgt. He was demoted to private in July 1861 at his own request. He fought at the Battle of Shiloh and was promoted to 1st lieut. in May 1862. He fought at the Battle of Baton Rouge and was promoted to captain, Nov. 25, 1863. He fought at the Siege of Jackson, New Hope Church, Ezra Church, Atlanta, Jonesboro, and Nashville. He was captured, Dec. 17, 1864, at Hollow Tree Gap near Franklin, Tenn. From there he was sent to Johnson's Island prison camp. His travel papers described him as twenty-five years old with dark complexion and dark hair, 5' 11" tall. He married Marie Amelie Bujol, Nov. 3, 1867. He is listed on the 1870 WBR census as a farmer, wife Amelia 28, Terese 1 year old, Catherine 6/12, and Narcisse 75, with $1000 in property. They had five children: Marie Therese, Mary Catherine, Thomas Belizaire, Moses Joseph, and Marie Manette. After the war he farmed, taught school, and in 1875 became Clerk of Court in WBR. In 1874 he was treasurer of the Poydras Fund. He signed the Father Vaudry petition in Dec. 1875, on which he was noted as "secretary of church wardens." He died of yellow fever, Feb. 18, 1879. He left his widow and five children destitute. His widow remarried to Pierre Magloire Babin. They had two children, Clemance and Albine. He is buried in St. John the Baptist Cemetery in an unmarked grave.

LEBLANC, URSIN 3rd Sergeant

He was born in 1822 in WBR Parish. Ursin was a veteran of the Mexican War. He served in the WBR Guards under Capt. Robertson, 5th LA Volunteers. He was an election commissioner from Ward 5 in an election held on May 20, 1861, in WBR. He was a neighbor of Narcisse Landry. Enrolled in the

Tirailleurs May 1861. Became 3rd sgt. in June, 1861. He was seriously wounded at Shiloh and sent home to WBR. He is listed on the 1870 census as a 48-year-old store clerk. He was buried in St. John the Baptist cemetery.

LEDIEU, ROMAULD ALPHONSE Private

Born in WBR, son of Jean Baptiste Ledieu and Gabriel Thomee. He was a private, Co. H., 4th LA, no information. The WBR Police Jury allotted $12 per month for his wife and child's subsistence. He married Cecelia Hebert, July 27, 1858 (Hippolite Hebert and Celeste Doiron). He was the brother-in-law of Lt. Numa Hebert. He died before 1870. His wife was listed on the 1870 WBR census as Cecilia Ledieu 31 F, and his children, Olivia 8 F, and Samuel 6 M.

LEJEUNE, THEODORE Private

Born January 18, 1838. His parents were Zenon Lejeune and Elizabeth Martin. He was the brother of Pvt. Joseph Theogene Lejeune and first cousin of Pvt. Theodule Lejeune. He enrolled as a private, May 1861. He went on furlough Dec. 28th, for seven days. He was killed at Shiloh. Probably buried somewhere in Davis' Wheat Field.

LEJEUNE, THEODULE ZENON Private

Born, March 6, 1841, and Baptized at St. Joseph's church, EBR. His parents were Severin Lejeune (1808) and Seraphine Aillet (Thomas Aillet and Julliene Marioneaux). His paternal grandparents were Jean Baptiste Lejeune and Marie Genevieve Dourand (Doiron). Nephew of Sosthene Aillet and first cousin of Pvts. Theodore and Theogene Lejeune. Deserted, May 1863. He married Theodorice Leblanc, April 27, 1865, (daughter of Pierre Paul Leblanc and Letitia Dodd). He married a second time, Feb. 13, 1888, to Olymph Penn (daughter of William Penn and Adele Hebert). He was the brother-in-law of Adamis Alexandre. He was probably the first cousin of Theodore and Theogene Lejeune. After the war he resided at Cinclare, La. He is listed on the 1870 WBR census as a 28-year-old farmer with Theodora 28 F, and Idalie 3 F. He died before 1911. He is probably buried in St. John the Baptist Cemetery, Brusly.

LEJEUNE, JOSEPH THEOGENE Private

Born Aug. 20, 1842. He enrolled in the Tirailleurs, May 25, 1861, at Camp Moore. His parents were Zenon Lejeune and Elizabeth Martin. He was the brother of Pvt. Theodore Lejeune. He was captured, May 21, 1863, near Port Hudson.

LEWIS, NORMON Private

Enrolled Dec. 13, 1861, by Lt. J. A. Leveque, at Berwick City. He was recruited from the neighborhood. He was AWOL at Berwick City in December 1862, and then listed as sick at his home in Berwick City. The next listing for him is Feb. 1865, detached in the Medical Department, Clinton, La.

LERAY, JOSEPH ALEXANDRE Private

Born 1836 in Brusly Landing, WBR parish. His parents were Charles Leray and Marie Julienne Aillet. He enrolled in May, 1861, as a private. He fought at Shiloh, Baton Rouge, Siege of Jackson, New Hope Church, Ezra Church, Jonesboro, and Nashville. He served the duration and was captured at Hollow Tree Gap. He was sent to Camp Douglas. After the war he married and had four children. His wife was Helena Landry, (Landry Xavier Landry and Helena Trahan). They married on January 25, 1866. He is listed on the 1870 WBR census as Joseph Leray 37, farmer, Helena 29, Leida 4, Azelia 14, and Levie 2. On his pension application he listed his occupation as laborer, at $.75 per day. He was living in Cinclare, Louisiana, and listed his comrades as Louis Kirkland and Jules Doiron. He is listed on the 1911 Confederate veterans census as seventy-four years old, living in WBR, Ward 2. He died Oct. 11, 1924, and was buried in St. John the Baptist Cemetery. His grave marker reads, "Joseph LeRay, Co. H, 4 La. Inf., C.S.A."

LEVEQUE, J. A., (JOSEPH AUGUSTUS) JR. 1st Lieutenant

Born Jan. 6, 1832. His parents were Joseph Augustus Leveque Sr. and Clarisse Doralise Landry. In 1860, Leveque Sr. owned sixty-two slaves. He was the brother-in-law of Lt. Belisaire Landry, Pvt. J. A. Landry, and Pvt. Alcide Landry. He graduated from Pennsylvania Medical College, Philadelphia, March 3, 1855. He started practice in Iberville in 1855. He married Marie Therese Kirkland (Vincent Kirkland and Pauline Hebert). They married, Dec. 22, 1862. He was also the brother-in-law of Pvt. Louis Kirkland. He was elected 1st lieut. from the beginning of the war. He fought in the Battle of Shiloh. On May 19, 1862, he resigned from the regiment. He became the surgeon for the Delta Rifles. He later became, major, surgeon, 8th LA Cavalry. The 8th LA Cav. formed in Oct.1864 and did skirmishing on Bayou Teche and the Atchafalaya. They were at Natchitoches at the surrender. After the war he practiced medicine in Natchitoches, La. He left Iberville parish after the war due to continued high water. He died in Bermuda, La., near Natchitoches, Dec. 11, 1893. He was buried in Common Street Cemetery, Lake Charles, La. His wife died June 19,

1902. They had two children, Lucy and Joseph. Lucy became a Broadway star (stage name Rhonda Cameron). Joseph became a newspaperman and was assassinated. The entire Leveque family moved away from WBR after the war. They were not Acadian and did not possess the tendency to patrilocality known to Acadians.

LEVEQUE, (JEAN ETIENNE) LOUIS Private

Born Aug. 14, 1835, in WBR. Enrolled May 1861 in the Tirailleurs. He was a brother of 1st Lt. J. A. Leveque and Pvt. Samuel Leveque. He was on furlough for three months, starting July 29, 1861. He was sick most of the war. On the Lake Charles 1870 census, he was a lawyer, living with his brother Justinian Daniel Leveque (Deputy Clerk of Court). It is listed as I. Daniel Leveque, 33 white male (deputy clerk of court?), Family: Marie J., 23 W F KH, La, Daniel J. 3 WM La, Marie 6/12 W F, Dec. La, Louis, 36 W M Attorney, Emily Clark, 24 W F KH LA. He married Emily Clark Richard. He died in 1878. No children. He was buried in the Common Street Cemetery, Lake Charles, La. His brother, Justinian Daniel Leveque, was born in 1837 in WBR. He served as a private in the Orleans Guards. After Shiloh, he joined the 30th LA. He developed chronic hepatitis and returned to WBR in the spring of 1864. He married Mary J. Mullell and died at Lake Charles, Louisiana.

LEVEQUE, (JOSEPH) SAMUEL Private

Born Sept. 9, 1840. Enrolled May 25, 1861. He was the sixth child of Joseph Auguste Leveque Sr. and his first wife, Clarice Doralise Landry. Clarice died in 1840. He was the brother of Lt. J. A. Leveque and Pvt. Louis Leveque. He also had a brother, Pvt. Justinian
Daniel Leveque, 30th LA. He was the brother-in-law of Lt. Belisaire Landry, Capt. Trasimond Landry, and Pvt. Simon Alcide Landry. He enrolled in the Tirailleurs in May 1861, and fought in the battles of Shiloh and Baton Rouge. He was wounded at Shiloh in the left thigh in the early part of the first day's fighting and returned home on sick leave, April 16, 1862, aboard the steamer *Laurel Hill*. He was listed as "missing" after the Battle of Baton Rouge, but turned up at Port Hudson. In May of 1863, he was on detached duty in the vicinity of Port Hudson. In Nov. 1862, Maj. Gen. Gardner assigned him to the "Secret Service" in WBR Parish. Toward the close of the war he was detailed into a special torpedo service along the Mississippi River "from Baton Rouge down the river." Samuel returned to WBR after the war and farmed on lands of J. A. Leveque Sr. He signed a petition, December 1875, along with Zoe, his wife, in support of Father T. A. Vaudry. Samuel and Zoe where the last Leveques to

leave WBR Parish and join the remainder of the family in Calcasieu Parish. He lived in West Lake. Among other things, he was a band leader. He and Zoe Marson (Eugene Marson and Euphrosie Hebert) had no children. He died March 31, 1909, at the home of Frank Christopher, in Gooseport. He applied for his pension, Aug. 1902, and listed his occupation as "gardener." He listed his attorney as D. B. Gorham and his references as Daniel B. Gorham of Lake Charles and Alcide Landry of West Lake. Zoe died July 3, 1907. They are both buried in the Common Street Cemetery, Lake Charles, La.

LIBBY, F. JACKSON Private

Born March 1821, Limington, Maine (Abner Libby/Salome Jackson). Listed on the 1850 census as an overseer. He was a member of the WBR Guards (Capt. Robertson's Company 5th LA Volunteers) in the Mexican War. He became ill at Camp Lovell and returned home. He rejoined the company before Shiloh, but burned his foot and was sent to a hospital in Jackson. He ended the war as a pvt., Co I., Ogden's LA Cav. Paroled at Gainsville, Ala., May 12, 1865. He married Amanda Flynn. One daughter, Martha Salome Libby, was baptized Catholic, April 1869, at age twenty. Jackson Libby died June 6, 1866.

LONGUEPEE, AUGUSTE Private

Born Jan. 4, 1826. Parents were Jean Baptiste Longuepee and Modest Genevieve Lejeune. He was the brother of Pvt. Edward Longuepee. Enrolled at Port Hudson, Feb. 4, 1863. He was sick in the hospital at Dalton, Ga., Dec., 1863. He married Carmelite Virginia Lejeune (Julian Lejeune and Elizabeth Gibson). He was a 23-year-old planter in 1850. He was killed at Jonesboro. His wife and four children received $75 from the Baltimore Ladies fund.

LONGUEPEE, EDWARD Private

Born Jan. 14, 1828. Parents were Jean Baptiste Longuepee and Modest Genevieve Lejeune. He was brother of Pvt. Auguste Longuepee. Enrolled in the Tirailleurs July 4, 1861, at Mississippi City. He fought at Shiloh, Baton Rouge, Siege of Jackson, New Hope Church, Ezra Church, Atlanta, Jonesboro, and Nashville. In Sept. 1864, he was detached as brigade provost guard. He was captured at Hollow Tree Gap near Franklin, Dec. 17, 1864. He was sent to Camp Douglas, paroled, and captured again at the mouth of the Red River, April 5, 1865. He was captured this second time along with Louis Kirkland.

LONGUEPEE, LOUIS ADAMIS, Jr. Private

He was born in WBR, Sept. 13, 1830. His parents were Louis Adamis Longuepee and Julie Comeaux. His grandfather arrived on the *LaVille d'Archangel*. He enrolled in the Tirailleurs, July 4, 1861. He fought at Shiloh and Baton Rouge. In June 1863 he was sick at Port Hudson and was captured there. He married Julia White, July 12, 1875.

LONGUEPEE, PIERRE HILIARE Private

He was born Jan. 10, 1843, EBR Parish. He was baptized at St. Joseph's Church, Baton Rouge. His parents were Simon Pierre Longuepee (a cotton planter) and Sophie Ludivine Comeaux. He enrolled in the Tirailleurs May 25, 1861, fought at Shiloh, and was wounded. He was also wounded at the Battle of Baton Rouge. He made no pension application. No information after the Battle of Baton Rouge. He married Ophelia Verdean, Nov. 15, 1880.

LYLE, ROBERT Private

His father was Dr. William W. Lyle, owner of Smithfield Plantation (3200 acres). Enrolled at Mississippi City, Co. H, 4th LA, Oct. 23, 1861. He was wounded at Shiloh. "Absent, left in hospital at Corinth, supposed dead" He died of his wounds. Buried somewhere in Corinth, Mississippi.

MARTIN, (F.) LOUIS Private

Enrolled May 24, 1861, at Baton Rouge, La. He was wounded at Shiloh. "Left at the hospital in Corinth, supposed dead." He died of his wounds. Buried somewhere in Corinth, Mississippi.

MARTIN, THEODORE Private

Enrolled in the Tirailleurs as a private. In the Fall of 1863 he was sick in a hospital in Mobile. Ross Hospital, Mobile, Ala., Oct. 26, 1863. He was wounded at Ezra Church, July 28, 1864.

MAYHART, EDWIN Private

No information.

MCKIMMINS, M. B. Private

Enrolled May 25, 1861, at Camp Moore. Wounded at Shiloh.

O'BRYAN, J. J. Private

Transferred to Scott's Cavalry.

PEYRONNIN, FENELON Private

Born in 1844. Listed on the 1870 census as son of Bernard Peyronnin, 50-year-old farmer, and Julienne 49 F. He died July 14, 1871 at twenty-seven years old. His mother was Julienne Granger (Pierre Granger and Genevieve Hebert).

PEYRONIN, JEAN LOUIS (J. L. PEYRONIN) Private

Parents were Jean Louis Peyronnin Sr. and Adelaide Granger. Enrolled as a private in Co. H, 4th LA, May 1861. He was on the rolls at the first pay period. The WBR Police Jury sent his mother $8 per month subsistence pay. No other information. His father died in 1856. He may have married Rosa Manning and died Aug. 23, 1923, in New Orleans. Possibly born in 1840.

PEYRONIN, OSCAR Private

Born Sept 11, 1841, WBR. Parents were Jean Louis Peyronin and Adelaide Granger. Enrolled at Baton Rouge by Capt. Aillet in August 1862. He deserted, July 17, 1863, at Jackson, Miss. He became a prisoner of war at Camp Moore and was released on Oath, May 22, 1865.

POPE, E. J. Private

Enrolled July 4, 1862, at Vicksburg by Capt. Aillet. He was detached duty, July 1863, at Port Hudson. He became 5th sgt., Oct. 14, 1863, and was transferred to Co. E, 2nd KY Regiment, in Aug. 1864.

RENAUD, JOHN Corporal

His father may have been Dr. William Reynaud. Enrolled Dec. 13, 1861, at Berwick City. He was appointed corporal, Oct. 14, 1862. He fought at Shiloh, Baton Rouge, the Siege of Jackson, and New Hope Church. He was wounded at Ezra Church on July 28, 1864. He fought in the Battle of Nashville and was captured at Hollow Tree Gap near Franklin, Tenn., Dec. 17, 1864. He was captured again at the mouth of the Red River, April 5, 1865. He was a member of Scott's cavalry battalion at the time.

RICHARD, OCTAVE Private

Enrolled Dec. 13, 1861, at Berwick City by Lt. J. A. Leveque. Deserted, Aug. 1863. He married Adelaide Broussard.

RIVAULT, CHARLES BERTRAND Private

Born in Bourdeaux, France, June 13, 1831. He arrived in Louisiana, Dec. 18, 1848, on the ship *Cabot*. He married Marie Antoinette Ferbos (Paul Ferbos and Cidalize Landry), Dec. 24, 1855, at Brusly Landing. Enrolled in Co. H., 4th Louisiana, and was on the rolls to Dec. 1862. Fought at Shiloh and Baton Rouge. Absent on detached duty to move machinery from the penitentiary in Baton Rouge to Clinton, La. After May 1863, he was absent on detached duty at Clinton, La. He was a cousin of Pvt. Joinville Doiron and brother-in-law of Pvt. Ulysse Ferbose. Listed on WBR census 1870 as a 38-year-old carpenter born in France, wife, Antoinette 33 F, Alphonse 14 M, Marie 13 F, Annie 5 F. He died in 1878 and was buried in St. John the Baptist Cemetery

RIVET, SIMON OCTAVE Private

Born in Iberville Parish, Aug 12, 1929. His parents were Isidore Rivet and Clothilde Morales. He enrolled Sept. 27, 1862, at Port Hudson. He is listed as deserted, Dalton, Ga., Dec. 1863. He fought at the Siege of Jackson. "I was paroled in WBR, La., and sick until the war ended. Affected in the kidney, bladder, and spitting up blood. Cared for by Dr. T. P. Vaughn." He married, July 12, 1862, to Marguerite Josephine Landry (Narcisse Landry and Marie Carmelite Hebert). He was a brother-in-law of Lt. Belisaire, Sgt. Amadee, Capt. Trasimond, and Pvt. Alcide Landry. Marie Josephine Rivet was born July 27, 1861 (Brusly). They had five children. He worked in the clerk of court's office in WBR, and was living in Mark, La. (Addis), in 1898. He died Jan. 15, 1903. His wife died Feb. 15, 1875. In 1870, he was farming and living next to Alcide and Trasimond Landry, with $1000 in property. He was buried at St. John the Baptist Church at Brusly Landing.

SERRET, GUSTAVE Private

Born 1822, WBR. He was a 28-year-old planter on the 1850 census. His parents were Celestin Serret and Reine Sophie LeBlanc. Enrolled in the Tirailleurs, May 1861. On the rolls till Dec. 1861. No other information.

SCOVAL, CHARLES Private

Enrolled in the West Feliciana Rifles, May 25, 1861. Transferred to the WBR Tirailleurs, Aug. 19, 1861. He was captured at Port Hudson.

SHERRON, GEORGE Private

Enrolled Sept. 30, 1862, at Port Hudson. "Absent sick at home," Dec., 1862. Never returned to regiment. Was probably a conscript.

SHERRON, THOMAS 5th Sergeant

Enrolled May, 1861. Fought at the battles of Shiloh and Baton Rouge. Deserted from Port Hudson, May 14, 1863. The WBR Parish Police Jury sent his wife $8 per month subsistence pay. He made no pension application.

TEMPLET, (JEAN) AMADEEE Private

Born in WBR, March 30, 1838. His parents were Marcelin Templet and Aglace Trahan. Enrolled May 25, 1861, at Camp Moore. He fought at Shiloh and Baton Rouge. He was sick in the hospital, May 1, 1863. In Aug. 1863 he was at Lauderdale Springs Hospital. Feb. 28, 1865, he was assigned to "light duty" at Selma, Ala. Nov. 15, 1864, he was in the Concert Hall Hospital, Montgomery, Ala. He married Marie Adelina Melancon, Oct. 9, 1865. It is interesting that Adelina vouched for Edward Gibson in a letter to the pension board, written in 1931. He is listed on the 1870 WBR census as a 31-year-old farmer with his wife Adelina 24, and Gusta (?) 4.

TULLIER, DORVAL Private

Born in WBR, Sept. 27, 1839. His parents were Flavien Tullier and Marie Adele Alexandre. He was the brother of Portalis and Ulysse Tullier. He was enrolled Sept. 26, 1862, by Capt. Aillet at Port Hudson. Left sick at Port Hudson and was taken prisoner. Paroled, July 12, 1863. He was alive in 1911. He married Adeline Hermine LeBlanc (Faustin LeBlanc and Julienne Bourgoyne), Sept. 24, 1860.

TULLIER, PORTALIS Private

Born December 3, 1837. His parents were Flavien Tullier and Alexandrine Daigre. He was baptized, March 19, 1838, at St. Joseph's Church, EBR. He married Celestine Olivia Raffray, Feb. 16, 1857. She was the daughter of Jean

Baptiste Raffray and Rosalie Tullier. He was an election commissioner from Ward l in an election, May 20, 1861, in WBR. He was the brother of Dorval and Ulysse Tullier. He enrolled in the Tirailleurs in May 1861. He was wounded at Shiloh and sent home on the steamer *Laurel Hill*. He fought at Baton Rouge, Siege of Jackson, New Hope Church, Ezra Church, Atlanta, Jonesboro, and Nashville, and was captured at Hollow Tree Gap near Franklin, Tenn., Dec. 17, 1864. He was sent to Camp Douglas, Ill. He married a second time to Zepheline Kirkland (Jeremy Kirkland and Zepheline Hebert), October 3, 1871.

TULLIER, ULYSSE Private

Born in 1846. Parents were Flavien Tullier (planter) and Marie Adele Alexandre. He was the brother of Portalis and Dorville Tullier. Enrolled Sept. 27, 1862, at Port Hudson. Oct. 1862, was in the hospital in Clinton, La. Dec, 1862, was sick at home in WBR. He never returned.

WAGNER (WAGGONER), WILLIAM Private

Enrolled in the Tirailleurs at age forty-nine. He was a carpenter. Married the widow Euphrosine Gibson. Was a Mexican War veteran. The WBR Police Jury provided subsistence to his wife and child of $12 per month. No other information.

WHITE, THOMAS C. 3rd Sergeant

Born in WBR Parish. His parents were Thomas D. White and Lusinda White of North Carolina. He married, May 12, 1856, to Adolphine Gibson (Isaac Gibson and Euphrosine Templet). He was a Mexican War veteran. He was promoted to 2nd corpl. in June 1861, and then to 4th sgt. He made 3rd sgt. Oct. 14, 1863. He was sick at Camp Hospital at a Port Hudson, Oct. 5, 1862. He fought in the battles of Shiloh, Baton Rouge, Siege of Jackson, New Hope Church, and was killed at the battle of Ezra Church and left on the field. The WBR Police Jury sent his wife $12 per month for her and her two children. He added two more children during the war. After the war his wife received $75 from the Baltimore Ladies Fund for the "relief of destitute widows and orphans of deceased Confederate soldiers of WBR." His widow married Hermogene Babin (Paul Babin and Caroline Lejeune), a farm laborer. T. C. White was the only Tirailleur veteran of the U.S. Army to die for the Confederacy.

WILLIAMS, FRANCIS A. Captain

Born 1824 and married Jane Dunbar, July 27, 1848. In 1850, Francis was a 26-year-old planter with $9000 in assets. Listed as a planter on the 1850 census. He was a commissioner for general elections in 1856, from Brusly Precinct. He was a member of the Tirailleurs in the Mexican War. Absent on furlough, Nov. 26, 1861. Sick in Nov. 1861. Not re-elected captain in May 1862. Dropped from the rolls and replaced by Sosthene Aillet.

WOODS, ISHAM Private

Born 1840, WBR. He was a student at St. Joseph's College, Bardstown, Kentucky, in 1856. His father was James C. Wood (from Kentucky and Tennessee). He was the brother of Patrick Woods. Enrolled in Co. H, 4th LA, in Dec., 1862. He was absent in the hospital in Jackson, La. In Oct 1863, he was at the hospital in Clinton. He died in the hospital at Woodville, Miss.

WOODS, LEWIS E. Private

Attended a military academy for six months prior to entering West Point Military Academy, class of '59. He resigned in 1861 and joined Co. H, 4th LA. He transferred to Miles' Legion and was elected 1st lieut., Co. A, in March 1862. He was captured at Port Hudson and imprisoned. He escaped, Aug. 8, 1863. He married after the war and lived in Iberville Parish. He wrote to Sec. War Seddon in April 1863, requesting transfer to a cavalry or light artillery unit. Lewis was a ward of Mr. E. D. Woods. L. E. Woods was from Plaquemine, Iberville Parish. On the 1880 census he is listed as a 36-year-old sugar planter (wife Nidonia, 32). They were listed as homestead No. 1. So they must have been living right on the parish line between Iberville and WBR.

WOODS, PATRICK Private

Born in WBR in 1843. He enrolled at St. Joseph's college, Bardstown, Ky., May 5, 1856, in the classical course. His father was James C. Woods (planter in 1850 with $19,000 in property assets), of Brusly Landing, WBR. Was the brother of Pvt. Isham Woods. No military information after enrollment in Co. H, WBR Tirailleurs, 4th LA, May 25, 1861.

COMPANY ROSTERS, 4TH LA, CSA

The rosters of the other companies of the 4th LA are listed below.
Abbreviations:
C   Captured
D   Deserted
K   Killed
M   Missing
S   Substitute
T   Transferred
W   Wounded
ex   exchanged
*   Present in November 1861
Rank listed is the highest rank obtained during the war.

FIELD AND STAFF

Robert Barrow*	Colonel	Resigned
H. W. Allen*	Colonel	Resigned
Samuel Eugene Hunter*	Colonel	Captured Nashville
J. G. Kilbourne*	Captain	Quartermaster
J. A. Godfrey*	Chaplain	Resigned
Ben Clark	Adjutant	Discharged May 1862
Clifford Belcher	Adjutant	Resigned May 1862
J. M. Doyle	Adjutant	W Jonesboro
B. S. Daniels	Sgt. Maj.	K Jonesboro
E. E. Dick	Quartmst. Sgt.	Passed through war
V. M. Purdy	Ordinance Sgt.	Passed through war
J. R. Giles	Color Sgt.	W Atlanta, C Nashville
J. M. Blou	Commissary Sgt.	W Bat. Rouge, W Span Fort

HUNTER RIFLES A
Roster of Company A, 4th Louisiana Volunteers (Old Co. K)

H. Obed. Acord*	Private	C 1864
John Adkins (Atkins)*	Private	K Baton Rouge
Carl Attler	Private	W Pickett's Mill
Napoleon B. Barfield*	2nd Lieut.	K Port Hudson
John Bresler (Bessler)	Private	C Jonesboro

William Bessell*(Biesel)	Private	Present to Feb. 1862
John Bisler	Private	
John W. Bradford*	Private	C Port Hud., W Jonesboro
D. M. Calliham*	Private	Absent 1862
Ed Calliham	Private	
Ed Cambell	Private	W Jonesboro
W. B. Carter*	Private	
W. P. Carter	Private	T Ogden's Cav.
John C. Cay	Private	C Resaca, May 16, 1864
R. L. Chaney*	Private	C Baton Rouge, C Clinton
B. E. Chaney*	Private	T
James E. Chaney*	Private	K Dec. 4, 1864
Levy R. Chaney*	Private	W Baton Rouge
William J. Chap(t)man*	Private	K Ezra Church
James Clark*	Private	Absent 1861
Charles L. Collins*	Private	Passed through the war
Royal E. Collins*	Corporal	K Atlanta, 6/4/64 skirmish
Peter Z. Colson*	Private	W Shiloh, T Apoethecary
William Hosea Cook*	Private	W Shiloh, W Jonesboro
W. J. Crane*	Lieut.	C Nashville
Arthur Crawford	Private	T Commissary
Thomas Crosby	Private	C Aug. 5, 1864
Joe Deaton	Private	AWOL 1863
E. E. Dick	Sergeant	Quartermaster Dept.
Henry Dietz	Private	Present Shiloh
W. P. Doughty*	Private	Died disease Apr. 9, 1862
J. F. Dupriest*(Depriest)	Private	K Shiloh
John Dwyer*	Private	W Shiloh, AWOL 1863
A. T. Fiester	Captain	W Baton Rouge W Jonesboro, died
Edward Goodman	Private	T from Wingfield's Co.
George Gourlay	Private	Discharged July 1861
Jacob Guth (Gouth)*	Musician	Present 1861
J. N. Grierson	Private	C
E. Griffin	Private	C Aug. 5, 1864, Atlanta
M. Griffin	Private	C Atlanta, Aug. 5, 1864
Jacob Habricht*	Private	C Clinton
G. W. Hamilton*	Private	W Shiloh
C. P. Harrall	Corporal	Absent after 1861
A.W. Hayes	Private	Present April 1865

E. A. (G) Hays	3rd Lieut.	
R. W. Hays*	Private	W Ezra Church
Guy M. Hearrell*	Private	Died Berwick City, 1861
W. H. Heatherington*	Private	W July 4, 1864
Gus Heckler*	Private	Sam Lambert's roster 1861
Henry Herchler*	Private	Sam Lambert's roster 1861
J. T. Hicklin*	Corporal	K Shiloh
E. W. Hobgood*	Private	W Shiloh, W Ezra Church
Meyer Hiltner*	Private	Died disease, Berwick 1862
Thomas M. Hudson*	Private	W, C Shiloh, W Nashville, lost leg, died
H. M. Huntington	Private	W Shiloh, friendly fire
William Jackson*	Sergeant	Accidentally shot Miss. City W Ezra Church?
C. P. Jarett*	Corporal	K Shiloh
John Jennings	Private	Present Feb. 1862
J. Jerolds	Private	C Baton Rouge
Thomas Lott Johnson*	Sergeant	W Shiloh, K Jonesboro
Howel W. Johnson*	Sergeant	W Shiloh, W Atlanta 8/5/64, W Jonesboro Died of gangrene
M. Johnson	Private	C Murphreesboro
William A. Knox*	3rd Lieut.	W Shiloh, W Ezra church, lost leg
Ernest Henry Kramer*	Private	W, C Shiloh
M. Kelley*	Private	Absent after Feb. 1862
Julius Keiffer	Musician	W Shiloh
Samuel A. Lambert*	Sergeant	W Ezra Church, DIARIST
Pryon W. Lea	Private	C Atlanta, 8/5/64 POW died
Hampton M. Lea	Sergeant	W Atlanta, Aug. 5, 1864
Willie D. Lea*	Corporal	K Jackson, July 12, 1863
Zacharia Lea*	2nd Lieut.	W Shiloh, friendly fire
J. N. Marbery	Private	C Nashville
Henry Marston Jr.	2nd Lieut.	T 15th TN, W Perryville W Chickamauga
James Marston	Sergeant	W Ezra Church, C Nashville
W. Wallace Mathews*	Private	W Atlanta, Aug. 5, 1864
William C. T. Maxwell*	Corporal	C Nashville
Abraham Mayer	Musician	Regimental Band

James Mays*	Private	K Shiloh
John P. McAdams*	Corporal	W Ezra Ch., died 8/5/64
Jason McAdams	Private	W Ezra Church, died
William R. McAdams*	Private	W Shiloh, W Pickett's Mill lost arm
W. D. McBride	Private	POW
J. McCombs*	Private	Present Feb. 1862
A. G. McDonald*	Private	W Shiloh
G. L. McDonald*	Private	C Jackson (?)
H. L. McDonell*	Private	K Shiloh
Robert F. McKie*	Private	K Shiloh
Joe A. McKneeley*	Sergeant	Passed through war
Samuel G. McKneeley*	Private	W Shiloh, died
William H. McKneeley	Private	T Secret Service
August Michell*	Private	Present Feb. 1862
John R. Montgomery*	Assistant Surgeon	
Thomas A. Moore*	Private	Accidentally shot, 8/10/64 left arm amputated
John Morgan*	Sergeant	W Shiloh, W Baton Rouge W Ezra Church, W Atlanta lost leg, Aug. 8, 1864
J. E. Morrison*	Private	Present Feb. 1862
Joseph Murrain*	Private	W Baton Rouge
J. P. Muyse	Private	Present to Feb. 1862
G. A. Neafus*	1st Lieut.	Not re-elected
Dan G. Odum*	Private	W Shiloh, died
C. J. Parkman	Private	W Shiloh
R. Draughan Patrick*	Private	T Commissary, DIARIST
David Pratt*	Private	C Jonesboro, exch 9/22/64 C Nashville
E. J. Pullen*	Major	W Ezra Ch., C Nashville
J. Pullen	Private	Present Feb. 1865
J. R. Quitsell	Private	
J. E. Ransom*	Private	W, C Shiloh, supposed dead, lost leg, died
Charles O. P. Ratcliff*	Sergeant	Accident, shot, Oct. 1863
George Ravenscraft	Private	Present Feb. 1862
J. Y. Richardson*	Private	W Shiloh, C Span. Fort
Frank M. Rivers*	Private	C Bat. Roug., T Navy 1864
Lawson T. Rheams*	Sergeant	W Ezra Church, lost leg

Eugene Rich*	Private	Present Feb. 1862
John Richerts	Muscian	C Nashville
John S. Rowe	Private	
Joseph Sanders*	Private	D New Orleans 1862
Henry Schroeter*	Private	Present Feb. 1862
W. S. Seymour*	Private	Prisoner after Feb. 1864
John Shea	Private	C Port Hudson
W. C. Shropshire*	Private	W Jonesboro
Henry Skipwith Jr.	Sergeant	T from 27th LA, T to Co. E
Thomas W. Skipwith*	Private	Died Jan. 1863
W. J. Smart	Private	AWOL April 1864
W. V. Smeltzer	Private	T Engineer Corps
Felix Smith*	Private	Discharged 1861
H. C. Smith*	Private	C Port Hudson
J. K. Smith	Private	K Shiloh
W. Henry Smith*	Private	AWOL
G. Sourly	Private	Sam Lambert's roster 1861
C. J. Sparkman*	Private	W Shiloh C Baton Rouge
C Ezra	Church,	died prison
T. J. Sparkman	Private	K Aug. 6, 1864, Atlanta
J. L. Spring	Sergeant	POW
Phillip Stevens	Private	C EBR Jan. 1865
A. R. Sterling	Color Sgt.	Present 1861
Leander Stewart*	Private	C Nashville
William M. Stone*	Private	C Port Hudson, shot Ratcliff
Thomas Sullivan	Private	C Port Hudson
Nic. W. Tate*	Private	K Shiloh
David C. Thompson*	Sergeant	W Shiloh, W Ezra Chrch
William A Thompson*	Private	W Shiloh, C Jonesboro, exchanged Sep. 22, 1864 C Nashville
J. E. Twiggs*	Private	Present Feb. 1862
Ira Bowman Wall*	Lieut.	T 19th LA, shot Tom Moore
Frank Weber*	Private	W Shiloh
Jarrret D. White*	Private	W Shiloh
John A. White*	Corporal	W Shiloh, W Jonesboro
Silas T. White*	Private	K Shiloh
S. B. Williams	Private	K Ezra Church
Joe Whitehead*	Hosp Steward	
Ferdinand Williams	Private	C Missionary Ridge

James S. Williams	Private	D
W. (S.?)B. Williams*	Private	K Ezra Church
W. D. Williams*	Private	Present Feb. 1862
Charles Wolf	Musician	W Shiloh
J. D. Worsham*	Sergeant	Severely W Jonesboro
Scott J. Worthy*	Private	Passed through war
William Yarborough	Private	K Jonesboro

NATIONAL GUARDS

Roster of Company B, 4th Louisiana Volunteers (Old Co. A)
G and C Roster indicates names that were on the roster printed in the Baton Rouge *Gazette and Comet* May 22, 1861, and that were on no other rosters.

Charles Albert*	Private	G and C roster
S. H. Albert	Musician	
Augustus Althaus*	Private	Died Aug. 7, 1863
Joseph R. Armistead	Hosp. Steward	
C. B. Austen	Private	Paid for substitute
J. M. Barron	Private	W Jonesboro
Charles Bates	Private	C Big Black, 1863
John Bates*	Private	C Big Black, 1863
Jacob Baum*	Private	G and C Roster
A Baumstark*	Sergeant	G and C Roster
Barth. Buckly*	Sergeant	W Ezra Church
M. Bellande	Private	C Aug. 5, 1864
John Belocq*	Private	Present to Feb. 1862
Charles Betz*	Captain	Not re-elected
Ed Biedel*	Sergeant	
Ovide Bisset	Private	Present Aug. 1864
A. Blum (Bloom)*	Lieutenant	Resigned 1862
T. J. Bluth	Private	
William J. Blythe	Private	Died in prison
Rudolph Bohn*	Private	Present Feb., 1862
Leopold Brodeck*	Private	Present Feb., 1862
Barholomew Buckley*	Private	W Ezra Church
John Caffrey*	Private	Joined 3rd LA
I. G. Carson	Private	
Joseph Caspar	Corporal	Substitute, A. W. Merriam K Jonesboro
Patrick Cavanaugh	Private	C Port Hudson

John (F?) Chaillet*	Sergeant	K Jonesboro
Louis J. Cohn*	Private	Hired substitute
Patrick Collins*	Private	Present Feb. 1862
Thomas Collins*	Private	D 1861
Severin Comeaux	Private	D Aug 7, 1863
John Councelman*	Private	
Thomas Crosby*	Private	K Atlanta, Aug 5, 1864
Jacob W. Christoffel*	Private	Absent 1861
R. De Leeun	Private	
N. P. DeLeuw*	Private	G and C roster
Jerry Deady*	Private	D July 8, 1863, US Army
Henry Dietz*	Private	Absent April 1862
		T Washington Artillery
J. W. H. Dils	Private	D July 18, 1863
Martin Donohoe*	Private	C Atlanta, 8/5/62
W. F. Downing	Private	Absent Dec. 1861
Charles Drumpt*	Private	G and C roster
John Dumke*	Private	G and C roster
Samuel Dupertuis	Private	D Mobile 1863, stood trial
Fred Eckles	Private	D Feb. 1863
Jerry Eddy	Private	
G. W. Emmons	Private	T 59 ALA
William Emmons	Private	T 59 ALA
Andrew Ernst*	Private	Shoemaker
John Evans*	Private	Absent after Feb. 1862
James Fearson*	2nd Lieut.	Dropped July 19, 1862
Andrew Fink (Finck)*	Private	D Ship Island
C. Focht	Private	Present 1861
Nicholas Fougerousse*	Private	Shoemaker, C P. Hud.
John Gaffrey*	Private	W Shiloh
Joseph Gaspard	Private	C Atlanta, Aug. 5, 1864
J. Garnell	Private	
Joseph Gearing*	Private	
A. L. Gibson*	Private	Present 1861
John Gibson	Private	W Jonesboro
S. (J.)L. Gibson*	Corporal	W Jonesboro
James Gill*	Private	Substitute for L. Cohn
G. Gimber (Gimler)*	Sergeant	Present 1861
W. W. Godwyn	Private	Discharged, underaged
Henry Gray*	Private	D New Orleans 1862

T. Gremillion	Private	Discharged 1864
John Gross*	Private	C Port Hudson
F. Guitreaux	Private	Passed through the war
John Hamlin (Hanlein)*	Private	
Charles Haller*	Corporal	Present Feb. 1862
Michael Hamall*	Private	W Shiloh
Henry Hardy*	Private	D Nov. 1861 New Orl.
William Harvey*	Corporal	Present Nov. 1863
Henry Hanmel*	Private	G and C roster
Charles Hanser (Houser)*	Private	
F. M. Hereford*	Private	G and C roster
Frank Hermogene	Private	T Tirailleurs D Shiloh
John Hermozen	Private	
Joseph Hester	Private	
P. Albert Hoff*	Private	T 27th LA
John Houser (Hauser)*	Private	
Hiram Holston	Private	C Nashville
Joseph P. Hutchinson*	Corporal	T Wingfield's Cav.
Theodore Junglebluth*	Private	Present Feb. 1862
Peter Jungen*	Private	Present Feb. 1862
A. Kaumstark	Private	
W. G. Kendall	Musician	Present Aug. 1864
James Kennedy*	Private	Present Dec. 1863
Patrick Kennedy*	Private	Present Feb. 1862
Anton Kerner*	Private	Present Feb. 1862
John (Jean?) Kohler*	Sergeant	Present Feb. 1862
John Kunzelman	Private	G and C roster
Hector Latil*	2nd Lieut.	W Shiloh
A. Laurent	Sergeant	C WBR Oct. 1864
George Lutz*	Private	Commissary Dept.
Jacob Maas*	Private	K Shiloh
Thomas Madingly*	Private	G and C roster
John Magenis	Corporal	C Nashville
Emile Major	Private	Died Feb. 22, 1863
Etienne Major	Private	Died March 1863
M. Magornan	Private	C Atlanta, Aug 5, 1864
Christian Mann*	Private	Present Feb. 1862
Moritz Mantz*	Private	G and C roster
Carl (Charles) Markstein*	Private	Absent, sick
Francis Martin*	Sergeant	M, C Shiloh, C Nashville

Joe Martin	Musician	
George Mathis	Musician	Substitute for E. Loeb D Port Hudson
G. W. Mazengo	Private	Present Nov. 1863
F. J. McClellan	Sergeant	
Charles McGuire	Sergeant	W Jonesboro neck, died
Jacob Mears*	Private	G and C roster
A. W. Merriam	Private	Bought substitute
Joseph Miller*	Private	
J. A. Miltz*	Private	C Baton Rouge
William Montan	Private	T Company F, commissary
Barney Moran*	Private	
Thomas B. Morgan	Private	W Baton Rouge, died
Frank Morton	Private	C Natchitoches
Joe Mullen	Private	
Jerry Mulvihil*	Private	W Shiloh, C Atlanta Aug. 5, 1864
Maretz (Moveck) Munsch*	Private	
G. (J?) Nachmann*	Private	Present 1861
James Neville*	Private	C Port Hudson
C. Nonnemacker	Private	C Port Hudson
John Oeschger*	Private	Present Feb. 1862
Joe Oster*	Private	D Aug. 7, 1863
F. Otto*	Corporal	G and C roster
John F. Paul*	Private	Present Feb. 1862
G. Pletzer*	Private	G and C roster
P. E. Porche	Private	T to Delta Rifles
Gideon Pritchett	Private	Sick (joined in Alabama)
John Prout	Sergeant	C Jackson (Deserted)
Cornelius Ragan	Private	
Ed Riedel*	3rd Lieut.	
Cornelius Regan	Private	G and C roster
L. Regan	Private	C Atlanta, Aug. 5, 1864
Richard Railey (Riley)*	Private	Discharged 1862
Henry C. Rauhman*	Captain	Resigned, Dec., 1861
Thomas Redman	Private	C Spanish fort
M. A. Roberts	Private	C August, Aug. 5, 1864
A. Richy	Private	S for C. B. Austen
John B. Rodgers	Private	C Nov. 7, 1863
Benjamin Roth (Rooth)*	Private	Present Feb. 1862

John Roth	Private	T Nat. Guards, D Aug. 1863
John Ryan	Private	C Atlanta, Aug. 5, 1864
Louis Saisan	Private	AWOL
Charles Schaeffer*	Private	Present Feb. 1862
John Schaeffer*	Private	AWOL May 1864
Frederick Schilling*	Sergeant	C Baton Rouge
Frederick Schmidt*	Private	Present April 1862
Mathias F. Schneider*	Sergeant	K Atlanta, Aug. 5, 1864
John Schneider	Private	D Jackson, MS 1863
J. Schneider*	Corporal	G and C roster
Jacob Schuler*	Private	Sam Lambert's roster 1861
Albert Schulsing	Private	Quartermaster Dept
Joe Schwab*	Private	D Aug. 1863
A. Scott	Lieut.	W Ezra Church
R. F. Sheffield	Private	C Spotsylvania
F. Smith	Private	G and C roster
(John) George Staff*	Private	Present Feb. 1863
Henry Stegal	Private	
William Stern*	Private	M Shiloh
George Stevens*	Private	G and C roster
A. Stingel	Sergeant	
Corn (John?) Sullivan*	Private	Present to Feb. 1863
Tim (Tom?) Sullivan*	Private	POW, May 1863
M. Snyder*	Private	K Atlanta, Aug. 5, 1864
Frederick Snyder*	Private	Sam Lambert's roster 1861
George Stephens	Drummer	Present Feb. 1863
Henry Stingel (Stengel)*	Sergeant	Elect Lt., resigned
F. Sullivan*		
J. M. Thompson	Private	Passed through war
Charles Trump*	Private	Suicide Pascagoula
Samuel Tynes	Private	Discharged 1864
Charles Vetters	Private	T Co. C, C Pt. Hud.
M. Vellandi	Private	C Atlanta, Aug. 5, 1864
Andrew Vink*	Private	Sam Lambert's roster 1861
Paul Vogel	Corporal	G and C roster
John Waldman*	Private	G and C roster
William Walter (Walker)*	Private	Present Feb. 1862
William Warten	Private	
John Weidner*	Private	G and C roster
A. Weinhardt*	Private	AWOL 1863

Max Weis*	Private	AWOL Mobile
Charles Weisser*	Private	D Jackson, 1863
John Wiltz*	Private	G and C roster
Charles Wick	Private	G and C roster
John L. Wolf*	1st Lieut.	Resigned April 1862
Simon Wolff*	Private	Absent Dec. 1863
Gustave Wolf*	Private	W Shiloh, C Nashville
Peter Younger	Private	M Shiloh

LAKE PROVIDENCE CADETS
Roster Company C, 4th LA Volunteers (Old Company B)

W. C. Adams*	Private	Discharged 1861
B. H. Alexander*	Private	W Shiloh
E. S. Alexander*	Private	W Shiloh, C Shiloh
William Alexander*	Private	Sick 1862
F. J. Alford	Private	
T. L. Alford*	Private	Present 1861
M. M. Allen (Allison)*	Private	Present to Dec. 1861
J. R. Armistead*	Private	Absent 1862, nurse
T. J. Barker*	Private	W Shiloh, discharged
James A Bass Jr.*	Private	Present Feb. 1862
W. J. Berry*	Private	Died Ship Island, 1861
J. L. Blase (Blatz)*	Private	Present Dec. 1861
A. J. Blount*	Private	C Port Hudson
William A. Blount*	Sergeant	C Port Hudson, C Carroll
J. K. Bovard	Private	C Port Hudson
William Bourke*	Private	Present Dec. 1861
Henry Bower*	Corporal	C Port Hudson
James M. Bradford*	Private	Present Dec. 1862
John Brannon (Banner)	Private	
R. H. Burke	Private	Hired substitute 1862
Mathew Butten	Private	
J. A. Caldwell*	Private	D Dec. 1862
Michael M. Carnay*	Private	C Jackson, La.
John Cliner	Private	
John D. Conn*	2nd Lieut.	C Port Hudson
J. F. Cottrell*	Private	
B. F. Crocket*	Private	C Port Hudson, C Sp. Fort
Daniel Cronan*	Private	Died disease Jan. 1862

J. A. Davenport	Private	D Little Rock, June 1861
K. (R.?) Davis*	Private	C Port Hudson
H. L. Deeson*	Private	C Port Hudson
W. L. DeFrance*	Surgeon	Post Surgeon
William Doran*	Corporal	Present Dec. 1861
F. Dreyfus*	Private	C Antietam, W Virginia
Thomas Eatmon	Private	
Thomas Egan*	Private	Present Dec. 1861
H. Fink (Frink)*	Private	Drowned Pass Christian
F. Flissner (Flessner)*	Private	C Port Hudson
William Frazer	Private	
Henry Galliway	Private	
Patrick Gerin*(Gerrin)	Private	
B. Gillbrida	Private	C Port Hudson
G. Gloker (Blecker)*	Private	Sick 1862
M. J. Grace*	Private	Absent, sick 1862
W. L. Grace*	Private	W Shiloh
John T. Green*	Corporal	C Port Hudson
D. Gutzmer*	Private	W Shiloh
J. W. Haynes*	Private	Discharged disability 1862
Mat Howley*	Private	C Port Hudson
E. J. Hynes*	Private	Present Dec. 1861
A. H. Hillman*	Private	Present Dec. 1861
Thomas E. Hogge*	Sergeant	W Shiloh
J. M. Jamison*	Private	Sick 1862
Robert Jamison*	Private	C Port Hudson
D. C. Jenkins*	2nd Lieut.	W, C Shiloh
B. C. Johnson*	Corporal	C Port Hudson
J. C. Jones	Private	Present Dec. 1861
J. M. Jones	Private	C Port Hudson
J. W. Keller*	Private	
L. Kibbe*	Private	C Port Hudson
Mat Kingsley*	Sergeant	C Jackson, La. May 1863
Louis Kirkland	Private	W Shiloh, T Tirailleurs
Ed L. Kleinpeter*	Private	C Port Hudson
L. A. Land*	Private	Present Dec. 1861
T. A. Laster*	Private	W Shiloh
Patrick Lawler*	Private	W Shiloh
George C. Lemmon	1st Lieut.	C Port Hudson
John Livey* (Levey)	Private	C Port Hudson (?)

Levi Levy*	Private	C Port Hudson
Charles D. Lewis MD	Surgeon	
Peter Lintz (Leutz)*	Private	
Nick Magorin*	Private	M Shiloh
John R. McAuley*	Private	Present Dec. 1861
J. W. McElroy*	Private	C Jackson, La. May 1863
Patrick McGuire	Private	No information
M. McHugh*	Private	Died disease, Nov. 1862
William T. McJilton*	1st Lieut.	T Co. E
George R. Medary*	2nd Lieut.	Present Dec. 1861
William M. Moon*	Private	W Shiloh
D. T. Murley (Murphy)*	Private	W Shiloh
John Murphy*	Private	W Shiloh
M. C. Noonan Jr.*	Private	Present Dec. 1861
John (James) O'Bryan*	Captain	C Port Hudson, Johnson's Island
W. F. Pennington*	Lt. Colonel	W Shiloh
James M. Pride*	Private	W Shiloh
William C. Potts*	Private	Absent after Dec. 1861
Charles R. Purdy*	Captain	K Port Hudson
V. Moreau Purdy*	Ordinance Sgt.	Passed through war
John Redus*	Private	Sam Lambert's roster 1861
T. J. Riley*	Private	Present Dec. 1861
A. W. Roberts*	2nd Lieut.	C Port Hudson, Johnson Is.
M. W. Roberts*	Private	C Port Hudson, C Atlanta Died Camp Chase
John S. Rowe*	Private	Present Dec. 1864
N. B. Russell*	Sergeant	W Shiloh C Port Hud.
B. F. Rust*	Private	Present Dec 1861
John Ryan*	Private	C Port Hud, C Jonesboro
Alfred H. Scott*	2nd Lieut	C Port Hudson
Charles Scovil	Private	C Port Hudson
Armond Selby	Private	Present Dec. 1862
Michael D. Shaffer	Sergeant	C Missionary Ridge, 1863
R. H. Shields*	Private	C Port Hudson
W.H.Simmers*(Simmons)	Private	C Baton Rouge
George W. Smith*	Lieutenant	W Shiloh
L. B. Smith*	Corporal	T
James M. Stafford*	Corporal	C Port Hudson

J. L. F. Stewart*	Private	Present 1862, T 8th Batt. La Art.
G. W. Taylor*	Private	C Nashville
R. S. Thompson*	Corporal	Died disease Feb. 1863 in Clinton Hospital
A. G. Tompkins*	Private	Present Dec. 1861
W. H. Tompkin*	Private	Present Dec. 1861
S. M. Tucker*	Sergeant	W Shiloh
A. V. Vernon	Private	C Port Hudson
Aaron W. Verter*	Captain	K Shiloh
Frank Whicher*	Captain	Died disease 1862
Thomas White	Lieutenant	C Winchester, Va. 1864
Henry Wilson, Jr.*	Drummer	AWOL Aug 1862
Thomas Wilson*	Private	T
Fred Winkleman*	Private	Died disease Berwick C.

WEST FELICIANA RIFLES
Roster Company D, 4th LA Volunteers (Old Co. E)

John Atchison	Private	W July 22, 1864
John D. Austen*	Corporal	Detailed telegrapher
L. S. Austin	Private	T from 27th LA, Teamster
George W. Bains	Private	C Scotts, Miss., Feb. 1864
L. Beleau*	Private	Sam Lambert's roster 1861
John Bennett*	Private	W Shiloh, D Bayou Sara
Eugene Bertus	Private	C St. Francisville
Puline Bisset*	Private	Died disease, March 1864
C. Bockel	Private	AWOL
Jules Bourquin*	Sergeant	C Nashville
John Brady*	Private	
C. G. Breckenridge*	Private	Present Feb. 1862
Joseph Brown	Private	T Quartermaster Corps
William Brown	Private	D Enterprise, MS, Aug. 1863
R. B. Burgess*	Private	Discharged disability 1861
John Campbell*	Sergeant	C Nashville Died at Camp Chase
J. F. Carpenter*	Private	Sam Lambert's roster 1861
L. Castenhoffer	Private	W Ezra church
J. H. Clark*	Private	T Scott's Cav.
L. S. Cline	Private	K Atlanta, Aug. 9, 1864

James S. Collins	Private	C Yazoo City, MS July 13, 1863, Enrolled US army
Levi K. Collins*	Private	W Shiloh, W Baton Rouge
Butler Cotton*	Private	W Whiloh, T Scott's Cav.
H. Clay Daugherty	Private	C Bayou Sara
John T. Davis*	Private	WC Shiloh, ex 10-9-62
John B. Dawson	Private	Sick, C Port Hudson
Thomas Dawson	Private	K Aug 7, 1864 Atlanta
Luke Dawson	Private	C Nashville
R. F. Dawson*	Sergeant	W Baton Rouge
Thomas Dawson	Private	K Atlanta Aug. 7, 1864
Richard Doherty*	Private	W Ezra Church, C Nashv. Died Camp Chase prison
John F. Elam*	Private	C Baton Rouge, D Jackson
John Elliot*	Private	K Shiloh
Charles L. Fischer*	Private	C June 15, 1864, Pine Mt.
Maximillian Fisher	Private	C June 15, 1864, Pine Mt.
James Fletcher	Private	C June 15, 1864, Pine Mt.
John Fletcher	Private	Sick
Willis Forrester*	Corporal	Sick
Victor Fortier	Private	C June 15, 1864, Pine Mt.
Julius Freyhan*	Musician	D July 15, 1863, Jackson
M. G. Gaither	Private	C June 15, 1864, Pine Mt.
Thomas Ga(r)tely*	Sergeant	C Morganza
Eugene Gardebled	Private	T Engineer Dept
Camille Gesselly*	Private	Present Apr. 1862
John Gibson	Private	W Ezra Church
John T. Gibbons	Private	W Ezra Church
James Gillingham	Private	T Qurtmstr. Corps, C Port Hudson
R. J. Gilmore	Private	C Nashville
Henry Goldsmith*	Private	C Port Hudson
Clement C. Gore*	Sergeant	W Ezra Church, lost leg
Joseph P. Gore*	Private	C Nashville
Napoleon B. Gore*	Private	Present April 1862
William A. Gore*	Private	W Shiloh, K Atlanta Aug. 7, 1864
Belmore Gossin*	Private	D Osyka May 8, 1863
Frank Gostenhofer*	Private	D on March to Baton Rouge
L. B. Gostenhofer*	Private	K Atlanta, Aug. 7, 1864

Aandrew Green	Private	C Port Hudson, T 27th LA
A. J. Green	Private	Discharge disabled 1861
Ephraim Gregory*	Private	Present April 1862
Victor Grosjean	Private	W Atlanta, 8/7/64 C Nashville
John Hanly	Private	Sam Lambert's roster 1861
Fergus D. Haralson	Private	W Atlanta, Aug.7, 1864
William Hearsey*	2nd Lieut.	Resigned Oct. 1861
John Hebert*	Private	Sam Lambert's roster 1861
Z. F. Henderson	Private	T Porche's Cav.
William Hess	Private	Present Aug. 1863
John H. Hobgood*	Sergeant	W Shiloh, W 7-4-63 C Nash
Dorson J. Hull*	Private	C Nashville
N. B. Hunter	Private	AWOL Nov 1863
John Hutchinson	Private	D July 17, 1863, Jackson
S. P. Insley*	Private	W Shiloh
B. F. Jones	Private	D 1863
J. C. Jones*	Private	Present Dec. 1862
Thomas Jones	Private	C (?)
T. Kelly*	Private	Sam Lambert's roster 1861
Zacharia Kelly	Drum Major	C Nashville
M. B. Key	Private	C June 21, 1864
O. C. Key*	Private	W Ezra Church
Patrick Kinney*	Private	Given up to civil aurtho-Ities, Ocean Springs 1861
Alonzo Klein	Private	K Atlanta, Aug.7, 1864
Eugene Kremer	Private	C Pointe Coupee
A. P. Lanna*	Corporal	K Ezra Church
August Lacour*	Private	Present Feb. 1862
William Laurens*	Private	K Picketts Mill
S. L. Lavergne*	Private	C Spanish Fort 1865
James R. Leake*	Private	T Scott's Cav.
John W. Leake*	Private	T Scott's Cav.
A. W. Lee*	Private	
William Leavenworth*	Drummer	K Shiloh
T. G. Lewis*	Private	D May 8, 1863, Osyka
H. Lies*	Private	Absent after Feb. 1862
John Lornorgan	Private	
Bella Lovassy*	Sergeant	Present Feb.1862
D. Lovemire	Private	W Ezra Church

David Lowrance	Private	D July 17, 1863, Jackson
R. G. Lurty	Private	T Cav.
Aaron Madera	Private	T Engineer Dept.
William H. Magearl	Private	C Port Hudson, W Atlanta
Israel McBright*	Private	C Port Hudson
Daniel McCarthy*	1st Lieut.	W Atlanta, 8/7/64, died
L. McGrindle	Private	C July 2, 1864
James McCu	Corporal	C Nashville
Hugh McDonald	Private	C Nashville
William McPherson*	Private	C Nashville
Abe Meyer*	Private	T Linton Light Artillery
J. L. Miller*	Private	Discharged disability 1861
A. T. Montgomery	Private	Sick
Charles G. Mourain*	Private	T Cavalry
William Taylor Mumford	Lieut.	Absent Dec 1863 T Art
John W. Mulholland*	Private	
John Newman*	Private	D Camp Moore, 1861
John T. Newton*	Private	Present Dec. 1863
John M. Nubling	Private	C Nashville
John Nugier*	Private	Present Dec. 1862
T. A. Obial*	Private	W Shiloh
John O'Neal	Private	D July 1863, Jackson
John Ortis*	Private	Died Miss. City, July 1861
Jules Oertis*	Private	Died disease 1862
William W. Packie	Private	Sick
Edward L. Paine	Private	T Scott's Cav.
William W. Paine*	Private	Passed through war
Samuel Parr*	Qtrmst. Sgt.	T Commissary
A. H. Pillet*	Private	Passed through war
Frank H. Pillet	Private	C Nashville
Leo L. Pillet	Private	W Atlanta, Aug.7,1864 lost leg, died
Daniel H. Pollard*	Private	Present Feb. 1862
Sam J. Powell	Private	T Quartermaster Dept.
Thomas Raynham	Private	C Nashville
John Reames*	Private	W Shiloh, C Nashville
James Reid*	Captain	C Nashville
Eugene D. Remondet*	Corporal	Passed through war
Henry H. Remondet*	Lieutenant	Sick, T Qurtmast.
Joseph E. Richard*	Private	D Sept 1863, Joined Cav.

E. Richards*	Private	Sick 1864
Henry H. Riley	Corporal	C Nashville
John B Riley*	Private	W Shiloh
Thomas Riley*	Private	C Nashville
Henry Rockner	Private	
George R. Rodgers*	Private	Present Feb. 1862, T Cav.
John Rowland*	Private	Discharged 1862
A. Rosentiel*	Private	T 27 LA
Omer Samson	Private	T Pointe Coupee Art, D
R. P. Saunders*	2nd Lieut.	Present Dec. 1862
Charles Scharch*	Private	T Navy
Simpson D. Scott*	Sergeant	C Port Hudson, K Atlanta, 7-22-64
Charles Scovil	Private	T Tirailleurs
John Seeders	Private	W Ezra Ch., C Jonesboro exchanged Sep. 22, 1864
Robert Seeders*	Private	W Baton Rouge
Thomas Sheehan*	Private	Present Feb. 1863
William Steward	Private	
W. M. Stiner*	Private	Present Nov 1862
Thomas Sullivan*	Private	Disability discharge 1861
Daniel T. Sulser*	Private	W Pickett's Mill, C Nashville
Charles S. Swayze*	Private	K Atlanta, Aug. 7, 1864
S. C. Swaze	3rd Lieut.	Sick 1864
L. J. Tansey*	Private	W. Shiloh
Joseph T. Tenny*	Corporal	K Ezra Church
Charles W. Temple*	Corporal	M Shiloh, C Nashville
Steven D. Thoms*	Hospital Steward	
Charles E. Tooraen*	Captain	K Shiloh
Edwin B. Turner*	Private	Present April 1862
Reason Turner*	Captain	Resigned Nov. 1862
W. R. B. Turner	Private	Present 1861
Jacob Ulm	Private	D Aug. 1863
James (Joe) Vicaro*	Private	W Shiloh, W Ezra Church
Arnold Vignes*	Private	W Shiloh
C. W. H. Walden*	Private	C Aug. 1863
F. Walplin*	Private	Sam Lambert's roster 1861
Richard I. Waldo*	Sergeant	Passed through war
August Walter*	Private	Discharged disability
R. C. Wederstrandt	Private	Present Dec. 1861

Cade D. White*	Private	W C Nashville, lost leg
Charles P. Whiteman*	Captain, Qtrmst	C Port Hudson, W Atlanta, Aug. 7, 1864 (?)
Edward W. Whiteman*	Private	C Jonesboro, C Nashville
McDaniel Whiteman*	Private	W Ezra Church, C Nashv.
James Williams	Private	AWOL
William F. Wilson*	Lieutenant	C Port Hudson
Gustave Wolf	Private	C Spanish Fort
Frank Wolfin	Private	Discharged 1861
J. S. Wooster*	1st Lieut.	C Near Morganza, 1863
Charles Zeigler*	Corporal	C Shiloh, Joined USA

LAFOURCHE GUARDS
Roster, Company E, 4th LA Volunteers (Old Co. H)

Ernest Allain*	Sergeant	W Shiloh, C Nashville
Louis Alain*	Corporal	W Shiloh
Maximillian Aucoin*	Private	Died disease, Marietta
Washington Austin*	Private	C Nashville
Adam Babin*	Private	W Shiloh
Joseph Babin*	Private	W Ezra Church, C Nashv. Died in prison
George F. Babin	Private	
Octave P. Babin*	Private	W Ezra Church, died
Adolphe Badeaux*	Private	C July 1863, Jackson, MS
Emile Badeaux*	Private	C July 1863, Jackson, MS
C. Batton	Private	
Clifford Belcher*	1st. Lieut.	Resigned May 1862
Christian Beldad*	Private	Present Dec 1861
Elisa Bennett	Private	
Philia Benoit*	Private	D
Victor H. Bernard*	Musician	Present Dec 1863
Phillip Bertin*	Private	Discharged 1861
Charles Bertrand*	Private	Absent after Feb 1862
Euphimon Bertrand*	Private	Absent sick 1861
John Besson*	Private	C Nashville
Joseph T. Besson*	Private	C Nashville
John S. Billieu*	3rd Lieut.	Present Feb 1862
I. (J.) L. Boney*(Bonner)	Corporal	K Atlanta, Aug.7, 1864
Henry R. Bonner*	Sergeant	C Nashville

J. M. Bonner	Private	Died disease Nov 1862
Arthur L. Boudreaux*	Corporal	Passed through war
Victorin Boudreaux*	Private	Discharged Ship Island
Feldey Bourgeois	Private	
Joseph Laurent Bourg*	Corporal	W Aug. 7, 1864, Died
Alciste Bourgeois*	Private	Present Feb. 1862
Alcee (Ilde) Bourgeois*	Private	C Nashville, joined US Arm.
Savinien Bourgeois	Private	K Ezra Church
Anthenor Bouvier*	Private	C Nashville, Died Prison
Henry C. Brasset*	Private	W July 23, 1864, C Nashv.
L. A. Roustan	Sergeant	W July 23, 1864
Henry Brockhoft*	Drummer	
Henry Bowmer	Private	
John W. Byers*	Sergeant	D June 16, 1863, Jackson
Andrew J. Carter*	Private	Present Feb. 1862
Joseph Chauvin*	Private	D July 16, 1862, Jackson
Theodore Chaisson*	Private	D July 16, 1863
Justinian Chaisson*	Private	
Ferdinand Clark*	Private	
Thomas Corbet*	Private	K Shiloh
H. Nicholas Coulon	Private	
Ernest Daigre (Daigle)*	Private	C Port Hudson
Onezime Dionne*	Private	M Shiloh
Joseph Dionne*	Private	W Shiloh
Aristide Daunis*	Private	D July 16, 1863, Jackson
Jackson L. Daunis*	Private	Detailed as post druggist
Onisime Daunis	Private	D July 16, 1863
William R. Darden*	Private	C Nashville
Hercules Dausereau*	2nd Lieut.	
George Durant*	Private	Sick
George Evans	Private	Sick 1864
Joseph M. Forest (Foret)*	Corporal	T Ord. Works, Selma, Ala.
Robert Forest (Foret)*	Private	W Ezra church, lost leg
Joseph A. Froehlicher*	Private	Died disease 1862
Alcee Gauthreaux	Private	W Ezra Church (killed?)
Neville Gauthreaux	Private	W Atlanta, Aug 7, 1864
A. P. Geautreaux	Private	K Atlanta
J. O. Grant	Private	T Cavalry
Nathan W. Grisamore*	Private	Present at Shiloh
Timothy Hanley*	Sergeant	W Ezra Church

Henderson H. Harris*	Private	W Shiloh
Cornelius Hart	Private	C Missionary Ridge, Nov. 1863, enlisted US Navy
William Lee Head*	Private	W Shiloh
Emile L. Hebert*	Private	C Port Hudson, T Cav.
Oscar F. Hebert*	Musician (Bugler)	Passed through war
Sosthene Hebert*	Private	W Shiloh, W Ezra church
S. Hendry	Private	T Cavalry
George Hill*	Private	T 26 LA, C Vicksburg
W. E. Hinson	Private	T 2nd ALA
Isaac D. Holliman	Private	T Cavalry
Amedie Hotard*	Private	D Aug. 7, 1863
William Key Howard	Private	No information
Alfred Hymel*	Private	C Nashville
Frank Imlasy (Imlay)	Private	Present 1865
H. Johnson	Private	Enrolled April, 1865
Joseph Jones*	Private	Sick
Theodore Journot*	Private	Sick
Ernest Lambert*	Private	Discharged 1862
John H. Lamberth	Private	T Cavalry
Jacob Leidner*	Private	Present Feb. 1862
Eugene Laperruque*	Private	Present Feb. 1862
Zephirin Lapeyrouze*	Private	W Shiloh
Jacob Leidner	Private	Present Feb. 1862
Aurelien Levron*	Private	W Jonesboro, lost arm
Charles LeBlanc*	Private	Present Feb. 1862
Prospere Leblanc*	Private	Present Feb. 1862
M. Hyppolyte Landry*	2nd Lieut.	C Nashville
J. Dennis Lorio*	Musician	
Peter Ernest Lorio*	Captain	Passed through war
James Lowden*(Louden)	Private	D June 6, 1861
Charles E. Lull*	Private	Died disease Nov. 1862
David (Dan) F. Marnell*	Private	Present Feb. 1862
Henry Maus(Maas/Maes)*	Private	
James McDonald*	Private	W Shiloh, W Ezra Church
L. T. Methvien	Private	T Cavalry
John L. Millam	Private	C Nashville
David Moore*	Private	Present Feb. 1864
George Moore	Private	Present Dec. 1863
Lucien F. Moorehead*	Sergeant	C Shiloh, discharged

James McDonald*	Private	W Shiloh, W Ezra Ch.
Myrtis Naquin*	Private (Fifer)	Died Oct. 1861
Mathew Narry (Nary)*	Private	C Jonesboro, ex 9/22/64
George O'Grady	Private	Hired substitute 1863
John L. Page*	1st Lieut.	Resigned Feb. 1864
Prospere Peligrin	Private	Present Dec. 1863
Rasselus Perkins*	Private	Present Feb. 1862
W. Perry	Private	T Cavalry
Edward B. Perryman*	Private	M Shiloh
Leander Dauradou Pitre*	Private	C Nashville
John H. Po(a)ttman*	Hosp. Steward	
George Quicksall	Corporal	Present Feb. 1862
William H. Quicksall*	2nd Lieut.	C Nashville
Arthur J. Roman*	Sergeant	W May 2, 1864
Adolphe Rossigno(l)e*	Private	W Shiloh
J. Abel Roussel*	Private	W Shiloh
L. Amos Roussel*	Private	W Ezra Church
Thomas Roussel*	Private	W, C Shiloh
Louis A. Roustan*	Sergeant	W July 23, 1864, K Ezra Church
Desire P. Robichaux*	Private	W Shiloh, W Aug. 7, 1864 C Nashville
Theophile P. Robichaux*	Private	Present Dec. 1863
Leander Robinett*	Private	Died of disease 1865
Adrien Roger*	Private	C Port Hudson
Joseph Sanchez	Private	W C Ezra church, lost arm
Hampton C. Smith*	Private	Died disease 1862
Frank Scanlan*	Private	W Shiloh
Robert M. Shephard	Sergeant	C Missionary Ridge 1863
Henry Skipwith	Sergeant	T from Co. A
John Smith	Private	
William H. Sparks*	Private	K Atlanta, Aug. 7, 1864
Peter Stanton	Private	T 3rd Md Cav, C Gettysburg
Thomas B. Stevenson*	Musician	C Port Hudson
John Stopman	Private	
Robert Torey	Private	W Atlanta, lost leg
Drauzin Toups*	Private	C Nashville Joined US Army
Thomas E. Vick*	Major	Dropped as Major 1862
Francois Vickner(nair)*	Private	D July 16, 1863

Charles Walls	Private	Present July 1863
John M. Walsh*	Sergeant	C Nashville
Charles White*	Private	Present Feb. 1864
Edward Wirtz* (Wiltz)	Private	

DELTA RIFLES
Roster, Company F, 4th LA Volunteers (Old Co. C)

Madison Adams	Private	C Vicksburg
Augustin Allain*	Sergeant	W Pickett's Mill, C Nashv.
F. E. Allain	Private	
H. W. Allen	Brigadier General	W Shiloh, W Baton Rouge
Edward Allsworth	Musician	D Jackson
C. P. Alverson*	Lieut	T Cavalry
H. T. Amaker	Sergeant	K Shiloh
Dudley Avery	Lieutenant	W Shiloh, T 18th LA
B. F. Babin*	Private	T Col. Mark's Regiment
Thomas W. Babin*	Private	Present Dec. 1861
A. D. Barrow	Sergeant	T
M. Barrow	Private	M Shiloh, Sick 1864
Wiley Barrow	Lieut	T 11th LA
William M. Barrow*	Corporal	C Shiloh, died disease DIARIST
E. C. Beasley	Private	C Baton Rouge
Charles B. Bergeron*	Private	D
F. V. Bergeron*	Private	Present Dec. 1861
Louis A. Bernard*	Private	Died of disease
Phillip Bernard*	Private	C Shiloh, W Ezra Ch.
J. B. Blanchard	Private	Present Dec. 1863
Samuel Blanchard*	Private	C Nashville
P. Blesiet	Private	C Baton Rouge
J. E. Blouin*	Private	T Stewart's Cav.
Samuel Blumhard	Private	
M. Bourke (Bourg)	Private	D July 30, 1863
O. Bourke (Bourg)	Private	D May 9, 1863
J. K. Boyard* (Bovard)	Private	
M. S. Bowman*	Private	W Shiloh, C Pt. Hudson
B. G. Bradford*	Private	W Shiloh
A. Brasseau	Private	Dec. 1862, sick at home
T. Bron	Private	

E. Broussard*	Private	T
Adolphe Broussard*	Private	C Port Hudson
W. Broussard	Private	W Ezra Church, died
Edward Brown	Private	W Shiloh (?)
Joseph Brown*	Private	D July 16, 1863, Jackson
Joshua Brown*	Private	W Shiloh
Llewellyn Brown*	Private	W Shiloh, D 1864
J. W. Bryant*	Private	T Tirailleurs
Henry Carl*	Private	W Shiloh, discharged 1862
John C. Carl	Private	W Shiloh, C Port Hudson
E. A. Carmouche*	3rd Lieut.	Resigned June 1863
A. Carter	Private	
C. A. Carson	Private	
Joseph Charle	Private	D
Frank A. Cheatham*	Private	T Ordinance Dept.
J. B. Chemin	Private	AWOL Port Hudson
V. Chemin	Private	AWOL Port Hudson
A. C. Chinn*	Private	Resigned 1861
Charles H. Chinn*	Hosp. Steward	
John Chutz	Private	AWOL
Ben W. Clark*	Adjutant	Discharged disabled 1862
E. C. Clouatre	Private	AWOL
P. Collier	Private	D April, 1863
G. Comeaux	Private	D July 30, 1863
H. M. Conn	Private	
John Conway		
W. H. Corlies*	Private	T Quartermaster
H. M. Conner*	Private	T Armory
Matt Conner*	Drummer	
Ben C. Cooly*	Lieutenant	T 14th LA
Robert Cooley	Private	C Pt. Hudson, W Ezra Church, C Nashville
W. B. Cooper*	Corporal	Present Dec, 1861
Stephen Crowley	Private	C
Polk Cunningham*	Private	Died disease Corinth 1862
Ed Davenport	Private	C Port Hudson
J. Dellahille	Private	Present Jan. 1862
William P. Denham*	Private	W Shiloh, T Cavalry
P. Deplaigne	Private	C Hagerstown

J. B. Desormes	Private	D July 17, 1863, Jackson
David Devall*	Captain	T Co B, C Nashville
Charles E. Dirmeyer*	Private	W Vicksburg
L. Doiron	Private	Died disease 1863
Oscar Doiron	Private	C Nashville
A. V. Dubroca*	Lieut.	T 13th LA (elected Lt.)
E. M. Dubroca*	Lieut. Col.	T 13th LA
J. J. Dudley	Private	C Baton Rouge
J. V. "Vick" Duralde Jr.*	Private	Present 1861
David Duval	Captain	
J. O. Edmonston	Private	Discharged underage, 1862
L. (V.?)Fabre	Private	D May 9, 1863
H. M. Favarot*	Colonel	Resigned, May 1862
St. Clair Favrot*	Corporal	C Spanish Fort
James Flower*	Private	T Quartermaster Dept.
Samuel Frazier	Private	W Ezra Church, died
M. J. Gaither	Private	C Altoona Valley June 1864
G. M. Garig*	Private	Discharged
Pierre Gaudier	Private	W Atlanta
Alfred B. Gibson*	Private	Present, 1861
J. A. Godfrey	Chaplain	Resigned, 1863
Desolive Gremillion	Private	D, C May, 1863
Pierre Grey	Private	C Port Hudson
Daniel B. Gorham*	Captain	T Tirailleurs, T Allen's Staff, T Cavalry
P. N. Guardia	Private	W Aug 4, 1864, Died
C. Guiraud	Private	D July 24, 1863
Pierre Guy*	Private	W Baton Rouge, D 1863
E. A. B. Hanks	Private	Discharged Disability 1862
Charles D. Hebert*	Corporal	Present Dec. 1861
Stephen Henderson*	Private	W Shiloh
J. B. Hereford	Private	T 8th LA
L. S. Hereford*	1st Lieut.	
F. B. Hillen	Private	T Dugue Guards
T. C. Hillen*	Private	Sam Lambert's roster 1861
R. Horton	Private	Court-martialed Mobile
A. J. Hudson	Private	Sick
A. Humphrey*	Sergeant	D
Samuel E. Hunter	Colonel	C Nashville
A. Jacneau	Private	W Ezra Church

Ernest Jarreau	Private	C Nashville
J. E. Jarreau*	Private	C Port Hudson, T Engineers
Leon Jarreau	Sergeant	C Nashville
William G. Jeter*	2nd Lieut.	C Port Hudson, escaped K Ezra Church
F. L. Jewell*	Private	Present Dec 1861
William Kitchen	Sergeant	D 1864
John Irwin Kendall*	1st Lieut.	C Pt. Hudson, escaped, C Nashville, T Co. B
William Keppler*	Private	C Shiloh
N. Sewell Key*	Private	W Shiloh
Oliver Key	Private	Sam Lambert's roster 1861
H. M. Kidd*	Corporal	D July 8, 1863
J. G. Kilbourne	Adj. Qtrmas.	
Isaac Kitchen*	Private	Present Dec. 1861
William Kitchen*	Private	
E. Kraft	Private	Passed through war
E. Labauve	Private	Present Aug. 1863
Pit Lafiton	Private	
Archibald H. Lamon*	Captain	C Jonesboro, ex 9/22/64
Charles Lancaster*	Private	T Pointe Coupee Rebels
O. Lawrence	Private	
E. Leblanc	Private	C Port Hudson
M. O. Leblanc*	Private	Discharged 1861, bad eyes
O. M. Leblanc	1st Lieut.	Resigned Oct. 1861
A. LeClerq	Private	W Ezra Church, C Span. F.
Dominique Lejendre*	Private	
Enos Lejeune*	Private	D May 9, 1863
J. Lejeune	Private	D July 16, 1863, died at Camp Morton, measles
Theodule Lejeune*	Private	K Pickett's Mill
George C. Lemmon*	2nd Lieut.	C Port Hudson
M. Lemoine	Private	D July 30, 1863
H. Levergne	Private	W Jonesboro
P. Levergne	Private	
L. S. Lobdell*	Lieut.	
Numa Longuepee	Private	
George McCausland*	Captain	ADC to Gen. Ewell
Marcus McCausland*	Private	Present 1861
W. S. McCrindell	Private	W Shiloh

John McGrath*	Captain	T 13th LA
F. McHattan	Private	Present 1861
August (Angus?) McKay*	Sergeant	T Selma Machine shop
D. McQuean	Private	Sick 1863
J. B. Magruder	Private	T Dugue Guards
Charles Mathis	Musician	D July 17, 1863
L. Metevier*	Private	
James Mitchell*	Private	
C. F. Mix	Private	D July 16 1863, died prison
H. Moebius	Private	Sick
W. Montgomery	Private	W Baton Rouge
T. G. Morgan Jr.	Lieutenant	Dropped 1861
William W. Montan*	Private	T Commissary Dept.
John Nesbit	Private	T to Co. B
T. J. Nolan Jr.*	Captain	C Port Hudson
John Ousset	Private	C Port Hudson
Francis F. Palms*	Lieut.	T Engineer, C Port Hudson
A. A. Patrick	Private	T Pargoud Guards
J. C. Patrick	Sergeant	T Carroll Guards
Thomas Percy*	Private	Present Oct. 1861, T Art Died of disease 1862
M. J. Pogue	Private	C Port Hudson
Marshall Pope	Surgeon, Capt.	R May 1862
Nathaniel Wells Pope	2nd Lieut.	Resigned 1861, T Cav.
E. Porche	Musician	Present to 1865
Francis Pousalvain	Private	D May 14, 1863
M. Prendergast	Private	AWOL April 1864
Robert L. Pruyn*	Major (fifer)	W Shiloh, T Co. B
John H. Putman	Hosp. Steward	AWOL 1862
O. J. Quiggins	Sergeant	C Port Hudson, C Nashville
D.H. Raymond	Private	AWOL 1863
Alvan S. Read	Lieutenant	T 1861 to Virginia
Auguste Retzner*	Private	Present Dec. 1861
L. F. Renaud*	Lieutenant	T Adjutant's Office
Fergus Richard*	Sergeant	Died or killed
J. Richard	Private	Discharged for substitute
Henry Rickner*	Private	T Qtrmst, C Port Hudson
C. A. Roberts*	Corporal	C Baton Rouge, C Livonia
Thom. Chinn Robertson*	Captain Qtrmst	Present Jan 1863

E. Sanchez	Private	W Ezra church
Joseph Sanchez*	Private	W Shiloh, C Bat. Rouge, W Ezra Church
P. Saulet	Private	C Nashville
F. Segain	Private	
Volmon Sequin	Private	C Nashville
Joseph Shanks*	Private	M Shiloh, D May 1863
Samuel Shanks*	Corporal	D May 1863
Oliver P. Skolfield*	Captain	W Shiloh, W Atlanta
Sam W. Skolfield*	2nd Lieut.	C Nashville
Benjamin S. Smith*	Sergeant	W Shiloh, C Nashville
John F. Smith	Private	W Ezra Church
John Smith	Private	Present Jan 1862
Abner G. Sparks*	Private	T Signal Corps, Richmond
John H. Stannard	Sergeant	C Port Hudson, W Aug. 5, 1864, C Nashville
J. Bailey Stuart	Private	W, C Shiloh
P. E. St. Martin	Private	C Port Hudson
W. L. Story	Private	D July 27, 1863, Forrest
A Tacneau	Private	W Ezra Church
Oscar L. Theodore*	Private	Present Dec. 1861
A. Thibodeaux*	Private	AWOL
Adonis Thibodeaux	Private	Present Dec. 1863
Alfred Thibodeau	Private	D Aug. 30, 1863
Alphonse Thibodeaux	Private	Present Dec 1861
Edgar Thibodeaux	Private	AWOL 1863
Joseph Thibodeaux	Private	AWOL 1863
Jules Thibodeaux	Private	D April 30, 1863
M. Tyindel	Private	
E. Trahan	Private	Died Disease Nov. 1862
J. Trahan	Private	Died disease Oct. 1862
J. E. Trahan	Private	C Nashville
T. Trahan	Private	W Atlanta Aug. 9, 1864
Joseph E. Trudeau	Private	C Nashville
John V. Van Pelt*	Private	M Shiloh
Joseph D. Vignes*	Private	T Quartermaster
M. Villeret	Private	Present Aug. 1863
Robert A Waddill*	Private	T Major Favrot's off
H. C. Walsh	Private	
W. T. Wills (Willis)*	Private	

Henry H. Walsh*	Captain	T Pargoud Guards
Sam Weathersbee*	Private	W Shiloh
Z. Pierre Yersin*	Private	W Shiloh
J. Young	Private	C Baton Rouge

HUNTER RIFLES B
Roster, Company G, 4th LA Volunteers (Old Co. I)

Gebhard D. Adams	Private	Passed through war
J. Adams	Private	Present Feb. 1865
Joseph J. Adams*	Lieutenant	W Shiloh, died
Stephen Ambrose Jr*	Private	Discharged 1861
T. J. C. Batchelor	Private	Present Dec. 1862, sick
Clarence Bell*	Sergeant	Passed through war
George H. Bell*	Private	C Atlanta, Aug. 5, 1864
John K. Bell	Private	C Port Hudson, returned
Robert P. Bell*	Private	W Ezra church, lost leg
J. Benge*	Private	Detailed as waggoner
Robert Benge	Private	Dropped, overaged
John J. Benton*	Sergeant	C Nashville
John Bivens	Private	C Nashville
William A. Blount	Private	C Port Hudson
Barnets G. Bradford	Private	
Patrick Brannon*	Private	Present Dec. 1863
Hugh P. Brashear*	Sergeant	W Pickett's Mill K Ezra church
Jake W. Brown*	Private	Died illness, Jackson, MS
R. P. Brown	Private	Present 1861
John H. Byrns (Burns)*	Private	W Ezra Church, C Nashville
G. Canton	Private	C Nashville
Olivier Canton	Private	C New Orleans, 1864
Fish Thomas D. Carney*	Private	
W. C. Carr	Private	Present 1861
Oliver Caucon	Private	
H. S. Causey	Private	AWOL
Ed Clark	Private	W Shiloh, Was clerk for Gens. French, Walthall, and Hood.
William A. Coe	Private	C Nashville
J. S. Conrad*	Private	C Port Hudson

R. E. Corcoran	Private	Sam Lambert's roster 1861
Timothy H. Corcoran*	Private	W Port Hudson, accident shot, lost leg
Cader R. Cornelius*	Captain	C Nashville
James Corbell	Private	K Ezra Church
B. S. Daniels*	Sgt. Major	W Jonesboro, died
Frank A. D'Armond	Sergeant	W Ezra Church, C Clinton
John D'Armond*	Sergeant	K Ezra Church
Thomas H. D'Armond*	1st Lieut.	C Nashville
T. Frank D'Armond*	Private	W Ezra Church
Morris B. Davis*	Musician	C Nashville
William Davis*	Sergeant	Present Oct. 1863
Henry C. Dawson	Private	W Jonesboro
John Delaney*	Private	W Shiloh Killed by Lt. Byars
William Young Dixon	Private	W Ezra Church (face)
Arch Doughty*	Private	W Shiloh (severe)
Timothy R. Doughty*	Private	W Shiloh, C Atlanta 8/5/64 died in prison
William E. Doughty*	Private	W Ezra Church, face
James "Jimmy" Doyle*	2nd Lieut.	W Shiloh, W Jonesboro
John Doyle*	Private	K Jonesboro
J. M. Draudy*	Private	
Timothy Drawdy	Private	K Jonesboro
J. D. Dulart (Dutart)*	Sergeant	Present Nov. 1862
W. H. Eatmon	Private	AWOL
S. Farris	Private	Present April 1862
J. M. Ford	Private	Present Dec. 1862
F. Gartner	Private	C
Caleb Oliver Gayle*	Corporal	W Shiloh
George A. Green*	Musician	
Peter A. Green*	Private	W Baton Rouge, W Ezra Church, lost leg
Ferdinand Gumbel*	Private	W Shiloh
William R. Haile*	Corporal	Present Oct. 1863, T Cav.
Robert Harp	Private	Discharged Dec. 1861
J. D. Hawsey (Hausey)*	Private	AWOL 1864
Augustus Heckler	Drummer	T Regimental Band
Henry Herchler	Musician	Present Feb. 1862
John W. Hobgood	Private	T from artillery

Harvin M. Hobgood*	Private	W, C Ezra Church, died in prison
E. C. Holmes*	2nd Lieut.	W Shiloh, died
Robert Hough*	Private	Discharged March 1862
David Hunt*	Private	Present Feb. 1862
Eli F. Huston*	3rd Lieut.	Resigned Jan. 1862
Henry Huston*	Corporal	W Ezra Church, C Atlanta Aug. 5, 1864
Joseph Huston	Private	C Atlanta, Aug. 5, 1864
Robert Hough	Private	Discharged March 1862
Beverly Hausey*	Private	Died Nov., 1861, disease
R. Harp	Private	Discharged 1861
John T. Hilliard*	Captain	K Shiloh
E. C. Holmes	2nd Lieut.	Present Aug. 1863
B. P. Irvin*	Private	Present Feb. 1862
George Irwin (Irvin)*	Private	Present Feb. 1862
David D. Jackson*	Private	Present Feb. 1862
Oliver P. Jelks*	Private	W Pickett's Mill C Nashville
Joe H. Joffrion*	Private	Died Disease 2-22-63 Port Hudson
B. C. Johnson	Corporal	
J. H. Jones	Private	K Near Clinton
William B. Jones*	Private	W Ezra Church, C Nashville
Thomas P. Kane*	Musician	Passed through war
Morris Keiffer*	Musician	Present Dec. 1862
Thomas G. Keller*	Private	Discharged 1861, artillery
M. Kennedy	Private	Present Dec. 1862
Lucien Kent*	Corporal	K Jonesboro
James Keoh*	Private	Present Dec. 1863
Ed. Kornblocker*	Private	Discharged 1862
Timothy Knight	Private	Present Dec. 1861
Jimmy H. Knighton*	Private	Died of disease 1862
O. P. Langworthy MD	Surgeon	
Charles Lea	Private	K Jonesboro
Ed Leblanc*	Private	C Port Hudson
Alfred P. Lacoq*	Private	
Winans Lloyd*	Private	Discharged 1862
J. B. Maryman*	Private	C Atlanta, Aug.5, 1864
William Maryman*	Corporal	C Atlanta, Aug.5, 1864

Ed Messey*	Private	M Shiloh
Joe Millican*	Private	Present Feb. 1862
Thad. C. Millican*	Private	Present 1861
Joel F. Mills	Private	W Shiloh
D. A. Moore*	Private	T 7th Miss
C. W. Mulkey	Private	Present 1861
Llewellyn Munson*	Hosp. Steward	Druggist
James E. Nash*	Corporal	Present Dec. 1863 T General Maury's staff
William N. Nash*	Private	W Baton Rouge
Edmond Neal*	Private	C Nashville, died prison
W. H. Neilson	Private	C Port Hudson
Wiley W. Noble	Private	C Nashville
T. L. Norwood	Private	D May 9, 1863
James Oliver	Sergeant	W Aug. 3, 1864, left leg
John J. Packer*	Private	Present April 1862
L. Packer	Private	K Jonesboro
Samuel Packer	Private	C Vicksburg, C Jonesboro
J. F. Y. Payne (Paine)*	Private	Discharged 1862
B. Frank Perry*	Private	W C Atlanta, 8-5-64, died
William M. Perry	Private	W Ezra church C Atlanta, Aug.5, 1864
Conrad H. Pierce	Private	Sick
William Pierce*	Private	Died Flux Mobile 9-20-63
Theodore Pinkney*	Lieut.	Present Dec. 1861, T Art.
William H. Pipes	Captain	Dropped, T 15th TN
L. Poole	Private	Absent after Oct. 1862
A. Pourciau	Private	W Ezra Church
Jacob Powell*	Private	C Nashville
Judge Powell	Private	Present March 1862
Littleton M. Powell*	Private	W Baton Rouge
William Robertson	Private	C Jonesboro, died Camp Douglas, Chicago
W. H. Robinson	Private	C Atlanta, Aug. 5, 1864
George W. Rogers*	Private	C Atlanta, Aug. 5, 1864
James P. Rogers*	Private	C Atlanta, Aug. 5, 1864
L. W. Rogers*	Sergeant	C Atlanta, Aug. 5, 1864
Moses Rogers*	Private	C Nashville
C. B. Rogillio*	Corporal	Present Feb. 1862
Henry S. Rogillio*	Corporal	K Port Hudson

Sidney Robins*	Private	Passed through war
A. Scarborough*	Private	C Port Hudson
Thomas J. Scott*	3rd Lieut.	K Jonesboro
William W. Scott*	Private	Present Feb. 1863
C. B. Sherbourne*	Private	Present Dec. 1863
H. Newton Sherbourne*	Private	T 10 LA Cav.
Enos L. Simpson*	Private	Present April 1862
J. W. Slocum*	Private	Present 1861
L. H. Smith*	Private	C Port Hudson
William C. Smith*	Sergeant	W Ezra Church K Jonesboro
Thomas Stafford*	Private	Present April, 1862
G. A. Steadman*	Private	Present April, 1862
E. Stephens	Private	
J. R. Sturgis	Private	T Artillery, Mobile
James J. Tate	Hospital Stew.	
Tom C. W. Taylor*	Private	W Jonesboro
Carl Taylor	Private	K Pickett's Mill
W. E. Trask*	Private	Discharged 1861
Robert Vinson*	Private	W Shiloh, W Pickett's Mill
B. Pife Veirs*	Private	Died disease 2-13-62
Jno W. Veirs*	Private	C Jonesboro, ex. 9/22/64
T. L. Vinning	Private	AWOL
L. B. Watkins	Private	Present Dec. 1862
Archibald Watson	Private	S for W. R. Haile, D Osyka May 10, 1863
Daniel J. Wedge*	Major	T Commissary Dept.
Ed L. Woodside	Private	W Shiloh
C. A. Younger*	Private	W Shiloh
John B. Zug	Private	C Atlanta, Aug. 5, 1864
Robert R. Zug*	Private	C Port Hudson

BEAVER CREEK RIFLES
Roster, Old Company G, 4th LA Volunteers
(Wingfield Rifles) (See Page 51)

O. P. Amaker*	Sergeant	T Wingfield's Cav. Port Hudson Promoted to Captain
Richard M. Amaker*	1st Lieut.	T Wingfield's Cav.

Thomas J. Andrews*	Corporal	W Shiloh, C Woodvill, MS.
Henry C. Berkley*	Private	T Wingfield's Cav.
Jno. Bestler*	Private	T Wingfield's Cav.
Guy Bridges*	Private	Sam Lambert's roster 1861
Ed. Briley (Bridges)*	Private	D
William V. Bosworth*	Private	C Port Hudson
Milton Bond*	Private	C Port Hudson
Thomas Bond*	Sergeant	C Port Hudson
M. Luther Bowman*	Private	C Port Hudson
Eugene F. Bunch*	Private	C Port Hudson
Theo C. Bunch	Corporal	
Dan B. Burleson*	Private	C Port Hudson
Robert Y. Burton*	3rd Lieut.	W Shiloh
Ed. Campbell*	Private	Present June 1862
Horace Carpenter*	Sergeant	C Port Hudson
S. B. B. Campbell*	Private	Present 1861
William Comish*	Private	C Port Hudson
John F. Day*	Corporal	Present April 1862
William A Day*	Private	Died Disease Oct. 1862
W. D. Davidson*	Private	C Port Hudson
George J. Decker*	Private	T Wingfield's Cav
S. H. Decker	Private	Present Oct. 1862
Hermann Delematre*	Private	
John W. Denmark*	Private	W Shiloh
Robert L. Draughon*	Private	C Port Hudson
John Durnin*	Private	C Port Hudson
William H. H. Dyer*	Private	W Shiloh
Franklin W. Eady*	Private	
Wesley F. Ferrill*(Fernell)	Private	
Benjamin F. Gill*	Private	
Calvin Gill	Private	W Shiloh
Jackson Gill*	Private	C Port Hudson
Joseph Glasscock*	Private	
Edward Goodman*	Private	T from Co. A, T to saddlery
Joseph D. Grice*	Private	C Port Hudson
John A. Hayden*	Private	
Joseph H. Hyde*	Private	
Augustus Jennings*	Private	Present Feb. 1862
John Jennings*	Private	
Michael Johnson*	Private	W Shiloh

Robert B. Kemp*	Private	
G. Kiptrell	Private	
R. B. Knight*	Private	Sam Lambert's roster 1861
T. Knight*	Private	
Robert Lamberth*	Private	
James W. Lee*	Private	
Obedia M. Lee*	Lieutenant	W Shiloh
William E. Ligon*	Sergeant	
John W. Lillard	Private	
Thomas M. Lillard*	Private	
Uriah Lucas*	Private	
Ed T. Manning*	Private	
A. Martin	Private	
Henry D. Martin*	Drummer	
J. B. McAllister*	Private	Present Feb. 1862
G. L. McConnell	Private	C Nashville
John McFarland*	Private	W Shiloh
N. McNabb*	private	C Port Hudson
Joseph Michel*	Private	T Hunter Rifles A
Brice F. Miller*	Corporal	
John W. Miller	Private	
George W. Mixon*	Private	
Joseph Mixon	Private	
S. C. Mixon	Private	C Port Hudson
J. T. Moore*	Private	No information
J. P. Muse*	Private	W Shiloh
William O'Connell*	Private	
Hermann Ohme*	Sergeant	W Shiloh
J. O'Sullivan*	Private	Present June 1862
Alfred Pitman*	Private	Present Feb. 1862
Jos. L. Perryman*	Private	C Baton Rouge
J. G. A. Powell*	Private	W Shiloh
J. W. Powell*	Private	C Port Hudson
W. A. Powell*	Private	C Port Hudson, escaped
R. L. Pray*	Private	C 1864
G. C. Ranier*	Private	
George W. Ravencraft*	Private	C Port Hudson
B. Richardson*	Private	Present Feb. 1862
J. W. Roberts*	Private	W Shiloh
William L. Russell*	Private	W Shiloh

Elias Self*	Private	Discharged
Jno. Sharkey*	Private	Present Feb. 1862
C. M. Sitman*	Private	Post Surgeon
William J. Smart*	Private	
James W. Smith*	Private	C Spanish Fort
J. E. Smith*	Private	
W. A. Smith*	Private	W Shiloh
E. L. Spring*	Private	W Shiloh
J. F. Stanly*	Private	Present Feb. 1862
William B. Stanly*	Private	Present Feb. 1862
A. R. Sterling	Private	
C. D. Strickland*	Private	Discharged
J. T. Strickland*	Private	Present Feb. 1862
S. D. Sutton	Private	
J. J. Tate*	Private	
A. M. Taylor*	Private	W Shiloh
A. J. Thompson*	Private	
W. L. Thompson*	Private	Present April 1862
William Trotter*	Private	Present April 1862
Robert H. Turnbull*	2nd Lieut.	Present Feb. 1862
M. J. Vaughn*	Private	Present Feb. 1862
Daniel A. Vernon	Private	
J. J. Vernon*	Private	Present Feb. 1862
M. W. W. Vernon*	Private	Present Feb. 1862
J. L. Van Zandt*	Private	Discharged 1861
C. J. Wall	Private	
S. F. Wall*	Private	Present 1862
R. M. Waller*	Private	Present April 1862
Alf Ward*	Private	Present Feb. 1862
John Weigle*	Private	W Shiloh
John C. White*	Private	W Shiloh
H. E. Williams	Private	Present April 1862
Henry Wilson, Jr.	Drummer	
John F. Wilson*	Private	Present Feb. 1862
J. T. Wilson*	Private	Present Feb. 1862
A. J. Wilson*	Private	Present Feb. 1862
James H. Wingfield*	Captain	W Shiloh, C Port Hudson
E. J. Young*	Private	Present Feb. 1862
W. M. Young*	Private	Present Aug. 1861

ST. HELENA RIFLES
Roster, Company I, 4th LA Volunteers (Old Co. F)

W. P. Addison	Sergeant	K Jonesboro
J. A. Addison*	Private	T Transmissippi Dist.
C. Dean Albert	Corporal	W Atlanta
J. H. Allen*	Corporal	Discharg Aug. 1862
John S. Allen	Sergeant	Wounded Atlanta 8-07-64
T. H. Allen*	Private	C Nashville
John S. "Sloch" Allen*	Private	W Atlanta, Aug. 7, 1864
Thomas H. Allen	Private	C Nashville
H. T. Amaker*	Sergeant	K Shiloh
John W. Arbuthnot*	Private	W Baton Rouge, Discharg.
William C. Arbuthnot*	Private	Died Disease 1862
Baldwin	Private	AWOL
H. W. Ballard	Private	Died Disease 1862
John W. Barrow*	Private	W Shiloh, C Nashville
J. L. Belue	Private	Died Disease 1861, CMoore
Elisha Bennett*	Private	T 1863
William T. Bennett*	Private	W, C Shiloh, W Baton Rouge, W Picket's Mill, W C Jonesboro
J. S. Bickham*	Private	Died disease 1862 Edward's Station
Thomas A. Bickham*	Private	C Nashville
James M. Blow*	Commissary Sergeant	W Baton Rouge, W Spanish Fort
John W. Bowen	Private	W Shiloh
R. W. Bradford*	Private	T 16 LA, Died disease 1864
A. A. Brewer*	Sergeant	W Jonesboro
J. H. Brewer*	Private	C Port Hudson, K Jonesboro
Peter R. Brewer*	Lieutenant	C Nashville
T. G. Brewer	Private	K Jonesboro
Guy Bridges*	Private	WShiloh, discharged underaged
A. Carter	Private (Fifer)	W Jackson, died
Charles W. Carter*	Private	C Nashville, Died prison
Haley M. Carter*	Captain	W Shiloh, T Ogden's Cavalry

Hannibal Carter*	Private	C Port Hudson
J. F. Carter*	Private	
Laban Carter	Private	W Shiloh, W Baton Rouge
Martin Carter	Private	K Jonesboro
M. R. Carter	Private	W, C Jonesboro
Robert J. Carter*	Lieutenant	T Wingfield's Battalion
William M. Carter*	Private	C Nashville
A. M. G. Chapman	Private	
John R. Clayton*	Private	K Shiloh
David Cohe	Private	Died disease 1863 Canton
James B. Corkren*	Major	T from Co. F, T Allen's Staff
S. C. Corkren*	Private	W 7/4/1862, K Jonesboro
B. P. Crittenden*	Private	T Pointe Coupee Art.
J. H. Crittenden	Private	Discharged 1861
Jules Daliet*	Private	C Allatoona Val, 6/30/64
Morton P. Day	Sergeant	C Nashville
Albert C. Dean*	Corporal	W Atlanta, Aug. 18, 1864
Jarvis Dennis	Private	C Port Hudson
E. S. Eady*	Private	T Army North Va. 1863
D. F. Easley	Private	D Aug. 8, 1863, joined cav.
George G. Easley	Private	K Shiloh
H. W. Easley	Private	D Aug. 1863, returned
J. Watterson Easley*	Private	T Wingfield's Cav
N. L. (Q) Easley*	Private	W Shiloh Dischar 1863
W. A. Easley	Private	W Baton Rouge
W. E. Easley	Private	Discharged 1863
P. Eddins	Sergeant	T from AL regiment
C. H. "Squad" Edwards*	Private	C Near Atlanta 1864
Columbus Friehland*	Private	T Allen's staff
W. G. Frierson*	Private	Left at P. Hud. C Nashville
John Furlow*	Private	C Nashville
John George*	Private	Discharged 1861 Ship Is.
G. W. Glasscock*	Private	W Shiloh, died as result
David Goodman	Private	C Spanish Fort
F. Goodman	Private	T Old Co. G 1861, K 1865
William Green	Private	Killed
A. Greuer	Private	W Jonesboro
John Guice	Private	C Port Hudson
John R. Gyles*	Ensign, 1st Lt.	W Ezra Ch., C Nashville
James Hart*	Private	Absent after Shiloh

F. W. Houet?	Private	Sam Lambert's roster 1861
T. W. Hurst*	Private	T Miss. Rgt., 1863
Joseph Houston	Private	
Merritt S. Hutchinson*	Private	K Jonesboro
Sam P. Hutchinson*	Private	K Baton Rouge
Charles H. Hyde*	Hosp. Steward	
William N. Hyde*	Sergeant	K Jonesboro
Reuben Jackson	Private	Present 1861
James H. Jenkins*	Private	Died disease 1862
A. O. Jones*	Private (sniper)	W, C Shiloh, C Nashville
S. W. Kemp*	Sergeant	W Jonesboro
T. D. Kemp*	Private	Discharged 1861
Char. Erasmus Kennon*	Captain	C Nashville
Thomas H. Kent	Corporal	T from 27LA, W C Nashville
John D. Killian*	2nd Lieut.	W Jonesboro, C Span. Fort
W. P. Kirk	Private	Disch. underaged, 1862
H. Knippers	Private	W Ezra Church, W Jonesboro
L. W. Knippers	Private	W July 1864, C Nashville
T. B. Knippers	Private	K Jonesboro
Joseph Lambert(h)*	Private	Died disease 1862
Richmond Lea	Private	T Mississippi Regiment 1864
William Leavensworth*	Drummer	K Shiloh
Patrick Long	Private	
J. M. Mayfield*	Private	Died at close of war
Samuel McMannus	Private	C Atlanta, Sept. 15, 1864(?)
Davis A. Morgan*	Private	K Baton Rouge
J. Monroe Nettles*	Lieutenant	Resigned Sept 1862
James Newson	Private	K Port Hudson
A. K. Nires	Private	C Nashville
W. J. Nichols	Private	Discharged 1861
J. George Parker*	Private	Died Smallpox, Mobile 1863
John H. Pipes*	Private	Overage, discharged 1862
W. J. Pearson*	Private	Present Oct. 1861
B. C. Quinn*	Lieut.	T Stockdale's Cav.
William L. Quinn*	Sergeant	Died Canton, MS 1862
Warren T. Rayborn*	Sergeant	W Shiloh, died Mobile 1863
William H. Ramsay*	1st Lieut.	Stabbed Feb. 1864
Amable P. Richards*	Sergeant	W Shiloh, W Atlanta Aug. 5, 1864, DIARIST

W. A. Sanders*	Private	W Jackson, died disease
William D. Self*	Corporal	C Port Hudson, W Kennesaw Mountain, K Jonesboro
J. W. Shaw	Private	AWOL 1864
William T. Spencer*	Private	T Medical Dept.
Thomas Spiller*	2nd Lieut.	T. Artillery died of disease
J. M. Staples*	Private	T Artillery, C Nashville
William Story	Private	D July 27, 1863, Forrest
C. D. Strickland	Private	W Ezra Church W Jonesboro
John Bunion Taylor*	Captain	K Shiloh
J. M. Taylor* Berwick	Private	Died typhoid 1862
B. W. Thompson*	Private	Discharged 1862
C. C. Thompson*	Corporal	K Shiloh
H. D. Travis*	Private	Died disease 1862
H. Kemp Viers*	Sergeant	Passed through war
H. C. Wagoner	Private	
G. W. Watson*	Private	W Jonesboro
Jason L. Watson*	Private	T 27th LA, K Vicksburg
John C. Watson*	Private	W Shiloh C Shiloh T 27 LA C Vicksburg
S. G. Watson	Private	C Jonesboro
T. G. Watson*	Sergeant	K Jonesboro
James Webb*	Private	W Port Hudson, C Port Hudson, died prison
M. C. Williams*	Private	W Ezra Church
G. W. Womack*	Sergeant	W Atlanta, K Jonesboro
John H. Womack*	Corporal	K Atlanta, Aug. 12, 1864
J. K. Womack*	Captain	Dropped May 1864
H. P. Womack	Private	T from 16th LA 1863
N. B. Womack	Private	W Ezra Church
William F. Womack*	Private	Discharged 1862
J. M. Wright*	Corporal	W Pickett's Mill
John T. Youngblood*	Private	Died disease 1862
W. D. (H) Youngblood*	Private	Died of disease
Thomas Yule	Private	Detached 1863
C. A. Zachary	Lieutenant	T Cavalry
Tom W. Zachary*	Sergeant	W Shiloh, K Jonesboro

PACKWOOD RIFLES
Roster, Company K, 4th LA Volunteers
(*) denotes original members of the company

A. Adler	Private	
Edward Barry	Private	Passed through war
Joseph Bemins	Private	Exchanged 10-9-62
Thomas W. Bishop*	Private	C Port Hudson
James Howell Booker	Private	D Jackson
J. L. Brown*	Private	C Port Hudson
Roderick Brown*	Private	W Ezra Church, both legs
D. Campbell*	Private	Sam Lambert's roster 1861
William R. Campbell*	Corporal	W July 25, 1864
William Caulifield*	Private	C Nashville, Joined US Army
Anderson R. Carle*	Private	C Atlanta, Aug.5, 1864
Tilmon Carle*	Private	
Anderson R. Carroll	Private	C Atlanta July 5, 1864
John Chance*	Private	Died of disease 1864
M. J. Chaney*	Private	Passed through war
William F. Chaney*	Private	C Died POW camp
W. J. Chapman*	Private	Sam Lambert's roster 1861
Ruffin D. Collier*	Private	Died of disease 1862
A. G. Cook*	Sergeant	K Ezra church
E. Craft*	Private	Sam Lambert's roster 1861
A. J. Dreher*	Private	enrolled 1864
William A. Dreher*	Private	W Jonesboro
Daniel Eades	Private	D Williams Bridge, 1863
F. W. Early*	Private	D Osyka, returned
Elam R. Felps*	Private	W Baton Rouge
William Felps*	Private	W Jonesboro, C Nashville
W. C. Foster	Private	D Williams Bridge, 1863
J. H. Green*	Private	D Jackson
William J. Gurney*	Private	C Clinton
Thomas B. Harris	2nd Lieut.	Sam Lambert's roster 1861
Samuel B. Haynes*	Lieutenant	
William Hedgepeth	Private	D Jackson
J. B. Hodges	2nd Lieut.	
Allen R. Jackson*	Private	C Jonesboro, ex 9/22/64
Calvin M. Jackson*	Private	C Atlanta, Aug. 5, 1864

William Johnson*	Private	Sam Lambert's roster 1861
Stephen Jones*	Private	K Atlanta, Aug. 5, 1864
S. J. Kelley*	Private	
Thomas Kelly*	Private	AWOL
William Kennedy	Private	
G. W. Kent*	1st Lieut.	Resigned Aug. 1863
John B. Knighton	Corporal	W Jonesboro
Isaac Lee	Private	W Ezra Church (hand)
J. A. Lee*	Private	Detached, wagonmaker
T. J. Lee*	Private	D Jackson
W. D. Lewis	Private	Sam Lambert's roster 1861
John W. Lipscomb*	Corporal	W Jonesboro, C Nashville
James A. Marchant*	Sergeant	W Jonesboro, lost arm
William Mattingly	Private	T Wingfield's Cav.
G. L. McConnell*	Private	C Nashville
John McDonald	Private	Sick, 1863
Joe. C. McMurry*	Private	C Nashville
John McPherson*	Private	D Port Hudson
Jacob Mercke*	Private	Detail, coffin maker
J. R. Miller*	Private	Sam Lambert's roster 1861
James P. Monahan*	Hospital Steward	
J. H. Morgan*	Private	D
John E. Morgan*	Private	K Ezra church
Morgan Morgan*	Private	W July 22, 1864 lost arm
T. B. Morgan*	Private	Sam Lambert's roster 1861
J. L. Mulder*	Private	C Port Hudson, ferryman
Joe Mulkey*	Private	D Port Hudson, T Cav.
Phillip H. Mulkey*	Private	AWOL
Alex J. Murphy*	Private	K Pickett's Mill
J. M. Murry	Private	W Ezra Church
Lewis Nauman*	Private	Detailed nurse
Willis J. Newton*	Private	D Aug. 8, 1863
James W. Oliver*	Private	W Jonesboro
J. F. Overton*	Private	Present Dec. 1862
George Hiram Packwood*	Captain	W C Atlanta, Aug. 5, 1864
John Peterson*	Private	W Nashville, lost arm
William Peterson*	Private	K Pickett's Mill
William Phillips	Private	W Atlanta, Aug. 5, 1864

Thomas Pilant	Private	D Sept. 1863, collaborator and scoundrel
H. A. Posey*	Private	D Sept 1863
James M. Pratt	Private	W June 25, 1864, C Nashville
John Rayborn	Private	W July 4, 1864
Daniel M. Rheams	Private	C Nashville
Wade H. Richardson*	Private	D Jackson, returned, C Nashville
Albert D. Richerts*	Sergeant	Passed through war
John Robinson	Private	W Atlanta, lost leg 8/5/64
George W. Rogillio*	Private	D July 1863, returned, C Nashville
John G. Rogillio*	Private	C Nashville
W. H. Rogillio*	Private	Present April 1863
T. F. Royster*	Private	Sam Lambert's roster 1861
G. W. Ward	Private	C Atlanta
T. H. Sessions*	2nd Lieut.	Resigned Aug 1863
J. M. Shull*	Private	Sam Lambert's roster 1861
Charles C. Simmons	Private	Present Dec. 1862
Henry Simon	Private	Discharged 1861
D. Ripley Slocomb*	Private	W Jackson
S. D. Smart*	Private	C Port Hudson
W. S. Smart*	Private	Sam Lambert's roster 1861
Edward Smith*	Private	Died disease 1864
Merrick M. Smith*	Private	C Spanish Fort
W. R. Smith*	Private	Passed through war
George A. W. Steadman*	2nd Lieut.	W Ezra Church, head
W. J. Stephens	Private	D 1863 Clinton Hosp.
William Stone	Private	D William's Bridge, May 1863, T Scott's Cav.
R. J. Thoms*	Private	AWOL
B. F. Turbeville	Private	Present Dec. 1862
P. B. Van Nor(au)man*	Private	W Ezra Church
E. Van Osdall	Private	D Port Hudson May 1863
J. Van Osdall	Private	D Port Hudson May 1863
M. Van Osdall	Private	D Port Hudson May 1863
George Vernon*	Private	Regimental Butcher
L. E. Virett*	Private	C Nashville
George W. Ward*	Private	C Aug 5, 1864, Atlanta

Gayden W. White*	Sergeant	C Nashville
T. S. Williams*	Private	
J. M. Williams*	Private	Present Dec. 1863
Dennis Woodmansee*	Private	C Nashville
Andrew J. Yarborough*	Corporal	C Nashville, Died prison
William J. Young*	Private	D William's Bridge, Died of disease

Members of the 4th LA of unknown companies:

John S. Blackman	Private	Possibly in Co. C
W. T. Carroll	Private	
John Demond	Private	D 1863
		O. Durio (Dureaux)
W. J. Essan	Private	D Died Ship Island
James W. Foutch	2nd Lieut.	Deserted Aug. 1864
Charles Graham	Private	Died Typhoid fever, 1862
R. H. Hadlock	Musician	
E. P. Hall		Co D 4th LA, listed as buried Camp Chase, Died Jan. 12, 1865.
J. A. Jones	Private	
John G. Jones	Captain	C Port Hudson
John W. Jones	Private	
William Kirkland	Private	Co. D, Died Clinton Hosp. Feb. 1863, Listed *Memphis Appeal* 3-17-63
_____ Moore	Private	See Barrow Diary, p. 720
R. Murry	Musician	D July 17, 1863
Joe Rogillio	Private	Died Vicksburg 7-12-62
Henry Scott	Private	C
William Smith	Private	D
Anton Wauhorat	Private	
Edward West	Captain	C Pointe Coupee, Feb. 1865
Lewis White	Private	D
Charles Wolf	Musician	
James W. Wyman	Private	Passed through war
Henry Simon	Private	Tirailleurs?
Joe Moore	Musician	Cater's Recollections
Theodore Bauer	Musician	Cater's Recollections

Physicians Associated with The 4th La Volunteers

Dr. Marshall Pope: Surgeon, resigned, May 19, 1962, replaced by O. P. Langworthy. Dr. Pope was at Shiloh.

Dr. O. P. Langworthy: Assistant Surgeon at Shiloh. Took Dr. Pope's position.

Dr. John Montgomery (1834-1910): Enrolled at Camp Moore, May 25, 1861. Appointed Post Surgeon, August 1861. Appointed Assistant Surgeon, May 1862. Was at Shiloh. Resigned, January 1863. Buried Magnolia Cemetery, Baton Rouge.

Dr. Charles D. Lewis: Regimental Surgeon, replaced Dr. Langworthy. Was at the Battle of Baton Rouge. Member of the Lake Providence Cadets.

Dr. J. M. Craig: Assistant Surgeon, replaced Dr. John Montgomery.

Dr. J. A. Leveque: Hired by the Delta Rifles as surgeon after Shiloh. (See Biographies)

Dr. Robert Francis Hereford: Post Surgeon at Port Hudson September 19, 1862

Dr. W. L. DeFrance: Post Surgeon, Member of the Lake Providence Cadets.

These physicians have been mentioned in letters from troops, but their exact role in the 4th LA is unknown:

Dr. Edward Deloney
Dr. Fenner (ran a hospital in Mobile)
Dr. Perkins
Dr. Camp
Dr. Cross
Dr. Covert (?)
Dr. Ware (?)

The physicians of the 4th LA were apparently quite skilled. The mortality rate for leg amputations in the War Between the States was 60%. Out of twelve known leg amputations of men of the 4th LA, only three died. Of ten arm amputations there were no deaths.

Notes

CHAPTER ONE

1. "East and West Baton Rouge, May 5, 1860," *Louisiana Historical Quarterly* Vol. 21, (1938): pp 1130–1133.

2. United States Census, *Slave Schedules West Baton Rouge Parish, Louisiana, 1860.*

3. "East and West Baton Rouge, May 5, 1860," *Louisiana Historical Quarterly* Vol. 21, (1938): pp 1130–1133.

4. Baton Rouge *Democratic Advocate*, 27 May 1846.

5. Baton Rouge *Gazette and Comet*, 25 May 1846.

6. Nancy Mertz, Midwest Jesuit Archives, 4511 West Pine Blvd, St. Louis, Missouri, 63108-2191.

7. Hughes, Nathaniel Cheairs, Jr., The *Pride of the Confederate Artillery: The Washington Artillery in the Army of Tennessee*, LSU Press, Baton Rouge, Louisiana, (1997), pp 1–2.

8. *Mexican War Companies* (Louisiana State Archives), Microfilm, no index.

9. "Aztec Club of 1847," *Mexican War Officer Search Page*: <<http://www.walika.com/aztec/searchlast.asp>>.

10. National Archives, Compiled Service Records of Confederate Soldiers Who Served in Organizations from the State of Louisiana, "Fourth Louisiana Infantry," Microcopy 320, Roll 137. Hereafter referred to as National Archives.

11. John D. Winters, *The Civil War in Louisiana*, LSU Press, Baton Rouge, Louisiana, 1963), pp 9–10.

12. John McGrath, *John McGrath Scrapbook*, Hill Memorial Library, LSU, Baton Rouge, Louisiana.

13. West Baton Rouge Parish *Sugar Planter*, 16 March 1861.

14. William Watson, *Life in the Confederate Army: Being the Observations and Experiences of an Alien in the South During the American Civil War*, LSU Press, Baton Rouge, Louisiana, (1995), p 75.

15. West Baton Rouge Parish *Sugar Planter*, 27 April 1861.

16. Baton Rouge *Daily Advocate*, 21 April 1861.

17. Carlton McCarthy, "Detailed Minutia of Soldier Life in the Army or Northern Virginia." *Southern Historical Society Papers*, Vol. 2, no. 3 (1876): pp. 120–130.

18. *Baton Rouge Gazette and Comet*, 25 May 1861.

19. Mark Twain, *Life on the Mississippi*, Penguin Books, New York, (1986), p 284.

20. West Baton Rouge *Sugar Planter*, 24 May 1861.

CHAPTER TWO

1. John D. Winters, *The Civil War in Louisiana*, LSU Press, Baton Rouge, Louisiana (1963), p 22.

2. John A. Morgan Papers, "Letter of May 16, 1861," Hill Memorial Library, LSU, Baton Rouge, Louisiana.

3. Sarah Dorsey, *Recollections of Henry Watkins Allen*, M. Doolady, New Orleans, Louisiana, (1866), pp 127–144. Hereafter referred to as the *Recollections of Henry Watkins Allen*.

4. Arthur Bergeron, *Guide to Louisiana Confederate Military Units, 1861–1865*, LSU Press, Baton Rouge, Louisiana, (1959), pp 79–80.

5. F. Jay Taylor, ed., *Reluctant Rebel: The Secret Diary of Robert Patrick, 1861–1865*, LSU Press, Baton Rouge, Louisiana, (1959), p 32. Hereafter refered to as the Diary of Robert Patrick.

6. West Baton Rouge Parish *Sugar Planter*, July 6, 1861.

7. Virginia Lobdell Jennings, *The Plains and the People: A History of Upper East Baton Rouge Parish*, Pelican Publishing Co., Gretna, Louisiana, (1998), pp 200–201.

8. "Letter of Alexis Hebert, July 5, 1861," translated by Jack Pastorek, West Baton Rouge Parish Museum.

9. John S. Kendall, ed. "Recollections of a Confederate Officer," *Louisiana Historical Quarterly* 29 (1946): pp 1041-1228. Hereafter referred to as the "Recollections of John I. Kendall."

10. McGrath, John, January 13, 1915, article for the *Baton Rouge Daily Advocate*, John McGrath Scrapbook, Hill Memorial Library, LSU, Baton Rouge, Louisiana.

11. West Baton Rouge Parish Museum, Letter of Alexis Hebert, July 26, 1861, translated by Jack Pastorek.

12. Silas T. White Papers, Letter of July 25, 1861, Hill Memorial Library, LSU, Baton Rouge, Louisiana. Hereafter referred to as Silas T. White letters.

13. Unknown Soldier, Anne E. Spears Papers, 1861-1864, letter of July 23, 1861 from Ship Island, Hill Memorial Library, LSU, Baton Rouge, Louisiana.

14. ibid.

15. Silas T. White letters, July 25, 1861.

16. Unknown Soldier, Anne E. Spears Papers, 1861-1864, letter of July 23, 1861 from Ship Island, Hill Memorial Library, LSU, Baton Rouge, Louisiana.

17. ibid.

18. West Baton Rouge *Sugar Planter*, June 29, 1861.

19. West Baton Rouge Parish Museum. Letter of Theodore Lejeune, July 26, 1861, translated by Jack Pastorek.

20. West Baton Rouge *Sugar Planter*, July 20, 1861.

21. ibid, June 28, 1861.

22. Garcia, Celine Fremaux, (Patrick J. Geary, Editor), *Celine, Remembering Louisiana, 1850-1871*, University of Georgia Press, Athens, Georgia, (1987), p 67.

23. Corkern, J. B., letter to his brother, July 16, 1861, Jeptha McKinney Papers, Hill Memorial Library LSU, Baton Rouge, Louisiana, hereafter referred to as Letter of James B. Corkern.

24. West Baton Rouge *Sugar Planter*, Aug. 17, 1861.

25. Jones, Terry L., *Lee's Tigers, The Louisiana Infantry in the Army of Northern Virginia*, LSU Press, Baton Rouge, Louisiana. (1987).

26. *The War of Rebellion: A Compilation of the Official Records of the Union and Confederate Armies*, 128 volumes (Washington, 1880-1902). Ser. I, Vol VI, Ch. XVI, p 742-743. Hereafter referred to as O. R.

27. Letter of James B. Corkern, August 27, 1861.

28. O. R. Ser. I, Vol VI, Ch. XVI, p 374.

29. Letter of Francis Palms to Henreitta Lauzan, September 19, 1861, Hill Memorial Library, LSU, Baton Rouge, Louisiana.

30. Letter of James B. Corkern, August 8, 1861.

31. Josiah Knighton Papers, Letters of Jimmy Knighton, Aug. 11, 1861, Hill Memorial Library, LSU, Baton Rouge, Louisiana.

32. Silas T. White letters, July 25, 1861.

33. Letter of Father Charles Menard (Thibodeaux, La.) to Archbishop J. M. Odin, October 8, 1861, Notre Dame Archives Calendar.http://cawley.archives.nd.edu/calendar/Cal1861l.htm.

34. Stephenson, Wendel H., and Edwin Adams Davis, "The Civil War Diary of Wyllie Micajah Barrow, September 23, 1861–July 13, 1862." *Louisiana Historical Quarterly*, Vol. XVII, (1934), p 442. Hereafter referred to as Diary of Wyllie Micajah Barrow.

35. West Baton Rouge Parish Museum, letter of Alexis Hebert, October 22, 1861, translated by Jack Pastorek.

36. Letter of James B. Corkern, August 27, 1861.

37. Letter of Francis Palms to Henrietta Lauzon, September 19, 1861, Hill Memorial Library, LSU, Baton Rouge, Louisiana.

38. ibid.

39. Winters, John D., *The Civil War in Louisiana*, LSU Press, Baton Rouge, Louisiana. (1963), P 66.

40. Diary of Wyllie Micajah Barrow, p 444.

41. Letter of James B. Corkern, November 12, 1861.

42. Recollections of John I. Kendall, p 1046.

43. National Archives, Roll 133, Fourth Louisiana.

44. Letter of James B. Corkern, November 12, 1861.

45. Diary of Wyllie Micajah Barrow, p 447.

46. O. R. Ser. I, Vol III, Ch. XVI, p 560.

47. Silas T. White letters, December 6, 1861, December 24, 1861.

48. Diary of Wyllie Micajah Barrow, p 451.

49. Letter of Francis Palms to Henrietta Lauzon, December 29, 1861, Hill memorial Library, LSU, Baton rouge, louisiana.

50. Silas T. White letters, December 6, 1861.

51. Letter of Francis Palms to Henrietta Lauzon, December 29, 1861, Hill Memorial Library, LSU, Baton Rouge, Louisiana.

52. National Archives, Roll 132, Fourth Infantry.

53. Letter of Francis Palms to Henrietta Lauzon, January 31, 1862, Hill Memorial Library, LSU, Baton Rouge, Louisiana.

54. Josiah Knighton Papers, Letter of Jimmy Knighton, Feb. 3, 1861, Feb. 8, 1861, Hill Memorial Library, LSU, Baton Rouge, Louisiana.

55. Silas T. White letter of February 2, 1862.

56. Letter of Francis Palms to Henrietta Lauzon, Jaunary 121, 1862, Hill Memorial Library, LSU, Baton Rouge, Louisiana.

57. Warner, Ezra J., *Generals in Gray*, LSU Press, Baton Rouge, Louisiana, (1959), pp 159-160.

58. Diary of Wyllie Micajah Barrow, p 718.

59. Winters, John D., *The Civil War in Louisiana*, LSU Press, Baton Rouge, Louisiana, (1963), p 82.

60. Diary of Wyllie Micajah Barrow, p 719.

61. Recollections of John I. Kendall, p 1048.

62. Letter of Francis Palms to Henrietta Lauzon, March 9, 1862, Hill Memorial Library, LSU, Baton Rouge, Louisiana.

63. National Archives, Roll 132 Fourth Louisiana.

64. Lettter of Francis Palms to Henrietta Lauzon, March 9, 1862, Hill Memorial Library, LSU, Baton Rouge, Louisiana.

65. ibid

66. Silas T. White letters, March 23, 1862.

67. Richardson, Frank L., "War as I Saw It. 1861-1865", *Louisiana Historical Quarterly*, Vol. 6, No. l, (1923), p 89. Hereafter referred to as Recollections of Frank L.Richardson.

68. Warner, Ezra J., *Generals in Gray*, LSU Press, Baton Rouge, Louisiana, (1959), p 104.

69. Ibid, p 265.

70. Diary of Robert Patrick, p 37.

71. Warner, Ezra J., Generals *in Gray*, LSU Press, Baton Rouge, Louisiana, (1959), p 30.

72. Diary of Robert Patrick, pp 80-81.

CHAPTER THREE

1. Diary of Robert Patrick, p 3.

2. Silas T. White letters, March 23, 1862.

3. West Baton Rouge Parish Museum, Letter of Alexis Hebert, March 23, 1862, translated by Jack Pastorek.

4. John A. Morgan Papers, Letter of March 26, 1862, Hill Memorial Library, LSU, Baton Rouge, Louisiana.

5. Grisamore, Silas T. (Edited by Arthur W. Bergeron, Jr.) *The Civil War Reminiscences of Major Silas T. Grisamore, CSA.*,LSU Press, Baton Rouge, Louisiana, (1993), p 57.

6. Diary of D. C. Jenkins, pp 389-39.

7. Warner, Ezra J., *Generals in Gray*, LSU Press, Baton Rouge, Louisiana, (1959), p 22.

8. Livaudais, Edmond Enoul, *The Shiloh Diary of Edmond Enoul Livaudais*, translanted by Stanley J. Guerin, New Orleans, Archdiocese of New Orleans, (1992) p 21. Hereafter referred to as the Diary of Edmond Livaudais.

9. Diary of D. C. Jenkins, pp 38-39.

10. T. C. Robertson, letter of April 9, 1862, Hill Memorial Library, LSU, Baton Rouge, Louisiana.

11. Josiah Knighton Papers, Letter of Jimmy Knighton, April 1, 1861, April 10, 1861, Hill Memorial Library, LSU, Baton Rouge, Louisiana.

12. T. C. Robertson, letter of April 9, 1862, Hill Memorial Library, LSU, Baton Rouge, Louisiana.

13. Shoemaker, Randall, Editor, *The St. Helena Rifles*, (1968), Privately Published, p 2. Hereafter referred to as the Recollections of A. P. Richards.

14. Diary of D. C. Jenkins, p 38-39.

15. Recollections of John I. Kendall, p 1062.

16. Recollections of Henry Watkins Allen, pp 127-144.

17. ibid., pp 127-144.

18. Recollections of A. P. Richards, p 2.

19. T. C. Robertson, letter of April 9, 1862, Hill Memorial Library, LSU, Baton Rouge, Louisiana.

20. West Baton Rouge Parish Museum, Letter of Alexis Hebert, April 8, 1862, translated by Johnnie Ruth Richey.

21. T. C. Robertson, letter of April 9, 1862, Hill Memorial Library, LSU, Baton Rouge, Louisiana.

22. ibid.

23. Diary of D. C. Jenkins, pp 38-39.

24. Recollections of Frank L. Richardson, p 100.

25. Diary of D. C. Jenkins, pp 38-39.

26. T. C. Robertson, letter of April 9, 1862, Hill Memorial Library, LSU, Baton Rouge, Louisiana.

27. Recollections of Frank L. Richardson, p 10.

28. McGrath, John, John McGrath Scrapbook, Hill Memorial Library, LSU, Baton Rouge, Louisiana.

29. Louisiana State Archives, Confederate Pension Application Records, microfilm roll CPl.80.

30. O. P. Skolfield, From a note written on a Confederate twenty dollar bill and in possession of his descendants.

31. T. C. Robertson, letter of April 9, 1862, Hill Memorial Library, LSU, Baton Rouge, Louisiana.

32. O. P. Skolfield, From a note written on a Confederate twenty dollar bill and in possession of his descendants

33. Diary of Edmond Livaudais, p 32.

34. Bierce, Ambrose, "What I Saw At Shiloh", *Civil War Stories*, Dover Publishing Company, (1994), p 10.

35. T. C. Robertson, letter of April 9, 1862, Hill Memorial Library, LSU, Baton Rouge, Louisiana.

36. Recollections of A. P. Richards, p 2.

37. Bierce, Ambrose, "What I Saw At Shiloh", *Civil War Stories*, Dover Publishing Company, (1994), p 16.

38. *O. R. Ser.* I, Vol. X/l, p 430.

39. Lambert, Samuel, "A Record of the Fourth Louisiana", *East Feliciana Democrat*, April 25, 1865, p 130. Hereafter referred to as "Recollections of Samuel Lambert."

40. New Orleans *Daily Picayune*, April 18, 1862.

41. Recollections of A. P. Richards, p 2.

42. T. C. Robertson, letter of April 9, 1862, Hill Memorial Library, LSU, Baton Rouge, Louisiana.

43. Recollections of Frank L. Richardson, p 225.

44. Baton Rouge *Daily Advocate*, April 16, 1862.

45. New Orleans *Crescent, March 5, 1868.*

46. Letter from Father Turgis to Archbishop J. M. Odin, April 16, 1862, University of Notre Dame Archives: Calendar, http://cawley.archives.nd.edu/calendar/cal1862d.htm.

47. Recollections of John I. Kendall, pp 1066-1067.

48. O. R., Ser. I, Vol. X/I, p 490.

49. Bergeron, Arthur W., Jr., *Guide to Louisiana Confederate Military Units, 1861-1865*, LSU Press, Baton Rouge, Louisiana, (1989), p 79-80.

50. Bergeron, Arthur W., Jr. *Confederate Mobile*, University Press of Mississippi, Jackson, Mississippi, (1991), p 20.

CHAPTER FOUR

1. *Memphis Daily Appeal*, April 9, 1862.

2. Recollections of John I. Kendall, p 1077.

3. Josiah Knighton Papers, Letter of J. M. Doyle, May 24, 1863, Hill Memorial Library, LSU, Baton Rouge, Louisiana.

4. Reminiscences of Spencer Talley, http://www.tennessee-scv.org/talleyC.html.

5. Davis, William C., *Diary of Confederate Soldier, John S. Jackman of the Orphan Brigade*, University of South Carolina Press, Columbia, South Carolina., (1990), pp 47-52. Hereafter referred to as Diary of John S. Jackman.

6. Dixon, William Young, family papers, Diary of William Dixon, June 28, 1862, Hill Memorial Library, LSU, Baton Rouge, Louisiana. Hereafter referred to as diary of William Dixon.

7. Winters, John D., ed. "Letter from a North Louisiana Soldier: The first Vicksburg Campaign, 1862." *North Louisiana Historical Association Journal*, VI (1975), pp 98-104.

8. Letter of James B. Corkern, July 6, 1862.

9. Diary of William Dixon, July 23, 1862.

10. Diary of a John S. Jackman, p 50.

11. Reminiscences of Spencer Talley, http://www.tennessee-scv.org/talleyC.html.

12. Scharf, Thomas J., *History of the Confederate States Navy*, Random House, New York, New York, (1989), pp 326-331.

13. Diary of John S. Jackman, p 45.

14. Winters, John D., ed. "Letter from a North Louisiana Soldier: The First Vicksburg Campaign, 1862." *North Louisiana Historical Association Journal*, VI (1975), 98-104.

15. Diary of William Dixon

16. Holmes, Richard, *Acts of War, The Behavior of Men in Battle*, The Free Press, New York, (1985), pp 128-129.

17. Dorman, James H., *The People Called Cajuns, An Introduction to Ethnohistory*, The Center for Louisiana Studies, University of Southwestern Louisiana, Lafayette, Louisiana, (1983), pp 67,77.

18. National Archives, Roll 133, Fourth Louisiana.

CHAPTER FIVE

1. *New Orleans Crescent*, March 5, 1868.

2. Allen, Henry W., Field Report dated August 3, 1862 on the Comite River Bridge. McCain Library and Archives, University of Southern Mississippi, Hattiesburg, Mississippi.

3. *Memphis Daily Appeal*, (Grenada, Mississippi), August 11, 1862.

4. ibid

5. O. R., Ser. I, Vol. XV, p 79.

6. Scharf, Thomas J., *History of the Confederate States Navy*, Random House, New York, New York, (1989), pp 332-337.

7. *Memphis Daily Appeal*, (Grenada, Mississippi), August 11, 1862.

8. O. R., Ser. I, Vol., XV, p 106.

9. Recollections of Henry Watkins Allen, pp 127-144.

10. O. R., Ser. I, Vol., XV, p 106.

11. Holmes, Richard, *Acts of War, The Behavior of Men in Battle*, The Free Press, New York, (1985), p 161.

12. Recollections of A. P. Richards, p 3-4.

13. O. R., Ser. I, Vol. XV, p 107.

14. ibid, p 102.

15. *Memphis Daily Appeal*, (Granada, Mississippi), August 13, 1862.

16. O. R., Ser. I, Vol. XV, p 107.

17. ibid, p 103.

18. Recollections of A. P. Richards, p 4-5.

19. Ibid, p 67.

20. Holmes, Richard, *Acts of War, The Behavior of Men in Battle*, The Free Press, New York, (1985), p 160.

21. O. R., Ser. I, Vol. XV, p 79.

22. Recollections of John I. Kendall, p 1088.

23. Diary of William Dixon, August 5, 1862.

24. O. R., Ser. I, Vol. XV, p 80.

25. O. R., Ser., I, Vol. LIIIa, p 534.

26. Isaac Erwin Diary, Entry of August 10, 1862, Hill Memorial Library, LSU, Baton Rouge, Louisiana.

27. Leblanc, Dudly, *The Acadian Miracle*, Evangeline Publishing Company, Lafayette, Louisiana, (1966), p 51.

28. Recollections of John I. Kendall, p 1090.

CHAPTER SIX

1. Winters, John D., *The Civil War in Louisiana*, LSU Press, Baton Rouge, Louisiana, (1963), pp 123-124.

2. McCarthy, Carleton, "Detailed Minutiae of Soldier Life In the Army of Northern Virginia", *Southern Historical Society Papers*, Vol II, Richmond, Virginia, September, 1876, No. 3, pp 129-130.

3. Diary John S. Jackman, p 55.

4. Diary of Isaac Erwin, entry of August 24, 1862, Hill Memorial Library, LSU, Baton Rouge, Louisiana.

5. Diary of William Dixon, August 21—23, 1862.

6. Letter of James B. Corkern, August 27, 1862.

7. Warner, Ezra J., *Generals in Gray*, LSU Press, Baton Rouge, Louisiana, (1959), pp 21-22.

8. Bonham, Milledge L., Jr. "Man and Nature at Port Hudson, 1863, 1917", *The Military Historian and Economist*, Vol III, No I, January 1918.

9. East, Charles, ed., *The Civil War Diary of Sarah Morgan*, University of Georgia Press, Athens, Georgia, (1991), p 277.

10. Diary of Isaac Erwin, entry of September 13, 1863, Hill Memorial Library, LSU, Baton Rouge, Louisiana.

11. Dorman, James H., *The People Called Cajuns, An Introduction to Ethnohistory*, The Center for Louisiana Studies, University of Southwestern Louisiana, Lafayette, Louisiana, (1983), p 39.

12. O. R., Ser. II, Vol. 3, pp 266-268.

13. Diary of Robert Patrick, p 52.

14. National Archives, Roll 133, Fourth Louisiana.

15. Diary of Robert Patrick, p 50.

16. Letter of James B. Corkern, November 30, 1862

17. National Archives, Roll 133, Fourth Louisiana.

18. Diary of Robert Patrick, p 59.

19. National Archives, Roll 129, Fourth Louisiana.

20. ibid., Roll 133, Fourth Louisiana.

21. O. R., Ser. I Vol. 15, pp 575-576.

22. Diary of Isaac Erwin, entry of December 21, 1862, Hill Memorial Library, LSU, Baton Rouge, Louisiana.

23. Diary of Robert Patrick, p 71.

24. Warner, Ezra J., *Generals in Gray*, LSU Press, Baton Rouge, Louisiana, (1961), p 218.

25. Hummel, Jeffrey Rodgers, *Emancipating Slaves, Enslaving Free Men, A History of the American Civil War*, Open Court, Chicago and LaSalle, Illinois, (1996), p 210.

26. Watson, William, *Life in the Confederate Army: Being the Observations and Experiences of an Alien in the South During the American Civil War*. LSU Press, Baton Rouge, Louisiana, (1995), pp 429-432.

27. Hewitt, Lawrence Lee, *Port Hudson, Confederate Bastion on the Mississippi*. LSU Press, Baton Rouge, Louisiana, (1987), p 181.

28. Hewitt, Lawrence and Arthur Bergeron, editors, *Post Hospital Leger, Port Hudson, 1862-1863* Published by Le Comite des Archives de la Louisiane, 1981.

29. Diary of Robert Patrick, pp 92-93.

30. Bartlett, Napier, *Military Record of Louisiana, Including Biographical and Historical Papers Relating to the Military Organizations of the State*, LSU Press, Baton Rouge, Louisiana, (1992), The Trans-Mississippi, pp 45-53.

31. Scharf, Thomas J., *History of the Confederate States Navy*, Random House, New York, (1996), pp 358-362.

32. Diary of Robert Patrick, pp 96-98.

33. O. R., Ser. I, Vol. XV, p 271.

34. Letter of A. H. Beauchamp, March 13, 1863. Private collection, Mr. Drew Burk.

35. Diary of Robert Patrick, pp 103-105.

36. Jennings, Virginia Lobdel. *The Plains and the People, A History of Upper East Baton Rouge Parish*, Pelican Publishing Co., Gretna, Louisiana, (1998), p 60.

37. O. R., Ser. I, Vol XV, p 276.

38. ibid., p 23.

39. Hewitt, Lawrence Lee, *Port Hudson, Confederate Bastion on the Mississippi*, LSU Press, Baton Rouge, Louisiana, (1987), p 181.

40. Letter of John Morgan, March 30, 1863 Hill Memorial Library, LSU, Baton Rouge, Louisiana.

41. Letter of A. H. Beauchamp, April 13, 1863, Private collection, Mr. Drew Burk.

42. ibid.

43. Diary of William Dixon, May 2, 1863.

44. Recollections of John I. Kendall, p 1144.

45. Diary of William Dixon, May 1, 1863.

46. Recollections of John I. Kendall, p 1108.

47. ibid, pp 1112-1117.

48. National Archives, Roll 133, Fourth Louisiana.

49. Hewlitt, Lawrence Lee, *Port Hudson, Confederate Bastion on the Mississippi*, LSU Press, Baton Rouge, Louisiana, (1987), p 174.

50. Edmonds, David C., *The Guns of Port Hudson*, The Acadian Press, Lafayette, Louisiana (1984), p 24.

51. ibid, pp 74-77.

52. Recollections of John I. Kendall, pp 1117-1131.

CHAPTER SEVEN

1. Diary of William Dixon, May 10-23, 1863.

2. Warner, Ezra J., *Generals in Gray*, LSU Press, Baton Rouge, Louisiana, (1959) p 161.

3. ibid., pp 93–94.

4. Diary of Robert Patrick, pp 118-119.

5. National Archives, Roll 129. Fourth Louisiana.

6. Lionel C. Levy, *Memoirs of Army Life in Fenner's Louisiana Battery*, American Jewish Archives, Cincinnati, Ohio, Melinda McMartin, Assistant Archivist. Hereafter referred to as Recollections of Lionel C. Levy.

7. National Archives, Roll No. 129, Fourth Louisiana.

8. ibid., Roll no 129, Fourth Louisiana.

9. Recollections of Samuel Lambert, p 86.

10. Diary of William Dixon, July 12, 1863.

11. Hughes, Nathaniel Cheairs, Jr., *The Pride of the Confederate Artillery, The Washington Artillery in the Army of Tennessee*, LSU Press, Baton Rouge, Louisiana, (1997), pp 107-11.

12. National Archives, Roll 129, Fourth Louisiana.

13. Recollections of Samuel Lambert, p 87.

14. Recollections of Lionel C. Levy.

15. Recollections of Samuel Lambert, p 88.

16. French, Samuel G., *Two Wars*, Blue Acorn Press, Huntington, West Virginia, (1999), p 183.

17. Diary of Robert Patrick, p 121.

18. Diary of William Dixon, July 21, 1863.

19. ibid.

20. Recollections of A. P. Richards, p 15.

21. Letter of James B. Corkern, August 25, 1863.

22. National Archives, Roll 129, Fourth Louisiana.

23. McCarthy, Carlton, "Detailed Minutia of Soldier Life in the Army of Northern Virginia", *Southern Historical Society Papers*, Vol. II, Richmond, Virginia, Sept. 1876, No. 3.

24. Diary of William Dixon, September 1, 1863.

25. Letter of Francis Palms to Henrietta Lauzon, January 22, 1862, Hill Memorial Library, LSU, Baton Rouge, Louisiana.

26. Diary of William Dixon, September 12, 1863.

27. Recollections of Samuel Lambert, p 90.

28. Warner, Ezra J., *Generals in Gray*, LSU Press, Baton Rouge, La., (1959), p 248-249.

29. National Archives, Roll 129, Fourth Louisiana.

30. Recollections of A. P. Richards, p 16.

31. Recollections of John I. Kendall, p 1147.

32. ibid., Roll 132. Fourth Louisiana.

33. Recollections of John I. Kendall, p 1147.

34. Bergeron, Arthur, Jr., *Confederate Mobile*, University Press of Mississippi, Jackson, Mississippi, (1991), pp 94.

35. National Archives, Roll 133, Fourth Louisiana.

36. ibid., Roll 133, Fourth Louisiana.

37. Josiah Knighton Papers, Letter of John Doyle, September 22, 1863, Hill Memorial Library, LSU, Baton Rouge, Louisiana.

38. Diary of William Dixon, September 25, 1863, September 27, 1863.

39. Letter from Father Turgis to Archbishop J. M. Odin, September 25, 1863, University of Notre Dame Archives: Calendar, http://cawley.archives.nd.edu/calendar/cal1863i.htm.

40. Bergeron, Arthur, Jr., *Confederate Mobile*, University Press of Mississippi, (1991), p 93.

41. Recollections of John I. Kendall, p 1148.

42. Bergeron, Aurthur, *Confederate Mobile*, University Press of Mississippi, Jackson, Mississippi (1991), p 94.

43. National Archives, Roll 129, Fourth Louisiana.

44. Recollections of Samuel Lambert, p 92.

45. Diary of William Dixon, November 22, 1863.

46. National Archives, Roll 129, Fourth Louisiana.

47. Recollections of Lionel C. Levy.

48. ibid.

49. Recollections of Samuel Lambert, p 92.

50. Recollections of Lionel C. Levy.

51. Diary of Robert Patrick, pp 138-139.

52. Diary of William Dixon, January 18, 1864.

53. National Archives, Roll 132, Fourth Louisiana.

54. ibid., Roll 133, Fourth Louisiana.

55. Diary of William Dixon, February 1, 1864.

56. Recollections of Samuel Lambert, p 95.

57. Warner, Ezra J., *Generals in Gray*, LSU Press, Baton Rouge, Louisiana, (1959) pp 193-194.

58. Recollections of Samuel Lambert, p 97.

59. Josiah Knighton Papers, Letter of John Doyle, Feb. 13, 1864, Hill Memorial Library, LSU, Baton Rouge, Louisiana.

60. O. R., Vol. XXIV, III/p 574.

61. *New Orleans Crescent*, March 5, 1868.

62. Bergeron, Arthur, *Confederate Mobile*, University Press of Mississippi, Jackson, Mississippi,(1991), p 96.

63. Diary of William Dixon, March 18, 1864.

64. Recollections of John I. Kendall, p 1150.

65. Recollections of Samuel Lambert, p 98.

66. Bergeron, Arthur, *Confederate Mobile*, University of Mississippi Press, Jackson, Mississippi, (1991) p 98.

CHAPTER EIGHT

1. Marsten, James, Diary entry of May 26, 1864. Henry Marsten Family Papers, Hill Memorial Library, LSU, Baton Rouge, Louisiana. Hereafter refrred to as Diary of James Marsten.

2. Warner, Ezra J., *Generals in Gray*, LSU Press, Baton Rouge, Louisiana. (1959) pp 53-54.

3. O. R., Ser. I, Vol. XXXVIII/3, p 725.

4. Recollections of A. P. Richards, p 20.

5. Diary of James Marsten, May 27, 1864.

6. Recollections of A. P. Richards, p 20.

7. Diary of James Marsten, May 27, 1864.

8. ibid.

9. Castel, Albert, *Decision in the West*, University Press of Kansas, Lawrence, Kansas, (1992), p 228.

10. Diary of James Marsten, May 31, 1864.

11. ibid, June 1, 1864.

12. ibid, June 3, 1864.

13. Recollections of John I. Kendall, p 1153.

14. Diary of Robert Patrick, p 182.

15. Diary of James Marsten, June 8, 1864.

16. Recollections of John I. Kendall, 1158.

17. Diary of James Marsten, June 12, 1864.

18. Hughes, Nathaniel Chiers, Jr., *The Pride of the Confederate Artillery, The Washington Artillery of the Army of Tennessee*, LSU Press, Baton Rouge, Louisiana, (1997), pp 188-189.

19. Recollections of Samuel Lambert, p 99.

20. Sketches of a Veteran—Louisiana Division, *Confederate Veteran*, VI (1898), p 577.

21. *Regulations of the Army of the Confederate States*, 1863. Published by National Historical Society, Harrisburg, Pennsylvania, (1980), p 60.

22. Recollections of John I. Kendall, p 1160.

23. Hughes, Nathaniel Chiers, Jr., *The Pride of the Confederate Artillery, The Washington Artillery of the Army of Tennessee*, LSU Press, Baton Rouge, Louisiana, (1997), p 192.

24. O. R. Ser. I, Vol. XXXVIII/3, p 879.

25. French, Samuel G., *Two Wars*, Blue Acorn Press, Huntington, West Virginia, (1999), p 211.

26. National Archives, Roll 129, Fourth Louisiana.

27. ibid., Roll 129, Fourth Louisiana.

28. Recollections of A. P. Richards, p 23.

29. O. R. Ser. I, Vol. XXXVIII/5, p 876.

30. Warner, Ezra J., *Generals in Gray*, LSU Press, Baton Rouge, Louisiana, (1959), pp 142-143.

31. Recollections of A. P. Richards, p 29.

32. Recollections of Samuel Lambert, p 110.

33. ibid, p 110.

34. Diary of Robert Patrick, p 201.

35. Warner, Ezra J. *Generals in Gray*, LSU Press, Baton Rouge, Louisiana, (1959), pp 183-184.

36. Recollections of John I. Kendall, pp 1177-1178.

37. Diary of James Marsten, July 28, 1864.

38. Recollections of Samuel Lambert, p 112

39. O. R. Ser. I, Vol. XXXVIII/3, pp 856-857.

40. Josiah Knighton Papers, Letter of John Doyle, Aug. 26, 1864, Hill Memorial Library, LSU, Baton Rouge, Louisiana.

41. *New Orleans Crescent,* March 5, 1868.

42. Castel, Albert, *Decision in the West*, University of Kansas Press, Lawrence Kansas, (1992), p 433.

43. Diary of James Marsten, July 28, 1864.

44. Recollections of John I. Kendall, p 1193.

45. Kendall, John S., ed. "The Diary of Surgeon Craig, Fourth Louisiana Regiment, C.S.A., 1864-1865," Louisiana *Historical Quarterly*, Vol. VII (1925), p 69. Hereafter referred to as Diary of Surgeon Craig.

46. Castel, Albert, *Decision in the West*, University Press of Kansas, Lawrence, Kansas, (1992), p 435.

47. Duff, W. H., *Six Months of Prison Life at Camp Chase, Ohio*, Orphan Helper Print, (1907), Lake Charles, Louisiana. www.civilwarancestor.com/store/files/ebook0030.htm

48. Scaife, William R., *The Campaign for Atlanta*, Civil War Publications, Cartersville, Georgia (1993), p 123-125.

49. Recollections of John I. Kendall, p 1195.

50. ibid., p 1193.

51. ibid., p. 1196.

52. Recollections of A. P. Richards, p 33.

53. French, Samuel G., *Two Wars*, Blue Acorn Press, Huntington, West Virginia, (1999).

CHAPTER NINE

1. Holmes, Richard, *Acts of War, The Behavior of Men in Battle*, The Free Press, New York, (1985), p 214.

2. Watkins, Sam, (Thomas Inge, Editor), *Company Aytch, or A Side Show of the Big Show*, Penguin Books, New York, New York, (1999), p 181-182.

3. Castel, Albert, *Decision in the West*, University of Kansas, Lawrence, Kansas, (1992), pp 498-502.

4. Recollections of A. P. Richards, p 34.

5. Recollections of John I. Kendall, p 1199.

6. Castle, Albert, *Decision in the West*, University of Kansas Press, Lawrence, Kansas, (1992), p 503.

7. Diary of Robert Patrick, p 221.

8. Diary of Surgeon Craig, p 58.

9. French, Samuel G., *Two Wars*, Blue Acorn Press, Huntington West Virginia, (1999), p 222.

10. Cater, Douglas John, *As It Was, Reminiscences of a Soldier of the Third Texas Cavalry and the Nineteenth Louisiana Infantry*, The State House Press, Austin, Texas, (1990), p 194.

11. French, Samuel G., *Two Wars*, Blue Acorn Press, Huntington, West Virginia, (1999), p 286.

12. Diary of Surgeon Craig, p 59.

13. Recollections of John I. Kendall, pp 1202-1204.

14. Recollections of Samuel Lambert, p 117.

15. Diary of Surgeon Craig, pp 60-61.

16. Hughes, Nathaniel Cheairs, Jr., *The Civil War Memoir of Philip Daingerfield Stephenson, D.D.*, LSU Press, Baton Rouge, Louisiana, (1995), p 259. Hereafter referred to as the Recollections of Phillip Stephenson.

17. Diary of Surgeon Craig, p 60.

18. ibid, p 60.

19. O. R., 38, I, 29

CHAPTER TEN

1. McCarthy, Carlton, "Detailed Minutiae of Soldier Life In the Army of Northern Virginia", *Southern Historical Society Papers*, Vol. III, Richmond, Virginia, January, 187, No. l, p 13.

2. Diary of Surgeon Craig, pp 60–61.

3. Recollections of John I. Kendall, p 1205.

4. Sword, Wiley, *The Confederacy's Last Hurrah, Spring Hill, Franklin, and Nashville*, Universtity of Kansas Press, Lawrence, Kansas, (1992), pp 170-233.

5. Recollections of John I. Kendall, pp 1206–1209.

6. Sword, Wiley, *The Confederacy's Last Hurrah, Spring Hill, Franklin, and Nashville*, University of Kansas Press, Lawrence, Kansas, (1992), pp 321-391.

7. Cater, Douglas John, *As It Was Reminiscences of a Soldier of the Third Texas Cavalry and the Nineteenth Louisiana Infantry*, State House Press, Austin, Texas, (1990), p202.

8. O. R., Ser. I, Vol. XLV/l, p 703.

9. Recollections of John I. Kendall, p 1210.

10. Lindsay, Colonel R. H., *Confederate Veteran*, Vol. VII, No. 3, Nashville, Tennessee, July, 1899

11. Diary of Surgeon Craig, p 61.

12. Recollections of Phillip Dangerfield Stevenson, p 327.

13. O. R., Ser. I, Vol. XLV/l, p 689.

14. Recollections of John I. Kendall, p 1211.

15. O. R., Ser I, Vol. XLV/l, p 690.

16. Cater, Douglas John, *As it Was Reminiscences of a Soldier of the Third Texas Cavalry and the Nineteenth Louisiana Infantry*. State House Press, Austin, Texas, (1999) pp 203.

17. Recollections of Samuel Lambert, p 132.

18. Diary of Surgeon Craig, pp 64–70.

19. Cater, Douglas John, *As it Was Reminiscences of a Soldier of the Third Texas Cavalry and the Nineteenth Louisiana Infantry*, State House Press, Austin, Texas, pp 210-211

20. Remarque, Erich Maria, *All Quiet on the Western Front*, Little Brown and Co., Boston, (1929), p 283.

CHAPTER ELEVEN

1. Brown, Dee Alexander, *Morgan's Raiders*, Konecky and Konecky, New York, New York, (1959), p 232.

2. ibid, p 233.

3. ibid, p 279.

4. Levy, George, *To Die in Chicago, Confederate Prisoners at Camp Douglas, 1862-1865*, Pelican Publishing Co., Gretna, Louisiana, (1999), p 296.

5. ibid, p 319.

6. ibid, pp 301-303.

7. Bush, David, "Johnson's Island", http://www.heidelberg, edu/~dbush/jrev2.html.

8. Bush, David, "Johnson's Island",
http://www.heidelberg.edu/~dbush/teachbr.html. p 5.

9. National Archives, Roll 129, Fourth Louisiana.

10. Pension Application Records for Soldiers in the Confederate States Army from Louisiana, Microfilm CPl, Louisiana State Archives.

0-595-27258-4

Printed in the United States
1425400003B/78